Contents

lonely planet

Rio de Janeiro

"All you've got to do is decide to go and the hardest part is over.

So go!"

TONY WHEELER, COFOUNDER – LONELY PLANET

5 255917 000

LONELY PLANET / GETTY IMAGES ©

EURASIA / GETTY IMAGES ©

(left) Maracanã Football Stadium (p146)

(above) Ipanema beach (p58)

(right) Cristo Redentor (p110)

ANDY CAULFIELD / GETTY IMAGES ©

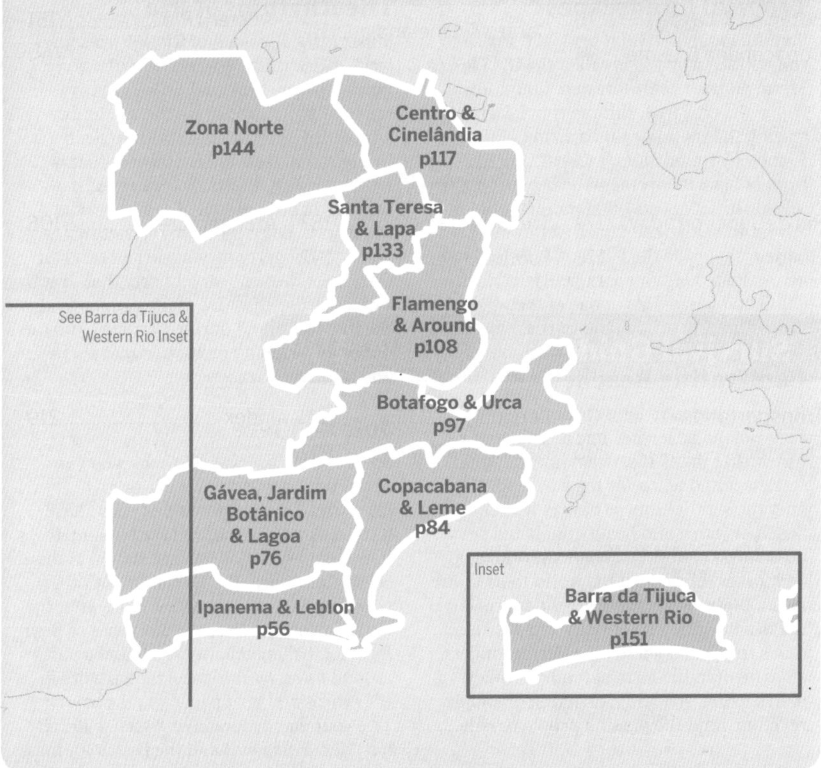

Welcome to Rio de Janeiro

Golden beaches and lush mountains, samba-fueled nightlife and spectacular football matches: welcome to the Cidade Maravilhosa (Marvelous City)

Tropical Landscapes

Standing atop the 710m peak of Corcovado, you will see why Rio is called the Cidade Maravilhosa. Lushly forested mountains fringe the city, with shimmering beaches tracing the shoreline and a string of tiny islands scattered along the seafront. Far from being a mere cinematic backdrop, this seaside beauty hosts outstanding outdoor adventures: hike the Tijuca rainforest, bicycle alongside the lake and beaches, sail across Baía de Guanabara, and surf, rock climb and hang glide in one of the world's most stunning urban landscapes.

Captivating Beaches

Rio's beaches have long seduced visitors. Copacabana beach became a symbol of Rio during the 1940s, when international starlets jetted down for the weekend. Hogging the spotlight these days is Ipanema beach, its fame and beauty unabated since bossa nova stars Tom Jobim and Vinicius de Moraes introduced the world to its allure in the 1960s. For *cariocas* (residents of Rio), the beach is Rio's backyard – a playground that's free and open to all, offering endless enjoyment in the form of football, volleyball, surfing, snacking, drinking or simply relaxing amid the passing people parade.

The Rhythms of Rio

Music is the lifeblood of Rio, with a soundtrack comprising rock, old-school bossa nova, hip-hop, funk and Brazil's many regional styles. Above all, there's samba, a rapid-fire style of music with African influences and an infectious beat that is synonymous with Rio. You can hear it all over town, but the soul of samba resides in Lapa, an edgy, red-light district that is home to dozens of live-music halls and an enormous weekend street party that draws revelers from all walks of life. Samba is also the integral sound during Carnaval and the danceable backing music to street parties and all-night parades.

Joie de Vivre

Speaking of Carnaval, Rio knows how to party. Whether you call it joie de vivre, *lebensfreude* or lust for life, *cariocas* have it in spades. Carnaval, and the build-up to it, is the most obvious manifestation of this celebratory spirit. But Rio has many other occasions for revelry – celebrations after the big Flamengo (or Vasco, Fluminense or Botafogo) football match, weekend samba parties around town, *baile* (dance) funk parties in the favelas and boat parties on the bay. Or save your energy for major fests like Reveillon (New Year's Eve) and the Festas Juninas.

Why I Love Rio de Janeiro

By Regis St Louis, Author

There's no other place like Rio. It's the combination of many things that I find so captivating: walking through parks inside the city and seeing monkeys and toucans, spending the evening catching music jams around Lapa, joining a few friends amid the roaring crowds at Maracanã or greeting the sunrise (after an early morning or late night) from Copacabana beach. It's those precious moments when you realize you're hooked. I also love the *carioca* spirit, spontaneous and good-natured, with the urge to live life to the fullest. It's no wonder that in a 2013 survey, Rio was rated the world's happiest city.

For more about our authors, see p256.

Top: Copacabana beach (p86)

Rio de Janeiro's Top 10

VIVIANE PONTI / GETTY IMAGES ©

Carnaval *(p26)*

1 Get plenty of sleep before you board the plane, because once you land, it's nonstop revelry until Ash Wednesday (sort of) brings it all to a close. With nearly 500 street parties happening in every corner of town, you will not lack for options. For the full experience, join a samba school and parade amid pounding drum corps and mechanized smoke-breathing dragons before thousands of roaring fans in the Sambódromo. Or assemble a costume and hit one of the Carnaval balls around town. The build-up starts weeks in advance.

Carnaval

Ipanema Beach *(p58)*

2 The enchanting beachfront attracts a wide mix of *cariocas* (residents of Rio), with a different crowd – surfers, volleyballers, bohemians, muscle boys – for each section (or *posto*), including famous Posto 9 where Ipanema's young and beautiful frolic. The principal activities of the day are people-watching, surfside walks and watching the sunset – best from Arpoador, at Ipanema's east end. You can also eat and drink on the sand. Roaming vendors bring the goods to you, and *barracas* (beach stalls) set you up with chairs, umbrellas and caipirinhas. All you need to do is show up.

Ipanema & Leblon

1

YADID LEVY / CORBIS ©

2

3

5

Copacabana Beach *(p86)*

3 The Copacabana experience is about many things: rising early and going for a run along the sands, playing in the waves on a sun-drenched afternoon or whiling away the evening over cocktails and appetizers at a beachfront kiosk. Regardless, you'll probably notice that incredibly seductive view: 4km of wide, curving sands framed by Rio's ubiquitous green peaks. Head uphill for even better views – rooftop bars and forts at either end of the beach make great settings for taking it all in.

Copacabana & Leme

Nightlife in Lapa *(p139)*

4 The Lapa Arches form the gateway to Rio's most animated nightlife. Pass through the 64m-high portal and stroll the packed, bar-lined streets while the rhythms of samba spill out of 19th-century facades. While there are drinks (curbside beer and caipirinha vendors) and music (impromptu jam sessions) all around, venture inside an old-school dance hall to see the city at its most dynamic. From the band on stage comes the rhythms of samba – one of the world's most infectious beats. Grab a partner and join the mayhem on the dance floor.

☆ ***Santa Teresa & Lapa***

Pão de Açúcar (Sugarloaf Mountain) *(p99)*

5 Some say to come around sunset for the best views from this absurd confection of a mountain. But in truth, no matter what time you come, you're unlikely to look at Rio (or your own comparatively lackluster city) in the same way. From here the landscape is pure undulating green hills and golden beaches lapped by blue sea, with rows of skyscrapers sprouting along the shore. The ride up is good fun: all-glass aerial trams whisk you up to the top. The adventurous can rock climb their way to the summit.

Botafogo & Urca

Cristo Redentor *(p110)*

6 The open-armed savior has stood atop his lofty perch (710m-high Corcovado), gazing peacefully over Rio, since 1931. The statue is a remarkable work of artistry, but most people don't come up here to admire the art deco design. They come for the mesmerizing panorama and combination of tropical rainforest, beaches, islands, ocean, bay and verdant peaks which surround this unlikely metropolis. There are several ways to reach the top. The steep cog train up through thick forest provides a memorable ascent.

Flamengo & Around

Santa Teresa *(p133)*

7 Overlooking downtown Rio, the hilltop neighborhood of Santa Teresa – where people live in houses rather than high-rises – has a villagelike vibe. Its aging 19th-century mansions and bohemian spirit offer a dramatic counterpoint to Rio's better-known seaside persona. Here you'll find old-school bars, art-loving B&Bs and lush backyards where marmosets often roam, with magical views over downtown and the bay. The downside: it's still rough around the edges. But the locals and expats who live here wouldn't have it any other way.

BAR DO GOMES (P139)

Santa Teresa & Lapa

6

Maracanã Football Stadium *(p146)*

8 Fresh from an R$800 million makeover in preparation for the 2014 World Cup and 2016 Summer Olympics, Maracanã is hallowed ground among Brazilians. It has been the site of triumph (Pele's 1000th goal) and catastrophe (losing to Uruguay in the final match of the 1950 World Cup). Games here are simply spectacular, with tens of thousands of cheering fans sending up an earth-shaking roar when the home team (and Rio has four of them) scores. Whether you're a football fan or not, don't pass up the chance to see a game inside this historic arena.

Zona Norte

Floresta da Tijuca (p156)

9 While New York has Central Park, Rio has the Floresta da Tijuca, a vast swath of rainforest with hiking trails, refreshing waterfalls and abundant greenery that make other parks look like playgrounds. There are a number of fine walks you can take here, as well as some climbs up rocky 900m-high peaks, where rewarding views await. If you prefer flying to walking, take the hang gliding flight from Pedra Bonita inside the Tijuca boundaries for a magnificent (if somewhat terrifying) view over Rio's wondrously green backyard.

Barra da Tijuca & Western Rio

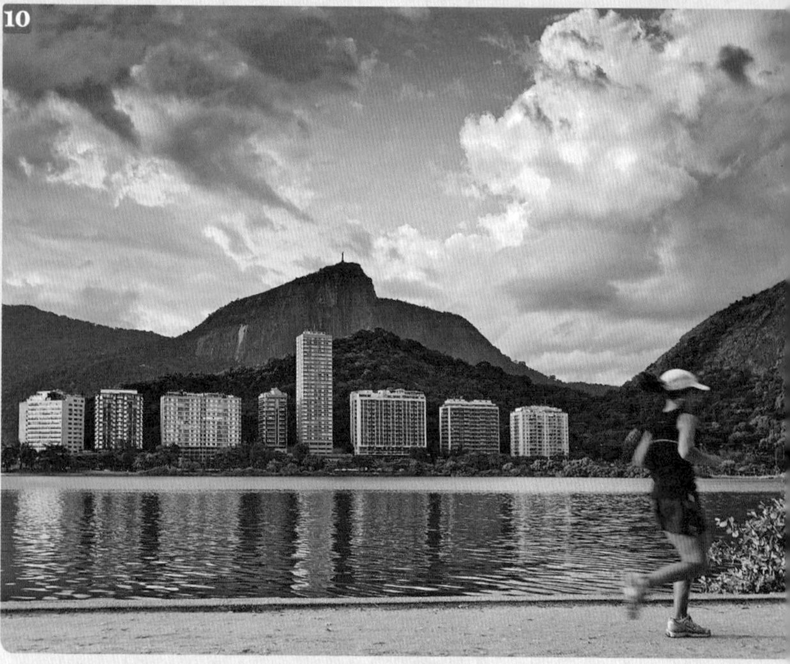

Lagoa Rodrigo de Freitas (p78)

10 'Saltwater lagoon' may not be the first thing you think of when you hear the words 'Rio de Janeiro', but this picturesque body of water plays a key role in the city's psyche. By day *cariocas* cycle, jog and stroll the 7km path that loops around it. By nightfall, a different crowd arrives to eat and drink in the open-air kiosks scattered along the shore. In December Lagoa is home to a massive floating Christmas tree, its glittering lights and nightly display pure magic for kids and adults alike.

Gávea, Jardim Botânico & Lagoa

What's New

Porto Maravilha

Among many new developments tied to the Summer Olympics, Rio is investing heavily in reinventing its derelict waterfront. The Porto Maravilha plan will bring light rail and several new museums, along with bike paths, public parks and thousands of new trees. The 15-year, R$8 billion project will happen in stages, with the Rio Art Museum opened in 2013, and the Museum of Tomorrow in 2014.

Maracanã Football Stadium

Brazil's most hallowed football arena received an R$800 million makeover in preparation for the World Cup and Summer Olympics, dramatically improving its on-site facilities while retaining its heritage-listed facade. (p146)

Cidade das Artes

The City of Arts Cidade das Artes finally opened in 2013. The high-tech Barra da Tijuca concert hall will host a wide-ranging repertoire and is the new home of the Brazilian Symphony Orchestra. (p157)

Museum of Image & Sound

In Copacabana, construction is underway on the high-tech Museu do Imagem e Som, an R$88 million waterfront project designed by the award-winning Diller Scofidio + Renfro. (p198)

Metro

Work continues on Rio's underground. The Linha 4 expansion, due for completion by 2016, will finally connect Barra da Tijuca in the west to Ipanema and Leblon. (p202)

Studio RJ & Bar Astor

The music has returned to Ipanema! Studio RJ is a great new concert space with diverse progamming (rock, jazz, samba). Downstairs is the new Bar Astor, an instant classic. (p71, p70)

Oro

Molecular gastronomy arrives in Rio with Oro (opened in 2010) top of the pack among a crop of celebrated new restaurants. Felipe Bronze prepares brilliantly imaginative dishes, up to nine courses. (p81)

Favelas

Rio is investing heavily in favela improvements, and security has improved markedly in recent years. Some favelas are drawing tourists, such as Complexo do Alemão, with its scenic cable car. (p148)

Theatro Municipal

After more than two years of renovations, the 1909 Theatro Municipal has been restored to its full gilded glory. Take a guided tour for an in-depth look. (p120)

Rodoviária Novo Rio

Rio's central bus station received a R$21 million facelift that ramped up security and turned the entire 2nd floor into a pleasant area with a respectable food court. (p200)

For more recommendations and reviews, see **lonelyplanet.com/Rio de Janeiro**

Need to Know

For more information, see Survival Guide (p199)

Currency
Real (R$)

Language
Portuguese

Visas
Many nationalities require visas, including citizens of the US, Canada and Australia.

Money
ATMs widely available. Credit cards accepted in most midrange and top-end hotels and restaurants.

Cell Phones
Local SIM cards can be used in unlocked European and Australian phones, and in US phones on the GSM network.

Time
Rio is three hours behind GMT. Daylight savings pushes the clocks one hour forward between mid-October and mid-February.

Tourist Information
Riotur (www.rioguiaoficial.com.br) has offices for getting maps, transport info and tips on attractions and events.

Your Daily Budget

Budget: less than R$200

- Hostel bed R$45 to R$60
- Sandwich and drink in a juice bar R$12
- Drinks on the street in Lapa R$6

Midrange: R$200 to R$600

- Standard double room in Copacabana R$350
- Dinner for two R$100 to R$150
- Guided tours R$90 to R$150
- Admission to a samba club R$20 to R$50

Top end: over R$600

- Boutique hotel room R$600
- Dinner for two at top restaurants with drinks R$300
- Hang gliding off Pedra Bonita R$350

Advance Planning

Nine months before Book a room if visiting during Carnaval or New Year's Eve.

Three months before Organize your visa (if you need one) and book accommodations.

Two weeks before Book guided tours and activities (such as rock climbing, rainforest tours, tandem gliding).

One week before Book a table at top restaurants. Check concerts and events on www.rioguiaoficial.com.br.

Useful Websites

- **Insider's Guide to Rio** (www.ipanema.com) Tips and planning info, with special sections on Carnaval and gay Rio.
- **Lonely Planet** (www.lonelyplanet.com/brazil/rio-de-janeiro) Destination information, travel forum and bookings.
- **Riotur** (www.rioguiaoficial.com.br) Rio's official tourism authority.
- **Rio Times** (www.riotimesonline.com) English-language resource on current events.

WHEN TO GO

High season runs from December to March, when Rio is festive, pricey and hot. To beat the crowds and higher prices, visit from May to September.

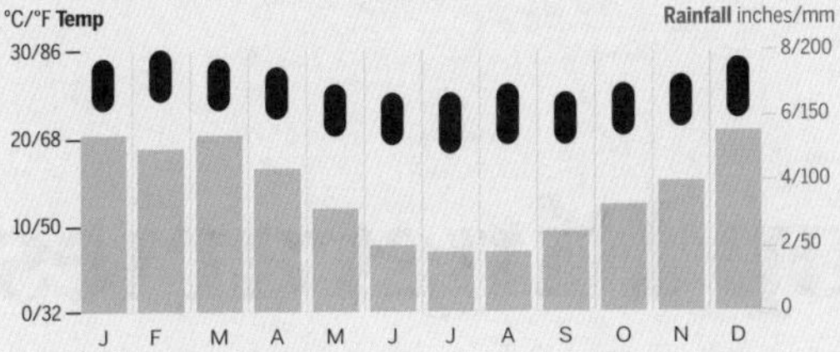

Arriving in Rio de Janeiro

Aeroporto Antônio Carlos Jobim Most international flights arrive at this airport (also called Galeão), located 15km north of the city center. From there, Premium Auto Ônibus (www.premiumautoonibus.com.br; R$12) operates buses approximately every 20 minutes to Flamengo, Copacabana, Ipanema, Leblon and other neighborhoods. It takes 75 minutes to two hours depending on traffic. Radio taxis charge a set fare of R$105 to Copacabana and Ipanema (45 to 90 minutes). Less-secure metered yellow-and-blue common *(comum)* taxis cost between R$50 and R$75.

For much more on **arrival**, see p200

Getting Around

➡ **Metro** The most convenient way to get around. Trains run from 5am to midnight Monday through Saturday, and 7am to 11pm on Sunday and holidays. Single rides cost R$3.20. Rates are higher at night and on Sundays.

➡ **Bus** Buses are frequent and cheap, with destinations listed above the windscreen. Fares on buses are around R$3.

➡ **Taxi** Useful at night. Rates start at R$4.50 plus R$1.60 per kilometer.

➡ **Bike** A shared-bike scheme, Bike Rio (www.mobilicidade.com.br/bikerio.asp) has numerous stations around town. You'll need a local cellphone number to release the bikes at each station.

For much more on **getting around**, see p201

Sleeping

Rio's most popular accommodations include high-rise hotels on the beachfront, small art-minded guesthouses (particularly in Santa Teresa) and stylish hostels. No matter where you stay, you probably won't get much value for the money. Rio's rates are inflated, and you'll pay a premium (double or triple the normal price) during Carnaval and New Year's Eve, with minimum stays (four to seven nights) usually required. You can save money by renting an apartment.

Book at least two or three months in advance during high season.

Useful Websites

➡ **Airbnb** (www.airbnb.com) Dozens of rooms and apartments listed in Rio.

➡ **Cama e Cafe** (www.camaecafe.com) Rent a room from local residents in Santa Teresa.

➡ **Blame It on Rio 4 Travel** (www.blameitonrio4travel.com) Excellent agency that rents apartments in Copacabana and Ipanema.

For much more on **sleeping**, see p159

DANGERS & ANNOYANCES

Crime in Rio is declining, but it's wise to be cautious.

➡ Take nothing of value to the beach.

➡ Avoid Centro on weekends, when it is deserted.

➡ Don't wear expensive-looking accessories.

➡ Carry a copy of your passport, one credit card and enough cash for the day; leave the passport, extra cash and cards in your hotel safe.

Top Itineraries

Day One

Ipanema & Leblon (p56)

Spend the first day soaking up the rays on **Ipanema beach**. Be sure to hydrate with *maté* (cold sweetened tea) and *agua de côco* (coconut juice), sample a few beach snacks (or a sandwich at **Uruguai**) and take a scenic stroll down to Leblon.

Lunch Market (p63) serves delectable fare on a well-concealed patio.

Ipanema & Leblon (p56)

In the afternoon, have a wander through the streets of Ipanema, doing some window-shopping on Rua Garcia d'Ávila, stopping for ice cream at **Vero**, and getting a coffee fix at **Cafeína**. Later, stroll over to **Ponta do Arpoador**, and watch the sunset behind Dois Irmãos.

Dinner Food with Eastern influences at romantic Zazá Bistrô Tropical (p65).

Ipanema & Leblon (p56)

Catch a concert at **Studio RJ**, a great new space for jazz, rock and samba. Afterwards, head downstairs to **Bar Astor**, which has a great cocktail menu. If you're not ready to call it a night, go to **Barzin**, a festive bar and live-music venue that stays open until 3am.

Day Two

Flamengo & Around (p108)

Starting off in Cosme Velho, take the cog train up Corcovado to admire the view beneath the open-armed **Cristo Redentor**. Nearby, visit the **Museu Internacional de Arte Naïf do Brasil**, which is full of colorful folk art from Brazil and beyond.

Lunch Have a leisurely lunch at Bar do Mineiro (p138), a Santa Teresa classic.

Santa Teresa & Lapa (p133)

Afterwards, wander through Santa Teresa, Rio's most atmospheric neighborhood. Browse for handicrafts at **La Vereda**, admire the views from the **Parque das Ruínas** and check out the eclectic art collection and lush gardens of **Museu Chácara do Céu**. Have a pick-me-up in **Cafecito**.

Dinner Feast on beautiful Amazonian dishes at Espírito Santa (p138).

Santa Teresa & Lapa (p133)

Take a taxi downhill to Lapa for a late night of samba and caipirinhas. Start the evening taking in the street party around the Arcos da Lapa, before making your way to **Rio Scenarium**, a beautiful antique-filled club where you can join samba-loving crowds on the dance floor – or just watch the evening unfold from an upper balcony.

Day Three

Barra da Tijuca & Western Rio (p151)

In the morning, go for a hike in **Floresta da Tijuca**, which has rainforest-lined hiking trails, refreshing waterfalls and spectacular views from craggy summits.

Lunch Pay-by-weight Frontera (p89) provides countless temptations.

Copacabana & Leme (p84)

In the afternoon take in the sun and surf on **Copacabana beach**. If you're feeling active, you can try your hand at stand-up paddle boarding. After a few hours in the sun, stroll to the southern end of the neighborhood, where you can visit the **Forte de Copacabana**. Here you'll find a small museum and several relaxing open-air cafes with memorable views across the sweep of Copacabana beach.

Dinner Enjoy a meal on the sand at one of the beachside kiosks (p89).

Copacabana & Leme (p84)

After an early dinner, wander over to **Bip Bip**, a hole-in-the-wall bar that hosts some of the best *samba de roda* (informal samba played in a circle) in the Zona Sul. Cap off the evening over drinks with beachfront views at **Horse's Neck**, or for something a little livelier hit the dance floor at **Fosfobox**.

Day Four

Centro & Cinelândia (p117)

Stroll around Centro for a look at Rio's historic district. Start off in the **Museu Histórico Nacional**, which has excellent exhibits tracing 500-plus years of history. Be sure to peek in some of the city's most impressive colonial churches, including **Igreja São Francisco da Penitência** and the **Igreja de Nossa Senhora do Carmo da Antiga Sé**.

Lunch Enjoy rich seafood dishes and bay views at AlbaMar (p129).

Botafogo & Urca (p97)

Spend the afternoon down in Urca. Take the cable-car to the top of **Pão de Açúcar**, where Rio spreads before you in a stunning panorama. Afterwards, head over to Botafogo to for drinks and predinner tapas plates at **Oui Oui**.

Dinner Sample the culinary wizardry at Oro (p81).

Gávea, Jardim Botânico & Lagoa (p97)

After dinner, go for amazing cocktails and even better views at the open-air lakeside setting of **Palaphita Kitch**. If you're still going strong, end the night at **00 (Zero Zero)**, which has a small, fired-up dance floor and top-notch DJs.

If You Like...

Beaches

Ipanema There's never a dull moment on Rio's most famous beach, with volleyball games, food and drink vendors and those inviting waves. (p58)

Copacabana Planted with high-rises and framed by mountains, curving Copacabana beach is truly magnificent. (p86)

Praia Vermelha Hidden near the cable-car station to Pão de Açúcar, this tiny, well-concealed beach boasts a magnificent panorama. (p100)

Barra da Tijuca A picturesque, seemingly endless stretch of sand located west of Leblon. (p153)

Prainha You'll find good surf and a striking setting of rainforest-backed beachfront with little development in sight. (p153)

Outdoor Adventures

Parque Nacional da Tijuca Lush rainforest, waterfalls, scenic views atop rocky cliffs – Tijuca National Park is a must for outdoor lovers. (p156)

Hang gliding Take the plunge off Pedra Bonita for an unforgettable airborne adventure. (p50)

Pão de Açúcar Forget the cable car; for an adrenaline rush sign up for a rock climbing excursion to the top. (p99)

Lagoa Rodrigo de Freitas By day you can jog or cycle around the picturesque lake; by night enjoy cocktails at waterside kiosks. (p78)

Pista Claudio Coutinho A short trail in Urca that skirts between the edge of Morro do Urca and the sea. (p100)

Igreja de Nossa Senhora do Carmo da Antiga Sé (p120)

Parks & Gardens

Jardim Botânico This beautifully set botanical garden makes a refreshing escape from the city. (p79)

Parque Lage Home to a historic mansion and rainforest-lined walking trails, including one challenging trail that ascends Corcovado. (p79)

Parque do Flamengo A long narrow park with magnificent bay views that makes a great setting for a bike ride. (p112)

Parque da Catacumba Trails that lead up to a peak with magnificent views over the lake and the peaks beyond. (p80)

Sítio Burle Marx It's a long journey, but this verdant wonderland will dazzle garden lovers. (p153)

Historical Sights

Museu da República The former presidential palace has historical artifacts, including an eerily preserved room where one president took his own life. (p112)

Igreja de Nossa Senhora do Carmo da Antiga Sé Magnificently restored church where several Portuguese kings were crowned. (p120)

Forte Duque de Caxias Stand atop an old colonial fort and enjoy stunning views over Copocabana and Pão de Açúcar. (p87)

Igreja São Francisco da Penitência This gilded masterpiece stands serenely overlooking Centro. (p120)

Museu Histórico Nacional The former royal arsenal houses provides a fascinating glimpse into Rio's royal days. (p119)

Mosteiro de São Bento A gold-laden work of art, and one of Brazil's finest colonial churches. (p121)

Art & Architecture

Museu Nacional de Belas Artes An impressive collection of 19th and early 20th century paintings in the heart of downtown. (p120)

Museu de Arte Moderna A massive post-modern building that houses works by some of Brazil's best known 20th-century artists. (p121)

Theatro Municipal One of Rio's most striking buildings, this theater was recently restored to its former splendor. (p120)

Museu do Índio A beautifully curated collection of indigenous objects, photos and sound recordings. (p100)

Museu Chácara do Céu You'll pass through lush gardens en route to this small museum, which has an outstanding collection of modern art. (p136)

Free Attractions

Centro Cultural Banco do Brasil Massive arts center home to some of the city's top exhibits. (p120)

Centro de Arte Hélio Oiticica A little visited gem that has cutting-edge contemporary exhibitions. (p121)

Real Gabinete Português de Leitura The elegant Portuguese reading room is one of Rio's few buildings of the manueline style. (p121)

Parque das Ruínas High up in Santa Teresa, the ruins of this former mansion has magnificent views over Rio. (p136)

Museu de Folclore Edison Carneiro A small but worthwhile collection of Brazilian folk art next door to the former presidential palace. (p113)

Instituto Moreira Salles Fascinating gallery of temporary exhibits in a restored villa surrounded by Burle Marx–designed gardens. (p79)

Centro Cultural Justiça Federal The handsome building that once housed Brazil's Supreme Court today hosts diverse exhibitions. (p124)

For more top Rio de Janeiro spots, see the following:

- Eating (p33)
- Drinking & Nightlife (p37)
- Entertainment (p41)
- Samba (p43)
- Shopping (p47)
- Sports & Activities (p49)

Month by Month

TOP EVENTS

Carnaval February

Festas Juninas June

Portas Abertas July

Gay Pride Rio November

Reveillon December

January

Following the excitement of New Year's Eve, Rio starts the year in high gear, with steamy beach days, open-air concerts, and the buzz of pre-Carnaval revelry.

Dia de São Sebastião

The patron saint of Rio is commemorated on January 20 with a procession that carries the image of São Sebastião from Igreja de São Sebastião dos Capuchinos in Tijuca to the Catedral Metropolitana in Lapa.

February

High season is in full swing, with people-packed beaches, sold-out hotel rooms and the unbridled revelry of Carnaval. Periodic thunderstorms bring some relief from the sweltering humidity.

Rio Music Conference

Despite the bland name, this event features a stellar line-up of electronic-music gurus. The 2013 edition, spread over seven nights, featured Fatboy Slim, Bob Sinclair and Richie Hawtin. Headliners appear in the Marina da Glória.

Carnaval

Brazil's biggest fest (p26) is celebrated with abandon in Rio, with hundreds of street parties as well as costume balls and elaborate samba-fueled parades that attract revelers from all corners of the globe.

Verão do Morro

In February or March, the Verão do Morro (summer on the mountain) party kicks off, with a month of weekend concerts in a fabulous setting – Pão de Açúcar – overlooking Rio. Top Brazilian bands and DJs headline the all-night fest.

March

After Carnaval the foreign crowds disperse, though the weather stays hot and tropical rain showers continue. Ongoing summer concerts and events make it a festive time to visit.

Dia da Fundação da Cidade

The city commemorates its founding in 1565 with a March 1 Mass in the church of its patron saint, Igreja de São Sebastião dos Capuchinos. A procession, concerts, a children's parade and one massive birthday cake are part of the festivities.

Sexta-Feira da Paixão

In March or April (depending on when Easter falls), Good Friday is celebrated throughout the city. The most important ceremony re-enacts the Stations of the Cross under the Arcos da Lapa, with more than 100 actors.

Festival Internacional de Documentários

Latin America's most important documentary film festival (www.itsalltrue.com.br) takes place over 10 days in March or April when more than 100 films from Brazil and abroad are screened at theaters in Rio and São Paulo.

April

After the sweltering heat of summer, April remains warm but pleasant with slightly cooler temperatures and fewer rainstorms. Following the festive January to March period, *cariocas* (residents of Rio) return to work, and the kids are back in school.

Dia do Índio

April 19 pays homage to Brazil's indigenous cultures, with a week of special events held at the Museu do Índio (p100). Exhibitions, dance and film presentations are staged daily.

Dia de São Jorge

On April 23 the city pays its respects to St George, an important figure in the Afro-Brazilian community. There's a Mass at Igreja de São Jorge (Rua da Alfândega 382, Centro) followed by a procession. Food vendors abound.

June

June brings milder weather, with temperatures in the low 20s (celsius) and little rainfall. Although it's low season, there's much merriment in the air during the fun-loving Festas Juninas.

Rio das Ostras Jazz e Blues Festival

Located 170km east of Rio, en route to Búzios, pretty Rio das Ostras hosts one of Brazil's best jazz and blues fests (www.riodasostrasjazzeblues.com), with five days of concerts on outdoor stages by international performers.

Festas Juninas

Spanning the month of June, the feast days of various saints mark some of the most important folkloric festivals in Brazil. Celebrations are held in various public squares, with food stands, music, fireworks and bonfires. The big days are June 13, 24 and 29.

Rio Marathon

Set along the coast, with the ocean always at your side, this marathon course ranks among the world's loveliest. The annual 42km run (www.maratonadorio.com.br) happens in late June or July, when the weather is mild. There are also 6km and 21km runs.

Festa da São Pedro do Mar

The fishing fraternity pays homage to its patron saint in late June in a maritime procession as decorated boats leave from the fishing community of Caju and sail to the statue of São Pedro in Urca.

July

The cooler days of winter arrive, with little rainfall, clear blue skies and mild temperatures. There aren't many visitors in town, and accommodation prices are near their lowest.

Portas Abertas

Artists in Santa Teresa open their studios for a week in July during this lively annual festival. Expect music, a diverse crowd and inventive installations that make good use of the atmospheric bohemian 'hood.

Festa Literária Internacional de Parati

This important literary festival (www.flip.org.br) brings authors from around the world to Paraty for five days in July or August. Well-known writers like Ian McEwan, Jennifer Egan and Hanif Kureishi were among the featured guests in years past.

August

With continuing cool weather but sunny skies, it's an excellent time to take advantage of outdoor activities – cycling, rock climbing and hikes in the Tijuca forest.

Festa de NS da Glória do Outeiro

On August 15 the historic church (p113) overlooking Glória and the bay holds a procession, stages a concert and hosts colorful stalls. Festivities start in the morning and continue all day.

Leblon Jazz Festival

Held over several weekends in November, this jazz festival is an opportunity for Rio's beautiful people to come together for great music. Free concerts happen along Rua Dias Ferreira in Leblon and feature jazz, samba-jazz, bossa nova, MPB and other styles.

September

The weather is getting warmer, and although Carnaval is still

months away, samba-school rehearsals get underway – making it a great opportunity to get a taste of the excitement out of season.

Rock in Rio

One of the biggest rock festivals on earth has recently returned to Rio (after rotating between Lisbon and Madrid). Expect a stellar line-up of bands and huge, celebratory crowds for this event, happening in Rio in 2013 and 2015. Check out www.rockinrio.com.br.

Samba-School Rehearsals

Samba schools begin hosting open gatherings once a week (usually on Friday or Saturday night). In spite of the name, these are less a dress rehearsal than just an excuse to dance (to samba, of course) and celebrate. All are welcome.

Dia de Independência do Brasil

Independence Day is celebrated on September 7 with a large military parade down Av Presidente Vargas in Centro. It starts at 8am at Candelária (p124) and goes down just past Praça XI.

Festival do Rio

Rio's international film festival (www.festivaldorio.com.br) is one of the biggest in Latin America. Some 400 films from over 60 countries are shown at 30 theaters. It runs from the last week of September through the first week of October.

(Top) Carnaval (p26)
(Bottom) Reveillon, Copacabana beach (p86)

October

October brings more beach days and a touch more daylight – Rio pushes the clock ahead for one hour from mid-October to mid-February. The comfortable temperatures make it an excellent time to be in the tropics.

Festa da Penha

Held on Sundays in October, this religious fest draws thousands of pilgrims who ascend the 365 steps to the dramatically set Igreja da Penha (p149) in the northern suburb of Penha. In the plaza below, food and drink stalls and live music create a festive environment.

November

Summer has nearly arrived and the city begins to gear up for festive days and nights ahead, with a big gay-pride parade, a dance festival and more activities on the city's sands.

Gay Pride Rio

Although not as large as São Paulo's massive parade, the Rio gay pride event (www.gaypridebrazil.org) gets bigger each year, with over a million people turning out in recent years. It usually takes place in November or October.

Festival Panorama de Dança

Spanning two weeks in November, the Festival Panorama (www.panoramafestival.com) showcases the work of dozens of contemporary dance groups from across the globe, bringing together a mix of experimental troupes as well as traditional performers.

December

While the northern hemisphere shivers, *cariocas* strip down to the bare essentials for hot days on the beach and steamy nights at samba parties around town.

Lighting of the Lagoa Christmas Tree

Throughout December, the world's largest floating Christmas tree (85m) glows brightly on Lagoa Rodrigo de Freitas (p78). To celebrate its lighting, a concert is held in Parque Brigadeiro Faria Lima, usually on the first Saturday in December.

Festa de Iemanjá

This December 31 Candomblé festival celebrates the feast day of Iemanjá, the goddess of the sea. White-clad participants place their petitions on small boats, sending them out to sea. If a boat returns, the prayer will not be answered.

Reveillon

Rio's biggest holiday after Carnaval takes place on Copacabana beach, when some two million people pack the sands to welcome the new year. Fireworks light up the sky as top bands perform on stages built on the sands.

With Kids

While Rio isn't the obvious choice for a family holiday, there are plenty of activities to keep kids amused: sandy fun on the beach, bike rides around Lagoa, aerial cable-car rides, adventure parks and rainforest walks, with plenty of great treats – fresh juices, ice creams, pastries – along the way.

ATLANTIDE PHOTOTRAVEL / CORBIS ©

Ipanema beach (p58)

Top Snacks

Sorvete

Buy ice cream from Vero (p61) or Felice Caffè (p63) especially.

Agua de Côco

Order coconut water straight from the nut at beachside kiosks.

Pão de Queijo

This small round cheese-filled bread is available at any juice bar.

Pastel de Nata

Sample these tasty custard tarts at the art deco beauty Confeitaria Colombo (p127).

Sucos

Try creamy *açaí* (juice made from an Amazonian berry) and many other juice flavors.

Green Spaces

Jardim Botânico

These verdant gardens (p79) are a fine break from the sun on a hot day, with a picturesque pond, a playground, a cafe and shaded walking trails.

Parque Lage

About 1km northeast of the Jardim Botanico, Parque Lage (p79) has extensive walking trails, including a challenging uphill climb to Corcovado (not for kids), and it's a great spot to see monkeys.

Floresta da Tijuca

At this vast wilderness (p156) northwest of the Zona Sul you can take short or long hikes, enjoy picturesque views and take a dip in a waterfall.

Stunning Panoramas

Cristo Redentor

Most kids will get a huge kick out of the steep cog train that takes visitors through dense forest to the massive Christ the Redeemer statue (p110).

Pão de Açúcar

The journey by aerial gondola to the summit of this peak (p99) is probably the best part of the experience for kids; afterwards, you can walk to the small picturesque beach of Praia Vermelha.

The Beach

For younger kids, check out **Baixo Bebê Leblon**. The family-friendly beach area (between posts 11 and 12) in Leblon has a netted-off play area with slides and such, and you can also hire a small plastic pool from a nearby kiosk (for around R$10).

For older kids, there's lots to see and do on the beach: pick-up football and volleyball games, boogie boarding, and sampling the snacks from roaming food vendors.

The Lake

At **Parque dos Patins**, on the west side of Lagoa, you can hire bikes, scooters, tricycles, toys and huge family-sized pedal bikes for a spin along the lakeside path.

On the east side of the lake, at **Parque do Cantagalo**, you can hire pedal boats (around R$15 for a half hour).

If you're around in December, pay a visit to the lake at night, when a giant floating Christmas tree lights up the lakeside.

Climbing Adventures

Near the east side of the lake you'll find Parque da Catacumba (p80), which is a great spot for older kids. The outfit known as **Lagoa Aventuras** (☎4105-0079; www.lagoaaventuras.com.br) has a zipline, rock climbing wall, treetop walks and rappelling (abseiling). There are also short but steep hiking trails which take you to a lookout with stunning views over the lake.

Boat Trips

Older kids might also enjoy a boat ride out on the bay. For a full-day outing you can take the ferry out to Ilha de Paquetá (p129). Once on the car-free island, you can get around by bicycle or horse-drawn carriage. There are also shorter cruises most days, as well as the cheap ferry to Niterói, which offers great views of the bay.

NEED TO KNOW

- **Admission** At most sites, kids under 13 pay half price; those under five or six typically get in free.
- **Attitudes** Brazilians are very family-oriented; you'll be welcomed with open arms at most restaurants. High chairs are readily available.
- **Accommodations** Many hotels let children stay free, although the age limit varies.

Top Attractions for Kids

Museu Naval

Checking out the submarine and nautical equipment (p121).

Ilha Fiscal

A Cinderella-esque castle (p127), reached by short boat ride.

Museu do Índio

Native music, headdresses, weaponry, recreated huts and activities for kids (p100).

Quinta da Boa Vista

The former home and gardens (p148) of the Portuguese royals now contains a natural history museum and a zoo (p148).

Rio Water Planet

A gigantic **water park** (Map p252; ☎2428-9000; Estrada das Bandeirantes 24000, Recreio dos Bandeirantes; admission R$89; ⏰10am-5pm Fri-Sun & holidays) where you can slip and slide along waterfalls; the downside is it's far west of the centre.

Markets

You'll find fruit markets (p35) all across town, and it's the perfect spot to assemble a picnic, while sampling fruits you won't find back home.

Planetário

Astronomic fun and stargazing (p79).

Carnaval

If you haven't heard by now, Rio throws one of the world's best parties, with music and dancing filling the streets for days on end. Officially, Carnaval is just five days of revelry – from Friday to Tuesday before Ash Wednesday – but the city begins partying months in advance.

ARY DIESENDRUCK / GETTY IMAGES ©

Samba schools parade, Sambódromo (p149)

Experiencing Carnaval

The culmination of the big fest is the brilliantly colorful parade through the Sambódromo (p149) – with giant mechanized floats, pounding drummers and whirling dancers – but there's lots of action in Rio's many neighborhoods for those seeking more than just the stadium experience.

Out-of-towners add to the mayhem, joining *cariocas* (Rio residents) in the street parties and costumed balls erupting throughout the city. There are free concerts to be found (in Largo do Machado, Arcos da Lapa and Praça General Osório, among other places), while those seeking a bit of decadence can head to the various balls.

Whatever you do, prepare yourself for sleepless nights, an ample dose of caipirinhas and samba, and mingling with the joyful crowds spilling out of the city.

Joining the *bandas* and *blocos* (street parties) is one of the best ways to have the *carioca* experience. These marching parades consist of a procession of brass bands (in the case of *bandas*) or drummers and vocalists (in the case of *blocos*) followed by anyone who wants to dance through the streets. Some *bandas* suggest costumes (drag, Amazonian attire etc), while others simply expect people to show up and add to the good cheer.

History

Although the exact origins of Carnaval are shrouded in mystery, some believe the fest originated as a pagan celebration of spring's arrival sometime during the Middle Ages. The Portuguese brought the celebration to Brazil in the 1500s but it took on a decidedly local flavor by adopting indigenous costumes and African rhythms. (The origin of the word itself probably derives from the Latin '*carne vale*' – 'farewell, meat' – whereby the Catholic population would give up meat and other fleshly temptations during the 40 days of Lent.)

The first festivals in Rio de Janeiro were called *entrudo,* with locals dancing through the streets in colorful costumes and throwing mud, flour and various suspect liquids at one another. In the 19th

NEED TO KNOW

➡ **Carnaval Dates** The following are the Carnaval dates (Friday to Shrove Tuesday) in coming years:

2014 February 28–March 4

2015 February 13–17

2016 February 5–9

➡ **Useful Contacts** Riotur (p209), the tourist organization in charge of Carnaval. **LIESA** (☎3213-5151; liesa.globo.com; Av Rio Branco 4 , Centro; ⏰10am-4pm Mon-Fri Sept-Carnaval) for information on buying tickets to the big parades in the Sambódromo.

century Carnaval meant attending a lavish masked ball or participating in the orderly and rather vapid European-style parade. Rio's poor citizens, bored by the finery but eager to participate in a celebration, began holding their own parades, dancing through the streets to African-based rhythms. Then, in the 1920s, the new sound of samba emerged in Rio. It was the music full of African flavors that was brought to the city by former slaves and their poor descendents – a sound that would forever more be associated with Carnaval.

Since those days, Carnaval has grown in leaps and bounds, with elaborate parades spreading from Rio de Janeiro to other parts of Brazil. It has also become a huge commercial enterprise, with visitors to the city spending in excess of R$1 billion each year.

Carnaval on the Streets

Rio's street parties – the *bandas* and *blocos* – have exploded in recent years. Ten years ago, there were only a handful of these events happening around town. In 2013 there were nearly 500 street parties, filling every neighborhood in town with the sound of pounding drums and old-fashioned Carnaval songs – not to mention thousands of merrymakers. For many *cariocas*, this is the highlight of Carnaval. You can don a costume (or not), learn a few songs and join in; all you have to do is show up – and for Zona Sul fests, don't forget to bring your swimsuit afterwards, for a dip in the ocean.

For complete listings, pick up a free *Carnaval de Rua* guide from **Riotur** (www.rioofficialguide.com). The following are some of the better-known street parties, each attracting anywhere from 1000 to hundreds of thousands. Although the dates usually stay the same, the times sometimes change, so it's wise to confirm before heading out.

AfroReggae (Posto 9, Ipanema; ⏰8am Carnaval Mon) A massive and hugely popular *bloco*, with a heavy rhythm section, that celebrates along the beachfront (Av Vieira Souto) in Ipanema.

Banda de Ipanema (Praça General Osório, Ipanema; ⏰4pm Sat of Carnaval and two Saturdays prior) This long-standing *banda* attracts a wild crowd, complete with drag queens and others in costume. Don't miss it.

Banda de Sá Ferreira (cnr Av Atlântica & Rua Sá Ferreira, Copacabana; ⏰4pm Sat, Sun, Mon & Tue of Carnaval) This extremely popular Copacabana *banda* marches along the ocean from Posto 1 to Posto 6.

Banda Simpatia é Quase Amor (Praça General Osório, Ipanema; ⏰2pm 2nd Sat before Carnaval & Carnaval Sun) Another Ipanema favorite, with a 50-piece percussion band.

Barbas (cnr Rua Assis Bueno & Rua Arnoldo Quintela, Botafogo; ⏰2:30pm Carnaval Sat) One of the oldest *bandas* of the Zona Sul parades through the streets with a 60-piece percussion band. A water truck follows along to spray the crowd, all decked out in red and white.

Carmelitas (cnr Rua Dias de Barros & Ladeira de Santa Teresa, Santa Teresa; ⏰1pm Carnaval Fri & 8am Carnaval Tue) A crazy mixed crowd (some dressed as Carmelite nuns) parades through Santa Teresa's streets.

Céu na Terra (Curvelo, Santa Teresa; ⏰3pm Carnaval Sat) Follows the tram tracks on a memorable celebration through Santa Teresa en route to Largo das Neves.

Cordão do Bola Preta (cnr Rua Evaristo da Veiga & Rua 13 de Maio, Centro; ⏰8am Carnaval Sat) The oldest and biggest *banda* still in action. Costumes are always welcome, especially those with black-and-white spots. More than two million join the festivities.

Dois Pra Lá, Dois Pra Cá (Rua da Passagem 145, Carlinho de Jesus Dance School, Botafogo;

DEMETRIO CARRASCO / GETTY IMAGES ©

Carnaval participant

⏲10am Carnaval Sat) This fairly long march begins at the dance school and ends at the Copacabana Palace.

Monobloco (Av Rio Branco near Pres Vargas, Centro; ⏲7am 1st Sun after Carnaval) Rise and shine! This huge *bloco* attracts upwards of 400,000 revelers. Nursing hangovers (or perhaps still inebriated), they gather in Centro for a final farewell to the Carnaval mayhem.

Que Merda É Essa? (Garcia D'Ávila near Nascimento Silva; ⏲noon Carnaval Sun) This playful gathering (which means 'What the shit is this?') is yet another big draw in Ipanema – and eventually makes its way along the beach.

Suvaco de Cristo (Rua Jardim Botânico near Rua Faro, Jardim Botânico; ⏲8am Sun before Carnaval) Very popular *bloco* (which means 'Christ's armpit' – in reference to the open-armed Redeemer looming overhead). It also meets on Carnaval Saturday, but doesn't announce the time (to avoid overcrowding), so ask around.

Carnaval Balls

Carnaval balls are giant, sometimes costumed, parties with live music and dancing, and an ambience that runs the gamut from staid and formal to wild and a bit tawdry. The most famous and formal ball (you'll need a tux) is held at the Copacabana Palace (p168), where you'll have the opportunity to celebrate with Rio's glitterati as well as international stars. Tickets cost upwards of R$1500.

Popular but less pricey balls (under R$100) are held at Rio Scenarium (p140) and at Circo Voador (p140) among other places. The most extravagant gay balls are found at Le Boy (p94). These are good places to don a costume to help get in the mood.

Tickets go on sale about two weeks beforehand, and the balls are held nightly during Carnaval. The *Veja Rio* insert in *Veja* magazine has details.

Samba School Parades

The highlight of any Carnaval experience is attending (or participating in) a parade at the Sambódromo (p149). There, before a crowd of some 90,000 (with millions more watching on TV), each of 12 samba schools has its 80 minutes to dance and sing through the open Oscar Niemeyer–designed stadium. The pageantry is not simply eye candy for the masses. Schools are competing for top honors in the parade, with winners announced (and a winner's parade held) on the Saturday following Carnaval.

The Big Event

Here's what to expect: each school enters the Sambódromo with amped energy levels, and dancers take things up a notch as they dance through the stadium. Announcers introduce the school, the group's theme colors and the number of *alas* (literally, wings – subgroups within a school, each playing a different role). Far away the lone voice of the *puxador* (interpreter) starts the samba. Thousands more voices join him (each school has 3000 to 5000 members), and then the drummers kick in, 200 to 400 per school. The pounding drums drive the parade. Next come the main wings of the school, the big allegorical floats, the children's wing, the drummers, the celebrities and the bell-shaped *baianas* (women dressed as Bahian aunts) twirling in elegant hoopskirts. The *baianas* honor the history of the parade itself, which was brought to Rio from Salvador da Bahia in 1877.

Costumes are fabulously lavish, with 1.5m feathered headdresses; long, flowing capes that sparkle with sequins; and rhinestone-studded G-strings.

Winner Takes All

The whole procession is also an elaborate competition. A handpicked set of judges chooses the best school on the basis of many components, including percussion, the *samba do enredo* (theme song), harmony between percussion, song and dance, choreography, costumes, story line, floats and decorations. The dance championship is hotly contested, with the winner becoming the pride not just of Rio but all of Brazil.

Getting Involved

Most visitors stay for three or four schools, and come to see their favorite in action (every self-respecting *carioca* has a school they support, just as they have a favorite football team). If you're really gung-ho, wear your school's colors and learn the theme song (the words are found on the website of each school) so you can sing along when it marches through the Sambódromo. Mangueira (pink and green) and Salgueiro (red and white) are two of the most popular schools.

Parade Nights

The Sambódromo parades start with the *mirins* (young samba-school members) on the evening of Carnaval Friday, and continue on through Saturday night when the Group A samba schools strut their stuff. Sunday and Monday are the big nights, when the 12 best samba schools in Rio (the Grupo Especial) parade: six of them on Sunday night and into the morning, and six more on Monday night. The following Saturday, the six top schools strut their stuff again in the Parade of Champions, which generally has more affordable tickets than on the big nights. Each event starts at 9pm and runs until 4am.

Tickets

Getting tickets for the parades at legitimate prices can be tough. **LIESA** (liesa.globo.com), the official samba school league, begins selling tickets in December or January, most of which get immediately snatched up by travel agencies – then later resold at higher prices). Check with Riotur about where you can get them, as the official outlet can vary from year to year.

Prices At face value, tickets run from R$130 to R$550, though you'll probably have to pay about twice that (or more) if you buy just before Carnaval.

Where to Sit The best seating areas, in order of preference, are sectors 9, 7, 11, 5 and 3. The first two (9 and 7) have great views and are in the center, which is the liveliest place to be.

Last-minute Options By Carnaval weekend, most tickets will have sold out, but there are lots of scalpers. If you buy a ticket from a scalper (no need to worry about looking for them – they'll find you!), make sure you get both the plastic ticket with the magnetic strip and the ticket showing the seat number. The tickets for different days are color coded, so double-check the date as well.

If you haven't purchased a ticket but still want to go, you can show up at the Sambódromo during Carnaval at around midnight, three or four hours into the show, when you can get grandstand tickets for about R$50 from scalpers outside the gate. Make sure you check which sector your ticket is for. Most ticket sellers will try to sell their worst seats.

And if you can't make it during Carnaval proper, there's always the cheaper Parade of Champions the following Saturday.

Getting to the Sambódromo

The best way to get to the Sambódromo is by metro, with several stations within walking distance of the arena. The metro runs round-the-clock during Carnaval, from Saturday morning until Tuesday evening. This is also a great opportunity to check out the paraders commuting in costume.

If you take the metro, the stop at which you get off depends on the location of your seats. For sectors 2, 4 and 6, exit at Praça Onze. Once outside the station, turn to the right, take another right and then walk straight ahead (on Rua Júlio Carmo) to Sector 2. For sectors 4 and 6, turn right at Rua Carmo Neto and proceed to Av Salvador de Sá. You'll soon see the Sambódromo and hear the roar of the crowd. Look for signs showing the entrance to the sectors. If you are going to sectors on the other side (1, 3, 5, 7, 9, 11 and 13), exit at the metro stop Central. You'll then walk about 700m along Av Presidente Vargas until you see the Sambódromo.

If you go by taxi, make sure you tell your taxi driver which side of the stadium your seats are on.

Carnaval Party Planner

by Marcos Silviano do Prado

Cariocas start partying long before the big Sambódromo parades take place, but the city is at its wildest from Friday to Tuesday before Ash Wednesday. To make the most of your time, check out the long-standing *festas* (parties) listed below. You can dance through the streets in a *banda,* party like a rock star at one of many dance clubs scattered throughout town or find your groove at one of the samba-school rehearsals (p45). Those looking for free, open-air, neighborhood-wide celebrations shouldn't miss Rio Folia, in front of Arcos da Lapa (Lapa Arches) in Lapa. For the location of events listed below see Carnaval on the Streets p27.

Saturday – Two Weeks Before Carnaval

➡ Banda de Ipanema at 4pm.

➡ Rehearsals at samba schools.

Weekend Before Carnaval

➡ Banda Simpatia é Quase Amor, Saturday at 2pm.

➡ Rehearsals at samba schools.

Carnaval Friday

➡ Carnaval King Momo is crowned by the mayor at 1pm.

➡ Shows start at Terreirão do Samba (Samba Land) from 8pm.

➡ Children's samba schools parade at the Sambódromo (p149) from 5pm.

➡ Costume ball at Rio Scenarium (p140).

➡ Gay ball at Le Boy (p94).

Carnaval Saturday

➡ Cordão do Bola Preta from 9:30am.

➡ Banda de Ipanema at 4pm.

➡ Parade of Group A samba schools at the Sambódromo from 7pm.

➡ Street band competition (Av Rio Branco, Centro; admission free) from 8pm.

➡ Shows at Terreirão do Samba (Samba Land) and Rio Folia from 8pm.

➡ Copacabana Palace Luxury Ball from 10pm – costume or black tie mandatory.

➡ Carnaval balls at Scala, Rio Scenarium and other venues from 11pm.

➡ Gay balls at Le Boy and The Week.

➡ X-Demente Party at Fundição Progresso (p142).

➡ Parties at 00 and other dance clubs.

Carnaval Sunday

➡ Banda Simpatia é Quase Amor at 2pm.

➡ Shows at Terreirão do Samba and Rio Folia from 8pm.

➡ Samba parade at the Sambódromo from 9pm.

➡ Carnaval balls at Rio Scenarium and other venues.

➡ Gay balls at Le Boy.

➡ Parties at dance clubs.

Carnaval Monday

➡ Shows at Terreirão do Samba and Rio Folia from 8pm.

➡ Samba parade at the Sambódromo from 9pm.

➡ Carnaval balls at Rio Scenarium and other venues.

➡ Gay balls at Le Boy.

➡ Parties at dance clubs.

Carnaval Tuesday

➡ Banda de Ipanema at 4pm.

➡ Shows at Terreirão do Samba and Rio Folia from 8pm.

➡ Parade of Group B samba schools at the Sambódromo from 9pm.

➡ Carnaval balls from 11pm.

➡ Gay balls at Le Boy and The Week.

➡ X-Demente Party at **Marina da Glória** (Map p241; www.marinadagloria.com.br; Av Infante Dom Henrique, Glória).

➡ Parties at dance clubs.

Weekend After Carnaval

➡ Parade of champions, Sambódromo, Saturday 9pm.

➡ Monobloco, Av Rio Branco in Centro, Sunday from 8am.

Joining a Samba School

Those who have done it say no other part of Carnaval quite compares to donning a costume and dancing through the Sambódromo before roaring crowds. Anyone with the desire and a little extra money to spare can march in the parade. Most samba schools are happy to have foreigners join one of the wings. To get the ball rolling, you'll need to contact your chosen school in advance; it will tell you the rehearsal times and when you need to be in the city (usually a week or so before Carnaval). Ideally, you should memorize the theme song as well, but it's not essential (you can always lip sync). The biggest investment, aside from the airfare to Rio, is buying a *fantasia* (costume), which will cost upwards of R$600. If you speak some Portuguese, you can contact a school directly; many Rio travel agencies can also arrange this. One recommended outfit is **Rio Charm** (☎2417-8018; www.riocharm.com.br), which brings a group of travelers together to parade with a Grupo A school (which some say is less formal and more fun). Costumes are around R$400.

Those seeking an insider's perspective on samba schools should read Alma Guillermoprieto's excellent book, *Samba*.

Rio Folia

Lapa becomes one of the major focal points during Carnaval. Rio Folia consists of open-air concerts held in front of the Arcos da Lapa on the Praça Cardeal Câmara. About half a dozen different bands play each night (samba, of course). The music starts at 10pm and runs until past 2am, though revelers pack Lapa until well past sunrise.

Samba Land & Samba City

Another festive space for concerts is the Terreirão do Samba (Samba Land), an open-air courtyard next to the Sambódromo's sector 1, where bands play to large crowds throughout Carnaval (beginning the weekend before). There are also dozens of food and drink vendors, and a wide variety of bands playing. The action starts around 8pm and continues until 5:30am. Admission is R$15.

One of the biggest developments in Rio's Carnaval world is Cidade do Samba (p148), which opened in 2006. Located north of Centro near the port, the 'city' is actually made up of 14 large buildings in which the top schools assemble the Carnaval floats.

Visitors can take a tour through the area (R$5) or attend a live show (R$190), which features costumed dancers, live music and audience participation, plus free drinks and appetizers. It's touristy and pricey, but some visitors enjoy the Carnaval-style show nonetheless. It's currently held every other Thursday, beginning at 8pm; confirm times with Cidade do Samba or check with Riotur.

Samba Glossary for Parade-Goers

Alas – literally the 'wings.' These are groups of samba-school members responsible for a specific part of the central *samba do enredo* (theme song). Special *alas* include the *baianas* (women dressed as Bahian 'aunts' in full skirts and turbans). The *abre ala* of each school is the opening wing or float.

Bateria – the drum section is the driving beat behind the school's samba and is the 'soul' of the school.

Carnavalesco – the artistic director of each school, responsible for the overall layout and design of the school's theme.

Carros alegóricos – the dazzling floats, usually decorated with near-naked women. The floats are pushed along by the school's maintenance crew.

Desfile – the parade. The most important samba schools *desfilar* (parade) on the Sunday and Monday night of Carnaval. Each school's *desfile* is judged on its samba, drum section, master of ceremonies and flag bearer, floats, leading commission, costumes, dance coordination and overall harmony.

Destaques – the richest and most elaborate costumes. The heaviest ones usually get a spot on one of the floats.

Diretores de harmonia – the school organizers, who usually wear white or the school colors; they run around yelling and 'pumping up' the wings, making sure there aren't any gaps in the parade.

Enredo – the central theme of each school. The *samba do enredo* is the samba that goes with it. Radio stations and dance halls prime *cariocas* with classic *enredos* on the weeks leading up to Carnaval.

Passistas – the best samba dancers of a school. They roam the parade in groups or alone, stopping to show off some fancy footwork along the way. The women are usually dressed in short, revealing skirts, and the men usually hold tambourines.

Puxador – the interpreter of the theme song. He (a *puxador* is invariably male) works as a guiding voice, leading the school's singers at rehearsals and in the parade.

HOLGER LEUE / GETTY IMAGES ©

Bar do Mineiro (p138), Santa Teresa

Eating

Despite top-notch chefs, ethnically diverse cuisine and a rich bounty from farm, forest and sea, Rio hasn't earned much of a culinary reputation abroad. Inside Brazil it's a different story, with cariocas (residents of Rio) convinced that there's no place quite like home for sitting down to a first-rate meal.

The Dining Scene

Variety comes in many forms in Rio, which is not surprising given the large immigrant population. Lebanese, Japanese, Spanish, German, French and Italian cuisines are among the standouts, though there's an equally broad selection of regional Brazilian restaurants.

Diners can sample rich, shrimp-filled *moqueca* (seafood stew cooked in coconut milk) from Bahia or tender *carne seca* (jerked meat) covered in *farofa* (toasted manioc flour), a staple in Minas Gerais. Daring palates can venture north into Amazonia, enjoying savory *tacacá* (*jambu* and dried-shrimp soup) or *tambaqui* (a large Amazonian fish) and other meaty fishes from the mighty Amazon. *Gaúchos* (cowboys) from the south bring the city its *churrascarias*, Brazil's famous all-you-can-eat barbecue restaurants, where crisply dressed waiters bring piping-hot spits of freshly roasted meats to your table.

Wherever you end up, try to pace yourself. Brazilian dishes are normally quite large – and some dishes are meant for two. When in doubt, ask the server to clarify.

NEED TO KNOW

Price Ranges

The price symbols in reviews indicate the cost of a main course.

$	under R$20
$$	R$20–40
$$$	over R$40

Opening Hours

Most restaurants open from noon to 3pm and 6pm to 11pm. On Sundays, many restaurants open only for lunch if at all. Juice bars open around 7am or 8am and close at midnight or later.

Tipping

In restaurants, a 10% tip is usually included in the bill. When it isn't included, it's customary to leave 10%.

Reservations

Most restaurants accept reservations for both lunch and dinner, so call ahead to avoid a wait. Reservations are essential at high-end restaurants, and the answering host will usually speak English.

Lunch Specials

Some restaurants serve multi-course lunch specials, which often provide decent value for money. Prices start around R$22 and can go upwards of R$40 for more elaborate offerings.

Dress Code

Cariocas are quite casual when it comes to dress, and dining out is no exception. At even the nicest places, a pair of smart jeans and a collared shirt or blouse will do just fine.

Etiquette

Brazilians can be fastidious when it comes to eating. Use a knife and fork when eating pizza, and naked hands should never touch your food – always use a napkin when eating sandwiches, bar snacks, etc.

Juice Bars

Most *cariocas* start their mornings off with a stop at the local juice bar, where they can enjoy two or three dozen varieties of vitamin-filled elixirs, including the very popular *açaí* (juice made from an Amazonian berry, and whipped up to a thick consistency – it's eaten with a spoon).

Other unique flavors to try: *cupuaçu* (Amazonian fruit), *caju* (fruit from the cashew nut tree), *acerola* (tropical cherry), *carambola* (star fruit), *graviola* (custard apple), *fruta do conde* (sugar apple) and *cacau* (made from the creamy pulp of the cocoa pod and nothing like cocoa). More traditional fruits include *maracujá* (passion fruit), *manga* (mango), *goiaba* (guava) and *tamarindo* (tamarillo).

Juices are made from frozen pulp, with added sugar. To order it without sugar, request *'sem açucar'*.

Juice bars also serve snacks (on display in the counters) as well as hot sandwiches (such as a *misto quente*, a toasted ham and cheese sandwich) and other bites served up in a hurry.

Per-Kilo Restaurants

At lunchtime, locals favor pay-by-weight restaurants, which range from simple, working-class affairs to sumptuous buffets lined with fresh salads, grilled meats, pastas, seafood dishes and a table packed with desserts. These are found all across the city, and are a great way to sample a wide variety of Brazilian dishes.

Most places charge around R$40 to R$50 per kilo, with a sizeable plate of food costing about R$25.

Snacks

Snack stands, juice bars and *botecos* serve up a wide variety of delicious, if utterly unhealthy *salgados* (bar snacks). After a day at the beach, they go quite nicely with a few rounds of *chope* (draft beer).

The following are a few top picks:

Pão de queijo Bite-sized cheese-filled rolls.

Esfiha Triangular pastry filled with meat and spices, spinach or other fillings.

Kibe Deep-fried Middle Eastern snack with a thin whole-wheat crust and a filling of ground beef and spices.

Bolinho de bacalhau Deep-fried codfish balls.

Coxinha Pear-shaped cornmeal balls filled with shredded chicken.

Pastel de carne/camarão/queijo Square of deep-fried dough filled with meat, shrimp or cheese.

Food Markets

The *feiras* (produce markets) that pop up in different locations throughout the week are the best places to shop for juicy mangos, papayas, pineapples and other fruits. For an authentic slice of homegrown *carioca* commerce, nothing beats wandering through and taking in the action. The best time to go is in the morning (9am to noon). The *feiras* end by 2pm or 3pm.

In addition to the markets listed below, stop in Ipanema's Hippie Fair (p72) on Sunday for delectable Bahian fare.

Cobal do Humaitá (Map p244; ☎2266-1343; Voluntários da Pátria 446, Botafogo; ⏰7am-4pm Mon-Sat) The city's largest farmers' market sells plenty of veggies and fruits; there are also cafes and restaurants, with a huge open-air pavilion for al fresco eating and drinking.

Cobal do Leblon (p70) Smaller than Humaitá's market, the Cobal do Leblon also has fruit stalls, as well as indoor-outdoor restaurants and bars.

Copacabana Markets are held Wednesdays on Praça Edmundo Bittencourt, Thursdays on Rua Ministro Viveiros de Castro and Rua Ronald de Carvalho, and Sundays on Praça Serzedelo Correia.

Gávea Friday market on Praça Santos Dumont.

Glória Sunday market on Av Augusto Severo.

Ipanema Markets are held Monday on Rua Henrique Dumont, Tuesday on Praça General Osório and Friday on Praça NS da Paz.

Jardim Botânico Saturday market on Rua Frei Leandro.

Leblon Thursday on Rua General Urquiza.

Leme Monday market on Gustavo Sampaio

Santa Teresa Friday on Rua Felicio dos Santos

Urca Sunday on Praça Tenente Gil Guilherme.

Feijoada

As distinctively *carioca* as Pão de Açúcar (Sugarloaf) or Cristo Redentor (Christ the Redeemer), the *feijoada completa* is a dish that constitutes an entire meal, which often begins with a caipirinha aperitif.

A properly prepared *feijoada* is made up of black beans slowly cooked with a great variety of meat – including dried tongue and pork offcuts – seasoned with salt, garlic, onion and oil. The stew is accompanied by white rice and finely shredded kale, then tossed with croutons, fried *farofa* (manioc flour) and pieces of orange.

Feijoada has its origins in Portuguese cooking, which uses a large variety of meats and vegetables; fried *farofa* (inherited from the indigenous inhabitants) and kale are also Portuguese favorites. The African influence comes with the spice and the tradition of using pork offcuts, which were the only part of the pig given to slaves.

Traditionally, *cariocas* eat *feijoada* for lunch on Saturday, though a few restaurants serve it on other days. Among the top places to sample the signature dish is Casa da Feijoada (p63), which is one of the few places in Rio that serves *feijoada* daily. Vegetarians can sample tasty meat-free versions of *feijoada* at Vegetariano Social Club (p66).

Eating by Neighborhood

➡ **Ipanema & Leblon** (p59) Best assortment of dining from inexpensive juice bars and per-kilo places to award-winning restaurants.

➡ **Gávea, Jardim Botânico & Lagoa** (p80) Charming upscale neighborhood options, plus dining with views at open-air lakeside kiosks.

➡ **Copacabana & Leme** (p87) Humble rotisseries, ethnic fare and beachfront kiosks, plus hidden gems on the side streets.

➡ **Botafogo & Urca** (p87) Botafogo has unique options, especially on the streets near the Cobal do Humaitá.

➡ **Flamengo & Around** (p113) Small selection of midrange and downmarket options and a few well-concealed surprises (Lebanese, Japanese, Amazonian).

➡ **Centro & Cinelândia** (p127) Loads of great-value lunch options on pedestrianized side streets, but few dinner options.

➡ **Santa Teresa & Lapa** (p137) Small but enticing collection of eateries, with the densest concentration around Largo do Guimarães.

Lonely Planet's Top Choices

Espírito Santa (p138) Superb Amazonian dishes and creative cocktails in Santa Teresa.

Sushi Leblon (p67) Famous for its inventive dishes and mouthwatering sashimi.

Oro (p81) Molecular gastronomy served with flair.

Zazá Bistrô Tropical (p65) Handsomely converted mansion with contemporary Asian-inspired fare.

Aprazível (p138) Beautiful setting with magical views over the city.

Porcão Rio's (p114) Sizzling juicy steaks coupled with fabulous views.

Best by Budget

$

Cafecito (p137)

Galeto Sat's (p88)

Yalla (p66)

Nega Teresa (p137)

Vero (p61)

$$

Meza Bar (p104)

Sobrenatural (p138)

Santa Satisfação (p88)

La Carioca Cevicheria (p81)

Guimas (p80)

$$$

Bazzar (p64)

Zuka (p67)

Olympe (p81)

AlbaMar (p129)

Térèze (p138)

Best for Seafood

Sobrenatural (p138)

La Carioca Cevicheria (p81)

AlbaMar (p129)

Best for Views

Azul Marinho (p64)

Arab da Lagoa (p81)

Emporium Pax (p104)

Bira (p157)

Best for Atmosphere

Confeitaria Colombo (p127)

Cais do Oriente (p129)

Bar do Mineiro (p138)

Santa Scenarium (p138)

Don Pascual (p156)

Best for Vegetarians

Vegetariano Social Club (p66)

Govinda (p128)

New Natural (p62)

Best Eat Streets

Rua Barão da Torre, Ipanema

Rua Dias Ferreira, Leblon

Rua Garcia D'Ávila, Ipanema

Rua Almirante Alexandrino, Santa Teresa

Rua do Rosário, Centro

Rua Conde de Irajá, Botafogo

Drinking & Nightlife

Any night of the week you'll find plenty of ways to experience Rio's fun-loving nightlife. A few places to start off the night: open-air bars by the lake, festive outdoor drinking spots on the colonial streets of Centro, beachfront kiosks, stylish lounges and nightclubs, and those warm and welcoming botecos (neighborhood bars) scattered all across the city.

The Scene

As in most places in the world, there are a few different subcultures (models and modelizers, surfers, hipsters and hippies) within the nightlife circuit, though there's plenty of crossover between groups. The well-heeled crowd from the Zona Sul, for instance, tends to favor high-end nightclubs in Gávea and Barra, while an alternative crowd heads to the clubs in Botafogo. Lapa's mix of bars and dance halls attracts a more diverse mix of people from all backgrounds who have little in common aside from a love of samba.

Venues come and go – and the best parties are often one-off events in unique spots – so it helps if you can get the latest from a local source. If you can read a bit of Portuguese, pick up the *Veja Rio* insert in *Veja* magazine, which comes out each Sunday. *Rio Show,* the entertainment insert that comes in the Friday edition of *O Globo,* also has extensive listings

Botecos

For an insight into Rio's drinking culture, familiarize yourself with one of the great sociocultural icons of the city: the *boteco*. These casual, open-sided bars are scattered all over town, and draw in a broad cross-section of society. You'll find young and old, upper class and working class, men and women, black and white mixing over ice-cold *chope* (draft beer) or caipirinhas, flirting and swapping the latest gossip as bow-tied waiters move deftly among the crowd.

Just as most *cariocas* (residents of Rio) have a favorite team, nearly every local also has a favorite *boteco* to call his or her own. These range from hole-in-the-wall joints where canned beer is handed out to drinkers slouched over plastic tables to classic, wood-paneled bar rooms, with murals on the walls, expertly mixed drinks and a history dating back several generations. Wherever you go in the city, you'll find food is an important part of the experience, as *cariocas* rate bars not just on the drinks and the vibe but on the menu as well.

Nightclubs

Rio has some great places to shake your *bunda* (booty). DJs pull from the latest house, drum 'n' bass and hip-hop favorites as well as more uniquely Brazilian combinations like electro-samba and bossa-jazz. In addition to local DJs, Rio attracts a handful of vinyl gurus from São Paulo, New York and

CONSUMPTION CARD

At many clubs in Rio, you'll receive a control card when you enter. Rather than paying for individual drinks, your card will be marked each time you order. At the end of the night, you'll head to the cashier and pay for your food and drinks, plus the admission charge. Don't lose it, as you'll be hit with a hefty fee (upwards of R$150).

NEED TO KNOW

Opening Hours

- **Bars** 6pm–2am Monday–Friday, from noon on Saturday and Sunday. Most places stay open later (typically till 4am) on Friday and Saturday nights.
- **Nightclubs** 11pm–5am Thursday–Saturday

How Much?

- **Drink Prices** A *chope* will set you back about R$4.50 to R$7, with cocktails running from R$13 to R$20 or even R$30 at pricier lounges. Most bars tack on a 10% service charge.
- **Club Admission** Prices vary, though women typically pay less than men. Fridays and Saturdays are the most expensive nights. On average, club admission on a weekend night is around R$50 for men and R$30 for women.

Getting In

- The dress code at clubs isn't strict in Rio. Neat shorts and sneakers are fine, though flip-flops and swimsuits are a no-no.
- Groups of single men will have a harder time getting in. Try to join up with a few females.
- Go well before midnight to beat the crowds.

London to spin at bigger affairs. Flyers advertising dance parties and raves (pronounced *hah*-vees) can be found in some boutiques in Ipanema and Leblon, and in the surf shops in Galeria River by Praia Arpoador. Most clubs give a discount if you've got a flyer.

Gay Rio

Rio has been a major destination for gay travelers since the 1950s. Back then the action was near the Copacabana Palace – and remnants of this distant past are still there, popular with a slightly older crowd (look for the rainbow-hued flag). Today, however, the party has mostly moved on, with the focal point of the GLBT (gay, lesbian, bisexual, transgender) scene, especially for visitors, in Ipanema. The gay beach at the end of Rua Farme de Amoedo (again, look for the rainbow flag) is the stomping ground of some of Rio's buffest men, sometimes known as 'barbies' in *carioca* slang. The bars and cafes of nearby streets – Rua Teixeira de Melo and Rua Farme – attract a mixed crowd and are a good spot to explore if you're not quite ready to jump into the beach scene.

Rio also hosts an enormously popular Gay Pride Rio festival. For more info on the gay scene in Rio, including recommendations on nightclubs, bars, cafes and guesthouses, visit Rio Gay Guide (p206).

Drinking & Nightlife by Neighborhood

- **Ipanema & Leblon** (p67) Lots of *botecos*, a handful of lounges and nightclubs.
- **Gávea, Jardim Botânico & Lagoa** (p82) Romantic lakeside drinking spots popular with couples.
- **Copacabana & Leme** (p91) Beach kiosks, hotel bars with views, *botecos* and several nightclubs.
- **Botafogo & Urca** (p104) Several popular spots in Urca; great *botecos* and several nightclubs in Botafogo.
- **Centro & Cinelândia** (p129) Atmospheric drinking spots on the pedestrian streets.
- **Santa Teresa & Lapa** (p139) Old-fashioned bars and bohemian haunts.

Lonely Planet's Top Choices

Palaphita Kitch (p82) Tasty imaginative cocktails in a picturesque setting facing the lake.

00 (Zero Zero) (p80) Nightclub of choice for the fashion-conscious, electronic-music-loving crowd.

Jobi (p70) Tiny, much-loved neighborhood watering hole open very late in Leblon.

Bar Urca (p105) Unfussy place with magical views over the bay.

Devassa (p70) Great drafts and always a fun crowd.

Bar Astor (p70) Excellent cocktail menu and a great location across from Ipanema beach.

Best Lounges

Baretto-Londra (p70)

Melt (p71)

Best for Meeting People

Hipódromo (p82)

Empório (p67)

Barzin (p67)

Blue Agave (p67)

Mud Bug (p91)

Best Views

Skylab (p94)

Très (p89)

Horse's Neck (p91)

Bar d'Hotel (p71)

Best for Dancing

Bar Bukowski (p105)

Nuth (p157)

Fosfobox (p94)

Best Botecos

Belmonte (p115)

O Plebeu (p105)

Botequim Informal (p91)

Bar do Gomes (p139)

Best Date Places

Caroline Café (p82)

Bar dos Descasados (p139)

Bar do Horto (p82)

Best for Beer Lovers

Delirium Cafe (p70)

Herr Brauer (p115)

Bar Luiz (p128)

Best Gay Clubs & Bars

The Week (p131)

Tô Nem Aí (p71)

Le Boy (p94)

TV Bar (p94)

Galeria Café (p71)

Entertainment

Rio has a celebrated music scene, with some enchanting settings to catch live performances, from cutting-edge concert halls to small and intimate neighborhood venues. Dance, theater, classical concerts and opera also have their small but loyal local following, while cinema is an even bigger deal, with Rio one of the leading film centers in Latin America.

Live Music

In addition to samba (p43), Rio is a showcase for jazz, bossa nova, Música Popular Brasileira (MPB), rock, hip-hop and the fusions among them. Brazil's many regional styles – *forró* (Brazilian music from the Northeast), *chorinho* (romantic, intimate samba) and *pagode* (relaxed and rhythmic samba) – are also a part of the music scene.

Venues range from megamodern concert halls seating thousands to packed samba clubs in edgy neighborhoods. Antiquated colonial mansions, outdoor parks overlooking the city, old-school bars, crumbling buildings on the edge of town and hypermodern lounges facing the ocean are all part of the mix.

CONCERT VENUES

In addition to small bars and clubs, Rio has a few large concert halls that attract Brazilian stars such as Gilberto Gil and Milton Nascimento, as well as well-known international bands visiting Rio on world tours. Major music festivals include the Rio Music Conference (p20), held in the Marina da Glória. In addition to established venues, during the summer months concerts sometimes take place on the beaches of Copacabana, Botafogo, Ipanema and Barra da Tijuca.

Dance

Rio has produced a number of successful dance troupes, including the contemporary Companhia de Dança Deborah Colker, which spends much of its time touring abroad. A home-grown talent you might catch in town is the Cia de Dança Dani Lima, an avant-garde troupe that weaves provocative pieces together through dance and aerial gymnastics. Also keep an eye out for the Lapa-based Intrépida Trupe, whose talented acrobat/dancers bring surreal works to the stage. There aren't any spaces dedicated solely to dance, and performances can take place at many of the venues listed here. Rio's biggest dance festival, Festival Panorama de Dança, is held in November. For classical dance, try to see a production by the Ballet do Theatro Municipal, which puts on highly professional performances at Rio's most venerable theater.

Theater

There's a long history of theater in Brazil, with literary greats from the 19th century, including the highly imaginative *carioca* (resident of Rio) Machado de Assis, giving vision to the stage. Talents from the 20th century, like the great Nelson Rodrigues and more recently Gerald Thomas, have kept the flame alive, and you can still see some of their work on Rio's stages. There are more than two dozen theaters in town. Unfortunately, if you don't speak Portuguese, you won't get a lot out of an evening at the theater.

Classical Music

In the classical music scene, Rio has several symphony orchestras and irregular appearances by chamber groups and soloists. The best venues are the Sala Cecília Meireles (p142), with its excellent acoustics, and the magnificent Theatro Municipal (p131). You might also attend a performance at the Centro Cultural Banco do Brasil (p120) or the Fundação Eva Klabin (p79), both of which host orchestral works periodically.

The biggest classical music festival is Música no Museu, held in museums, churches and cultural centers around town.

Cinema

There's plenty of variety at Rio's many cinemas. The market here is remarkably open to foreign and independent films, documentaries and avant-garde cinema. This isn't to say that mainstream Hollywood films are in short supply. The latest American blockbusters get ample airtime at movie megaplexes, while cultural centers, museums and old one-screen theaters offer a more diverse repertoire. Films are shown in the original language with Portuguese subtitles. On weekends, popular shows often sell out, so buy your ticket early. Prices range from R$16 to R$32 per ticket, with cheaper matinee prices Monday through Thursday and the highest prices (and longest lines) on Friday to Sunday.

The Rio film fest is one of the biggest in Latin America, with more than 400 films representing 60 countries shown at theaters all across Rio, and occasional screenings at the Marina da Glória and other open-air spots around town. In past years, the two-week festival has attracted over 300,000 attendees. It runs from the last week of September to the first week of October. Although there's a wide variety of international fare screened here, the festival often sets the stage for the success of Brazilian films aimed at wide release. For more info, visit www.festivaldorio.com.br.

Music in the Museum

Classical-music lovers should attend a concert held during the four-month-long event **Música No Museu** (Music in the Museum; www.musicanomuseu.com.br). Held from January to April, this event has been growing in popularity, and now features dozens of free concerts at museums and cultural spaces around the city, including inside the Museu de Arte Moderna (p121), Museu da República (p112), Centro Cultural Banco do Brasil (p120) and Parque das Ruinas (p136). Most concerts are held during the daytime (typically starting sometime between noon and 3pm), making it an alternative to the beach if you need a break. Visit the website or pick up a brochure from any tourist office for the current schedule.

NEED TO KNOW

Tickets & Reservations

➡ **Tickets for Fun** (p157) Sells tickets to big shows at Citibank Hall and Arena HSBC, both in Barra da Tijuca. It also sells through various stores in Rio including Lojas Saraiva, in **Shopping Rio Sul** (www.riosul.com.br).

➡ **Ingresso.com** (www.ingresso.com.br) Sells tickets to various venues, including Theatro Municipal, Studio RJ and Miranda. Purchasing online or over the phone requires Portuguese, though you can also buy from a distributor like **Lojas Americanas** (www.americanas.com.br).

Listings

➡ **Rio Guia Oficial** (www.rioguiaoficial.com.br/en) Rio's tourism authority maintains up-to-date listings of major events.

➡ **Time Out** (www.timeout.com.au/rio-de-janeiro) Maintains a weekly calendar of key concerts and events.

➡ **Rio Show** Published inside the Friday edition of *O Globo* newspaper and has extensive listings in Portuguese.

➡ **Veja** Another good (but Portuguese only) source of info is the *Veja Rio* insert included with this magazine, which comes out on Sundays.

Entertainment by Neighborhood

➡ **Ipanema & Leblon** (p71) A handful of theaters, cinemas and live-music venues.

➡ **Gávea, Jardim Botânico & Lagoa** (p82) Live-music spots at lakeside kiosks.

➡ **Botafogo & Urca** (p106) Several cinemas.

➡ **Flamengo & Around** (p115) Several arts spaces.

➡ **Centro & Cinelândia** (p130) Large selection of concert halls and theaters.

➡ **Santa Teresa & Lapa** (p140) Many live-music venues in Lapa.

➡ **Barra da Tijuca & Western Rio** (p157) Home to mega-sized concert halls.

Lonely Planet's Top Choices

Theatro Municipal (p120) Architecturally stunning building that showcases some of Rio's best performing arts.

Studio RJ (p71) Excellent line-up of rock and MPB in a fine new venue in Ipanema.

Cidade das Artes (p157) Stunning R$515 million home to the Brazilian Symphony Orchestra, opened in 2013.

Odeon Petrobras (p130) Classic old-fashioned cinema on Praça Floriano in Centro.

Circo Voador (p140) Creative space for top concerts in the heart of Lapa.

Best Cinemas

Estação Botafogo (p106)

Estação Ipanema (p72)

Teatro Leblon (p72)

Espaço Museu da República (p116)

Best Jazz & Bossa Nova

Maze Inn (p116)

TribOz (p141)

Vinícius Show Bar (p72)

Best Rock

Melt (p71)

Fundição Progresso (p137)

Citibank Hall (p157)

Miranda (p82)

Far Up (p106)

Best Theaters

Teatro do Leblon (p72)

Espaço SESC (p94)

Teatro Carlos Gomes (p131)

Teatro do Centro Cultural Banco do Brasil (p131)

LOOK DIE BILDAGENTUR DER FOTOGRAFEN GMBH / ALAMY ©

Samba da mesa, Bip Bip (p94)

Samba

Samba, the great soundtrack of Rio, plays all across town, though if you're looking for its heart, you'll probably find it in the bohemian neighborhood of Lapa. There addictive rhythms spill out of old-fashioned dance halls, drawing music-lovers from far and wide. Samba also takes center stage during Carnaval, with those percussive beats and singsong lyrics essential to the big fest.

Samba Clubs

Gafieiras (dance halls) have risen from the ashes of a once-down-at-heel neighborhood and reinvigorated it with an air of youth and song. The neighborhood in question is Lapa, and after years of neglect it has reclaimed its place as Rio's nightlife center. In the 1920s and '30s Lapa was a major destination for the bohemian crowd, who were attracted to its decadent cabaret joints, brothels and *gafieiras*. Today its vintage buildings hide beautifully restored interiors set with wide dance floors.

Inside you'll find some of Rio's top samba groups, playing to crowds that often pack the dance floor. The nostalgic settings inside the clubs add to the appeal, and even if you don't feel like dancing, the music and festive crowd set the scene for a great night out.

Samba da Mesa

by Carmen Michael

On Friday night Rio's samba community congregates in front of the faded colonial facades of Rua do Mercado under a canopy

NEED TO KNOW

Opening Hours

There's always something going on in Lapa, though many clubs are closed from Sunday to Wednesday. Typical opening are from about 8pm to 1am during the week, and till 3am or 4am on weekends.

When to Go

On weekends, Lapa packs huge crowds; and many people come for the festive ambience on the streets. If you plan to visit a samba club on Friday or Saturday, go early to beat the lines, and have a few backup options just in case.

Cover Charges

Cover charges typically range from R$20 to R$50, and women generally pay less than men. Often a portion of the charge covers drinks. As with other clubs, you'll be given a consumption card to keep track of your drinks, which you'll pay for at the end of the night.

Security

Lapa is still scruffy around the ages, so keep your wits about you. Stick to well trafficked areas, be mindful of pickpockets in crowded areas, and leave the valuables at home.

Resources

➡ **Lá Na Lapa** (www.lanalapa.com.br) If you can read some Portuguese, this is a handy site for finding out what's on in Lapa.

➡ **Rio Carnival** (www.rio-carnival.net) A decent website for checking times and reading up on other Carnaval-related activities.

of tropical foliage to play *samba da mesa* (literally, samba of the table). On the worn cobblestones a long table stands, altarlike. Around it the musicians sit and the crowd gyrates, paying homage to their favorite religion. *Samba da mesa* in Rio today is a grassroots movement of musicians and appreciators passionately committed to keeping their music on the street and in an improvised form.

It typically involves a table, at least one *cavaquinho* (small, ukulelelike instrument) player, an assortment of *tambores* (drums) and any number of makeshift instruments like Coke cans, knives and forks that will make a rattle. The standard of the music can be outstanding, and it is not uncommon to catch sight of a samba *bamba* (big-name samba performer) keeping the beat for the group or belting out one of its tunes. Depending on which bohemians have blown through for the night, you might even catch a duel, in which two singers will pit their wits against each other in a battle of rhymes. It is a challenge of the intellect, and the topics include everything from love to poverty to the opponent's mother. Even if you speak some Portuguese, you probably won't understand the slang and local references, but the delight of the crowd is infectious.

Street samba has taken a battering from the commercialization of music and space, the rising popularity of funk in the favelas and the police clampdown on 'noise pollution' in public spaces. However, for those still interested in a little piece of bohemian Rio, there are several established places that support free, improvised street music. On Friday night Rua do Mercado and Travessa do Comércio near Praça Quinze in Centro attract the younger radical chic set. On Sunday and Thursday night Bip Bip (p94), a tiny bar in Copacabana, caters for hard-core *sambistas* (samba singers). If you're around on December 2, Dia de Samba (Samba Day), then you can join the samba train bound for Oswaldo Cruz with the rest of Rio's samba community. The musicians disembark in the dusty backstreets of this working-class suburb, which is transformed every year into a labyrinth of makeshift bars and stages that host a 24-hour marathon of *samba da mesa*.

Impromptu street gatherings in Rio are more elusive at other times and finding them can sometimes be challenging. But it's an unforgettable experience if you find one. There are few fixed places for these parties, and they move from one week to the next. The *bairro* (neighborhood) of Lapa, in particular Rua Joaquim Silva, generally has something going on, but if not, keep your ears open for the unmistakable sound of the *samba bateria* (percussive-style samba) – follow that sound and you will find a party. Pay heed to the local etiquette: ensure you do not talk over the music, don't use cameras with a flash and don't sit down unless you are a contributing musician.

Samba Schools

In preparation for Carnaval, most big samba schools open their weekly rehearsals to the public, starting around September. An *escola de samba* (samba school) is a professional troupe that performs in the grand samba parade during Carnaval. They typically charge between R$10 and R$30 at the door (admission can go upwards of R$40 as Carnaval nears), and you'll be able to buy drinks. These are large dance parties, not specific lessons in samba (although you may learn to samba at some of them), that are fun to watch and visitors are always welcome to join in.

Keep in mind that many samba schools are in the favelas, so use common sense and consider going with a *carioca* (resident of Rio) for peace of mind. It's best to take a taxi, which there are usually plenty of in front. Mangueira and Salgueiro are among the easiest schools to get to.

Following is a list of samba schools, contact information and rehearsal days – they all get incredibly packed as Carnaval approaches. The schools that are most popular with tourists are generally Salgueiro and Mangueira. It's always best to confirm if there is going to be a rehearsal.

Beija-Flor (☑2233-5889; www.beija-flor.com.br; Praçinha Wallace Paes Leme 1025, Nilópolis; ☺9pm Thu)

Grande Rio (☑2671-3585; www.academicosdogranderio.com.br; Wallace Soares 5-6, Duque de Caixas; ☺9pm Tue)

Imperatriz Leopoldinense (☑2560-8037; www.imperatrizleopoldinense.com.br; Professor Lacê 235, Ramos; ☺8pm Sun)

Mangueira Map p254 (☑2567-4637; www.mangueira.com.br; Visconde de Niterói 1072, Mangueira; ☺10pm Sat)

DANCE CLASSES

Given samba's resurgence throughout the city, it's not surprising that there are several places where you can learn the moves. You can also find places to study *forró* (dance accompanied by the traditional, fast-paced music from the Northeast) and other styles. A dance class is a good setting to meet other people while getting those two left feet to step in time.

A few good places to learn:

➡ Casa de Dança Carlinhos de Jesus (p107)

➡ Centro Cultural Carioca (p132)

➡ Fundição Progresso (p137)

➡ Rio Samba Dancer (p96)

Mocidade Independente de Padre Miguel (☑3332-5823; www.mocidadeindependente.com.br; Av Brasil 31146, Padre Miguel; ☺10pm Sat)

Porta da Pedra (☑3707-1518; www.unidosdoportodapedra.com.br; Av Lúcio Tomé Feteiro 290, Vila Lage, São Gonçalo; ☺8pm Wed)

Portela (☑2489-6440; Clara Nunes 81, Madureira; ☺9pm Fri)

Rocinha (☑3205-3318; www.academicosdarocinha.com.br; Bertha Lutz 80, São Conrado; ☺10pm Sat)

Salgueiro (☑2238-0389; www.salgueiro.com.br; Silva Teles 104, Andaraí; ☺10pm Sat)

São Clemente Map p254 (☑2671-3585; www.saoclemente.com.br; Av Presidente Vargas 3102, Cidade Nova; ☺10pm Fri)

Unidos da Tijuca Map p254 (☑7590-1290; www.unidosdatijuca.com.br; Francisco Bicalho 47, Santo Cristo; ☺10pm Sat)

Vila Isabel (☑2578-0077; www.gresunidosdevilaisabel.com.br; Av Blvd 28 de Setembro 382, Vila Isabel; ☺10pm Sat)

Lonely Planet's Top Choices

Salgueiro (p45) Wonderfully festive, well-located samba school.

Rio Scenarium (p140) Touristy, but still a fantastic setting for live samba.

Democráticus (p140) Long-running club with first-class musicians.

Beco do Rato (p141) Low-key and welcoming spot, never a cover.

Bip Bip (p94) Copacabana gem famed for its *samba de roda* (informal samba played in a circle).

Pedra do Sal (p130) Outdoor samba in a historic locale north of Centro.

Best Samba Schools

Mangueira (p45)

Vila Isabel (p45)

Unidos da Tijuca (p45)

São Clemente (p45)

Best Lapa Samba Clubs

Carioca da Gema (p141)

Semente (p141)

Favellas (p141)

Best Live Samba Outside Lapa

Trapiche Gamboa (p130)

Casa Rosa (p115)

Shopping

Not surprisingly, beach and casual wear are a big part of the shopping scene in Rio, but less well known is the great variety of stores selling antiques, custom-made handicrafts, wine and spirits, handmade jewelry, records and CDs, coffee-table books and one-of-a-kind goods found only in Rio.

Markets of Rio

Rio's many markets are ideal places for exploring the subcultures beneath the city's skin – whether brushing elbows with antique lovers, recent migrants from the northeast or the youthful flocks of fashionistas from the Zona Sul. Several markets, such as the Feira Nordestina and the monthly Feira do Rio Antigo, are as much about food and music as they are about shopping.

The following are a few top markets:

Hippie Fair (p72)

Av Atlântica Fair (p236)

Feira do Rio Antigo (p143)

Feira Nordestina (p148)

Photography and Image Fair (p241)

Praça do Lido Market (p236)

Praça Santos Dumont Antique Fair (p234)

Rio Souvenirs

Music Expand your CD collection with local favorites such as singers Maria Rita, Diogo Nogueira or Mart'nália.

Cachaça (cane liquor) Buy a quality *cachaça* from Minas for around R$35 and up.

Swimwear Flaunt your new tan in a tiny *sunga* (Speedo) or *fio dental* (string bikini). Ipanema, along Rua Visconde de Pirajá, is the place to look.

Maracatu drum If the massive northeastern instrument won't fit on your coffee table, consider the smaller ukelelelike *cavaquinho*.

Havaianas (p95) Find a pair for every mood at the spacious shop in Copacabana.

Paintings Artists showcase their works at the Sunday Hippie Fair (p72).

Soccer jersey Score a jersey for one of Rio's teams. Loja Fla (p95) is the go-to place for Flamengo fans.

Folk art Tap into Brazil's handicraft traditions at stores scattered about town.

Shopping by Neighborhood

➡ **Ipanema & Leblon** (p72) Loads of boutiques; high prices.

➡ **Gávea, Jardim Botânico & Lagoa** (p83) Several small-scale but atmospheric shopping streets.

➡ **Copacabana & Leme** (p94) Loads of stores, a few markets, tourist fare.

➡ **Centro & Cinelândia** (p131) Wine shops, bookstores, downnmarket clothing shops, Medinalike browsing in the pedestrian streets of Saara.

➡ **Santa Teresa & Lapa** (p142) A few handicrafts shops and galleries near Largo do Guimarães.

NEED TO KNOW

Opening Hours

- Stores 9am-6pm Monday-Friday, 9am-1pm Sat
- Malls 10am-10pm Monday-Saturday, 3pm-10pm Sunday

Consumer Taxes

Most stores list their prices with the tax already included, so what you see on the price tag is the total price you'll pay for the goods.

Language Barriers

Many sales assistants in high-end shops speak English.

Bargaining

A little bargaining is expected when making purchases at markets, but keep in mind that sellers generally don't over-inflate their prices and so aren't willing to haggle very much.

Lonely Planet's Top Choices

Pé de Boi (p116) Eye-catching handicrafts made by artists from around Brazil.

Hippie Fair (p72) Have fun browsing – and eating street food – in Ipanema.

Maria Oiticica (p74) Elegant jewelry made from Amazonian seeds and fibers.

Osklen (p73) Attractive men's and women's fashion from Brazil's best-known designer.

Granado (p131) High-end skin-care products in an old-fashioned pharmacy.

Gilson Martins (p95) Wallets, bags and other accessories with iconic Rio imagery.

Best Handicrafts

Artíndia (p106)

La Vereda Handicrafts (p143)

O Sol (p83)

Best Jewelry Stores

Antonio Bernardo (p74)

H Stern (p74)

Amsterdam Sauer (p74)

Best Fashion Boutiques

Dona Coisa (p83)

Forum (p73)

Isabel Capeto (p73)

Redley (p73)

Best Bookshops

Nova Livraria Leonardo da Vinci (p131)

Livraria da Travessa (p132)

Argumento (p75)

Best Music Stores

Berinjela (p132)

Toca do Vinícius (p74)

Plano B (p143)

Arlequim (p132)

Bossa Nova & Companhia (p95)

Best Stores for Buying Musical Instruments

Maracatu Brasil (p116)

Casa Oliveira (p132)

Best Shopping Malls

Shopping Leblon (p74)

Fashion Mall (p157)

Shopping da Gávea (p83)

Botafogo Praia Shopping (p106)

Rio Sul Shopping (p107)

Barra Shopping (p157)

Sports & Activities

Tropical rainforest, towering peaks and sparkling beaches set the stage for a wide range of adventures in this outdoors-loving city. Hiking, rock climbing, hang gliding, surfing and cycling are just a few ways to spend a sun-drenched afternoon. Rio is also a great place to watch sport; nothing quite compares to seeing the mad spectacle of a football match at hallowed Maracanã.

Walking, Jogging & Cycling

Splendid views and the sounds of the ever-present ocean are just two of the features of the many good walking and jogging paths of the Zona Sul. Parque do Flamengo (p112) has plenty of paths stretching between city and bay. Further south Lagoa Rodrigo de Freitas (p78) has a 7.5km track for cyclists, joggers and inline skaters. At the lakeside Parque do Cantagalo you can rent bicycles (R$10 per hour), tricycles or quadricycles (around R$20 per hour). The popular option is the seaside path from Leme to Barra da Tijuca. Sunday is the best day to go, as the road is closed to traffic but open to the city's many outdoor enthusiasts.

Closed to bikes but open to walkers and joggers is the short Pista Cláudio Coutinho (p100), between the mountains and the sea at Praia Vermelha in Urca. It's open 7am to 6pm daily.

Hiking

Rio has some outstanding hikes along the trails coursing through Floresta da Tijuca. You can also go for hikes through wilderness areas around Corcovado, Morro da Urca and Pão de Açúcar (Sugarloaf Mountain; p99).

Jungle Me (☎4105-7533; www.jungleme.com.br; tour R$150) This top-notch outfit offers excellent hiking tours through Parque Nacional da Tijuca (p156) led by knowledgeable guides. The peaks-and-waterfalls tour offers challenging walks up several escarpments that offer stunning views of Rio followed by a refreshing dip in a waterfall. The wild-beaches-of-Rio tour takes you on a hike between scenic beaches in Rio's little-visited western suburbs.

Rio Adventures (☎2705-5747; www.rioadventures.com; hiking/climbing/rafting tours from R$90/220/400) Offering a range of outdoor activities, Rio Adventures leads hikes through Parque Nacional da Tijuca, including short treks up Pico Tijuca and more challenging ascents up Pedra Bonito. It also runs sightseeing tours, rock climbs, rafting excursions (to Paraibuna River, 175km northwest of Rio) and parachuting and paragliding trips.

Rio Hiking (☎2552-9204; www.riohiking.com.br; full-day tour from R$150) Founded by a mother-son team back in 1999, this popular outfit offers hiking

LONELY PLANET'S TOP CHOICES

Best Football Experience Seeing a game at Maracanã (p146).

Best Bike Outing Riding the beachside path from Leblon to Leme.

Best Climb The ascent up Pão de Açúcar (p99).

Best Hiking Scrambling through rainforest and up craggy overlooks in Floresta da Tijuca (p156).

Best Surfing The waves off Prainha.

Best Airborne Experience Taking the hang gliding plunge off Pedra Bonita.

NEED TO KNOW

Football at Maracanã

➡ **Going to Maracanã** You can take the metro to Maracanã station, and buy tickets at the gate; or go with a group organized by Brazil Expedition (p203), Be a Local (p204) or Sergio Manhães (http://futebolnomaracana.blogspot.com.au).

➡ **Game Days** Games take place year-round on Saturday or Sunday, and less frequently on Wednesday or Thursday.

➡ **Information** For results, schedules and league tables visit Samba Foot (p147).

Surf Rio

➡ **Surf Bus** To get to the great surf spots outside Rio, catch a ride on the Surfbus, which will take passengers and their boards down to Prainha, with stops along the way. It departs at 7am, 10am, 1pm and 4pm from Largo do Machado (and picks up passengers in the Zona Sul en route).

➡ **Surf Conditions** Find detailed information on all the breaks around Rio at www.wannasurf.com. If you can read Portuguese, check out www.riosurfpage.com.

➡ **Boards** For boards and other gear, visit Galeria River. Some hostels also rent boards.

➡ **Classes** Beginners who want to learn to surf can take classes through informal *escolinhas* (schools) off Ipanema beach and off Barra. Rio Surf 'N Stay (p172) offers lessons (in English) and overnight accommodations.

trips ranging from easy to strenuous and covering a variety of terrains around Rio. You can also arrange kayaking, diving, river rafting and numerous other adventure sports here.

Rock Climbing

Rio is the center of rock climbing in Brazil, with 350 documented climbs within 40 minutes of the city center. In addition to organized outings, you can also try your hand at the rock-climbing wall in Parque da Catacumba (p80).

Crux Ecoadventure (☎3474-1726, 9392-9203; www.cruxecoaventura.com.br) This reputable outfit offers a range of climbing excursions and other outdoor adventures. The most popular is the ascent up Pão de Açúcar (R$170), which isn't as daunting as it looks. Other possibilities include rappelling down waterfalls, full-day hikes through Floresta da Tijuca, and cycling and kayaking trips.

Climb in Rio (☎2245-1108; www.climbinrio.com; half-day climb R$230) This respected agency offers half- and full-day climbing trips led by experienced guides. Navigating more than 400 routes around Rio and the state, this is a good pick for climbing junkies.

Hang Gliding

If you weigh less than 100kg (about 220lb) and have a spare R$350 to spend, you can do the fantastic hang glide off 510m Pedra Bonita – one of the giant granite slabs that tower above Rio – onto Pepino beach in São Conrado. Flights last about seven to 10 minutes, and no experience is necessary. Guest riders are secured in a kind of pouch that is attached to the hang glider. The winds are quite safe here and accidents are rare.

The price of the flight includes pick-up and drop-off from your hotel.

Delta Flight in Rio (☎9693-8800, 3322-5750; www.riobyjeep.com/deltaflight) With more than 20 years' experience, Ricardo Hamond has earned a solid reputation as a safety-conscious and extremely professional pilot; he has flown more than 12,000 tandem flights.

Just Fly (☎2268-0565; http://justflyinrio.blogspot.com) Paulo Celani is a highly experienced tandem flyer with over 6000 flights to his credit.

Tandem Fly (☎2422-6371; www.riotandemfly.com.br) Two brothers – both very experienced pilots – run this outfit, and they also give lessons for those wanting to learn how to fly solo.

Capoeira

The only surviving martial art native to the new world, capoeira was invented by Afro-Brazilian slaves about 400 years ago. In its original form, the grappling martial art developed as a means of self-defense against the slave owners. Once the fighting art was discovered, it was quickly banned and capoeira went underground. The slaves, however, continued to hone their fighting skills; they merely did it out of sight, practicing secretly in the forest. Later the sport was disguised as a kind of dance, allowing them to practice in the open. This is the form that exists today.

Capoeira, which is referred to as a *jogo* (game), is accompanied by hand clapping and the plucking of the *berimbau* (a long, single-stringed instrument). Initially the music was used to warn fighters of the boss' approach; today it guides the rhythm of the game. Fast tempos dictate the players' exchange of fast, powerful kicks and blows, while slower tempos bring the pace down to a quasi-dance. The *berimbau* is accompanied by the *atabaque* (floor drum) and a *pandeiro* (Brazilian tambourine).

You can see musicians and spectators arranged in the *roda de capoeira* (capoeira circle) at the weekly Feira Nordestina (p148) in São Cristóvão. If you're in town for a while, you can also sign up for classes. Fundição Progresso (p143) in Lapa offers classes three nights a week.

Surfing

Rio has some fine options when it comes to surfing, with some great breaks just outside the city. If you're not ready to leave the Zona Sul, there are a few options, including fairly consistent breaks in front of Posto 10 in Ipanema and Posto 11 in Leblon. Copacabana gets an OK break between Posto 4 and 5. You'll find better waves near the spit of land dividing Copacabana from Ipanema. On the west side, off **Praia do Diabo** (Map p236), you get right and left breaks, which can reach up to 2m high, but it's not a good spot for beginners. On the other side of the rocks is Arpoador, which is generally more consistent with fast, hollow breaks to the left ranging from 0.5m to 3m. The big drawback here is that the place gets crowded, making maneuvering extremely difficult. To beat the crowds, go early on weekday mornings.

If you're serious about surfing, you'll want to head down to the beaches west of Rio. Just past Barra and Recreio is **Macumba** beach, with left and right breaks, which draws both long-boarders and beginners. After Macumba is lovely **Prainha**, which is widely considered the best surf spot in the area, with waves reaching 3m on good days. If it's too packed, you can continue on to **Grumari**, where the swell isn't as good but the crowds are thinner.

Sports & Activities by Neighborhood

- **Ipanema & Leblon** (p58) Cycling or jogging the beach path.
- **Gávea, Jardim Botânico & Lagoa** (p78) Cycling or jogging the lakeshore path. Hikes in Parque Lage.
- **Copacabana & Leme** (p86) Cycling or jogging the beach path.
- **Botafogo & Urca** (p99) Rock climbing up Pão de Açúcar. Walking the short Pista Claudio Coutinho.
- **Flamengo & Around** (p116) Cycling or jogging through Parque do Flamengo.
- **Zona Norte** (p146) Watching a football game at Maracanã.
- **Barra da Tijuca & West of Rio** (p156) Hikes and climbs in Floresta da Tijuca.

Explore Rio de Janeiro

RIO DE JANEIRO'S TOP SIGHTS

Neighborhoods at a Glance

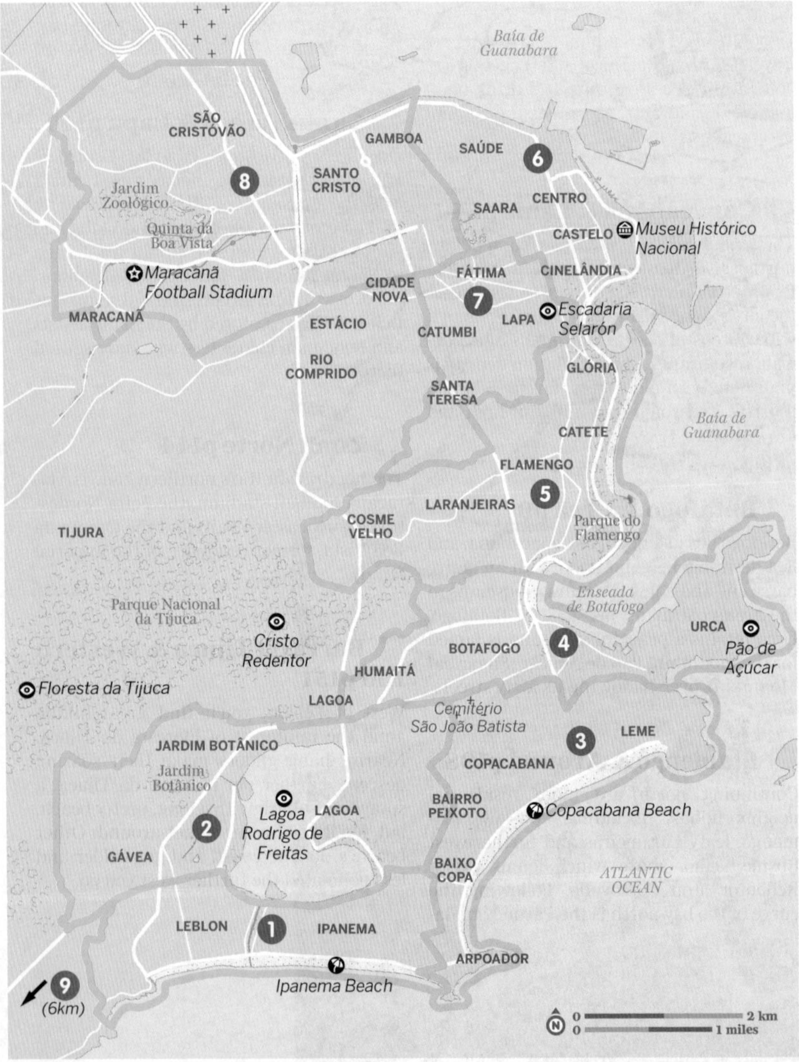
Baía de Guanabara
SÃO CRISTÓVÃO
GAMBOA
SAÚDE
6
SANTO CRISTO
8
Jardim Zoológico
SAARA
CENTRO
Quinta da Boa Vista
CASTELO
Museu Histórico Nacional
Maracanã Football Stadium
FÁTIMA
CINELÂNDIA
CIDADE NOVA
7
MARACANÃ
ESTÁCIO
CATUMBI
LAPA
Escadaria Selarón
RIO COMPRIDO
GLÓRIA
SANTA TERESA
Baía de Guanabara
CATETE
FLAMENGO
LARANJEIRAS
5
Parque do Flamengo
TIJURA
COSME VELHO
Parque Nacional da Tijuca
Enseada de Botafogo
Cristo Redentor
BOTAFOGO
4
URCA
Pão de Açúcar
HUMAITÁ
Floresta da Tijuca
LAGOA
Cemitério São João Batista
LEME
3
JARDIM BOTÂNICO
COPACABANA
Jardim Botânico
Lagoa Rodrigo de Freitas
LAGOA
BAIRRO PEIXOTO
Copacabana Beach
2
GÁVEA
BAIXO COPA
ATLANTIC OCEAN
LEBLON
1
IPANEMA
ARPOADOR
Ipanema Beach
9
(6km)
0
2 km
0
1 miles

❶ Ipanema & Leblon p56

Ipanema and Leblon share the same stretch of south-facing shoreline. Rio's beautiful people flock to these beaches, while the tree-lined streets just inland hide some of the best eating, drinking and shopping in the city.

❷ Gávea, Jardim Botânico & Lagoa p76

The northern border of Ipanema and Leblon is the Lagoa Rodrigo de Freitas, a saltwater lagoon fronted by the high-rent districts of Gávea, Jardim Botânico and Lagoa. Here you'll find open-air dining and drinking at lakeside restaurants, as well as the verdant botanical gardens to the west.

❸ Copacabana & Leme p84

The scalloped beach of Copacabana begins northeast of Ipanema. Once a destination for international jetsetters, Copacabana is the city's somewhat ragged tourist magnet, with dozens of oceanfront hotels and sidewalk restaurants. The population density is high here with old-timers, favela kids and tourists, and you'll find a mix of high and low culture.

❹ Botafogo & Urca p97

Botafogo lies just north of Copacabana, and is a desirable neighborhood with an active bar scene and a few intriguing museums in the area's old mansions. East of Botafogo, Urca retains a peaceful vibe, and is famed for the mountain, Pão de Açúcar (Sugarloaf Mountain), overshadowing its leafy streets.

❺ Flamengo & Around p108

Continuing north are more residential neighborhoods, including low-key Flamengo, leafy Laranjeiras and further west Cosme Velho, above which looms Cristo Redentor atop Corcovado. Following the curve of the bay north is the Parque do Flamengo, home to cycling trails, sports fields and several monuments and museums. Inland from there, Catete and Glória hide history in their battered streets, including the former presidential home.

❻ Centro & Cinelândia p117

Centro is Rio's business hub with wide boulevards crisscrossed by narrow pedestrian lanes; it's also one of Rio's oldest areas, with baroque churches, former palaces and excellent museums. There are also a few theaters (including historic Theatro Municipal) and some lively outdoor bars that draw happy-hour crowds.

❼ Santa Teresa & Lapa p144

On the southwestern edge of Centro is Lapa, a ramshackle neigborhood that's also the epicenter of Rio's nightlife with dozens of samba-filled bars and clubs and late-night street parties. Uphill from Lapa is Santa Teresa, a picturesque neighborhood of winding streets and old mansions that have been restored by the many artists and bohemian characters who have settled there.

❽ Zona Norte p144

The big draw in Rio's northern zone is Maracanã football stadium, the Feira Nordestina (Northeastern Fair) and the Quinta da Boa Vista, former residence of the imperial family.

❾ Barra da Tijuca & Western Rio p151

West of Leblon, you'll find great hiking amid the rainforest of Floresta da Tijuca. Nearby, hang gliders make their soaring descent. Further out is Barra da Tijuca, a sprawling suburb with a long, pretty beach, but you'll need a car to get around. Other beaches dot the coast, and get wilder and less populated the further west you go.

Ipanema & Leblon

IPANEMA | LEBLON

Neighborhood Top Five

❶ Frolicking in the waves, sipping refreshing *maté* (sweetened tea) and watching the passing people parade on lovely **Ipanema beach** (p58).

❷ Joining fishermen, couples and tourists on rocky **Ponta do Arpoador** (p59) for the nightly spectacle of sunset.

❸ Learning about the craftsmanship involved in reshaping rare stones at the **Museu H Stern** (p59).

❹ Gazing out over the length of Leblon and Ipanema at the **Mirante do Leblon** (p59).

❺ Catching a live concert at the handsomely located **Studio RJ** (p71).

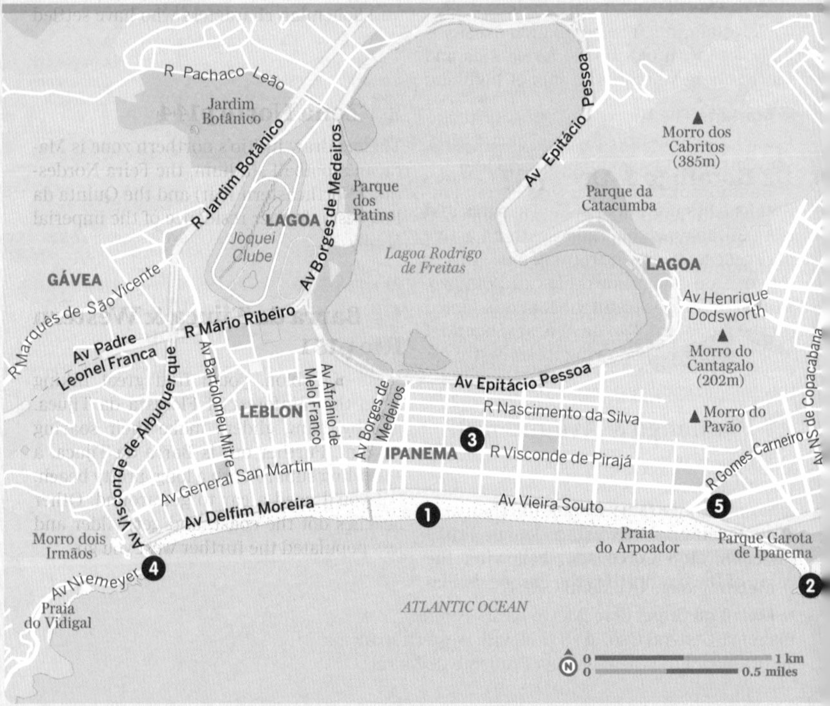

For more detail of this area see Map p228 and p232

Explore Ipanema & Leblon

The favored address for young, beautiful and wealthy *cariocas* (residents of Rio), these twin neighborhoods boast magnificent beach and tree-lined streets full of enticing open-air cafes, restaurants and bars. They're also the epicenter of the city's high-end shopping, with dozens of colorful boutiques and multistory *galerias* (shopping centers) selling pretty things that can quickly deplete a budget. While traditional sights are few, you can frolic on the beach and explore the leafy streets. Ipanema is also Rio's gay district, which revolves around the cafe and bar scene on and near Rua Farme de Amoedo.

Ipanema acquired international fame in the early '60s as the home of the bossa nova character 'Girl from Ipanema.' It became the hangout of artists, intellectuals and wealthy liberals, who frequented the sidewalk cafes and bars. These days, the artists and intellectuals have moved on, and the area is better known for its high-priced apartments and luxury lifestyle. This is, after all, Rio's most affluent district. While few *cariocas* can afford to live here, the streets and beach attract a wide cross-section of society, from surf kids from the outskirts to long-time residents and fashion-conscious 20- and 30-somethings who pack the open-sided bars by night. Ipanema and Leblon are among the city's top destinations for dining and drinking.

Local Life

➡ **Markets** The Hippie Fair (p72), held on Sundays on Praça General Osório, features handicrafts, artwork, souvenirs and tasty Bahian street food.

➡ **Restaurant Strips** Rua Dias Ferreira in Leblon is packed with tempting restaurants, and makes a fine setting to explore your options.

➡ **Hangouts** The Cobal do Leblon (p70) is a market by day and a festive drinking spot by night. Jobi (p70) draws the late-night drinking crowd.

➡ **Rainy-Day Escapes** Shopping Leblon (p74) has plenty of rainy-day amusement; top-end shops, a movie theater and good restaurants – some with views.

Getting There & Away

➡ **Bus** Botafogo (574); Corcovado train station (570); Urca (512); Copacabana (570); São Conrado (177); Centro (132); Novo Rio bus station (474).

➡ **Metro** Ipanema/General Osório.

➡ **Metrô na Superfície** 'Metro buses' connect Ipanema/General Osório station with western Ipanema and Leblon. Find them on Rua Prudente de Morais.

Lonely Planet's Top Tip

On Sundays, the east-bound lane of the beach road closes to traffic, and fills with cyclists, joggers and inline skaters. It's a great time to go for a run (all the way up through Copacabana to Leme for the ambitious).

Best Places to Eat

➡ Zazá Bistrô Tropical (p65)

➡ Zuka (p67)

➡ Bazzar (p64)

➡ Sushi Leblon (p67)

➡ Azul Marinho (p64)

➡ Market (p63)

For reviews, see p59 ➡

Best Places to Drink

➡ Devassa (p70)

➡ Bar Astor (p70)

➡ Barzin (p67)

➡ Empório (p67)

➡ Academia da Cachaça (p70)

➡ Delirium Cafe (p70)

For reviews, see p67 ➡

Best Places to Shop

➡ Gilson Martins (p72)

➡ Osklen (p73)

➡ Maria Oiticica (p74)

➡ Aquim (p72)

➡ Forum (p73)

For reviews, see p72 ➡

TOP SIGHT
IPANEMA BEACH

You've probably seen the photos and heard the jazzy theme song ('Girl from Ipanema'), but nothing quite compares to the experience of kicking off your Havaianas and strolling along the golden sands of Rio's most famous beach. The beach is the city's great backyard, free and open to all, with amusements of all kinds: from surfing and jogging along the shore to sitting back, *agua de côco* (coconut water) in hand – and watching Rio at play.

One long stretch of sun-drenched sand, Ipanema beach is marked by *postos* (posts), which marks off subcultures as diverse as the city itself. Posto 9, right off Rua Vinícius de Moraes, is Garota de Ipanema, which is where Rio's most lithe and tanned bodies tend to migrate. The area is also known as the Cemetério dos Elefantes because of the handful of old leftists, hippies and artists who sometimes hang out there. In front of Rua Farme de Amoedo the beach is known as Praia Farme, and is the stomping ground for gay society. Posto 8 further east is mostly the domain of favela kids. Arpoador, between Ipanema and Copacabana, is Rio's most popular surf spot.

Whatever spot you choose, you'll enjoy cleaner sands and sea than those in Copacabana. Keep in mind that if you go on Saturday or Sunday, the sands get crowded. Go early to stake out a spot.

Once on the beach, head to your favorite *barraca* (beach stall), where you can hire chairs and a sun umbrella. There are also food and drink stalls, though roving vendors will come to you, proffering cold drinks (try the sweet-tea like *maté*) and snacks (like crunchy donut-like *globos*).

Bring just enough cash for the day, and keep a close watch on your belongings. Petty theft is rife on the beach.

DON'T MISS...

- Sandwiches with fresh-grilled meat from Uruguai (p61).
- *Globos* and *maté*.
- Rehydrating *agua de côco*.
- Watching *cariocas* show off their skills at volleyball and *futevolei* (volleyball without using hands).

PRACTICALITIES

- Map p232
- Av Vieira Souto

SIGHTS

Ipanema

PONTA DO ARPOADOR — VIEWPOINT

(Map p236; far eastern end of Av Vieira Souto) This rocky point juts out into the water and serves as one of Rio's best places for watching the sunset. Throughout the day, you'll spot fishermen casting off the rock, couples stealing a few kisses and photographers snapping that iconic stretch of Ipanema beach stretching off toward the peaks of Dois Irmãos.

You'll also see large flocks of surfers jockeying for position offshore. Around the western edge of the rock is the tiny, secluded Praia do Diabo (Devil's Beach), a fine place to take in the views – but swim with caution. A very rustic gym is built into the rocks (think Fred Flinstone–style barbells with concrete weights and chin-up bars).

MUSEU H STERN — MUSEUM

(Map p228; ☎2106-0000; www.hstern.net; Garcia D'Ávila 113; ⊙9am-6pm Mon-Fri, 9am-2pm Sat) FREE The famous jeweler H Stern allows visitors to get a glimpse behind the scenes at the gemmological headquarters. A 12-minute audio tour shows the process of turning the rough stones into flawlessly cut jewels, and you can peer behind the laboratory windows to see craftsmen, cutters, goldsmiths and setters at work.

You can also ask to visit the small museum with its display of rare mineral specimens and a large collection of tourmalines. Following the tour, you'll meet with a sales rep, which some people find uncomfortable. A polite 'no thank you,' will usually see you to the next level (the showroom) and on to the exit. Free shuttle service to and from any major hotel in Rio.

MUSEU AMSTERDAM SAUER — MUSEUM

(Map p228; ☎2512-1132; www.amsterdamsauer.com; Garcia D'Ávila 105; ⊙9am-7pm Mon-Fri, 9am-4pm Sat) FREE Next door to Museu H Stern, the Amsterdam Sauer Museum houses an impressive collection of precious stones – over 3000 items in all. Visitors can also take a peek at the two replicas of mines.

PARQUE GAROTA DE IPANEMA — PARK

(Map p236; off Francisco Otaviano, near Bulhões Carvalho; ⊙7am-7pm) This small park next to the Arpoador rock features a tiny playground, a concrete area popular with skaters and a lookout with a view of Ipanema beach. On weekends in summer, there are occasional concerts here.

ELEVADOR DO MORRO DO CANTAGALO — VIEWPOINT

(Map p228; Barão da Torre & Teixeira de Melo) FREE Connected to the metro station off Praça General Osório, this elevator whisks passengers up to Cantagalo, a favela that's wedged between Ipanema and Copacabana. The sparkling sea views are quite fine, though local residents are happy simply to have a convenient way to get home that doesn't mean ascending hundreds of steps. From the top, keep heading uphill for even finer views over Ipanema and the lake.

As far as security goes, Cantagalo has been safe to visit since the police pacification units arrived in 2009. Recent high-profile visitors include Lady Gaga, Carla Bruni and even Brazil's president, Dilma Rousseff.

Leblon

MIRANTE DO LEBLON — LOOKOUT

(Map p232; Av Niemeyer) A few fishermen casting out to sea mingle with couples admiring the view at this overlook at the western end of Leblon Beach. The luxury Sheraton Hotel looms to the west, with the not so luxurious favela of Vidigal nearby.

PRAIA DE LEBLON — BEACH

(Map p232) Separated from Ipanema by the gardens and canal of Jardim de Alah, Leblon Beach attracts more families and has a slightly more sedate vibe than its eastern counterpart. Parents with little ones may want to check out Baixo Bebê, between posts 11 and 12, where you'll find a small playground on the sand and other young families.

EATING

Ipanema

Rio's best restaurants lie in the neighborhoods of Leblon and Ipanema. Here, along the tree-lined side streets abutting the major thoroughfares, you'll find a mix of trendy eateries, outdoor cafes and juice

HOPE IN RIO'S FAVELAS

Residents of Rio de Janeiro's favelas (shanty towns) face enormous obstacles. Many families live in communities lacking basic essentials (sewers, medical clinics, roads). Children attend some of the city's worst schools (many, indeed, drop out). The long bus commute to work can often take hours on traffic-snarled roads for a salary that may not even meet living expenses. There's also the social stigma of living in the slums, some of which – particularly those far from tourist eyes – are still run by local drug lords.

Yet it isn't all gloom for Rio's estimated one million favela residents. In the last two decades locally managed organizations have begun appearing in favelas across the city. While small in scale, these nonprofits offer residents the chance to learn new skills, gain a sense of pride, and give something often in short supply: hope.

For many poor favela children, the Grupo Cultural Afro Reggae (GCAR; www.afroreggae.org) is a lifeline. In 1997 in the Vigário Geral favela, GCAR opened a cultural center offering workshops in music, theater, dance, hip-hop and capoeira (Brazilian martial art). The center provided kids with a chance to get off the street, tap into their Afro-Brazilian heritage and gain self-esteem in setting and fulfilling goals. Owing to the center's wide popularity, the ideas have spread. GCAR and its favela affiliates now offer more than 60 different programs for poor residents around Rio.

Rocinha, Brazil's largest favela, creates similar opportunities for local residents at its Casa da Cultura. Founded in 2003 by Gilberto Gil, Minister of Culture, singer and neighbor, the center draws on the favela's rich artistic tradition, and offers classes in music, theater and painting. The favela next door, Vidigal, perched on a hillside overlooking Ipanema beach, is the base of the group Nós do Morro (Us From the Favela; www.nosdomorro.com.br). This theater group won fame after some of its young actors appeared in the award-winning film, *Cidade de Deus* (City of God). Ten of its members performed in *The Two Gentlemen of Verona* for the Royal Shakespeare Company in August 2006.

As many have discovered, the favela has a deep well of talent, but few opportunities. Opportunity is exactly what sociologist Maria Teresa Leal had in mind when she founded a sewing collective in Rocinha in the 1980s. The idea began during Leal's repeat trips to the favela where she encountered many talented seamstresses who had no chance to earn money for their skills. So began Coopa Roca (www.coopa-roca.org.br), a small group of women, each working from home to produce quilts, pillows and craft items made of recycled fabrics and other materials. Today the co-op employs some 100 women, and makes pieces for Brazilian and international designers; and its work has been displayed at museums in Rio, New York and Paris among other places.

For their part, favelas have made numerous contributions to the city. Rio's biggest party, Carnaval, was born in the favelas, and they continue to be pivotal to the fest. That favelas throw the best parties has long been known to many *cariocas*. Today, Baile Funks are a well-known aspect of the party scene, luring both rich and poor to the gritty neighborhoods on the hillsides. There, DJs spin a blend of Rio's bass-heavy tunes (with almost no relation to American-style funk) to packed dance floors.

Those who want a closer look at life inside the favela should consider overnighting inside one (p170).

bars. Price and quality generally run high here, though the stylish new flavor of the month doesn't always live up to the hype.

DELÍRIO TROPICAL BRAZILIAN $

(Map p228; ☎3624-8162; www.delirio.com.br; Garcia D'Ávila 48; salads R$11-15; ⌚11am-9pm Mon-Sat, noon-7pm Sun; ✎) Delírio Tropical serves a tempting array of salads, which you can enhance by adding on grilled trout, salmon carpaccio, filet mignon and other items. The open layout has a pleasant, casual ambience, though you'll need to go early to beat the lunchtime crowds.

FONTES VEGETARIAN $

(Map p228; ☎2512-5900; Visconde de Pirajá 605D; mains R$10-21; ⌚11am-10pm Mon-Sat, noon-8pm

Sun) Hidden in a nondescript shopping plaza, this tiny, low-key restaurant is worth seeking out if you're after a decent vegetarian meal. The menu changes daily but features shiitake-filled manioc pastries, green salads, roasted eggplant and the like. On Saturday and Sunday, the rich, smoked-tofu *feijoada* (black bean stew) always draws a crowd.

KONI STORE — JAPANESE $

(Map p228; ☎2521-9348; Maria Quitéria 77; hand roll around R$12; ⏰11am-3am Sun-Wed, to 6am Thu-Sat) With nearly two dozen branches in Rio, the Koni craze shows no sign of abating. The recipe is simple – *temaki* (a seaweed hand roll) stuffed with salmon, tuna, shrimp, roast beef or a combination – which can then be devoured at one of the tiny bistro tables. It's stylish, tasty and cheap – a few reasons why you'll have to wait in line among nightclub kids for a roll at 4am on a Friday night. Other branches: **Ipanema** (Map p228; Farme de Amoedo 75); **Leblon** (Map p232; Av Ataulfo de Paiva 1174); Copacabana (p88).

GALITOS GRILL — ROAST CHICKEN $

(Map p228; ☎2287-7864; Farme de Amoedo 62; mains R$14-36; ⏰noon-10pm) A handy spot in the neighborhood is this open-sided purveyor of roast chicken. Grab a seat at the counter and enjoy inexpensive nicely seasoned lunch specials (R$14 to R$17) whipped up in a hurry.

LA VERONESE — PIZZA $

(Map p228; ☎2247-3152; Visconde Pirajá 29; mini pizzas R$4; ⏰9am-7pm Tue-Fri, to 6pm Sat, to 2:30pm Sun) If Rio is fast destroying your budget, head to this friendly stand-up snack counter for one of the best deals in the Zona Sul: the R$4 mini pizza with crispy crust is excellent value, and you can top it off with a few strangely addictive *palmeiras* (palm-shaped cookies).

POLIS SUCOS — JUICE BAR $

(Map p228; ☎2247-2518; Maria Quitéria 70; juices around R$6; ⏰7am-midnight; 🖉) One of Ipanema's favorite spots for a dose of freshly squeezed vitamins, this juice bar facing the Praça NS de Paz has dozens of flavors, and you can pair those tangy beverages with sandwiches or *pão de queijo* (balls of cheese-stuffed bread).

YOGOBERRY — FROZEN YOGURT $

(Map p228; ☎3281-1512; Visconde de Pirajá 282; small/medium yogurt R$7/9; ⏰10am-10pm) Ever popular, Yogoberry has been sating the hunger for low-fat frozen yogurt since 2007. It comes in just three flavors: *natural* (plain), diet and *chá verde* (green tea), but the fresh fruit, cashews, chocolate chips and other toppings help turn it into a delicacy.

SORVETE BRASIL — ICE CREAM $

(Map p228; ☎2247-8404; Maria Quitéria 74C; ice cream one/two scoops R$9/16; ⏰10am-10pm) A delightful pit stop on a sunny day in Ipanema, Sorvete Brasil scoops up more than 50 different ice-cream flavors including Amazonian *cupuaçu* (acidic, pear-like fruit), lychee, star fruit and guava.

URUGUAI — SNACK STAND $

(Map p228; Posto 9, Ipanema beach; sandwiches R$8-12; ⏰noon-5pm) Of the many *barracas* (food stalls) on the beach, Uruguai is a long-term favorite, serving scrumptious chicken, beef or sausage sandwiches, which are grilled up fresh on the sands. Look for the blue-and-white striped Uruguayan flag flying high over the beach.

VERO — ICE CREAM $

(Map p228; ☎3497-8754; Visconde de Pirajá 260; small/medium/large ice cream R$9/12/15; ⏰11:30am-7:30pm) An instant hit after opening in 2011, this artisanal gelato maker whips up over two dozen rich and creamy varieties, including Amazonian fruits like *açaí* and *cupuaçu* and innovative combinations like *caramelo com flor de sal* (caramel with sea salt) and *figo com amêndoas* (fig with almond).

LAFFA — KEBAB $

(Map p228; ☎2522-5888; Visconde de Pirajá 175; sandwich small/large R$13/19; ⏰11:30am-midnight) A new hit on the street food scene, this is a lively little eatery where harried staff whip up satisfying, piping hot grilled lamb or turkey shwarma, falafel sandwiches or slightly more exotic inventions like strawberry and Nutella wraps – all of which are served on *laffa* bread, made fresh with each order.

AMAZÔNIA SOUL — AMAZONIAN $

(Map p228; ☎2247-1028; Teixeira de Melo 37; snacks R$12-22; ⏰9am-9pm) This tiny new cafe doles out small plates of *caranguejo* (crab meat), *vatapá* (a puree of manioc, dried shrimp, coconut and dendê oil) and *tacacá,* a complicated soup made of tapioca, shrimp and manioc root. You can also sample juices and ice creams made from Amazonian fruits. The small shop inside sells handicrafts and edible items from the Amazon.

MIL FRUTAS ICE CREAM **$**

(Map p228; ☎2521-1384; www.milfrutas.com.br; Garcia D'Ávila 134; ice cream from R$10; ⏰11am-1am) On chic Garcia D'Ávila, Mil Frutas serves ice cream that showcases fruits from the Amazon and abroad. *Jaca* (jackfruit), lychee and *açaí* are among the several dozen varieties.

CAFEÍNA CAFE **$$**

(Map p228; ☎2521-2194; www.cafeina.com.br; Farme de Amoedo 43; quiches R$7-9, sandwiches R$20-30; ⏰8am-11:30pm; 📶) In the heart of Ipanema, this inviting cafe (and its sidewalk tables) is a fine spot for an espresso while watching the city stroll by. You'll also find freshly made sandwiches, salads, quiches and some very rich desserts.

NEW NATURAL VEGETARIAN **$$**

(Map p228; ☎2287-0301; Barão da Torre 167; per kg R$45; ⏰8am-10:30pm; 🖉) Featuring an excellent vegetarian lunch buffet, New Natural was the first health-food restaurant in the neighborhood. Fill up on fresh pots of soup, rice, veggies and beans at the healthy buffet. After 9pm the price drops to R$35 per kilo.

PINTXO SPANISH **$$**

(Map p228; ☎3586-4963; Gomes Carneiro 130; tapas R$6-14; ⏰11am-10pm Mon-Thu, to 2am Fri & Sat) A short stroll east of Praça General Osório, tiny Pintxo serves creative Basque cooking amid a charming interior of old film posters and colorful ceramic-tile floors. Stop in at lunchtime for good-value two-course specials (R$17) or in the evening for pintxos like the Amalur (foie gras with caramelized onions and mango), Txistorra (sausage, quail egg and spicy pepper) or less fussy slices of tortilla (Spanish omelet) or gazpacho. All go down nicely with bottles of Estrella or Voll-Damm beer.

TERZETTO CAFE CAFE **$$**

(Map p228; ☎2247-3243; cnr Jangadeiros & Visconde de Pirajá; mains R$16-42; ⏰9am-midnight) Fronting Praça General Osório, Terzetto is a bright and bustling cafe with an assortment of prepared salads and antipasti as well as focaccio sandwiches, ravioli, bruschetta, grilled dishes, pizzas (after 2pm) and desserts. There's a pricier Terzetto next door, which isn't really worth the money.

FRONTERA BUFFET **$$**

(Map p228; ☎3289-2350; Visconde de Pirajá 128; per kg R$53-60; ⏰11:30am-11pm) Run by a Dutch chef, Frontera offers more than 60 plates at its delectable lunch buffet, featuring a mouthwatering assortment of grilled meats, baked casseroles, and seafood pastas, plus salads, fresh fruits, grilled vegetables and desserts. Sushi is extra. If you're famished, opt for the all-you-can-eat (R$56). Dark woods and vintage prints give the place a cozier feel than most per-kilo places.

GULA GULA BRAZILIAN **$$**

(Map p228; ☎2259-3084; Henrique Dumont 87A; mains R$30-53; ⏰noon-midnight) In a cozy villa on the western edge, Gula Gula remains one of Ipanema's culinary favorites – which means a lot in a neighborhood ever in search of the new. Grilled meats are tops at this casual spot, but those in search of something lighter can opt for quiches and salads. Gula Gula is also in Centro and **Leblon** (Map p232; ☎2284-8792; Rita Ludolf 87A) among other places.

VIA SETE INTERNATIONAL **$$**

(Map p228; ☎2512-8100; Garcia D'Ávila 125; mains R$28-56; ⏰noon-midnight) This restaurant on upscale Garcia D'Ávila serves a good selection of salads and grilled vegetable wraps, as well as heartier fare like grilled tuna and a high-end steak burger. Best of all, Via Sete uses 100% organic ingredients (beef included). The pleasant front-side patio is a prime spot for sipping tropical cocktails while practicing the discreet art of people-watching.

GAROTA DE IPANEMA BRAZILIAN **$$**

(Map p228; ☎2523-3787; Vinícius de Moraes 49; mains R$30-80; ⏰noon-2am) A mix of tourists and neighborhood regulars pack the tables at the former bar where Tom Jobim and Vinícius de Moraes once held court. Although the food is fairly standard Brazilian fare, one dish stands out – the *picanha Brasileira* (R$80 for two), a scrumptious skillet of sliced sirloin brought sizzling to your table.

Wash it down with a few glasses of ice-cold *chope* (draft beer) and you'll realize why Garotas have been springing up all over the city.

ARTIGIANO ITALIAN $$

(Map p228; ☎2512-6107; Av Epitácio Pessoa 204; mains R$36-55; ⊙6:30pm-midnight Mon-Sat, noon-11pm Sun) Overlooking the Jardim de Alah, Artigiano is set in a picturesque villa with more than a hint of the old-world about it. Here, you will find an older, well-dressed crowd enjoying classic Italian fare, including some 20 superb varieties of handmade pasta amid the oil paintings and antique furnishings.

MARKET BRAZILIAN $$

(Map p228; ☎3283-1438; Visconde de Pirajá 499; mains R$30-50; ⊙noon-5pm Mon, 9am-midnight Tue-Sat, to 6pm Sun) Market serves inventive seafood dishes, grilled meats, creative salads and gourmet sandwiches, and breakfast (waffles, eggs Benedict) is served until 5pm. Hidden from the street, Market is reached by a narrow corridor to a shaded plant-trimmed patio and a cozy dining room beyond. Two-course lunch specials (R$31) are good value.

VENGA! SPANISH $$

(☎2247-0234; Garcia D'Ávila 147; tapas R$15-30; ⊙noon-midnight) A festive spot to eat and drink, Venga! became Rio's first authentic tapas bar when it opened back in 2009. Classic wood details and a good soundtrack set the scene for noshing on *patatas bravas* (spicy potatoes), *pulpo a la Gallega* (grilled octopus), *gambas al ajillo* (garlic prawns) and other Iberian hits. Match those small plates with a Spanish rioja. Also in Leblon.

FELICE CAFFÈ CAFE $$

(Map p228; ☎2522-7749; Gomes Carneiro 30; mains R$26-50; ⊙noon-midnight Mon-Fri, 10am-midnight Sat & Sun) Half a block from the beach, Felice has a small shaded front terrace for taking in the passing people parade. Head inside for air-conditioned splendor, where locals and travelers enjoy gourmet sandwiches (grilled veggies, steak, thick burgers), juicy grilled dishes, bountiful salads, and, most importantly, rich Italian-style ice cream (R$10 for two scoops), pulled from the highly enticing display counter in front.

CAPRICCIOSA PIZZA $$$

(Map p228; ☎2523-3394; Vinícius de Moraes 134; small/large pizzas around R$45/60; ⊙6pm-1am) Inside this trendy high-end pizzeria, you'll find tasty thin-crust pizzas made with fresh ingredients. The price is high, but the chefs – working in an open kitchen next to the brick oven – are at least generous with the toppings. Among many flavorful combinations is the signature *capricciosa* (ham, bacon, egg, artichoke hearts and mushrooms).

BENKEI JAPANESE $$$

(Map p228; ☎2540-4829; Av Henrique Dumont 71; all-you-can-eat R$41-57; ⊙noon-4pm Tue-Sun, 7pm-midnight daily) This casual Japanese restaurant is a favorite haunt for after-the-beach meals on weekends. Benkei does have a menu, though nearly everyone here comes for the all-you-can-eat sushi buffet, with a wide variety of rolls and sashimi, plus miso soup. You can dine on the small front patio or in the cooler dining room inside.

NIK SUSHI JAPANESE $$$

(Map p228; ☎2512-6446; Garcia D'Ávila 83; all-you-can-eat lunch R$42-48, dinner R$55-60; ⊙11:30am-midnight Tue-Sat, 1-11pm Sun) This simple but stylish Japanese restaurant has earned many loyal customers for its all-you-can-eat sushi lunches and dinners. Prices are slightly lower on weekdays.

ALESSANDRO E FEDERICO PIZZA $$$

(Map p228; ☎2522-5414; Garcia D'Ávila 151; pizzas around R$50; ⊙noon-1am) Dominated by the wood-burning oven at center stage, this stylish two-story restaurant serves some of Ipanema's best thin-crust pizzas. A more casual Alessandro e Federico further south on the same street has a menu of freshly made panini, salads and pastas (but no pizza), with sidewalk seating.

TEN KAI JAPANESE $$$

(Map p228; ☎2540-5100; Prudente de Morais 1810; mains R$45-90; ⊙7pm-1am Mon-Fri, 1pm-midnight Sat & Sun) In the top tier of the city's Japanese restaurants, Ten Kai serves mouthwatering sashimi and sushi, and maintains the strong culinary traditions of the East. The ambience is pure charm, with an interior lit by glowing paper lanterns.

CASA DA FEIJOADA BRAZILIAN $$$

(Map p228; ☎2247-2776; Prudente de Morais 10B; feijoada R$73; ⊙noon-midnight) Admirers of Brazil's iconic *feijoada* (black beans and pork stew) needn't wait until Saturday when it's traditionally eaten to experience the meaty meal. The casual Casa da

Feijoada serves the rich black-bean and salted-pork dish every day of the week. It comes with the requisite orange slices, *farofa* (garnish of manioc flour sautéed with butter) and grated kale (cabbage), and goes nicely with a caipirinha.

BRASILEIRINHO BRAZILIAN $$$
(Map p228; ☎2523-5184; Jangadeiros 10; mains R$34-57; ⏰noon-11pm) Facing Praça General Osório, this rustically decorated restaurant serves good, traditional Mineiro cuisine. Favorites include *tutu a mineira* (mashed black beans with manioc), *carne seca* (dried beef) and *picanha* (rump steak). The *feijoada* here is tops – not surprising given that Brasileirinho is run by the same owner as the nearby Casa da Feijoada.

AZUL MARINHO SEAFOOD $$$
(☎2513-5014; Av Francisco Bhering, Praia do Arpoador; mains R$62-100; ⏰noon-midnight) Below the Arpoador Inn, Azul Marinho serves an assortment of tasty seafood dishes, and the outdoor tables facing the ocean have the best beachside setting you'll find in the Zona Sul (there's no traffic between you and the sea, only palm trees and sand). Try one of the *moquecas* (seafood stews cooked in coconut milk) or the octopus vinaigrette salad.

BAZZAR INTERNATIONAL $$$
(Map p228; ☎3202-2884; Barão da Torre 538; mains R$48-70; ⏰noon-1am Mon-Sat, to 7pm Sun) Set on a peaceful tree-lined street, this nicely designed restaurant with relaxing front terrace serves creative, beautifully executed dishes. Recent hits include duck with crispy plantains, *cavaquinha* (a lobster relative) and inventive risottos. There's a smaller branch hidden with more of a bistro menu on the 2nd floor of Ipanema's **Livraria da Travessa** (Av Rio Branco 44, Centro).

THE GIRL FROM IPANEMA

Her name was Helô Pinheiro, and in 1962, tall, tanned, young (she was 17 at the time) and quite lovely, she went frequently to the beach of Ipanema. Her route from her home a few blocks away took her past the small Bar Veloso, where several men made overtures to her, though she hardly noticed them.

Flash forward to August 1962. Inside a cramped club in Copacabana, Tom Jobim takes the stage (along with João Gilberto). They play a song composed by Jobim and poet, Vinícius de Moraes. It's a nostalgic, sorrowful tune, with unusual chord progressions and a jazzy beat, and titled 'Garota de Ipanema' (the Girl from Ipanema). The song becomes a smash hit and helps launch the sound of bossa nova, a still budding movement barely known even in Rio.

When Pinheiro later heard the tune, she never suspected that she was the inspiration for the song. She heard rumors, but didn't believe them – at least until 1965, when De Moraes declared in a press conference that Helô was indeed the inspiration behind the song, describing her as 'a golden girl, a mixture of flowers and mermaids, full of light and grace, but whose sight is also sad because it carries within it, on the way to the sea, the sense of youth that passes, of beauty that doesn't belong only to us.'

Pinheiro got to know De Moraes and Jobim – who both proposed to her. She was impressed with their obvious musical gifts, but never became involved with either of them. In an interview with the *Guardian* in 2012, Pinheiro said, '...The two of them drank too much. They were always at the bar drinking whisky, caipirinhas, beer.' Instead she initially shirked the fame, marrying her high school sweetheart and initially living a sedate life as a housewife – there was pressure from her father, an army general, to settle down.

Years later, circumstances changed, and Pinheiro returned to the spotlight. She became a model, posing for Playboy (once alongside her daughter in 2003), a radio host, a TV announcer and wrote an autobiography in 1996. Although she never earned any money directly from the song, it helped pave the way to success in a variety of enterprises – including a boutique of swimwear (named Garota de Ipanema, naturally) on the street next to the former Bar Veloso (now also called the Garota de Ipanema). And even the Rua Montenegro has been renamed as Vinícius de Moraes, in honor of the songwriter. Today Helô lives in São Paulo, though for bossa nova fans she'll always be the girl from Ipanema.

ZAZÁ BISTRÔ TROPICAL FUSION $$$

(Map p228; ☎2247-9101; www.zazabistro.com.br; Joana Angélica 40; mains R$51-65; ⏰7:30pm-midnight Mon-Thu, 1:30pm-1am Fri & Sat, 12:30pm-6pm Sun) Inside an art-filled and whimsically decorated converted house, Zazá serves beautifully prepared dishes with Asian accents, and uses organic ingredients when possible. Recent favorites include grilled squid and octopus with wild rice and lemon confit, flambéed prawns with risotto and grilled *namorado* served with caramelized plantains. Upstairs, diners lounge on throw pillows amid flickering candles. You can also sit at one of the tables out the front.

VIEIRA SOUTO INTERNATIONAL $$$

(Map p228; ☎2267-9282; Av Vieira Souto 234; mains R$44-98; ⏰noon-4pm & 7pm-midnight Tue-Sun) In a converted 1930s villa facing the beach, Vieira Souto serves up excellent pastas as well as grilled meats and seafood, and you can also stop in for a gourmet prix-fixe lunch (couvert, appetizer, main course and dessert for R$68).

CAVIST BRAZILIAN $$$

(Map p228; ☎2123-7900; Barão da Torre 358; mains R$50-110; ⏰noon-3pm & 7pm-midnight Mon-Sat) Overlooking leafy Praça Nossa Senhora da Paz, this elegant restaurant is a must for wine aficionados. In the shop in back, you'll find a decent selection of wines from the old and new worlds, and you can select any bottle to be served with your meal. Menu highlights include duck in a wine reduction sauce, shrimp fettuccine, baked cod and mixed cheese plates. The open-air terrace upstairs is a magical spot for dinner. There's also a branch in Leblon.

FASANO AL MARE SEAFOOD $$$

(Map p228; ☎3202-4000; Av Vieira Souto 80; mains R$90-120; ⏰noon-3:30pm & 7pm-1am) Under the helm of award-winning Italian chef Luca Gozzani, the lavish Fasano Al Mare serves excellent seafood dishes. Top picks include risotto with saffron and rock lobster, seared tuna and whole fish baked in salt. Reservations are essential.

Leblon

BIBI CREPES CREPERIE $

(Map p232; ☎2259-4948; Cupertino Durão 81; crepes R$16-28; ⏰noon-1am) This small, open-sided restaurant attracts a young, garrulous crowd who enjoy the more than two dozen sweet and savory crepes available, as well as design-your-own salads (choose from 40 different toppings). Come early to beat the lunch crowds.

VEZPA PIZZA $

(Map p232; ☎2540-0800; Av Ataúlfo de Paiva 1063; slice R$6-8; ⏰noon-2am Sun-Thu, to 5am Fri & Sat) Vezpa is a New York–style place, with brick walls and high ceilings, where you can order pizza by the slice. The crusts are thin and crunchy and there are decent selections on hand (try the mozzarella with tomatoes and basil). Vezpa also has locations in Ipanema (Farme de Amoedo) and Copacabana (Djalma Ulrich).

ARMAZÉM DO CAFÉ CAFE $

(Map p232; ☎2259-0170; Rita Ludolf 87B; snacks R$5-10; ⏰9am-midnight Sun-Thu, to 1am Fri & Sat) Dark-wood furnishings and the fresh-ground coffee aroma lend an authenticity to this Leblon coffeehouse. Connoisseurs rate the aromatic roasts much higher here than neighboring Cafeína. It also serves waffles, snacks and desserts.

BIBI SUCOS JUICE, FAST FOOD $

(Map p232; ☎2259-4298; www.bibisucos.com.br; Ataúlfo de Paiva 591A; açaí R$6-14; ⏰8am-2am) Among Rio's countless juice bars, Bibi Sucos is a longstanding favorite. Here you'll find over 40 different varieties, and a never-ending supply of the favorite *açaí*. Sandwiches will quell greater hunger pangs.

EMPÓRIO ARABE MIDDLE EASTERN $

(Map p232; ☎2512-7373; Av Ataúlfo de Paiva 370; savory pies R$4; ⏰9am-8pm Mon-Sat) There are only a few tables inside this tiny restaurant in Leblon, but most people stop by just long enough to down a quick bite from the counter facing the sidewalk. *Esfirras* (triangular pies) filled with chicken, spinach or ricotta, make for a speedy snack on your way back from the beach.

HORTIFRUTI SUPERMARKET

(Map p232; ☎2586-7000; Dias Ferreira 57; ⏰8am-8pm Mon-Sat, to 2pm Sun) This popular grocer and produce market sells a wide variety of fruits and vegetables, plus fresh juices and all the supermarket essentials.

ZONA SUL SUPERMARKET SUPERMARKET

(Map p232; ☎2259-4699; Dias Ferreira 290; ⏰24hr Mon-Sat, 7am-midnight Sun) A Rio institution for nearly 50 years, Zona Sul supermarket has branches all over the city. This one is the best of the bunch, with freshly baked breads, imported cheeses and olives, wines, cured meats and other items. The adjoining pizza and lasagna counter serves decent plates. A handy **Ipanema branch** (Map p228; Prudente de Morais 49) is near Praça General Osório.

YALLA MIDDLE EASTERN $

(Map p232; ☎2540-6517; Dias Ferreira 45; mains R$18-25; ⏰noon-4pm & 6-11pm) One of the few nonfancy options on this culinary street, Yalla is a small, quick-serving restaurant where you can pick up fresh tabbouleh or couscous salads, sandwiches on lavash bread (shwarma, falafel, shish kebab) or pasties filled with ricotta, beef or spinach. Don't miss baklava for dessert.

TALHO CAPIXABA SANDWICHES $

(Map p232; ☎2512-8760; Av Ataúlfo de Paiva 1022; sandwiches around R$18-35; ⏰8am-10pm) This deli and gourmet grocer is one of the city's best spots to put together a takeout meal. In addition to pastas, salads and antipasti, you'll find excellent sandwiches (charged by weight) made from quality ingredients. You can also dine inside or at the sidewalk tables in front.

GALETO DO LEBLON BRAZILIAN $

(Map p232; ☎2294-3997; Dias Ferreira 154; mains for two R$30-80; ⏰11am-2am) One of the pioneers on this street, Galeto do Leblon has been around for over 35 years. Although a recent renovation has created an airy, modern feel, with floor-to-ceiling glass windows, Galeto still serves the traditional Brazilian dishes that have made it such a neighborhood favorite over the years. On Saturday, stop in for excellent *feijoada* (R$58 for two).

CAFÉ SEVERINO CAFE $

(Map p232; ☎2239-9398; Dias Ferreira 417; mains R$17-30; ⏰9am-midnight Mon-Sat, 10am-midnight Sun) In the back of the Argumento bookshop, this charming cafe is a cozy place to hide away with a book or a new friend, and enjoy coffees and lighter fare – sandwiches, salads and desserts.

VEGETARIANO SOCIAL CLUB VEGETARIAN $

(Map p232; ☎2294-5200; Conde Bernadotte 26L; lunch buffet R$30; ⏰noon-11pm Mon-Sat, noon-5:30pm Sun; ☑) Vegetarians interested in sampling Brazil's signature dish should visit this small charmer on Thursday or Sunday when tofu *feijoada* is served. At other times, they serve a small (10-dish) lunch buffet, while the more elaborate evening à la carte menu features risottos, yakisoba, heart-of-palm stroganoff and other inventive dishes.

UNIVERSO ORGÂNICO VEGETARIAN $

(Map p232; ☎3874-0186; store 105, Conde Bernadotte 26; mains R$8-28; ⏰8am-7pm Mon, to 9:30pm Tue-Sat, 11am-8pm Sun) In the back of a small shopping center, Universo Orgânico whips up delicious fruit and veggie shakes – such as the carrot, ginger, apple and linseed combo – best enjoyed with a veggie burger or savory nonmeat *salgados* (bar snacks). The small grocery store sells organic goodies. It's a great option for raw-food craving vegans.

PRIMA BRUSCHETTERIA ITALIAN $$

(Map p232; ☎3592-0881; www.primab.com.br; Rainha Guilhermina 95; bruschetta R$7-10, mains R$23-43; ⏰noon-1am) Prima showcases an Italian delicacy not often seen in these parts, with imaginative ingredients like goat's cheese, olive tapenade, prosciutto, smoked salmon and even caviar appearing atop its char-grilled bread. You'll also find fresh salads, antipasto plates and various risottos.

JUICE CO INTERNATIONAL $$

(Map p232; ☎2294-0048; Av General San Martin 889; mains R$27-65; ⏰6pm-midnight Mon-Fri, noon-midnight Sat & Sun) This stylish two-story restaurant serves much more than just tasty, freshly squeezed juices. In an uberdesigned loungelike setting, you can sample a wide range of fare – foccacia sandwiches, salads, risottos, grilled fish and roast meats, any of which can be paired nicely with one of 60 juice concoctions.

FELLINI BUFFET $$

(Map p232; ☎2511-3600; General Urquiza 104; per kg R$63-74; ⏰11:30am-4pm & 7:30pm-midnight) One of Leblon's top buffet restaurants, Fellini has an enticing selection of dishes: salads, pastas, grilled fish and shrimp, a sushi counter and the hallowed roast-meat counter. The modest dining room attracts a mix of hungry patrons – tourists, neighborhood folk and the beautiful crowd included.

RÁSCAL ITALIAN $$$

(Map p232; ☎2259-6437; Shopping Leblon, Av Afrânio de Melo Franco 290; all-you-can-eat R$58; ⏲noon-3pm & 7pm-10:30pm) This popular São Paulo chain arrived in Rio a few years back and quickly earned top marks for its fantastic buffet. The huge spread of Italian cuisine includes salads, bruschetta, pizzas, pastas (six different kinds) and a few juicy grill choices.

ZUKA INTERNATIONAL $$$

(Map p232; ☎3205-7154; Rua Dias Ferreira 233, Leblon; mains R$57-90; ⏲7pm-1am Mon, noon-4pm & 7pm-1am Tue-Fri, 1pm-1am Sat & Sun) One of Rio's best restaurants, Zuka prepares delectable mouthwatering cuisine – zingy ceviche or the confectionlike delicacy of Zuka's original foie gras to start, followed by rack of lamb with passion fruit, grilled fish of the day with *mandoquinha* (a kind of sweet root vegetable) purée, seared tuna over heart-of-palm tagliatelle and many other imaginative dishes. All the grilling action happens at the open kitchen to the right (you can sit at the counter and watch the chefs in action), and the cocktails (particularly the lychee saketinis) and desserts are excellent.

NAM THAI THAI $$$

(Map p232; ☎2259-2962; Rainha Guilhermina 95B; mains R$50-75; ⏲7pm-1am Mon, noon-4pm & 7pm-1am Tue-Fri, noon-1am Sat, to 11pm Sun) Thai cuisine is a rarity in Rio, which makes charming Nam Thai even more of a star. The French colonial interior is a cozy setting for the eclectic Thai cooking. Favorites are the squid salad and spicy shrimp curry with pineapple. No less intoxicating are Nam Thai's tropical drinks, such as the *caipivodca de lychee* (lychee vodka caipirinha).

PLATAFORMA CHURRASCARIA $$$

(Map p232; ☎2274-4022; Adalberto Ferreira 32; mains around R$80; ⏲noon-midnight) This well-known *churrascaria* (barbeque restaurant) still draws a garrulous mix of politicians, artists and tourists. Dark, mellow woods in the dining room match the tones of the roast meats traveling from table to table. Also in this complex is the Plataforma Show – the over-the-top touristy Carnaval spectacle (headdresses, sequins and lots of skin).

SUSHI LEBLON JAPANESE $$$

(Map p232; ☎2512-7830; Dias Ferreira 256; mains R$50-70; ⏲noon-4pm & 7pm-1:30am Mon-Sat, 1pm-midnight Sun) Leblon's top sushi destination boasts a Zenlike ambience with a handsome dark-wood sushi counter setting the stage for succulent cuisine. In addition to sashimi and sushi, you'll find grilled *namorado* with passion fruit *farofa,* sea-urchin ceviche and refreshing sake to complement the meal.

DRINKING & NIGHTLIFE

Ipanema has a mix of stylish and classic bars attracting a 20- and 30-something crowd. For drinking al fresco, you will find peacefully set tables along the east side of Praça General Osório. Leblon has even more bars on offer than Ipanema, with venerable *botecos* (small bars) and a few lounges as well. A particularly good place to wander in search of a drink is toward the west end of Av General San Martin.

Ipanema

BLUE AGAVE BAR

(Map p228; Vinícius de Moraes 68; ⏲noon-2am) On a lively bar-lined street, this small bar gathers a largely gringo crowd who come for margaritas, bottles of Sol and a small selection of Tex-Mex fare (tacos, enchiladas, burritos). TVs over the bar show the latest NFL games.

BARZIN BAR, LIVE MUSIC

(Map p228; Vinicius de Moraes 75; ⏲11am-3am Tue-Sun) Barzin is a popular spot for post-beach drinks, with an open-sided ground-floor bar that fills with animated chatter at all hours. Upstairs, you can catch a changing line-up of bands playing surf rock, hip hop and other popular Brazilian music (cover charge R$20 to $60).

EMPÓRIO BAR

(Map p228; ☎3813-2526; Maria Quitéria 37; ⏲8:30pm-late) A young mix of *cariocas* and gringos stirs things up over cheap cocktails at this battered old favorite in Ipanema. A porch in front overlooks the street – a fine spot to stake out when the air gets too heavy with bad '80s music. From Wednesday to Saturday you can catch live rock shows on the 2nd floor (entrance R$10 to R$20). Don't come early; Empório doesn't get lively until after midnight.

1

2

BEN LEWIS / ALAMY ©

1. Ipanema beach (p58) 2. Surfer, Praia do Arpoador (p58)
3. *Futevolei* (no-hands volleyball), Copacabana beach (p86)

Beach Life

The beaches of Rio are the city's wondrous and carefree backyard. It's where *cariocas* (residents) from all walks of life – rich and poor, young and old, black and white, model-thin and beer-bellied – come to play and socialize against a backdrop of crashing waves and the ever-present green peaks towering over the city.

The Perfect Crowd

Although the mix is incredibly democratic, *postos* (posts) subdivide the beach into different sections, with each subculture drawn to its particular *posto*, whether drawing favela kids, volleyballers, well-heeled families or the beauty crowd.

Seaside Sport

Sports are a big seaside draw, and entail surfing, stand-up paddle boarding, jogging, cycling and skating the beachside path, football, volleyball and *futevolei* – that uniquely Brazilian combination of volleyball played with football-style rules (no hands allowed!). There's also *frescobol*, a simple game where two players with wooden rackets stand 10m apart and pound a rubber ball back and forth.

Sit Back & Relax

Many beachgoers, however, would rather just relax and enjoy the scene. For sun-lovers, there's much to take in: the sand, the sea, the food and drink vendors, the passing people parade and much more.

BEACH ETIQUETTE

- Leave valuables back at the hotel. Take only the cash you need for the beach.
- Don't use a towel on the beach – instead, sit on a chair or a *kanga* (sarong); Brazilian men stand or sit on the sand.
- Choose your spot; find a *barraca* (stall) you like, hire chairs and sunshades from it.
- Don't bother bringing food or drink to the beach; support the local vendors.

DELIRIUM CAFE BAR

(Map p228; ☎2502-0029; Barão da Torre 183; ⏲5pm-midnight Sun-Thu, to 2am Fri & Sat) This small cozy pub has more than 300 varieties of brew, with labels from across Europe, the US, Australia and beyond. If you've been to the original Delirium in Brussels, you might be a bit disappointed by its modest sister enterprise. Nevertheless, it's probably Rio's best destination for beer lovers.

BARTHODOMEU BOTECO

(Map p228; ☎2247-8609; Maria Quitéria 46; ⏲noon-2am) Barthodomeu is a friendly bar that has *boteco* charm – open-sided, wood tables, minimal decor and waiters bustling about under trays of *chope*, *feijoada* (good value at R$37), grilled meats and piping hot appetizers.

DEVASSA BOTECO

(Map p228; ☎2522-0627; Prudente de Moraes 416; ⏲noon-2am) Serving some of Rio's best beer, Devassa makes its own creamy brews, before offering them up to chatty *cariocas* at this bar and restaurant – one of 10 in the Rio chain. The choices: *loura* (pilsner), *sarará* (wheat beer), *ruiva* (pale ale), *negra* (dark ale) and *Índia* (IPA). The food menu features well-prepared pub fare – burgers, steak, pastas, grilled fish and lots of appetizers.

BAR ASTOR BAR

(Map p228; www.barastor.com.br; Veira Souto 110; ⏲6pm-1am Mon-Fri, noon-3am Sat, to 10pm Sun) Won't make it to São Paulo? No problem. One of Sampa's best bars has arrived in Rio in spectacular fashion. This gorgeous art deco bar on prime Ipanema real estate does meticulously prepared caipirinhas, some 20 exotic flavors in all, and great food to help soak up the quality *cachaça* (potent can spirit).

GAROTA DE IPANEMA BAR

(Map p228; ☎2523-3787; Vinícius de Moraes 49) During its first incarnation, this small, open-sided bar was called Bar Veloso. Its name and anonymity disappeared once two scruffy young regulars – Tom Jobim and Vinícius de Moraes – penned the famous song, 'Girl from Ipanema', here that changed history (and the name of the street, too). Today, you'll find a mix of tourists and *cariocas* here, as well as sizzling platters of grilled steak.

BARETTO-LONDRA LOUNGE

(Map p228; ☎3202-4000; Av Vieira Souto 80; ⏲7pm-2am Mon-Thu, to 4am Fri & Sat) One of Rio's glammiest bars is inside the Hotel Fasano, and offers a vision of decadence matched by few of the city's nightspots. The intimate space, designed by Philippe Starck, has an enchantingly illuminated bar, leather armchairs and divans, and a DJ spinning world electronica. The crowd is A-list, the drinks are pricey (cocktails are around R$27), and unless you're a model (or have one draped on your arm), prepare for a long wait at the door.

SHENANIGAN'S BAR

(Map p228; Visconde de Pirajá 112A; admission R$5 to R$25; ⏲6pm-2am) Overlooking the Praça General Osorio, Shenanigan's is an English-style pub with exposed brick walls, imported beers and a couple of tiny balconies perched above the street. Sunburnt gringos and the odd working girl mix it up over games of pool and darts to the occasional backdrop of live bands.

Leblon

JOBI BOTECO

(Map p232; ☎2274-0547; Av Ataúlfo de Paiva 1166; ⏲9am-5am) A favorite since 1956, Jobi has served a lot of beer in its day, and its popularity hasn't waned. The unadorned *botequim* (bar with table service) still serves plenty; grab a seat by the sidewalk and let the night unfold. If hunger beckons, try the tasty appetizers – the *carne seca* (jerked beef) and the *bolinhos de bacalhau* (codfish croquettes) are tops.

COBAL DO LEBLON BAR

(Map p232; ☎2239-1549; Rua Gilberto Cardoso; ⏲closed Mon) Leblon's flower-and-produce market features a number of bars and restaurants, many of which open onto the large terrace in back. A vibrant, youthful air pervades this place, and it's a major meeting spot on weekends and on game days.

ACADEMIA DA CACHAÇA BAR

(Map p232; ☎2239-1542; Conde de Bernadotte 26G; ⏲noon-1am Sun-Thu, to 2am Fri & Sat) Although *cachaça* has a sordid reputation in some parts, here the fiery liquor is given the respect it nearly deserves. Along with traditional Brazilian cooking, this pleasant indoor-outdoor spot serves over

100 varieties of *cachaça,* and you can order it straight, with honey and lime, or disguised in a fruity caipirinha. For a treat (and/or a bad hangover), try the passion fruit *batida* (*cachaça* and passion fruit juice).

TÔ NEM AÍ GAY BAR

(Map p228; ☎2247-8403; cnr Farme de Amoedo & Visconde de Piraja, Ipanema; ⊙noon-3am) On Ipanema's gayest street, this popular bar is a great after-beach spot.

GALERIA CAFÉ GAY BAR

(Map p228; ☎2523-8250; www.galeriacafe.com.br; Teixeira de Mello 31, Ipanema; ⊙Thu-Sat) This bar with a very mixed crowd has lovely decor.

PIZZARIA GUANABARA BAR

(Map p232; ☎2294-0797; Av Ataulfo de Paiva 1228; ⊙9am-7am) One of the pillars of Baixo Leblon, this popular drinking spot serves lousy pizza – but that hasn't stopped patrons from packing this place at all hours of the night. Expect simple ambience and a young, flirtatious, beer-drinking crowd.

BAR VELOSO BOTECO

(Map p232; ☎2274-9966; Aristides Espínola 44; ⊙11am-1am Sun-Wed, to 3am Thu-Sat) Named after the original bar (now occupied by Garota de Ipanema) where Jobim and Vinícius penned the famous song 'Girl from Ipanema', the open-sided Bar Veloso attracts a young, good-looking crowd who spill out onto the sidewalk on busy weekends. Upstairs, is a quieter air-conditioned retreat where men (mostly) watch the game in peace.

LORD JIM PUB

(Map p228; ☎2294-4881; Paul Redfern 44; ⊙6pm-2am Mon-Thu, to 3am Fri, 1pm-3am Sat & Sun) Something of a novelty for *cariocas,* Lord Jim is one of several English-style pubs scattered about the Zona Sul. Darts, English-speaking waiters and a few expat beers – Guinness, Harps, Bass etc – are on hand to complete the ambience. The R$30 all-the-beer-you-can-drink nights (currently Thursdays from 6pm to 10pm) get messy.

Unlike many bars, there's always a cover charge (from R$20 to R$30), though drink specials lessen the hurt.

MELT CLUB

(Map p232; ☎2249-9309; www.meltbar.com.br; Rita Ludolf 47; admission R$30-60; ⊙10pm-4am Mon & Thu-Sat, 11pm-4am Tue & Wed) The Melt club gathers a young, attractive crowd in its candlelit main-floor lounge, sipping brightly colored elixirs. Upstairs, DJs break beats over the dance floor, with the occasional band making an appearance.

BRACARENSE BOTECO

(Map p232; ☎2294-3549; José Linhares 85B; ⊙9am-midnight Mon-Sat, 10am-10pm Sun) Opened in 1948, Bracarense is a classic *carioca* watering hole, famous for its simple, unpretentious ambience and its heavenly *salgados* (bar snacks). A steady stream of neighborhood regulars enjoy over 20 varieties of the snacks (try the *aipim com camarão* – cassava with shrimp) to the accompaniment of ice-cold *chope.*

BAR D'HOTEL LOUNGE

(Map p232; ☎2172-1112; 2nd fl, Marina All Suites, Av Delfim Moreira 696; ⊙noon-2am) The waves crashing on the shore are just part of the background of this texture-rich bar overlooking Ipanema beach. The narrow bar is like a magnet for the style set, who gather in the intimate space to enjoy tropical drinks to the backdrop of sea and ambient electronic music. The adjoining restaurant serves high-end fusion fare (mains around R$80).

ESCH CAFÉ CIGAR BAR

(Map p232; ☎2512-5651; Dias Ferreira 78; ⊙noon-1:30am Mon-Sat, noon-midnight Sun) Billing itself as the House of Havana, Esch offers a blend of Cuban cigars and jazz. The dark-wood interior combined with the well-dressed over-30 crowd will probably make you feel like you're stepping into a Johnnie Walker photo shoot.

★ ENTERTAINMENT

STUDIO RJ LIVE MUSIC

(Map p228; ☎2523-1204; http://studiorj.org; Vieira Souto 110, Ipanema; admission R$20-60; ⊙from 9pm Mon-Sat) Above Bar Astor, Studio RJ has given a much-needed jolt to Ipanema's dormant music scene. The spacious, acoustically fit music hall sees an eclectic line-up throughout the week, from old-school jazz nights (currently on

Tuesdays) to innovative samba, MPB, hip hop and indie rock. Shows kick off around 9:30pm on weekdays and midnight on weekends, with DJs keeping the party going afterwards till the early hours.

VINÍCIUS SHOW BAR LIVE MUSIC
(Map p228; ☎2523-4757; www.viniciusbar.com.br; 2nd fl, Prudente de Morais 34, Ipanema; admission R$30-40) Billing itself as the 'temple of bossa nova,' this place has been an icon in the neighborhood since 1989. The intimate space makes a fine setting to listen to first-rate bossa nova (and occasional MPB and samba). Shows start between 9:30pm and 11pm.

TEATRO DO LEBLON PERFORMING ARTS
(Map p232; ☎2529-7700; Conde Bernadotte 26, Leblon) This conveniently located theater shows a mix of drama, cutting-edge and children's performances on three different stages. In the same complex is an assortment of lively eating and drinking spots.

CASA DA CULTURA LAURA ALVIM CINEMA
(Map p228; ☎2332-2015; Av Vieira Souto 176, Ipanema) Across from the beach in Ipanema, this small center stages plays and hosts art exhibitions; the atrium cafe is a pleasant spot for a bite.

ESTAÇÃO IPANEMA CINEMA
(Map p228; ☎2279-4603; Visconde de Pirajá 605, Ipanema) On the 1st floor of a small shopping complex in Ipanema, this cinema screens popular contemporary films from Brazil and abroad. Its single theater seats 140.

TEATRO LEBLON CINEMA
(Map p232; ☎2461-2461; Av Ataúlfo de Paiva 391, Leblon) Leblon's popular theater has two screens showing the latest Hollywood releases.

SHOPPING

Ipanema

Ipanema and Leblon are the best hunting grounds for top fashion designs (both home-grown and foreign labels). You'll also find curio and novelty stores, galleries, bookshops, liquor stores and plenty of cafes for refueling along the way. There's a lot going on along the main thoroughfare (Rua Visconde de Pirajá in Ipanema and Av Ataúlfo de Paiva in Leblon).

HIPPIE FAIR MARKET
(Map p228; Praça General Osório; ⏲9am-6pm Sun) The Zona Sul's most famous market, the Hippie Fair (aka Feira de Arte de Ipanema) has artwork, jewelry, handicrafts, clothing and souvenirs for sale. Stalls in the southeast and northeast corners of the plaza sell tasty plates of *acarajé* (croquettes, with a sauce of *vatapá* and shrimp, R$7), plus excellent desserts (R$3). Don't miss it.

AQUIM CHOCOLATE
(Map p228; ☎2523-5090; Garcia D'Ávila 149; ⏲11am-7pm Mon-Sat) This artisanal chocolatier carefully sources its cacao from a single environmentally conscious grower in Bahia, and has garnered international awards for its high-quality (and delicious!) products. Stop by this jewel-box-sized store for rich truffles, macarons, chocolate cakes and mini tarts that look nearly too lovely to eat. Baristas whip up an excellent cappuccino, which you can enjoy at one of the two cafe tables out front.

GILSON MARTINS ACCESSORIES
(Map p228; ☎2227-6178; Visconde de Pirajá 462; ⏲9am-8pm Mon-Sat) Designer Gilson Martins transforms the Brazilian flag and silhouettes of Pão de Açúcar and Corcovado into eye-catching accessories in his flagship store in Ipanema. In addition to glossy handbags, wallets, passport covers, key chains and iPad covers, the shop has a gallery in the back with ongoing exhibitions.

Products are durable and use recycled and sustainable materials – and are not available outside of Rio. Gilson also has several other branches, including a spacious Copacabana showroom.

LIVRARIA DA TRAVESSA BOOKS, MUSIC
(☎3205-9002; Visconde de Pirajá 572; ⏲9am-midnight Mon-Sat, 11am-midnight Sun) One of several branches around town, Livraria da Travessa has a small selection of foreign-language books and periodicals, with CDs upstairs. The buzzing 2nd-floor cafe (a branch of Bazzar) serves salads, sandwiches, quiches and desserts. There's an even larger Livraria da Travessa inside the mall, Shopping Leblon.

ESPAÇO FASHION CLOTHING

(Map p228; ☎2512-8419; Av Aníbal de Mendonça 114; ⏰9am-8pm Mon-Sat, 10am-6pm Sun) This long, narrow boutique has a decor and aesthetic aimed at attracting a young, hip, somewhat fashion-forward group of shoppers with its form-fitting skirts, dresses and tops, flashy sneakers and one-of-a-kind jewelry. Electronic music plays overhead, and there's a tiny lounge area at the back with some art books – for the gents while the gals shop.

FORUM CLOTHING

(Map p228; ☎2521-7415; www.forum.com.br; Barão da Torre 422; ⏰10am-6pm Mon-Fri, 10am-2pm Sat) Much touted Brazilian designer Tufi Duek reigns over this curiously designed flagship store. Here you'll find beautifully made pieces from his men's and women's collections.

ISABELA CAPETO CLOTHING

(Map p228; ☎2523-0052; Garcia d'Ávila 173; ⏰10am-8pm Mon-Fri, 10am-3pm Sat) One of Brazil's fashion stars, Isabela Capeto creates beautifully made clothing with seductive lines. Many of her pieces are embroidered and feature add-ons of vintage lace, sequins or fabric trims. This shop is a good place to see dresses and skirts that have earned her accolades from *O Globo*, *Vogue* and other publications.

OSKLEN CLOTHING

(Map p228; ☎2227-2911; Maria Quitéria 85; ⏰9am-8pm Mon-Fri, 10am-7pm Sat, 11am-5pm Sun) One of Brazil's best-known fashion labels outside the country, Osklen is known for its stylish and well-made beachwear (particularly men's swim shorts and graphic T-shirts), sneakers and outerwear. The company was started in 1988 by outdoor enthusiast Oskar Metsavaht, the first Brazilian to scale Mont Blanc.

REDLEY CLOTHING

(Map p228; ☎2267-1573; Maria Quitéria 99; ⏰9am-8pm Mon-Sat) In the heart of Ipanema, this new multilevel fashion store is a fine place to browse for couture beach duds and streetwear. Unlike most other Ipanema boutiques, this one's aimed at the men, with an excellent assortment of T-shirts, shorts and swimsuits.

CATHERINE LABOURÉ CLOTHING, ACCESSORIES

(Map p228; ☎2287-9630; Rua Visconde de Pirajá 207, 2nd fl, Ipanema; ⏰10am-6:30pm Mon-Fri, 10am-4pm Sat) Tucked away inside an otherwise humdrum shopping center, this intriguing shop sells vintage dresses, skirts, silk scarves, handbags, shoes and sunglasses, with labels by top international designers. There's a smaller selection for men – mostly T-shirts and button-downs – as well as a few small antiques and collectibles for the home.

ESPAÇO BRAZILIAN SOUL CLOTHING, ACCESSORIES

(Map p228; ☎2522-3641; Prudente de Morais 1102; ⏰9am-8pm Mon-Fri, 10am-7pm Sat, 11am-5pm Sun) Set in a picturesque little villa, Espaço Brazilian Soul is a two-story boutique selling designer clothes (Osklen among them) in the form of board shorts, T-shirts, flip-flops and button-downs. There's more men's apparel than women's, though the dresses are worth a peek.

GAROTA DE IPANEMA CLOTHING, ACCESSORIES

(Map p228; ☎2521-3168; Vinícius de Moraes 53; ⏰10am-6pm Mon-Fri, noon-4pm Sat) Next to the famous restaurant of the same name, this tiny boutique is an excellent place to browse for attractive, reasonably priced bikinis and beachwear. There are also eye-catching T-shirts (for men and women) as well as bags and other accessories.

LUKO CLOTHING, ACCESSORIES

(Map p228; ☎2540-0589; http://luko.com.br/lojas; Store 111, Visconde de Pirajá 547; ⏰10am-8pm Mon-Fri, 10am-5pm Sat) This charming boutique has an eclectic collection of youthful women's couture. Slim, beaded necklaces and bracelets, silk scarves, form-fitting tops and skirts, and slinky lingerie are among the items you'll find here. Rumor has it that Luko is a favorite among TV production companies looking for pieces. Visit the website for locations of Luko's other stores.

WÖLLNER OUTDOOR CLOTHING, ACCESSORIES

(Map p228; ☎2512-6531; Visconde de Pirajá 511; ⏰10am-9pm Mon-Fri) The great outdoors, and the shirt and shorts you'll need to enjoy it, seem to be the inspiration for Wöllner. Clothes and accessories are ruggedly styled, not unlike Abercrombie and American Eagle.

HAVAIANAS SHOES

(Map p228; ☎2267-7395; Farme de Amoedo 76; ⏰9am-8pm Mon-Fri, 10am-6pm Sat & Sun) This small shop is a great place to stock up on

Brazil's iconic rubber sandals. You'll find a colorful variety of Havaianas for men, women and children, covering all price points (from R$20 to R$72). There's a bigger branch in Copacabana.

BRASIL & CIA HANDICRAFTS
(Map p228; ☎2267-4603; www.brasilecia.com.br; Maria Quitéria 27) This handicrafts shop sells colorful works in papier-mache, porcelain and glass, showcasing Brazil's rich artisan traditions. Figurines, wooden boxes, dolls and other crafts are made by artists from Pernambuco and Alagoas. Perfect for keepsakes of your travels.

ANTONIO BERNARDO JEWELRY
(Map p228; ☎2512-7204; Garcia D'Ávila 121; ⏰10am-8pm Mon-Fri, 11am-4pm Sat) Designer-goldsmith Antonio Bernardo has garnered attention for his lovely bracelets, earrings and necklaces. The designs here are unique and artfully done, and Bernardo uses high-quality materials.

AMSTERDAM SAUER JEWELRY
(Map p228; ☎2279-6237; www.amsterdamsauer.com; Visconde de Pirajá 484; ⏰9am-7:30pm Mon-Fri, 10am-4pm Sat) Well known for its impressive collection of precious stones, Amsterdam Sauer also sells finely crafted jewelry. Watches, pens, wallets and other accessories are available too. Visitors can also check out their museum on Garcia D'Avila while they are here.

H STERN JEWELRY, ACCESSORIES
(Map p228; ☎2274-3447; www.hstern.com.br; Visconde de Pirajá 490; ⏰9:30am-6:30pm Mon-Fri, 10am-4pm Sat) The famous jeweler H Stern has an array of finely crafted jewelry, watches and other accessories for sale. At the company's headquarters you can also take a tour of the H Stern gem museum.

TOCA DO VINÍCIUS MUSIC
(Map p228; ☎2247-5227; www.tocadovinicius.com.br; Vinícius de Moraes 129; ⏰10am-7pm Mon-Fri, 10am-6pm Sat & Sun) Bossa nova fans shouldn't miss this store. In addition to its ample CD selection of contemporary and old performers (prices run from R$30 to R$35), they also sell music scores and composition books. Upstairs a tiny museum displays memorabilia of the great songwriter and poet, Vinícius de Moraes.

CASA & VIDEO PHOTOGRAPHY, ELECTRONICS
(Map p228; ☎2508-3030; Visconde de Pirajá 371; ⏰9am-10pm) If you've lost your digital camera (or forgot to bring one), this electronics chain is a handy store to get a replacement. All the name brands are here as well as some you probably haven't heard of. Prices are higher than what you'd pay back home (owing to high import taxes). Casa & Video has numerous other branches around town, including inside Rio Sul shopping center.

CAVIST WINE
(Map p228; ☎2123-7900; Rua Barão da Torre 358; ⏰9:30am-midnight Mon-Sat) One of Rio's best-stocked wine shops, with a high-end attached restaurant, where you can try out any of the bottles in the shop.

Leblon

SHOPPING LEBLON SHOPPING CENTER
(Map p232; ☎2430-5122; www.shoppingleblon.com.br; Av Afrânio de Melo Franco 290; ⏰10am-10pm Mon-Sat, 3-9pm Sun) The best shopping destination in Leblon is this glittering multistory shopping center packed with top-name Brazilian and foreign labels. There are plenty of tempting stores that will drain your vacation funds, as well as good restaurants, a cinema and a Starbucks, complete with a live piano player in the evenings.

MARIA OITICICA JEWELRY
(Map p232; ☎3875-8025; Shopping Leblon, Av Afranio de Mello Franco 290, Leblon; ⏰10am-10pm Mon-Sat, 3-9pm Sun) Using native materials found in the Amazon, Maria Oiticica has created some lovely handcrafted jewelry inspired by indigenous art. Seeds, plant fibers and tree bark are just some of the ingredients of her bracelets, necklaces, earrings and sandals (there are even some striking handbags made from fish 'leather'), and her work helps support struggling local communities with craft-making traditions. It's located on the main floor of the Shopping Leblon mall.

LIDADOR WINE, SPIRITS
(Map p232; ☎2512-1788; Av Ataúlfo de Paiva 1079; ⏰10am-8pm Mon-Fri, 10am-5pm Sat) Lidador stocks Chilean and Argentinean wines as well as vintages from Europe and beyond. *Cachaças,* rums and even Brazilian wines are available if you're looking for something

with a little more bite. There's also a handy location in Ipanema.

ARGUMENTO BOOKS, MUSIC

(Map p232; ☎2239-5294; Dias Ferreira 417; ⏲9am-midnight Mon-Sat, 10am-midnight Sun) One of Leblon's fine neighborhood bookstores, Argumento stocks a small but decent selection of foreign-language books and magazines. The charming cafe in the back is the perfect place to disappear with a book.

KOPENHAGEN CHOCOLATE

(Map p232; ☎2511-1112; Av Ataúlfo de Paiva 1025; ⏲9am-7pm Mon-Fri, 9am-5pm Sat) Serving up tasty bonbons and other decadent chocolate treats, Kopenhagen has been satisfying children and chocoholics since 1928. Recent favorites include tiny bottle-shaped liqueur-filled chocolates, chocolate-dipped cookies and giant rum balls. There's another store in Copacabana.

ESCH CAFÉ CIGARS

(Map p232; ☎2512-5651; Dias Ferreira 78; ⏲noon-1:30am Mon-Sat, to midnight Sun) This restaurant-bar is also the 'house of the Havana,' which means if you have a taste for the Cubans, this is your place. The humidor is stocked with a decent selection, which you can enjoy there over a glass of port, or a few blocks away on the beach. It also has a Centro branch.

SPORTS & ACTIVITIES

DIVE POINT DIVING

(Map p232; ☎2239-5105; www.divepoint.com.br/english; Shop 04, Av Ataúlfo de Paiva 1174, Leblon) Scuba divers can rent equipment or take classes from Dive Point. It also offers diving courses, and dive tours around Rio's main beaches and Ilha Cagarras (the island in front of Ipanema), as well as the premier dive spots in Arraial do Cabo, west of Rio.

ESCOLINHA DE VÔLEI VOLLEYBALL

(Map p228; ☎9702-5794; near Garcia D'Avila, Ipanema beach) Those interested in improving their volleyball game, or just meeting some *cariocas*, should pay a visit to Escolinha de Vôlei. Pelé, who speaks English, has been hosting volleyball classes for over 10 years. Lessons range from one to two hours. Look for his large Brazilian flag on the beach near Rua Garcia D'Ávila. Pelé's students are a mix of *cariocas* and expats, who then meet for games after honing the fundamentals.

SPA MARIA BONITA DAY SPA

(Map p228; ☎2513-4050; www.spamariabonita.com.br; Level P, Prudente de Morais 729, Ipanema) Although better known for its lush spa resort in Friburgo, Maria Bonita does offer a full range of treatments for those who'd rather not trek out to the countryside. Options here include aromatherapy baths, deep tissue massage, shiatsu and acupuncture. There is also a new organic and raw food restaurant on-site.

BODY TECH GYM

(Map p232; ☎2529-8898; General Urquiza 102, Leblon; day pass R$100; ⏲6am-11pm Mon-Fri, 9am-8pm Sat, 9am-2pm Sun) Body Tech has gyms all over the Zona Sul, which offer a full range of services: swimming pool, free weights and cardio machines, and classes such as dance, gymnastics and spinning. The best of the bunch is this three-story branch, but there are also a couple of Body Techs in **Ipanema** (Rua Barão de Torre 577 & Rua Gomes Carneiro 90), and one in **Copacabana** (Av NS de Copacabana 801). If you're in town for a week or so, the staff will usually negotiate a discounted rate.

BLYSS YÔGA YOGA

(Map p228; ☎3627-0108; www.blyss.com.br; Ste 211, Visconde de Pirajá 318, Ipanema; per class R$30) Near Praça Nossa Senhora da Paz, this peaceful center offers a full schedule of morning, afternoon and evening classes Monday to Saturday in Vinyasa, Iyengar and Hatha yoga. Some instructors speak English.

Gávea, Jardim Botânico & Lagoa

GÁVEA | JARDIM BOTÂNICO | LAGOA

Neighborhood Top Five

❶ Hiring a bike and going for a spin around the **Lagoa Rodrigo de Freitas** (p78).

❷ Taking a stroll through the lush and flower-filled **Jardim Botânico** (p79), followed by lunch at a lakeside kiosk.

❸ Looking for monkeys in the tropical rainforest-lined **Parque Lage** (p79).

❹ Sipping cocktails in an open-air setting while admiring the view from **Palaphita Kitch** (p82).

❺ Checking out the latest exhibit at the **Instituto Moreira Salles** (p79).

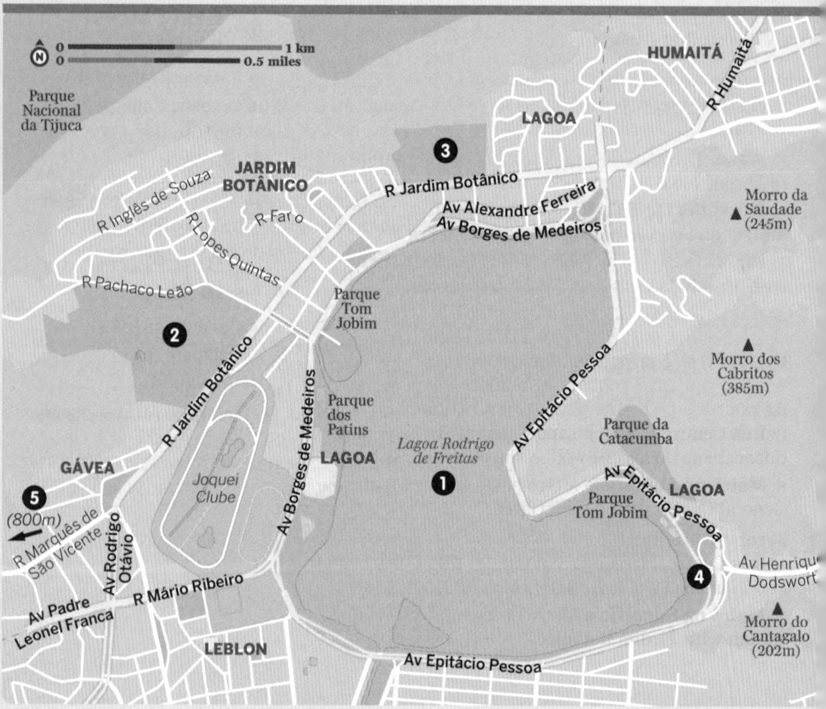

For more detail of this area see Map p234

Explore Gávea, Jardim Botânico & Lagoa

Rio's picturesque lake is the focal point of these well-heeled neighborhoods. The Lagoa Rodrigo de Freitas is actually a saltwater lagoon and is much utilized by *cariocas* (residents of Rio). Joggers and cyclists zip along the shoreline trail by day, while the lakeside restaurants fill with people enjoying a meal and live music in the open air by night. This area includes the north, east and west sides of the lake. The streets on the south side of Lagoa are generally considered part of Ipanema and Leblon.

West of the lake are the botanical gardens for which the neighborhood, Jardim Botânico, is named. Here you'll find stately palms and a variety of flowering plants. South of the gardens is Gávea, home to Rio's premier horse-racing track, and a planetarium. Aside from their natural attractions, these neighborhoods also have some excellent restaurants, lively nightlife and one of the Zona Sul's best cultural centers.

Much of the development of this area is linked to the lake, which is named Rodrigo de Freitas in honor of the Portuguese settler who made his fortune off the sugarcane fields surrounding the lake in the 16th century. Factories blighted the landscape in the 1900s, and it took much of the 20th century for the area to recover. Although the lake is still too polluted for swimming, some wildlife has returned, and visitors might see egrets on the lookout for fish in the lake.

Local Life

- **Walks** There are several fine walks amid rainforest in Parque Lage or Parque da Catacumba.
- **Markets** Praça Santos Dumont hosts an antiques market on Sunday and a fruit market on Friday.
- **Nightlife** Bars near Praça Santos Dumont attract a large mostly student crowd during the week.

Getting There & Away

Gávea

- **Bus** Centro, Flamengo and Catete (170); Ipanema and Copacabana (571, 572, 574); Leblon (432, 435, 593).
- **Metrô na Superfície** Metro buses connect Ipanema/General Osório station with Gávea.

Jardim Botânico

- **Bus** Centro, Flamengo and Catete (170); Copacabana and Ipanema (570, 162, 584); Leblon (512, 574, 584).
- **Metrô na Superfície** Metro buses connect Botafogo station with Jardim Botânico.

Lonely Planet's Top Tip

One of Rio's often overlooked attractions, the Instituto Moreira Salles is well worth a visit with a picturesque setting and a museum that stages first-rate exhibitions. If you have kids in tow, Saturdays are a good time to visit, when they offer special (free) activities (crafts, music and the like).

Best Places to Eat

- Oro (p81)
- Olympe (p81)
- Bráz (p81)
- La Carioca Cevicheria (p81)
- Lagoon (p81)

For reviews, see p80

Best Places to Drink

- Palaphita Kitch (p82)
- Caroline Café (p82)
- Hipódromo (p82)
- 00 (p82)

For reviews, see p82

Best Places to Shop

- Dona Coisa (p83)
- Gabinete (p83)
- O Sol (p83)

For reviews, see p83

MARCO GUNIER / GETTY IMAGES ©

TOP SIGHT
LAGOA RODRIGO DE FREITAS

Blessed with mountains, beaches and rainforest, it's perhaps a little unfair that Rio would also have a picturesque lake – surrounded by highly desirable neighborhoods no less. *Cariocas* however take it in their stride and make ample use of the watery expanse, running the lakeside path, dining near the water's edge or simply admiring the view from nearly any vantage point.

No matter the time of year, you'll always find runners and cyclists making good use of the 7.2km path that encircles the lake. If you'd like to join them, there are various places to hire bikes, including the Parque dos Patins on the west side.

For an even better view over the lake, book a seat on a scenic helicopter flight that departs from a helipad on the west side of the lake. A much cheaper way to admire the view is to hike to the top of Parque da Catacumba.

Another way to experience the lake is to get out on the surface. Pollution makes swimming a bad idea, though you can hire pedal boats from the eastern side near the Parque do Cantagalo.

For those who prefer caipirinhas to plastic swan boats, the kiosks scattered along the shore make a memorable setting for a sundowner. You can also dine in the open air at one of a dozen or so kiosks serving Brazilian, Middle Eastern, sushi and bistro fare. Many places have live music on weekends – making it a popular draw with couples. You'll find the kiosks near Parque do Cantagalo and Parque dos Patins. There's also a new lakeside complex Lagoon, which has restaurants, a cinema and a live-music venue.

One of the major events in the city's calendar is the lighting of the floating Christmas tree on the lake each year. If you're around in December, don't miss a visit by night.

DON'T MISS...

- ➡ Cycling around the lake.
- ➡ Skimming over the surface on a pedal boat.
- ➡ Drinks and live music at a lakeside kiosk.

PRACTICALITIES

- ➡ Map p234

SIGHTS

Gávea

INSTITUTO MOREIRA SALLES CULTURAL CENTER
(☎3284-7400; www.ims.com.br; Marquês de São Vicente 476; ⏲11am-8pm Tue-Sun) FREE This beautiful cultural center is next to Parque da Cidade and contains an archive of more than 80,000 photographs, many portraying old streets of Rio as well as the urban development of other Brazilian cities over the last two centuries. It also hosts impressive exhibitions, often showcasing the works of some of Brazil's best photographers and artists; check its website for details.

The gardens, complete with artificial lake and flowing river, were designed by Brazilian landscape architect Burle Marx. There's also a craft shop and a quaint cafe here that serves lunch or afternoon tea.

MUSEU HISTÓRICO DA CIDADE MUSEUM
(☎2512-2353; www.rio.rj.gov.br/cultura; Estrada de Santa Marinha 505) Currently closed for renovation, the 19th-century mansion located on the lovely grounds of Parque da Cidade houses the City History Museum. In addition to its permanent collection, which portrays Rio from its founding in 1565 to the mid-20th century, the museum has exhibitions of furniture, porcelain, photographs and paintings by well-known artists. The park itself is free, open from 7am to 6pm.

PLANETÁRIO PLANETARIUM
(Map p234; ☎2274-0046; www.planetariodorio.com.br; Av Padre Leonel Franca 240; adult/child R$10/5; ⏲9am-5pm Mon-Fri, 3-6pm Sat & Sun) Gávea's stellar attraction, the Planetário (Planetarium) features a museum, a *praça dos telescópios* (telescopes' square) and a couple of state-of-the-art operating domes, each capable of projecting over 6000 stars onto its walls (40-minute sessions in the domes take place on weekends and holidays). Visitors can also take a peek at the night sky (R$20) through the telescopes on Tuesday, Wednesday and Thursday from 7:30pm to 8:30pm (6:30pm to 7:30pm June to August). The modern **Museu do Universo** (Universe Museum) houses sundials, a Foucault's Pendulum and other permanent exhibitions, plus temporary displays.

Jardim Botânico

JARDIM BOTÂNICO GARDENS
(Map p234; ☎3874-1808; www.jbrj.gov.br; Jardim Botânico 920; admission R$6; ⏲9am-5pm) This exotic 137-hectare garden, with over 8000 plant species, was designed by order of the Prince Regent Dom João (later to become Dom João VI) in 1808. The garden is quiet and serene on weekdays and blossoms with families and music on weekends. Highlights of a visit here include the row of palms (planted when the garden first opened), the Amazonas section, the lake containing the huge Vitória Régia water lilies and the enclosed **orquidário**, home to 600 species of orchids. Also on-site is the **Museu do Meio Ambiente** (Environmental Museum; Map p234; ☎3204-2504; Jardim Botânico 1008; ⏲10am-5pm Tue-Sun), which houses temporary environmentally focused exhibits. English-language tours can be arranged by appointment. A pleasant outdoor cafe overlooks the gardens. Be sure to take insect repellent.

PARQUE LAGE PARK
(Map p234; ☎3257-1800, guided visits 3257-18721; www.eavparquelage.rj.gov.br; Jardim Botânico 414; ⏲8am-5pm) FREE This beautiful park, at the base of Floresta da Tijuca, is about 1km from Jardim Botânico. It has English-style gardens, little lakes and a mansion that houses the **Escola de Artes Visuais** (School of Visual Arts), which hosts free art exhibitions and occasional performances. The park is a tranquil place and the cafe here is a fine setting for coffee or a meal. Native Atlantic rainforest surrounds Parque Lage, and you can sometimes see monkeys and toucans among the foliage. This is the starting point for challenging hikes up Corcovado.

Lagoa

FUNDAÇÃO EVA KLABIN MUSEUM
(Map p234; ☎3202-8557; www.evaklabin.org.br; Av Epitácio Pessoa 2480; admission R$10; ⏲guided visits by appointment 2:30pm & 4pm Tue-Fri) An old mansion full of antiques, the former residence of Eva Klabin houses the works of art she collected for 60 years. Reflecting Eva's diverse interests, the collection has 1100 pieces from ancient Egypt, Greece and

CATACUMBA

Lagoa is one of the few neighborhoods in Rio that doesn't have a neighboring favela. This wasn't always the case, the Parque da Catacumba was once the site of a favela, and home to more than 10,000 residents at its height in the 1960s. According to the historical records, the area was part of an estate belonging to a wealthy landowner in the 19th century. Upon her death, she left the lands to her slaves, though the first constructions didn't begin to appear until the 1930s. According to some former favela residents, the name Catacumba predates the favela, and refers to an indigenous burial ground – although no remains were ever found on the site.

Under the strong-armed government of Francisco Negrão de Lima, the *favelados* (slum dwellers) were removed in 1970 and their houses razed – in large part owing to the commercial value of the occupied lands. The expelled residents went on to form the Complexo da Maré, a favela near the airport that later became known as the 'Gaza Strip' because of its high murder rate.

Catacumba was subsequently reforested and turned into a public park. You can still see a few vestiges of the old favela on a hike to the Mirante do Sacopã lookout.

China including paintings, sculptures, silver, furniture and carpets.

PARQUE DA CATACUMBA PARK

(Map p234; ☎2247-9949; www.parquedacatacumba.com.br; Av Epitácio Pessoa; ⏰8am-5pm Tue-Sun) On the edge of the lake (but across the busy road), this park and sculptural garden added some new adventure activities in 2010, including a 7m rock-climbing wall (R$20), a zipline (R$20), rappelling down a rockface (R$100) and a canopy walk (R$30) through the treetops. It's operated by Lagoa Aventuras. It's free to simply stroll through the park, and there's a short but steep trail (15 minutes' walking) to the **Mirante do Sacopã** (Map p234), which offers scenic views from a height of 130m above Lagoa (also where the rappelling begins).

EATING

The open-air restaurants around the peaceful Lagoa Rodrigo de Freitas are big draws here. On warm evenings music fills the air as diners eat, drink and enjoy the views across the water. The hot spots for drinking and dining are at the Parque dos Patins on the west side (where some places host live music) and Parque do Cantagalo on the east side. Gávea has a few dining and drinking spots around Praça Santos Dumont, while Jardim Botânico's thickest concentration of eateries is on Rua JJ Seabra and Rua Pacheco Leão.

Gávea

BRASEIRO DA GÁVEA BRAZILIAN $$

(Map p234; ☎2239-7494; www.braseirodagavea.com.br; Praça Santos Dumont 116, Gávea; mains for 2 R$62-90; ⏰noon-1am Sun-Thu, to 3am Fri & Sat) This family-style eatery serves large portions of its popular *linguiça* (sausage) appetizers, *picanha* (rump steak) and *galetos* (grilled chicken). On weekends, the open-air spot fills with the din of conversation and the aroma of freshly poured *chope* (draft beer) drifting by. As the evening wanes, a younger crowd takes over drinking late into the night.

00 (ZERO ZERO) CONTEMPORARY $$

(Map p234; ☎2540-8041; Av Padre Leonel Franca 240, Planetário da Gávea, Gávea; main R$20-50; ⏰7:30pm-1am Wed-Sun) Housed in Gávea's planetarium, 00 (Zero Zero) is a sleek restaurant-lounge that serves top-end bistro fare. Filet mignon sandwich with Gruyère, mozzarella and pesto ravioli, ceviche, a full sushi counter and well mixed cocktails are best enjoyed on the open-air veranda. After dinner, have a few cocktails and stick around: some of Rio's best DJs spin at parties here.

GUIMAS CONTEMPORARY $$$

(Map p234; ☎2259-7996; Rua José Roberto Macedo Soares 5, Gávea; mains R$42-60; ⏰noon-1am) An upscale *carioca boteco* with a creative flair, Guimas has been going strong for over 30 years. Winning dishes include the *bacalhau à bras* (codfish mixed with potatoes, eggs and onions), shrimp risotto and the juicy *picanha no sal grosso* (grilled rump-steak). There's outdoor seating in front.

Jardim Botânico

DRI CAFE CAFE $

(☎2226-8125; off Rua Jardim Botânico 414, Jardim Botânico; mains R$14-24; ⏰9am-6pm) Inside the lush Parque Lage, this beautifully sited cafe serves tasty sandwiches, salads, quiches, pastas and desserts. On weekends it's a popular gathering spot for young families who come for the brunch (from R$27 to R$32), which features fresh breads and jams, fruits, juices and the like.

JOJÖ CAFE $$

(Map p234; ☎3565-9007; www.jojocafe.com.br; Pacheco Leão 812; mains R$37-45; ⏰8am-midnight Tue-Fri, 1pm-1am Sat, to 8pm Sun) This small, charming neighborhood cafe and bistro serves up delectable salads, pastas and Asian-inspired dishes such as Thai chicken curry. There are a handful of sidewalk tables on this peaceful corner in Jardim Botânico.

Lagoa

ARAB DA LAGOA MIDDLE EASTERN $$

(Map p234; ☎2540-0747; www.restaurantearab.com.br; Borges de Medeiros, Parque dos Patins; mains R$22-40; ⏰9am-1:30am) This is one of the lake's most popular outdoor restaurants, serving traditional Middle Eastern specialties such as hummus, baba ghanoush, tabbouleh, kibbe and tasty thin-crust pizzas. The large platters for two or more are good for sampling the tasty varieties. During the day, it's a peaceful refuge from the city, while at night you can hear live samba, *choro* (romantic, intimate samba) or jazz from 9pm on weekdays, 7pm on Saturdays and Sundays (cover charge is R$6).

LAGOON BRAZILIAN $$

(Map p234; ☎2529-5300; www.lagoon.com.br; Av Borges de Medeiros 1424, Lagoa; mains R$30-60; ⏰noon-2am) This sparkling new eating and entertainment complex houses half a dozen restaurants as well as a cinema and a bar-live music venue. The best tables are on the second floor, and offer photogenic views over the lake. Italian, seafood, bistro fare and traditional Brazilian cooking are among the options – and no matter where you sit, you can order from any menu.

LA CARIOCA CEVICHERIA SEAFOOD $$

(Map p234; ☎2226-8821; Maria Angélica 113, Jardim Botânico; ceviches R$20-30; ⏰6:30pm-1am) True to its name, this new Peruvian place specializes in ceviche, serving up over a dozen varieties of the tangy, tender seafood dish in small portions that are perfect for sharing. Have a seat on the inviting terrace in front and fortify yourself with fiery pisco (Peruvian brandy) or poetry (placemats bear a poem by Neruda).

ORO CONTEMPORARY $$$

(Map p234; ☎7864-9622; www.ororestaurante.com; Frei Leandro 20; three-/16-course dinner R$120/395; ⏰7:30pm-midnight Mon-Sat) Felipe Bronze heads this acclaimed restaurant, which celebrates Brazilian produce and its cooking traditions while serving up some of the most imaginative plates in the city. The low-lit Zenlike interior contrasts with the culinary pyrotechnics on display in most dishes.

Utilizing the tools of molecular gastronomy (centrifuges, liquid nitrogen and other gadgetry), chefs whip up whimsical flavor-rich concoctions like compressed watermelon with sardine slices, pork belly with *jabuticaba* (an Amazonian fruit) and a shot of Jerez-infused vinaigrette, and elfin steak and pineapple sandwiches. If your holiday budget is particularly well-endowed, you can also order wine pairings with each course.

OLYMPE CONTEMPORARY $$$

(Map p234; ☎2539-4542; Custódio Serrão 62, Lagoa; mains R$79-110; ⏰7:30pm-midnight Mon-Sat, noon-4pm Fri) One of Rio's top chefs, Claude Troisgros, and his son Thomas, dazzle guests with unforgettable meals at this award-winning restaurant set in a peaceful villa on a sleepy, tree-lined street. Originally from France, Troisgros mixes the old world with the new in dishes like duck with passion fruit, endive and foie gras or shrimp risotto with white truffle oil and mushroom foam.

BRÁZ PIZZA $$$

(Map p234; ☎2535-0687; Maria Angélica 129; pizzas R$45-65; ⏰6:30pm-12:30am) The much-touted pizzeria from São Paulo won a huge *carioca* following after it opened in Rio in 2007. Perfect crusts and super-fresh ingredients are two of the components that make

Bráz the best pizza place in town. This is no secret, so arrive early and plan on having a few quiet *chopes* on the front patio before scoring a table.

DRINKING & NIGHTLIFE

Gávea has one of Rio's liveliest young drinking spots – an area called Baixo Gávea, near Praça Santos Dumont. The bars here almost always draw in a crowd, with imbibers spilling onto the plaza most nights. Jardim Botânico has a youthful population that comes out en masse to the bars along Rua JJ Seabra. Meanwhile, the lakeside kiosks offer a more sedate experience, with couples gathering for live music to the backdrop of Lagoa and Christ the Redeemer.

Gávea

HIPÓDROMO BAR

(Map p234; Praça Santos Dumont 108, Gávea; ⏲noon-1am) In an area more commonly referred to as Baixo Gávea, Hipódromo is one of several bars in the area responsible for the local residents' chronic lack of sleep. Most nights, you'll find a college-age- and 20-something crowd celebrating here, with patrons spilling onto the facing Praça Santos Dumont.

00 (ZERO ZERO) LOUNGE, CLUB

(Map p234; http://00riodejaneiro.com.br/riodejaneiro.html; Av Padre Leonel Franca 240, Gávea; ⏲8pm-late) Housed in Gávea's planetarium, 00 starts the evening as a stylish restaurant and transforms into lounge and nightclub around midnight. A mix of *cariocas* joins the fray here, though it mostly tends to be a fashion-literate, Zona Sul crowd. Top-notch DJs spin at rotating parties here, and on Tuesday nights, party promoter Bem Brasil (www.bembrasilrio.com.br) throws a bash for the hostel crowd – a good place to be if you want to mingle with other travelers.

Jardim Botânico

CAROLINE CAFÉ LOUNGE

(Map p234; ☎2540-0705; JJ Seabra 10, Jardim Botânico; ⏲4pm-2am Mon-Sat) Caroline Café has long been a major draw for couples. There are a few outdoor tables, but inside is where you'll find most of the action, which here means a sizeable drink menu – including 'flambeed' cocktails like the Vizoovio (Jack Daniels, tequila and amaretto served alight) – and an assortment of dishes (thick burgers, sushi and pizzas).

BAR DO HORTO BAR

(Map p234; ☎3114-8439; Pacheco Leão 780, Jardim Botânico; ⏲noon-2am Sun & Tue-Thu, to 3am Fri & Sat) The colorful Bar do Horto is one of Jardim Botânico's most charming bars. The decor is festive and kitsch: with walls covered with shimmering fabric and an interior festooned with brightly hued paper lanterns, butterfly appliques, bottle-cap curtains and other recycled ephemera. On Thursdays to Saturdays, the sidewalk tables gather a festive crowd (largely couples) who come for live MPB and international tunes.

Lagoa

PALAPHITA KITCH LOUNGE

(Map p234; ☎2227-0837; www.palaphitakitch.com.br; Av Epitácio Pessoa s/n, Lagoa; ⏲6pm-1am) A great spot for a sundowner, Palaphita Kitch is an open-air, thatched-roof wonderland with rustic bamboo furniture, flickering tiki torches and a peaceful setting on the edge of the lake. This is a popular spot with couples, who come for the view and the creative (but pricey) cocktails – particularly the caipirinhas made from unusual fruits from the Northeast and Amazonia.

BAR LAGOA BOTECO

(Map p228; ☎2523-1135; Av Epitácio Pessoa 1674; ⏲6pm-2am Mon-Fri, noon-2am Sat & Sun) With a view of the lake (but separated by a busy road), Bar Lagoa is one of the neighborhood's classic haunts. Founded in 1935, this open-air spot hasn't changed all that much since then: the bar still has surly waiters serving the excellent beer to ever-crowded tables and, in spite of its years, a youthful air pervades.

ENTERTAINMENT

MIRANDA LIVE MUSIC

(Map p234; ☎2239-0305; www.mirandabrasil.com.br; Av Borges de Medeiros 1424, Lagoa; admission from R$40) New in 2012, Miranda is a classy but inviting bar and live-music venue that hosts a range of shows and events, including *feijoada* and live samba on Sundays (R$60), MPB groups and well-known Brazilian artists like Mart'nalia and BossaCucaNova (a group that blends bossa nova with electronica). It's located inside the Lagoon complex in Lagoa.

SHOPPING

Aside from a few scattered shops, there isn't much of a shopping scene in Jardim Botânico or Lagoa. Residents from the neighborhood typically head to Ipanema, Leblon or the huge Shopping da Gávea mall to satisfy their retail cravings. On weekends, however, an interesting market on the Praça Santos Dumont makes the journey here worthwhile.

Gávea

SHOPPING DA GÁVEA — SHOPPING CENTER

(Map p234; ☎2294-1096; Marquês de São Vicente 52, Gávea; ⏰10am-10pm Mon-Sat, 3-9pm Sun) Shopping da Gávea touts itself as the preferred mall of artists and intellectuals, which may or may not matter to you when you're laying down serious cash for those sneakers. There are 200 stores, a five-screen cinema, several theaters and numerous restaurants, including **La Pastaciutta**, which serves tasty pastas and appetizers.

Jardim Botânico

DONA COISA — FASHION

(Map p234; ☎2249-2336; www.donacoisa.com.br; Lopes Quintas 153, Jardim Botânico; ⏰11am-8pm Mon-Fri, 10am-6pm Sat) One of Rio's top boutiques, Dona Coisa sells top labels by Brazilian and international designers, including one-of-a-kind pieces you won't find elsewhere (such as snakeskin Converse by Missoni). The multiroom design house also has original objects for the home – delicate ceramics by Heloisa Galvão, engraved wine-glasses – in addition to skin and beauty products by Phebo and Granado.

GABINETE — HOMEWARES

(Map p234; ☎3173-8828; Lopes Quintas 87, Jardim Botânico; ⏰11am-8pm Mon-Fri, 10am-6pm Sat) On a street with a growing number of shops and cafes, Gabinete is a fun place to browse for unusual curios – decorative brass mooseheads, vintage glassware, illuminated teapot lampos, wind-up circus miniatures and earth-toned pottery – which line the artfully lit display shelves of this intriguing curiosity cabinet.

O SOL — HANDICRAFTS

(Map p234; ☎2294-5099; Corcovado 213, Jardim Botânico; ⏰9am-6pm Mon-Fri, 10am-2pm Sat) O Sol is run by Leste-Um, a nonprofit social-welfare organization. This delightful store displays the works of regional artists and sells Brazilian folk art in clay, wood and porcelain. It also sells baskets and woven rugs.

SPORTS & ACTIVITIES

NIRVANA — DAY SPA

(Map p234; ☎2187-0100; www.enirvana.com.br; Jockey Club, Rua Jardim Botânico, near Praça Santos Dumont, Gávea; ⏰10am-10pm Mon-Fri, to 8pm Sat) Inside the Jockey Club, this sunny full-service spa offers an enticing array of relaxing treatments, and you can also use the sauna. If you want to make a day of it, book a day-spa package, which includes a yoga class, lunch, exfoliating treatment, a selection of various treatments (reflexology, reiki, hot rocks massages, etc) and aromatherapy bath.

JOQUEI CLUBE — HORSE RACING

(Map p234; ☎3534-9000; www.jcb.com.br; Jardim Botânico 1003, Gávea; ⏰2-8pm Sat & Sun) One of the country's loveliest racetracks, with a great view of the mountains and Corcovado, the Joquei Clube (Jockey Club) seats 35,000 and lies on the Gávea side of the Lagoa Rodrigo de Freitas opposite Praça Santos Dumont. Local race fans are part of the attraction – it's a different slice of Rio life.

Tourists are welcome in the members' area, which has a bar overlooking the track. Races are held on weekends and ocasionally on Mondays and Fridays. The big event is the Brazilian Grand Prix (the first Sunday in August).

Copacabana & Leme

COPACABANA | LEME

Neighborhood Top Five

❶ Soaking up the sunshine on **Copacabana beach** (p86), followed by a meal at an oceanfront eatery.

❷ Exploring the **Forte de Copacabana** (p87) and taking in the peaceful views across the sands.

❸ Walking to mountaintop heights along a forested trail inside the **Forte Duque de Caxias** (p87).

❹ Admiring the breathtaking sea views from the **Skylab Bar** (p94).

❺ Listening to samba jam sessions at **Bip Bip** (p94).

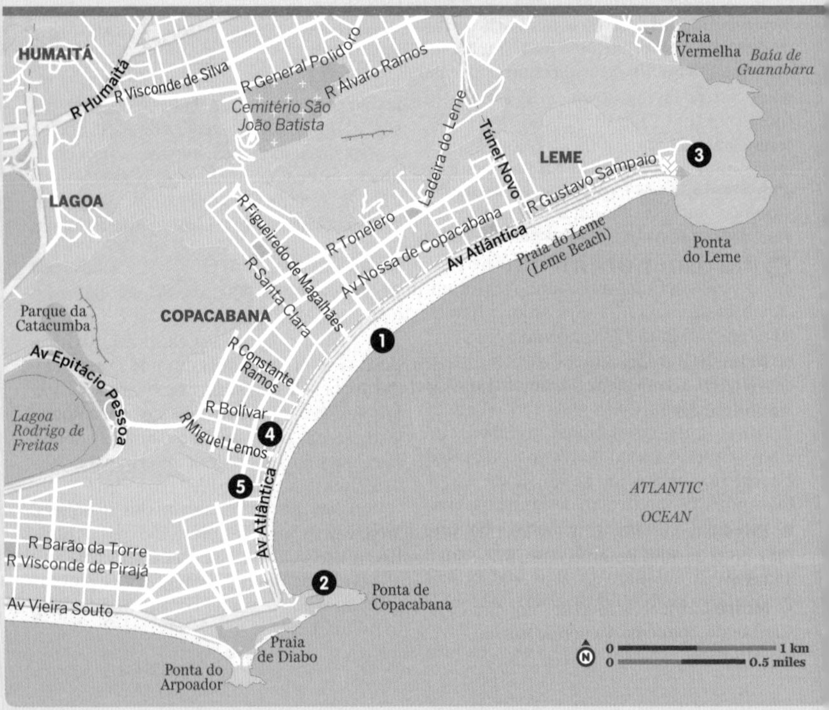

For more detail of this area see Map p236 and p240

Explore Copacabana & Leme

With the construction of the neoclassical Copacabana Palace Hotel in 1923, Copacabana – and Rio – became South America's most elegant destination, one frequented by international celebrities. Copacabana remained Rio's untarnished gem until the 1970s, when the area fell into decline. Today's Copa is a chaotic mix of discount stores and noisy traffic-filled avenues, with a humming red-light district and slightly edgy streets. While paradise it clearly is not, the beach remains beautiful. Framed by mountains and deep blue sea, the magnificent curve of shoreline stretches more than 4km.

Packing the beach are sun-worshippers of every age and background – from favela kids to aging socialites, to tourists and families from the Zona Norte. Copacabana's democratic mix, old-school *botecos* (small neighborhood bars), eclectic restaurants and nightclubs, myriad shops and of course the handsome shoreline still entrance many visitors. While the cool kids cling to Ipanema and Leblon, Copacabana seems poised on the edge of a renaissance. Its glassy kiosks have brought class to the neighborhood, while 'Baixo Copa' is becoming a nightlife destination.

The small neighborhood of Leme, just northeast of Copacabana (Av Princesa Isabel divides the two), has a village feel, with its mix of old-timers, upper-middle-class families and favela residents. The lack of major roads through Leme creates a more peaceful vibe, and the oceanfront restaurants make for a more relaxing setting for a drink than the buzzing Copacabana strip.

Local Life

- **Markets** Copacabana has a handful of weekly produce markets (p35) held at various locales. Our favorite happens in peaceful Bairro Peixoto (p87).
- **Hangouts** One of Copacabana's liveliest areas for a drink is Baixo Copa, a bar- and restaurant-lined strip just back from Av Atlântica around Rua Domingos Ferreira and Barão de Ipanema.
- **Arts** Little frequented by tourists, Espaço SESC often hosts an excellent line-up of dance and theatre performances.

Getting There & Away

- **Bus** Ipanema (161, 573), Leblon (511, 161, 583), Gávea (161, 583), Jardim Botânico (161, 573, 583) Centro (121, 123, 124).
- **Metro** Cardeal Arcoverde, Siqueira Campos, Cantagalo, Ipanema/General Osório.

Best Places to Eat

- Azumi (p90)
- Zot (p90)
- Santa Satisfação (p88)
- Amir (p88)
- Le Blé Noir (p88)

For reviews, see p87

Best Places to Drink

- Mud Bug (p91)
- Sindicato do Chopp (p94)
- Botequim Informal (p91)
- Ponto da Bossa Nova (p91)

For reviews, see p91

Best Places to Shop

- Havaianas (p95)
- Loja Fla (p95)
- Bossa Nova & Companhia (p95)

For reviews, see p94

IAN TROWER / GETTY IMAGES ©

TOP SIGHT
COPACABANA BEACH

A magnificent confluence of land and sea, the long, scalloped beach of Copacabana extends for some 4km, with a flurry of activity along its length: over-amped soccer players singing their team's anthem, *cariocas* (residents of Rio) and tourists lining up for caipirinhas at kiosks, favela kids showing off their football skills and beach vendors shouting out their wares among the beached and tanned bodies.

As in Ipanema, each group stakes out its stretch of sand. The area between the Copacabana Palace hotel and Rua Fernando Mendes is the gay and transvestite section, known as the Stock or Stock Market – easily recognized by the rainbow flag. Young football and *futevôlei* (volleyball played without hands) players hold court near Rua Santa Clara. Posts 5 and 6 are a mix of favela kids and *carioca* retirees, while the beach next to Forte de Copacabana is the fishermen's community beach. In the morning, you can buy the fresh catch of the day. As Copacabana beach curves north you get into the quieter sands of Leme (Av Princesa Isabel forms the demarcation between the two neighborhoods). Here you'll find a mix of older Leme residents as well as kids from the nearby favela.

Aside from frolicking in the waves and people watching, the main attraction is running or cycling the beach path; like Ipanema the beachside lane closes to traffic on Sundays. Early risers can greet the sunrise while exercising. Another way to get physical is to try your hand at stand-up paddle boarding, which you can hire from both ends of the beach (hire outfits also offer lessons). By afternoon and nightfall, the beach kiosks are a great place to be, rehydrating over *agua de côco* (coconut water), snacking and having a few libations before the night begins.

DON'T MISS...

- Stand-up paddle boarding along the coast.
- Evening drinks at a beachfront kiosk.
- A sunday run or bike ride along the beach boulevard.

PRACTICALITIES

- Map p236
- Av Atlântica

SIGHTS

FORTE DE COPACABANA FORT

(Map p236; ☎2521-1032; Av Atlântica & Rua Francisco Otaviano; admission R$6; ⏱10am-6pm Tue-Sun) Built in 1914 on the promontory of the old Our Lady of Copacabana chapel, the fort of Copacabana was one of Rio's premier defenses against attack. You can still see its original features, including walls up to 12m thick, defended by Krupp cannons. Inside is a museum with several floors of exhibits tracing the early days of the Portuguese colony to the mid-19th century, and the views across the full length of Copacabana are striking. There are several cafes with fine vantage points, including Confeitaria Colombo.

FORTE DUQUE DE CAXIAS FORT

(Forte do Leme; Map p240; ☎3223-2034; Praça Almirante Júlio de Noronha; admission R$4; ⏱9:30am-4:30pm Tue-Sun) More commonly known as Forte do Leme, this military base is now open to the public, and visitors can walk to the top of Morro de Leme (Leme mountain) along a steep 800m trail that passes through Atlantic rainforest. At the top stands an 18th-century fort affording magnificent views of Pão de Açúcar (Sugarloaf mountain) and the Cagarras Islands.

BAIRRO PEIXOTO NEIGHBORHOOD

(Map p236; Rua Anita Garibaldi) A world away from the bustle of Copacabana's busy avenues, the Bairro Peixoto is a peaceful enclave centered on the leafy Praça Edmundo Bittencourt. There you'll find a playground, park benches and tables where folks play dominoes and read the paper, all of which seem to lend the setting more of a village-like air than a big-city neighborhood. You might even see a few marmosets up in the trees. A good day to visit is on Wednesday, when the weekly fruit market is on.

SAFETY

The beach is lit at night and police are in the area, but it's still not wise to wander the sands after dark. It's fine to go for a drink at one of the kiosks at night, just try to avoid walking along deserted stretches.

Av NS de Copacabana (NS stands for Nossa Senhora, meaning Our Lady) is also sketchy late at night and on weekends, when the shops are closed and few locals are around.

EATING

Rio's most visited neighborhood has an enormous variety of restaurants, from award-winning dining rooms to charming old bistros from the 1950s, as well as creperies, *churrascarias* (restaurants serving barbequed meat), sushi bars and other ethnic haunts. In general, you will encounter less experimentation here, but if you're looking for excellent traditional cuisine – both Brazilian and international – you will find plenty of delectable options in Copacabana. The restaurant strip along Av Atlântica has fine views of the seaside, but generally unexceptional food. The narrow roads crisscrossing Av NS de Copacabana from Leme to Arpoador contain many fine dining establishments – and many mediocre ones. Do some exploring, trust your instincts and *bom proveito* (happy eating).

O REI DAS EMPANADAS EMPANADAS $

(Map p236; ☎3258-3003; Rua Barata Ribeira 48; empanadas R$3-4; ⏱9am-11pm) 'The king of empanadas' serves up piping-hot pasties, baked fresh throughout the day. There are about a dozen varieties, including *carne picante* (spicy beef), *camarão* (shrimp) and dessert options (banana with chocolate).

BIBI SUCOS SNACK STAND $

(Map p236; ☎2513-6000; Rua Miguel Lemos 31, Copacabana; mains R$9-22; ⏱9am-1am) Offering much the same recipe for success as its Leblon branch, Bibi serves dozens of juices, along with savory and sweet crepes, sandwiches, burgers and build-your-own salads. It has outdoor tables and a bustling vibe.

BOULANGERIE GUERIN BAKERY $

(Map p236; ☎2523-4140; Av NS de Copacabana 920, Copacabana; pastries R$8-10; ⏱8am-9pm) Serving Rio's best croissants, *pains au chocolat* and eclairs, this classic French patisserie was an instant success upon opening in 2012. Prices for those delectable raspberry-covered tarts and creamy *millefeuilles* are high, but so is the quality, and you can watch the bakers at work through the oversized windows adjoining the small bakery-cafe.

O CRACK DOS GALETOS ROAST CHICKEN $

(Map p236; ☎2236-7001; Domingos Ferreira 197; mains R$20-28; ⏲noon-midnight) If you're on a budget, Rio's unfussy roast chicken restaurants are a must. Here, you can sidle up to the wrap-around counter and enjoy juicy plates of chicken fresh off the roaster.

CERVANTES BRAZILIAN $

(Map p236; ☎2275-6147; Av Prado Júnior 335B, Copacabana; sandwiches R$13-21; ⏲noon-4am Sun & Tue-Thu, to 6am Fri & Sat) A Copacabana institution, the late-night Cervantes gathers *cariocas* who come to feast on Cervantes' trademark meat and pineapple sandwiches. Its waiters are famed for their fussiness, along with their speed to the tap when your *chope* (draft beer) runneth dry. Around the corner, Cervantes' stand-up **boteco** (Map p236; Barato Ribeiro 7; ⏲noon-4am Sun & Tue-Thu, to 6am Fri & Sat) serves up tasty bites in a hurry.

GALETO SAT'S ROAST CHICKEN $

(Map p236; ☎2275-6197; Barato Ribeiro 7, Copacabana; mains R$15-45; ⏲noon-5am) One of Rio's best roast chicken spots, laid-back Galeto Sat's has earned many fans since its opening back in 1962. Grab a seat along the mirrored and tiled wall, order a *chope* and enjoy the scent of grilled spit-roasted birds before tucking into a filling meal.

RESTAURANTE NATURALEVE VEGETARIAN $

(Map p236; Travessa Cristiano Lacorte, Copacabana; per kg R$39; ⏲11am-4pm Mon-Sat; 🥕) Set just off Rua Miguel Lemos, this tidy health-conscious restaurant cooks up a reasonably priced lunch buffet, with vegetarian black beans, *moqueca* (seafood stew cooked in coconut milk) with salmon, grilled tofu, various baked dishes and fresh salads.

KONI STORE JAPANESE $

(Map p236; Constante Ramos 44; hand roll around R$12; ⏲noon-3am Sun-Thu, to 5am Fri & Sat) This popular spot serves tasty *temaki*, which are seaweed hand rolls filled with tuna, salmon and other bites. It stays open late, making for an ideal post-bar snack.

SANTA SATISFAÇÃO BRAZILIAN $$

(Map p236; ☎2255-9349; www.santasatisfacao.com; Santa Clara 36C, Copacabana; mains R$20-42; ⏲closed Sun) Oozing farmhouse charm, this always-packed bistro is worth forking over a bit extra for outstanding daily lunch specials of upscale Brazilian comfort food and sophisticated sandwiches.

AMIR MIDDLE EASTERN $$

(Map p236; ☎2275-5596; Ronald de Carvalho 55C, Copacabana; mains R$25-50; ⏲noon-midnight Mon-Sat, to 11pm Sun) Step inside Amir and you'll enter a world of delicate aromas and handsomely dressed waiters in embroidered vests. Daytime crowds come for the buffet (R$50 on weekdays, R$60 weekends), while at night the a la carte menu features all the favorites, including delicious platters of hummus, *koftas* (spiced meat patty), falafel, kibbe and salads. There's a belly dancer Friday nights (at 9pm), while other nights you can smoke from a hookah if you snag a balcony seat.

LE BLÉ NOIR FRENCH $$

(Map p236; ☎2267-6969; Xavier da Silveira 19A; crepes R$35-60; ⏲7:30pm-midnight) Flickering candles and subdued conversation make this restaurant a real date-pleaser. Le Blé Noir offers over 50 different varieties of crepe, pairing rich ingredients such as shrimp and artichoke hearts or Brie, honey and toasted almonds.

CONFEITARIA COLOMBO CAFE $$

(Map p236; ☎3201-4049; Forte de Copacabana, Praça Coronel Eugênio Franco, Copacabana; mains R$20-30; ⏲10am-8pm Tue-Sun) Far removed from the hustle and bustle of Av Atlântica, this cafe has magnificent views of Copacabana beach. At the outdoor tables, you can sit beneath shady palm trees, enjoying cappuccino, omelets, pastas, salads or sandwiches as young soldiers file past. To get here, you'll have to pay admission (R$6) to the Forte de Copacabana (Copacabana Fort).

THE BAKERS CAFE $$

(Map p236; ☎3209-1212; www.thebakers.com.br; Santa Clara 86, Copacabana; desserts R$7-10, lunch specials R$27-30; ⏲9am-8pm) The Bakers is a fine spot for flaky croissants, banana Danishes, apple strudels and other treats. There are also salads, gourmet sandwiches (like prosciutto and mozzarella on ciabatta), quiches (ricotta with sun-dried tomatoes), and filling lunch specials (such as grilled salmon or penne pasta).

ECLIPSE BRAZILIAN $$

(Map p236; ☎2287-1788; Av NS de Copacabana 1309, Copacabana; mains R$27-45; ⏲24hr) One

THE KIOSKS OF COPACABANA

The *quiosque* (kiosk) has long been a presence on the beachfront of Rio, doling out cold drinks and snacks to *cariocas* on the move, with plastic tables and chairs providing a fine vantage point for contemplating the watery horizon. In recent years Copacabana beach has seen a new crop of flashy kiosks replacing the old-fashioned wooden ones (angering traditionalists – not to mention a few disenfranchised kiosk owners). Now it's possible to get a decent meal (the kitchens are cleverly concealed underground), an ice-cold draft beer or gourmet snacks without ever leaving the sand.

The new kiosks are sprinkled all along the beach, with the most options between about Rua Siqueira Campos and the Copacabana Palace. Here are a few current favorites:

Très (Map p236; ☎4106-7185; www.tres-restaurant.com; Copacabana beach near Siqueira Campos; snacks R$3-19, sandwiches R$18-28) A top choice for foodies and Francophiles, Très whips up tasty crepes both savory (blue cheese and walnuts) and sweet (Nutella with strawberry and banana), as well as cheese and charcuterie plates, gourmet sandwiches, salads, milkshakes and appetizers (pan-fried shrimp with garlic).

Itaipava (Map p236; near Copacabana Palace; ⏲9am-2am) A popular gathering spot, Itaipava serve up very cold *chope* and plenty of satisfying snacks – including cheese-covered *fritas* (fries).

Carioca Com Você (Map p240; near Praça Julio de Noronha; snacks R$12-20; ⏲24hr) At the northeast end of Leme, elevated over the beach, this peacefully set kiosk serves small plates of sardines (six for R$12) as well as strong drinks. Nearby, you can watch fearless *carioca* kids diving off the seawall.

of the few 24-hour restaurants in town, Eclipse is equal parts juice bar, pizzeria and traditional Brazilian restaurant, with outdoor seating, a stand-up counter and a sit-down air-conditioned restaurant for escaping the heat. It can be a great (and lively!) destination when hunger strikes in the *madrugada* (the wee hours of the night).

FRONTERA — BUFFET $$

(Map p236; ☎3202-9050; Av NS de Copacabana 1144, Copacabana; per kg R$53-60; ⏲11:30am-midnight) Much like its Ipanema branch, Frontera spreads an excellent lunch buffet. You'll find dozens of Brazilian dishes plus salads, individual counters for grilled meats, sushi, fried dishes and desserts. At night they serve all-you-can-eat pizzas from R$22 to R$27 per person.

FAENZA — BUFFET, PIZZA $$

(Map p236; ☎2257-1427; Siqueira Campos 18, Copacabana; lunch per kg R$45; ⏲noon-midnight) Warmly lit, with exposed brick walls, Faenza offers an extensive lunch buffet of Brazilian dishes and a nightly all-you-can-eat pizza feast (at R$30 per person). Steaming thin-crust pizzas are brought to your table by harried waiters, and there are even dessert options (such as strawberry with Nutella).

DEVASSA — BRAZILIAN $$

(Map p236; ☎2236-0667; Bolívar 8, Copacabana; mains R$30-50; ⏲11am-2am) The popular Rio chain of upscale *botecos* is well known for its excellent beers. Devassa also serves tasty pub fare, including juicy burgers, veggie quesadillas, seafood pastas and the usual bar food. The open-sided restaurant enjoys a good location on the edge of Av Atlântica.

DON CAMILLO — ITALIAN $$

(Map p236; ☎2549-9958; Av Atlântica 3056, Copacabana; pastas R$35-55; ⏲noon-1am) One of the few decent restaurants on the Copa strip, this handsomely appointed Italian restaurant has flavorful pastas and lasagnas, as well as some excellent seafood dishes. Antique tile floors, distressed wood beams and black-and-white photos make a nice setting to add to your dining pleasure. For pure decadence, try the linguini with lobster, shrimp and cherry tomatoes.

LA TRATTORIA — ITALIAN $$

(Map p236; ☎2255-3319; Fernando Mendes 7A, Copacabana; mains R$28-55; ⏲noon-midnight) Old photos, simple furnishings, hearty dishes and the constant din of conversation have made this trattoria a neighborhood favorite since 1976. Shrimp dishes are the Italian family's specialty – its won over many diners with its *espaguete com camarão e óleo tartufado* (spaghetti with shrimp and truffle oil).

ARATACA AMAZONIAN **$$**

(Map p236; ☎2548-6624; Domingos Ferreira 41D, Copacabana; mains for two around R$55; ⏲10am-9pm) The casual, no-nonsense Arataca serves the exotic cuisine of the Amazon. While there's better *tacacá* (spicy soup) on offer in Rio (Flamengo's Tacacá do Norte is the city's best), Arataca is a handy spot to grab a savory bowl of the soup. There's also *pirarucu* (a kind of fish), *pato no tucupi* (roast duck flavored with garlic) or *vatapá* (seafood dish with a thick sauce of manioc paste and coconut), all of which go nicely with real guarana juice.

LA FIORENTINA ITALIAN **$$**

(Map p240; ☎2543-8395; Av Atlântica 458A, Leme; mains R$35-80; ⏲11:30am-2am) One of Leme's classic Italian restaurants, La Fiorentina attracted Rio's glitterati in the '60s. Today, its beach-facing outdoor tables draw a loyal, mostly neighborhood crowd, who come to feast on oysters, risottos and pizzas.

GALERIA 1618 BISTRO **$$**

(Map p240; ☎2295-1618; Gustavo Sampaio 840, Leme; mains R$37-58; ⏲noon-midnight) Opened by two French expats in 2006, the art-filled Galeria 1618 offers beautifully prepared *boeuf bourguingnon*, Toulouse-style cassoulet or Tunisian lamb couscous. You can also opt for freshly made pastas, risottos and grilled fish or meat dishes, plus a dozen varieties of crepes.

CARRETÃO CHURRASCARIA **$$$**

(Map p236; ☎2542-2148; Ronald de Carvalho 55, Copacabana; all-you-can-eat R$49-54; ⏲noon-midnight) It's all about the meat at this decent but (relatively) inexpensive *churrascaria*. With several branches throughout the city, including an Ipanema Carretão, this popular chain serves up bountiful portions. There's a small salad bar, and you can order sides from the menu at no added charge.

CHURRASCARIA PALACE CHURRASCARIA **$$$**

(Map p236; ☎2541-5898; Rodolfo Dantas 16; all-you-can-eat R$70; ⏲noon-midnight) For the price, this is one of the best-value *churrascarias* in town. You'll find high-quality cuts of meat and attentive service at this elegant place. Waiters make frequent rounds with the goods; don't be shy about saying no otherwise you'll end up with more than you could possibly eat.

CAPRICCIOSA PIZZA **$$$**

(Map p236; ☎2255-2598; Domingos Ferreira 187, Copacabana; pizza from R$50; ⏲6pm-2am) Like its better-known version in Ipanema, Capricciosa serves excellent thin-crust pizzas.

BAR MÔNACO SEAFOOD **$$$**

(Map p236; ☎2521-0195; Miguel Lemos 18, Copacabana; mains for 2 R$100-120; ⏲8am-2am) The fresh fish counter gives it all away: the casual Bar Mônaco is the neighborhood destination for sizzling plates of grilled squid, fresh cherne (grouper), shrimp and a mean bowl of Leão Veloso (a rich seafood soup). Sidewalk tables provide a relaxing point for a meal or a drink on a fairly untrafficked street.

SHIRLEY SPANISH **$$$**

(Map p240; ☎2275-1398; Gustavo Sampaio 610, Leme; mains R$50-90; ⏲noon-1am) The aroma of succulent paella hangs in the air as waiters hurry to and from the kitchen bearing platefuls of fresh seafood. Shirley, opened in 1954, was one of the first Spanish restaurants in town, and attracts a local following in its small Leme dining room. In addition to paella, the mussel-vinaigrette appetizer and the oven-baked snapper in white wine sauce are also recommended.

AZUMI JAPANESE **$$$**

(Map p236; ☎2541-4294; Ministro Viveiros de Castro 127, Copacabana; meals R$70-150; ⏲7pm-midnight Tue-Thu & Sun, to 1am Fri & Sat) Some claim Azumi is the bastion of traditional Japanese cuisine in the city. This laid-back sushi bar certainly has its fans – both in the *nisei* (second generation Japanese born in Brazil) community and from abroad. Azumi's *sushiman* (sushi chef) masterfully prepares delectable sushi and sashimi, though tempuras and soups are also excellent. Be sure to ask what's in season.

ZOT CONTEMPORARY **$$$**

(Map p236; ☎3489-4363; Bolívar 21, Copacabana; mains around $40; ⏲6pm-midnight Tue-Sat, from noon Sun) Set amid the bars of Baixo Copa, Zot is a sleek and stylish gastrobar featuring an inventive menu that showcases Brazilian ingredients and an excellent drink selection, including dozens of wines by the glass. On Tuesdays Zot hosts nights of live jazz (cover charge R$15).

MARIUS BRAZILIAN $$$

(Map p240; ☎2104-9002; Av Atlântica 290; all-you-can-eat meat/seafood R$120/170; ⊙noon-midnight) Although the price is sky-high here, this spacious all-you-can-eat restaurant spreads a feast before a mostly tourist-filled dining room. You can opt either for grilled meats or a meat-and-seafood combination: with lobster, mussels, oysters, tuna, salmon, scallops and more brought to your table.

SIRI MOLE & CIA BRAZILIAN $$$

(Map p236; ☎2267-0894; Rua Francisco Otaviano 50, Copacabana; mains R$75-140; ⊙7pm-midnight Mon, noon-midnight Tue-Sun) Rated one of Rio's best Bahian restaurants, Siri Mole & Cia serves outstanding *vatapa*, *moqueca de camarão* (shrimp stew) and *ensopada de peixe* (fish and coconut milk stew). Stop in on Saturday (before 5pm) for the all-you-can-eat seafood buffet (R$75). Around the corner is Siri Mole's smaller, cheaper and more casual *boteco,* **Toca do Siri** (Map p236; Rua Raul Pompeia 6; ⊙noon-midnight Tue-Sun), which serves tasty *acarajé* (spicy shrimp-filled croquettes).

DRINKING & NIGHTLIFE

Although it is often overshadowed by its younger, hipper neighbor, Ipanema, to the south, Copacabana has seen marked improvement in its nightlife offerings, boosted in part by its ocean-fronting kiosks, which make a great spot for a late afternoon drink. On the other side of the busy road are the open-air restaurants and bars of Av Atlântica, which are generally – with a few exceptions – overpriced tourist traps. More authentic is the emerging nightlife area that some have dubbed 'Baixo Copa' (Lower Copa), with a dozen or so lively bars and restaurants sprinkled along a quiet street just back from Av Atlântica. To explore this area, head along Rua Aires Saldanha and Rua Domingos Ferreira, between Rua Almirante Gonçalves and Rua Constante Ramos. For something more upscale, the best options are at high-end hotel bars, some of which have million-dollar views.

MUD BUG BAR

(Map p236; ☎2235-6847; www.mudbug.com.br; Rudolfo Dantas 16; ⊙5pm-2am) Mud Bug is a warmly lit sports bar that has a rustic, all-wood interior where *cariocas* and foreigners mingle over football games, bar bites and a broad beer selection. There's also live music – typically classic rock on most weekends. A second Copacabana location is a few blocks west on Rua Paula Freitas.

BAR DO COPA LOUNGE

(Map p236; ☎2548-7070; Copacabana Palace hotel, Av Atlântica 1702, Copacabana; admission R$40-80; ⊙8pm-2am Wed, 9pm-4am Thu-Sat) Inside Copacabana's most recognizable landmark, this poolside bar received a dramatic R$4 million makeover in 2009, raising the stakes in the hotelier design game. The ceiling, with its 10,000 points of light, aims to mimic the night sky, while crystal chandeliers, glowing column-sized luminaries and gilded mosaics add a vaguely futuristic element to the spacious lounge. There are live bands and DJs; Palace guests get in free.

BOTEQUIM INFORMAL BOTECO

(Map p236; ☎3816-0909; Domingos Ferreira 215, Copacabana; ⊙noon-1am) Botequim Informal is a lively drinking spot with an elevated open-sided deck, frothy drafts and tasty appetizers (including a fried polenta with gorgonzola sauce). There are 10 other branches of Botequim Informal in Rio. It lies amid half a dozen open-sided bars in a sub-neighborhood known as Baixo Copa.

PONTO DA BOSSA NOVA BAR

(Map p236; ☎2235-4616; Domingos Ferreira 215, Copacabana; ⊙noon-1am Sun & Mon, till 3am Tue-Sat) On a lively street sprinkled with bars, Ponto da Bossa Nova is a cozy wood-lined space with a small outdoor patio that makes a peaceful spot for sampling daily lunch specials (R$13 to R$17), appetizers like *carne seca com aipim* (jerked beef with fried cassava) and well-made caipirinhas. True to its name, there's live bossa nova on Tuesday and Saturday nights.

HORSE'S NECK BAR

(Map p236; ☎2525-1232; Av Atlântica 4240, Sofitel Rio de Janeiro, Copacabana; ⊙noon-2am) This bright and airy bar has potted palms, wood furnishings and ocean breezes that give it a tropical vibe. This is the place to come to nurse a Belgian beer, while taking in that magnificent stretch of coastline from one of the tables on the terrace.

1. Samba band **2.** Rio night life **3.** Rio Scenarium (p140), Lapa
4. Al fresco dining, Centro (p127)

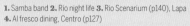

DAVID BANK / CORBIS ©

Nightlife

By night, the energy on Rio's streets is electric. All-night street parties in Lapa, old-school *gafieiras* (dance halls), impromptu jam sessions at outdoor bars, riotous dance floors presided over by celebrated DJs – Rio's nightlife is all this and much more. The only thing you have to do is show up.

Lapa

Epicenter of Rio's samba scene, there's always something afoot in this atmospheric neighborhood on the edge of Centro. On weekends the party takes over, and the city closes the streets to traffic.

Nightclubs

Lapa aside, some of the best spots for dancing are in the Zona Sul, with trendy places like 00 (Zero Zero) (p80) and Melt (p71) bringing in the well-dressed club kids.

Botecos

A much-loved institution in Rio, the *boteco* is a casual open-sided bar where *cariocas* (residents of Rio) gather over ice-cold *chopes* (draft beer) and snacks. Eating is an essential part of Rio's drinking culture.

Al Fresco

Cariocas make good use of the warm nights, with open-air drinking spots all around town. Try the Travessa do Comércio (p124) in Centro for colonial flavor, Bar Urca (p105) for great views, or the Copacabana kiosks for afternoon cocktails on the beachfront.

Lagoa

The pretty lagoon (p78) behind Ipanema and Leblon is a favorite spot among couples at night. Lakeside kiosks serve up cocktails and live music (as well as food) in tranquil open-air settings.

LE BOY GAY CLUB

(Map p236; ☎2513-4993; www.leboy.com.br; Raul Pompéia 102, Copacabana; cover R$10-30; ⏰closed Mon) Open since 1992, Le Boy is Rio's gay temple. There are theme nights with drag shows and go-go boys.

SINDICATO DO CHOPP BAR

(Map p236; ☎2523-4644; Av Atlântica 3806, Copacabana; ⏰11am-3am) A Copacabana institution, this open-air bar looks out on the wide avenue, with the beach in the background. Owing to its breezy location, it attracts a wide mix of people, all playing a part in Copa's inimitable street theater. The food isn't so great here, but the beers are icy cold and the ocean is, well, right there. A second **Sindicato do Chopp** (Map p240; Av Atlântica 514, Leme) is an even more peaceful beach-fronting refuge.

SKYLAB BAR

(Map p236; ☎2106-1666; 30th fl, Rio Othon Palace, Av Atlântica 3264, Copacabana; ⏰7pm-midnight) It's all about the view at this modestly decorated bar in the Rio Othon Palace. From 30 floors up, the coastline unfolds, allowing a glimpse of the Cidade Maravilhosa (Marvelous City) at its most striking.

TV BAR GAY BAR

(Map p236; www.bartvbar.com.br; Av NS de Copacabana, 1417, Shopping Cassino Atlântico, Copacabana; cover R$10-40) The trendy new boy in town, with DJs spinning amid an audiovisual assault in the space of a former TV station.

FOSFOBOX CLUB

(Map p236; ☎2548-7498; www.fosfobox.com.br; Siqueira Campos 143, Copacabana; admission R$15-30; ⏰11pm-4am Thu-Sat) This subterranean club is hidden under a shopping center near the metro station. Good DJs spin everything from funk to glam rock, and the crowd here is one of the more eclectic in the club scene.

☆ ENTERTAINMENT

BIP BIP LIVE MUSIC

(Map p236; ☎2267-9696; Almirante Gonçalves 50, Copacabana; ⏰6pm-midnight Sun-Fri) FREE For years, Bip Bip has been one of the city's favorite spots to catch a live *samba da mesa* (informal samba played around a table). Although it's just a storefront with a few battered tables, as the evening progresses the tree-lined neighborhood becomes the backdrop to serious jam sessions, with music and revelers spilling into the street. The schedule at the time of writing was samba on Thursday, Friday and Sunday, *choro* (short for *chorinho* – romantic, intimate samba) on Monday and Tuesday, and bossa nova on Wednesday. Music kicks off around 8pm.

ESPAÇO SESC PERFORMING ARTS

(Map p236; ☎2547-0156; www.sescrj.org.br; Domingos Ferreira 160, Copacabana) Hosting an excellent assortment of theater and dance performances, Espaço SESC is a bulwark of the Copacabana arts scene. The repertoire tends toward the experimental and avant-garde, particularly during annual dance and theater festivals.

SALA MUNICIPAL BADEN POWELL PERFORMING ARTS

(Map p236; ☎2548-0421; Av NS de Copacabana 360, Copacabana) One of the few music halls in the Zona Sul, the 500-seat Sala Baden Powell hosts a broad range of concerts throughout the year, with MPB (Música Popular Brasileira) and jazz figuring prominently (the hall even hosts a 10-day jazz fest in January). Most tickets are around R$20, with shows taking place Thursday through Sunday nights starting around 9pm.

ROXY CINEMA

(Map p236; ☎2461-2461; Av NS de Copacabana 945, Copacabana) Copacabana's only cinema is a good retreat when the weather sours. The Roxy shows the usual films on wide release.

SHOPPING

Copacabana's shops, just like its local residents, are a diverse bunch, with everything from *cachaça* (potent cane spirit) to football jerseys on hand, as well as shoe stores, surf shops and record stores thrown in the mix. Fashion hunters will find more lower-tier labels than in Ipanema, along with lower prices to match. Between Copa and Ipanema is the Galeria River, a low-rise shopping mall lined with surf and swimwear shops.

HAVAIANAS SHOES

(Map p236; ☎2267-2418; Xavier da Silveira 19, Copacabana; ⏰9am-8pm Mon-Fri, 10am-6pm Sat & Sun) If you're out of ideas for gifts to take home, head to this sizeable Havaianas shop, where the ubiquitous Brazilian rubber sandal comes in all different styles – sporting the flags of Brazil, Argentina, Portugal, England and Spain – plus snazzy designs for the ladies, and even logo-bearing bags, key chains and beach towels.

LOJA FLA CLOTHING, ACCESSORIES

(Map p236; ☎2541-4109; Av NS de Copacabana 219, Copacabana; ⏰10am-6pm Mon-Fri, to 4pm Sat) With more than 30 million fans worldwide, Flamengo is one of the most-watched football teams in all of Brazil. This new shop sells all the Flamengo goods, including jerseys, logo-emblazoned socks and footballs, posters and other memorabilia. The prices aren't cheap (jerseys run R$80 to R$180), but that hasn't dented the popularity of this often-packed little store.

BOSSA NOVA & COMPANHIA MUSIC

(Map p236; ☎2295-8096; Duvivier 37A, Copacabana; ⏰9am-7pm Mon-Fri, 9am-5pm Sat) Here you'll find a decent assortment of bossa, *choro* and samba CDs and LPs, as well as musical instruments, coffee-table books, sheet music and biographies of top Brazilian composers.

GILSON MARTINS ACCESSORIES

(Map p236; Av Atlântica 1998, Copacabana; ⏰10am-10pm Mon-Sat, 2-8pm Sun) Like its flagship store in Ipanema, this colorful shop sells well-made wallets, bags, keychains and other items with images of Christo Redentor (Christ the Redeemer), the Brazilian flag and other iconic designs.

DRACO STORE CLOTHING

(Map p236; ☎2227-7393; Francisco Otaviano 55, Ipanema; ⏰10am-8pm Mon-Sat, noon-5pm Sun) Like Galeria River a few doors down, this menswear store specializes in stylish beachwear, including well-made swimshorts. You'll also find jeans, button-downs and T-shirts (in the R$50 to R$90 range) – the best of which bear the names of Rio neighborhoods (Copacabana, Ipanema, Arpoador).

MUSICALE MUSIC

(Map p236; ☎2267-9607; Av NS de Copacabana 1103C, Copacabana; ⏰10am-7pm Mon-Fri, 10am-4pm Sat) Musicale has a small but well-curated selection of used CDs (and a few new titles), most of which cost around R$20 or R$25. Albums run the gamut between samba, MPB and regional sounds, plus American and British rock and indie as well as world music (French pop, *nueva cancion*), and you can listen to used discs on one of several CD players scattered around the store. Musicale also buys and trades CDs.

LOMOGRAPHY GALLERY STORE PHOTOGRAPHY

(Map p236; ☎2267-2226; www.lomography.com.br; Barata Ribeiro 369; ⏰10am-8pm Mon-Fri, 10am-7pm Sat) This colorful shop and gallery specializes in the Lomo Kompakt Automat, a compact Russian film camera known for saturated colors and surreal effects (halos, shadowing). You can purchase different models here at the store, check out the LomoWall (of photographic art) and learn more about the growing fan base worldwide who are devoted to these analog cameras.

GALERIA RIVER SHOPPING CENTER

(Map p236; Francisco Otaviano 67, Arpoador; ⏰10am-6pm Mon-Sat) Surf shops, skateboard and rollerblade outlets, and shops selling beachwear and fashions for young nubile things fill this shopping gallery in Arpoador. Shorts, bikinis, swim trunks, party attire and gear for outdoor adventure are in abundance. The shops here – like BoardsCo – are a good place to inquire about board rentals.

DEU LA DEU VINHOS WINE, SPIRITS

(Map p236; ☎2235-7287; Domingos Ferreira 66, Copacabana; 9am-9pm Mon-Sat, to 4pm Sun) Copacabana's best wine shop is hidden on a quiet street one block from the beach. In addition to a fair assortment of Chilean and Argentine vintages, you'll find a few decent Brazilian labels like Casa Vadulga and Miolo. A wide assortment of *cachaças* and other spirits round out the offerings.

MUNDO VERDE FOOD

(Map p236; ☎2257-3183; www.mundoverde.com.br; Av NS de Copacabana 630, Copacabana; ⏰9am-6pm Mon-Fri, 9am-2pm Sat) Brazil's largest health-food retailer, Mundo Verde sells organic products, including: *salgados* (bar snacks), and other snacks; jams made from Amazonian fruits; and other assorted goods. The sun-care products are usually cheaper here than in pharmacies – and much better for your skin.

SHOPPING

SIQUEIRA CAMPOS SHOPPING CENTER

(Map p236; ☎2549-0650; Siqueira Campos 143, Copacabana; ⏲10am-8pm Mon-Sat) One of Rio's first malls, this quirky shopping mall packs an intriguing mix of stores in a no-nonsense parking garage-like interior. You'll find numerous antique shops, used book and record stores, internet cafes, art galleries and dozens of other surprising finds that you won't come across in Leblon.

SPORTS & ACTIVITIES

SURF RIO WATER SPORTS

(Map p236; ☎7779-2003; www.surfrio.com.br; Posto 6, Copacabana beach; per hr R$50-60; ⏲7am-5pm) The latest sporting novelty on the beaches of Rio is stand-up paddle boarding, a sport that's been around since the 1960s but has only recently attracted a worldwide following. Near the southern end of Copacabana, Surf Rio is one of several places on the beach where you can hire gear. If you've never tried it, Surf Rio also offers one-hour classes (R$60 per person) where you can learn the basics.

ANTARYAMIN YOGA

(Map p236; ☎3201-1355; www.antaryamin.com.br; room 202, Francisco Sá 31, Copacabana) This recommended yoga studio offers Hatha, Vinyasa and Iyengar yoga, and offers a range of workshops, retreats and meditation courses on the side. Individual classes cost R$40, with discounts for longer commitments.

RIO SAMBA DANCER DANCE

(Map p236; ☎8229-2843; riosambadancer.com; Barata Ribeiro 261A, Copacabana; 90min private lesson per person R$80) English-speaking dance instructor Hélio Ricardo offers private one-on-one dance classes (in samba or *forró*), and he'll even provide a partner for you if you're a male. He also will take you out to dance places around town where you can practice your new moves (R$120 per person including dance lesson).

Botafogo & Urca

BOTAFOGO | URCA

Neighborhood Top Five

❶ Gliding up to the top of **Pão de Açúcar** (Sugarloaf Mountain; p99) by cable car for the awe-inspiring view of Rio at your feet.

❷ Learning about Brazil's many indigenous cultures at the interactive **Museu do Índio** (p100).

❸ Walking between forest and sea on the peaceful **Pista Cláudio Coutinho** (p100).

❹ Having a glimpse into the past at the well-preserved **Museu Casa de Rui Barbosa** (p100).

❺ Snapping a few photos at **Praia Vermelha** (p100), one of Rio's prettiest little beaches.

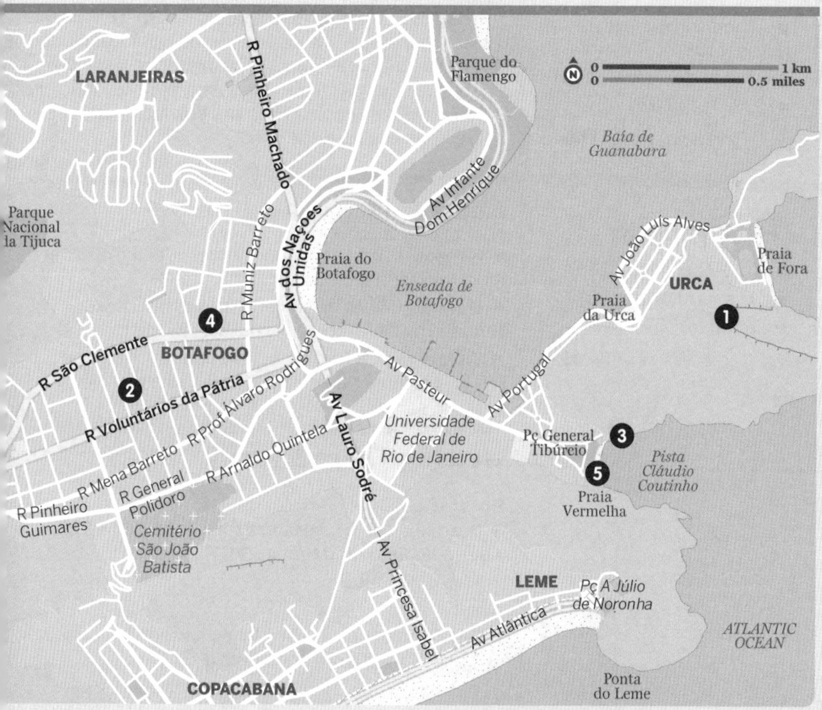

For more detail of this area see Map p244 ➡

Lonely Planet's Top Tip

Although Urca is home to one of Rio's top attractions, few visitors venture into the neighborhood beyond Pão de Açúcar. Its quiet tree-lined streets (like Rua Otávio Correia) make for some intriguing exploring, and there are picturesque views from the bayside roads (like Av João Luís Alves).

Best Places to Eat

- Meza Bar (p104)
- Oui Oui (p104)
- Emporium Pax (p104)

For reviews, see p104

Best Places to Drink

- Champanharia Ovelha Negra (p105)
- Espírito do Chopp (p105)
- O Plebeu (p105)

For reviews, see p104

Best Nightclubs

- Bar Bukowski (p105)
- Casa da Matriz (p105)
- Far Up (p106)

For reviews, see p104

Explore Botafogo & Urca

The traditional, middle-class neighborhood of Botafogo may not have the beaches of its neighbors to the south, but it doesn't lack for much else, with intriguing museums, movie theaters, quaint bookshops, a shopping center, and festive, open-air bars on tranquil back streets. There are also two vibrant nightclubs and a boulevard dotted with old mansions.

Neighboring Urca is even more idyllic, with shaded, quiet streets. It's eclectic architecture includes art-deco and modernist houses backed by manicured gardens. Along the seawall, which forms the northwestern perimeter of Pão de Açúcar, fishermen cast for dinner as couples lounge beneath palm trees, taking in views of Baía de Guanabara (Guanabara Bay) and Cristo Redentor (Christ the Redeemer). Tiny Praia Vermelha in the south has one of Rio's finest beach views. A pleasant walking trail begins there.

Botafogo is named after the Portuguese settler, João Pereira de Souza Botafogo, and grew in importance following the arrival of the Portuguese court in the late 1800s. Dona Carlota Joaquina, the wife of Dom João VI, had a country villa, and she used to bathe in the Baía de Guanabara. With royalty established in the area, arriving aristocrats built many mansions, some of which still stand as schools, theaters and cultural centers.

In the 19th century, development was spurred by the construction of a tram that ran to the botanical garden (Jardim Botânico), linking the bay with the lake (Lagoa Rodrigo de Freitas). This artery still plays a vital role in Rio's traffic flow, though Botafogo's main streets are now extremely congested.

Local Life

- **Hangouts** At Bar Urca, locals gather in the open air for drinks with great views.
- **Markets** Browse the produce stands of Cobal do Humaitá by day and sample the bars by night.
- **Shopping** Botafogo Praia Shopping has numerous stores, plus upper-floor restaurants with great views.

Getting There & Away

Botafogo

- **Bus** Ipanema, Leblon and Copacabana (161 & 573), Jardim Botânico and Gávea (170, 176, 592).
- **Metro** Botafogo.

Urca

- **Bus** Centro (107), Leblon, Ipanema and Copacabana (511), Jardim Botânico and Gávea (512).

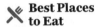

TOP SIGHT
PÃO DE AÇÚCAR

One of Rio's dazzling icons, Pão de Açúcar (Sugarloaf Mountain) offers a vision of Rio at its most disarming. Following a steep ascent up the mountain, you'll be rewarded with superb views of Rio's gorgeous shoreline, and the city planted among the green peaks. From the summit, 395m above above Rio and the Baía de Guanabara, it's quite clear why Rio is called the Cidade Maravilhosa (Marvelous City).

The most traditional way to reach the top is to board the two-stage cable car that departs from Urca every 20 minutes or so. The glass-and-steel cars are good fun in themselves, and ascend 215m to Morro da Urca. From here, you can see Baía de Guanabara and along the winding coastline. On the ocean side of the mountain is Praia Vermelha, in a small, calm bay. Morro da Urca has a restaurant, souvenir shops, a playground, outdoor theater and a helipad. In the summer, concerts are sometimes staged in the amphitheater.

The second cable car goes up to Pão de Açúcar. At the top, the city unfolds beneath you, with Corcovado mountain and Cristo Redentor off to the west, the twinkling lights of Niteroi across the bay to the east, and the long curve of Copacabana Beach to the south. If the breathtaking heights unsteady you, a cafe is on hand to serve caipirinhas and other drinks. There's also a restaurant, an ice-cream shop and the obligatory souvenir shop.

Those who'd rather take the long way to the top should sign up with one of the granite-hugging climbing tours offered by various outfits in Rio. Morro da Urca is much easier to climb, and you can do it on your own. The short but steep path takes about 30 minutes to climb. You'll find the unmarked trail along the Pista Cláudio Coutinho.

For prime views of the Cidade Maravilhosa, go around sunset on a clear day.

DON'T MISS...

- Drinking caipirinhas while watching planes land beneath you.
- Summer concerts up top.
- The walking trail up Morro da Urca.

PRACTICALITIES

- Map p244
- 2546-8400
- www.bondinho.com.br
- Av Pasteur 520, Urca
- adult/child R$53/26
- 8am-7:50pm

SIGHTS

Botafogo

MUSEU CASA DE RUI BARBOSA MUSEUM

(Map p244; ☎3289-4663; www.casaruibarbosa.gov.br; São Clemente 134; admission R$4, free on Sun; ⏲10am-5:30pm Tue-Fri, 2-6pm Sat & Sun) The former mansion (completely restored in 2003) of famous Brazilian journalist and diplomat, Rui Barbosa, is now a museum housing his library and personal belongings, along with an impressive archive of manuscripts and first editions of other Brazilian authors, such as Machado de Assis and José de Alencar. Barbosa played a major role in shaping the country's socioeconomic development in the early 20th century.

MUSEU DO ÍNDIO MUSEUM

(Map p244; ☎3214-8736; www.museudoindio.org.br; Rua das Palmeiras 55; admission R$3; ⏲9am-5:30pm Tue-Fri, 1-5pm Sat & Sun) Featuring multimedia exhibitions on Brazil's northern tribes, the small Museu do Índio provides an excellent introduction to the economic, religious and social life of Brazil's indigenous people. Next to native food and medicinal plants, the four life-size dwellings in the courtyard were actually built by four different tribes.

As a branch of Funai (the National Indian Foundation), the museum contains an excellent archive of more than 14,000 objects, 50,000 photographs and 200 sound recordings. Its indigenous ethnography library containing 16,000 volumes by local and foreign authors is open to the public during the week.

PRAIA DE BOTAFOGO BEACH

(Map p244; Av dos Naçoes Unidas) Although the waters of the bay are too polluted for swimming, the beach overlooking the Enseada de Botafogo (Botafogo Inlet) makes a photogenic setting for a stroll. Hopeful football stars play pick-up games along the shore, against the backdrop of sailboats bobbing on the water and Pão de Açúcar off in the background.

PASMADO OVERLOOK LOOKOUT

(Map p244; Rua Bartolomeu Portela) Sweeping views of Enseada de Botafogo, Pão de Açúcar and Corcovado await visitors who make the journey up Pasmado. It's best reached in early morning or late afternoon, when the light is at its best for capturing the postcard panorama. Visitors will also be able to see details of a favela from above. The overlook is best reached by taxi via Rua General Severiano.

MUSEU VILLA-LOBOS MUSEUM

(Map p244; ☎2266-3845; www.museuvillalobos.org.br; Sorocaba 200; ⏲10am-5pm Mon-Fri) FREE Housed in a century-old building, this modest museum is dedicated to the memory of Brazil's greatest classical composer – and founder of the Brazilian Academy of Music – Heitor Villa-Lobos. In addition to scores, musical instruments – including the piano on which he composed – and personal items, the museum contains an extensive sound archive. Classical concerts are sometimes held in the adjoining courtyard.

Urca

PISTA CLÁUDIO COUTINHO WALKING TRAIL

(Map p244; ⏲6am-sunset) Everyone loves this paved 2km trail winding along the southern contour of Morro do Urca. It's a lush area, with the waves crashing on the rocks below. Look out for families of marmosets with their gray fur, striped tails and tiny faces. To get there, walk 100m north along the edge of Praia Vermelha (with your back to the cable-car station) and you'll see the entrance to the path straight ahead, just past the beach.

About 300m along the path, there's a small unmarked trail leading off to Morro da Urca. From there you can go up to Pão de Açúcar by cable car, saving a few reais. Pão de Açúcar can also be climbed – but it's not recommended without an experienced guide and climbing gear.

PRAIA DA URCA BEACH

(Map p244; Av João Luis Alves) This tiny beach is popular with neighborhood kids who gather here for pick-up football games when school is not in session (and sometimes when it is).

PRAIA VERMELHA BEACH

(Map p244; Praça General Tibúrcio) Beneath Morro da Urca, narrow Praia Vermelha has superb views of the rocky coastline from the shore. Its coarse sand gives the beach the name *vermelha* (red). Because the beach is protected by the headland, the water is usually calm.

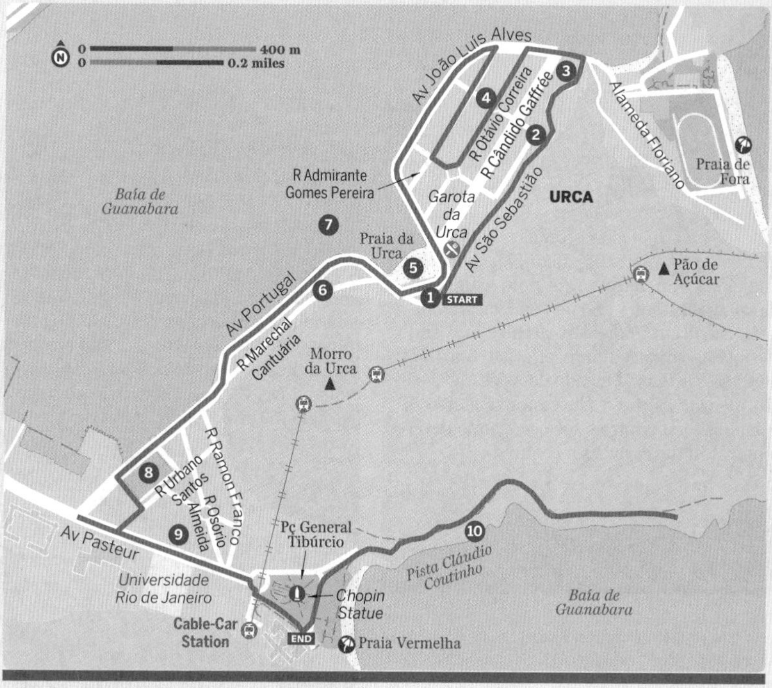

Neighborhood Walk
Urca, the Village by the Sea

START RUA MARECHAL CANTUÁRIA
END PRAIA VERMELHA
DISTANCE 5KM
DURATION THREE HOURS

One of Rio's most charming neighborhoods is also one of its least explored. Our walk begins where Rua Marechal Cantuária meets Av São Sebastião. On your left, you'll see the former 1 **Cassino da Urca**, a once-popular gambling and nightspot, where Carmen Miranda and Josephine Baker both performed.

Veer to the right along Av São Sebastião, following the road uphill. You'll pass 2 **Carmen Miranda's former residence** at No 131 and soon reach the wall that separates the military fort from the neighborhood.

At the end of the street, take the steps down to Av João Luis Alves. Stop for a cold drink at 3 **Bar Urca** (p105), while admiring the views.

Explore the tree-lined backstreets by heading down 4 **Rua Otávio Correira** and looping back along Rua Admirante Gomes Pereira.

Cut back to Av João Luis Alves and follow it to 5 **Praia da Urca**, a tiny beach with more fine views of the bay.

Stay on the bay side as the road forks. Peek inside 6 **Igreja de Nossa Senhora do Brasil** (the chapel is on the ground floor; the church upstairs), noting the small Brazilian flag on the Madonna's cloak.

Facing the church is the floating 7 **statue of São Pedro no Mar**. On June 29, St Peter's feast day, the fishermen process across the bay, past the statue, scattering flowers across the water.

Go along what is now Av Portugal to a bridge. On the left is 8 **Quadrado da Urca**, a harbor.

Follow 9 **Avenue Pasteur** southeast past majestic buildings such as Companhia de Pesquisa de Recursos Minerais (Av Pasteur 404), guarded by a lion and a winged creature.

Follow paved 10 **Pista Cláudio Coutinho** out and back.

CHRISTOPHER PILLITZ / CORBIS ©

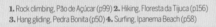

1. Rock climbing, Pão de Açúcar (p99) **2.** Hiking, Floresta da Tijuca (p156) **3.** Hang gliding, Pedra Bonita (p50) **4.** Surfing, Ipanema Beach (p58)

2

PAUL EDMONDSON / GETTY IMAGES ©

4

Outdoor Adventures

Blessed with tropical rainforest, towering peaks and sparkling seaside, the Cidade Maravilhosa (Marvelous City) offers some captivating ways to spend a sun-drenched afternoon. You can go hang gliding, surfing, biking, hiking, running and rock climbing amid spectacular scenery without leaving the city limits.

Hang Gliding

Although it will cost you a fair bit, hang gliding off Pedra Bonita (p50) is an unforgettable experience: just the pilot and you, soaring high over treetops and landing near the sea.

Rock Climbing

Sure, you can take the cable car to the top of Pão de Açúcar (Sugarloaf Mountain), but for an adrenaline rush and mesmerizing scenery, sign up for a rock-climbing trip (p50) to the top. The view will be all the sweeter.

Surfing

Superb waves (p51) are all around Rio. For a quick fix, you can join the locals off Arpoador. More serious surfers should get a ride on the surf bus and head west to Macumba or Prainha.

Hiking

Rio's tropical rainforest makes a fine setting for a hike (p49). Head to Floresta da Tijuca for hikes through lush forest, followed by a dip in a waterfall.

Cycling

The beachside bike path is great anytime for cyclists, and you can plot a route from Leblon up through Flamengo, riding waterside for most of the journey. You can also take a scenic spin around Lagoa.

MUSEU DE CIÊNCIAS DA TERRA MUSEUM
(Map p244; ☎2295-7596; Av Pasteur 404; ⏲10am-4pm Tue-Sun) FREE With curved staircases and statues out the front, this majestic building went through many incarnations before it housed the Earth Science Museum. The four-room exhibit gives an overview of the natural history of Brazil. Other rooms showcase the museum's extensive collection of minerals, rocks and meteorites – 5000 pieces in all.

EATING

Botafogo generally has a better drinking than dining scene, though there are some top picks hidden in these old streets. Urca, largely untouched by commercial development, has only a few choices.

CAFÉ BOTÂNICA CAFE $$
(Map p244; ☎2535-2465; Capitão Salomão 14B, Botafogo; mains R$23-35; ⏲9am-7pm Mon-Fri, to 2pm Sat; 🚸) This letterbox-sized cafe and bistro serves tasty bites, like goat's milk cheese quiche, pumpkin soup and homemade sandwiches. Don't neglect the tasty pie and cake selection.

EMPORIUM PAX BRAZILIAN $$
(Map p244; ☎3171-9713; 7th fl, Praia de Botafogo 400, Botafogo; lunch buffet R$37-47; ⏲noon-midnight) One of many eateries at Botafogo Praia Shopping, Emporium Pax is a more polished affair than the adjoining food court and offers spectacular views of Pão de Açúcar and Baía de Guanabara. The big draw is the extensive lunch buffet, though for something lighter you can order salads, sandwiches and quiches – plus tasty desserts – all a big draw for shoppers and film-goers.

MEZA BAR TAPAS $$
(Map p244; www.mezabar.com.br; Capitão Salomão 69, Botafogo; tapas R$10-25; ⏲6pm-1am) Botafogo's see-and-be-seen hot spot serves up delectable, Brazilian-slanted tapas to a sophisticated and trendy crowd. Creative cocktails and delightful staff round out the fun here.

OUI OUI FRENCH, BRAZILIAN $$
(Map p244; ☎2527-3539; Conde de Irajá 85, Humaitá; small plates R$32-36; ⏲noon-3pm Mon-Fri, 8pm-1am Tue-Sat) On a tranquil street in Humaitá, elegantly set Oui Oui serves innovative tapas plates designed for sharing – grilled trout with leeks and almonds, duck risotto, haddock croquettes and a zesty quinoa salad are a few recent hits. Several other good restaurants lie along the same street. Although evenings are best, Oui Oui also offers three-course lunch specials for R$33.

GAROTA DA URCA BRAZILIAN $$
(Map p244; ☎2541-8585; João Luís Alves 56, Urca; mains R$30-60; ⏲noon-1am Sun-Thu, to 2:30am Fri & Sat) Overlooking the small Praia da Urca, this neighborhood restaurant serves good-value weekday lunch specials, and you can enjoy views over the bay from the open-air veranda. By night, a more garrulous crowd converges for steak and *chope* (draft beer).

MIAM MIAM CONTEMPORARY $$$
(☎2244-0125; General Goés Monteiro 34, Botafogo; mains around R$50; ⏲8pm-12:30am Tue-Sat) Exposed brick walls and a mishmash of retro furnishings set the scene for dining in style at Botafogo's culinary darling. Chef Roberta Ciasca serves up her own brand of comfort food, which means bruschetta with pesto and tapenade, codfish ragout and pumpkin curry with Moroccan couscous and other unique dishes. Don't miss the creative cocktail menu or the desserts.

ZOZÔ BRAZILIAN $$$
(Map p244; ☎2542-9665; Ave Pasteur 520, Urca; lunch buffet R$55, mains around R$70; ⏲noon-4pm Tue-Sun & 8pm-midnight Tue-Sat) Next door to the cable car station, Zozô serves a good lunch buffet that's popular with tourist groups. All glass walls and ceiling give fine views onto the mountain, and the tree in the middle of the dining room adds a whimsical touch. By night the elegant restaurant serves innovative cuisine (the head chef trained under Daniel Boloud in New York).

On weekends, Zozô transforms into a nightclub after dinner, attracting Rio's beautiful people. Come for dinner to ensure you can get in.

DRINKING & NIGHTLIFE

Botafogo is the place to go for lively, authentic *carioca* (resident of Rio) bars, with fun, mixed crowds and little of the pretense you might encounter in bars further south. Rua Visconde de Caravelas

is a good place to browse the pub scene. Relatively uncommercial Urca has a few gems including a new trendy nightclub and a more downmarket live-music spot overlooking Praia Vermelha.

CHAMPANHARIA OVELHA NEGRA BAR

(Map p244; 2226-1064; Bambina 120, Botafogo; 5:30am-11:30pm Mon-Fri) One of Rio's best happy-hour scenes, Ovelha Negra draws a mostly local crowd who come for the lively conversation and the 40 different varieties of champagne and *prosecco* (Italian sparkling white wine) – the specialties of the house.

ESPÍRITO DO CHOPP BAR

(Map p244; 2266-5599; Cobal do Humaitá, Voluntários da Pátria 446, Botafogo; 9am-midnight Sun-Thu, to 2am Fri & Sat) One of many open-air venues in the Cobal, Espírito do Chopp fills up its plastic tables most nights with a festive, low-key crowd. The beer flows in abundance and there's always music nearby – either here or at one of the neighboring bars.

O PLEBEU BAR

(Map p244; 2286-0699; Capitão Salomão 50, Botafogo; noon-4am Mon-Sat, to 9pm Sun) In the liveliest stretch of Botafogo, O Plebeu is a welcoming, open-sided two-story bar with tables spilling onto the sidewalk and a 2nd-floor balcony. Neighborhood regulars pack this place, drawn by ice-cold beer (served in bottles), codfish balls and an unpretentious crowd befitting the name ('The Commoner').

BAR URCA BAR

(Map p244; 2295-8744; Cândido Gaffrée 205, Urca; 9am-11pm Mon-Sat, to 8pm Sun) This simple neighborhood bar and restaurant has a marvelous setting near Urca's bayside waterfront. At night, young and old crowd along the seaside wall as waiters bring cold drinks and appetizers.

BEERJACK HIDEOUT BAR

(Map p244; 2226-0267; Martins Ferreira 71, Botafogo; 5pm-11pm Sun-Wed, to 2am Thu-Sat) Serious beer drinkers will want to toss their Skol cans aside and pay a visit to this fairly new addition to Botafogo, a classy but low-key bar set inside a converted two-story villa. You'll find over 200 varieties on hand, including some fine unique Brazilian microbrews (like the Diabólica Indian Pale Ale) as well as plenty of international choices.

BOTEQUIM BAR

(Map p244; 2286-3391; Visconde de Caravelas 184, Botafogo; noon-1am) Another of Botafogo's great neighborhood bars, Botequim is an old-school, down-at-the-heels watering hole serving a friendly crowd. The menu has plenty of appetizers and more substantial dishes if you need something to accompany those *chopes*.

COBAL DO HUMAITÁ BAR

(Map p244; Voluntários da Pátria 446, Humaitá; 7am-2am Mon-Sat) A large food market on the western edge of Botafogo (technically in Humaitá), the Cobal transforms into a festive nightspot when the sun goes down, complete with live music and open-air eating and drinking.

GAROTA DA URCA BAR

(Map p244; 2541-8585; João Luís Alves 56, Urca; noon-1am Sun-Thu, to 2:30am Fri & Sat) A neighborhood crowd gathers over *chope* and *salgados* (snacks) in the evening at this low-key spot.

BAR BUKOWSKI CLUB

(Map p244; 2244-7303; Álvaro Ramos 270, Botafogo; admission R$35; 10pm-6am Thu-Sat) Paying homage to the bohemian American writer, this club has a downstairs dance floor and bar, and an upstairs level for live bands playing rock, pop and blues. It's a great scene, and usually attracts a fun crowd. There's also a pool table, darts and you can have a go at one of the water pipes.

CASA DA MATRIZ CLUB

(Map p244; 2266-1014; www.casadamatriz.com.br; Henrique de Novaes 107, Botafogo; admission R$15-30; from 11pm, closed Tue & Sun) Artwork lines this space in Botafogo. With numerous rooms to explore (lounge, screening room, dance floors), this old mansion embodies the creative side of the *carioca* (resident of Rio) spirit. It usually attracts a student crowd. Check the website for party listings.

PISTA 3 CLUB

(Map p244; 2266-9691; São João Batista 14, Botafogo; admission R$20-35; midnight-4am Wed-Sat) Pista 3 is another good dance spot, with notable DJs spinning a wide mix of rock, electronica and funk. It has two floors: one for dancing, one for lounging (complete with pool table and an area for drinking and snacking).

ENTERTAINMENT

FAR UP LIVE MUSIC

(Map p244; ☎2286-2614; Cobal do Humaitá, Voluntários da Pátria 446, Botafogo; admission R$10-30; ⏰9pm-2am Tue-Sun) Featuring live music most nights of the week, Far Up is a good destination if you're hanging out in Humaitá. The program leans toward rock and Música Popular Brasileira (MPB), although the Wednesday night karaoke session mixes things up.

CIRCULO MILITAR DA PRAIA VERMELHA LIVE MUSIC

(Map p244; ☎2295-3397; Praça General Tibúrcio; ⏰noon-midnight Mon-Sat) Perched over the beach of the same name, Praia Vermelha has gorgeous views of Pão de Açúcar looming overhead. By night, jazzy MPB bands play from 8pm onward, making for an enviable open-air setting. The food is less spectacular, and it's best to stick to drinks and appetizers.

ESTAÇÃO RIO CINEMA

(Map p244; ☎2226-9952; Voluntários da Pátria 35, Botafogo) This two-screen cinema in Botafogo shows a range of films – Brazilian, foreign, independent and the occasional Hollywood film. It has a lovely cafe inside, as well as a shop selling used records and books with a number of works focusing on the film arts.

ESTAÇÃO BOTAFOGO CINEMA

(Map p244; ☎2226-1988; Voluntários da Pátria 88, Botafogo) One block from Estação Rio, this small three-screen theater shows a mix of Brazilian and foreign films. The small cafe in front is a good place to grab a quick *cafezinho* (small black coffee) before the movie.

SHOPPING

Shopping in Botafogo usually means heading to the high-rise mall overlooking the bay. There are, however, other options, such as the Museu do Indio's small handicrafts shop (with all pieces made by Brazilian tribes) as well as a cozy bookshop near the cinemas with a back-room cafe. Urca, quiet old soul that she is, has nothing in the way of shopping.

LIVRARIA PREFÁCIO BOOKS, MUSIC

(Map p244; ☎2527-5699; Voluntários da Pátria 39, Botafogo; ⏰10am-10pm Mon-Fri, 2-10pm Sat & Sun) This charming bookshop stocks a small selection of foreign titles as well as music. And perusers need not go hungry or thirsty while they browse for titles: a slender bar in front delivers refreshing glasses of *chope*, while seating upstairs and in the cafe in back offers heartier fare. The bookshop hosts an occasional poetry reading or record-release party.

ARTÍNDIA HANDICRAFTS

(Map p244; ☎3214-8702; Museu do Índio, Rua das Palmeiras 55, Botafogo; ⏰9am-5:30pm Mon-Fri, 1-5pm Sat & Sun) Inside the grounds of the Museu do Índio, Artíndia sells a variety of indigenous handicrafts – masks, musical instruments, toys, pots, baskets and weapons. Regional artists, mostly from northern tribes, create objects crafted from native materials like straw, clay, wood and feathers.

BOTAFOGO PRAIA SHOPPING SHOPPING CENTER

(Map p244; ☎3171-9872; Praia de Botafogo 400, Botafogo; ⏰10am-10pm Mon-Sat, 2-9pm Sun) Botafogo's large shopping center has dozens of stores, featuring Brazilian and international designers to suit every style – and clothe every part of the body. The 3rd floor's the best for top designers: check out stores such as Philippe Martins, Giselle Martins, Osklen and Equatore. The mall also has a cinema and several top-floor restaurants, such as Emporium Pax, with great panoramic views.

CASA & GOURMET SHOPPING CENTER

(Map p244; ☎2542-5693; www.casaegourmetshopping.com.br; General Severiano 97, Botafogo; ⏰10am-10pm Mon-Sat, 3-9pm Sun) Near Rio Sul Shopping, Casa & Gourmet is dedicated to home design and furnishings. It also has a handful of good restaurants, serving everything from sushi to traditional Brazilian.

RIO SUL SHOPPING SHOPPING CENTER

(Map p244; ☎2545-7200; www.riosul.com.br; Lauro Müller 116, Botafogo; ⏲10am-10pm Mon-Sat, 3-10pm Sun) The biggest shopping center you can reach without heading to Barra, Rio Sul has over 400 shops, featuring both the prominent and the obscure, cinemas, restaurants and, on weekends, overwhelming crowds.

SPORTS & ACTIVITIES

CASA DE DANÇA CARLINHOS DE JESUS DANCE

(☎2541-6186; www.carlinhosdejesus.com.br; Álvaro Ramos 11, Botafogo) At this respected dance academy in Botafogo, Carlinhos and his instructors offer evening classes in samba, *forró,* salsa and tango. On some Friday nights, open dance parties for students and guests are held. One of Botafogo's colorful *bloco* (street) parties, Dois Pra Lá, Dois Pra Cá begins from here during Carnaval.

Flamengo & Around

FLAMENGO | COSME VELHO | CATETE | GLÓRIA | LARANJEIRAS

Neighborhood Top Five

❶ Taking the steep cog train up Corcovado for a panoramic view beneath Rio's open-armed **Cristo Redentor** (Christ the Redeemer; p110).

❷ Exploring Rio's past days of demagogues and political intrigue in the **Museu da República** (p112).

❸ Admiring the colorful works of talented but little-known artists at the **Museu Internacional de Arte Naïf do Brasil** (p112).

❹ Making the short but steep climb up to the 18th-century **Igreja de Nossa Senhora da Glória do Outeiro** (p113).

❺ Taking a bike ride through the expansive **Parque do Flamengo** (p112).

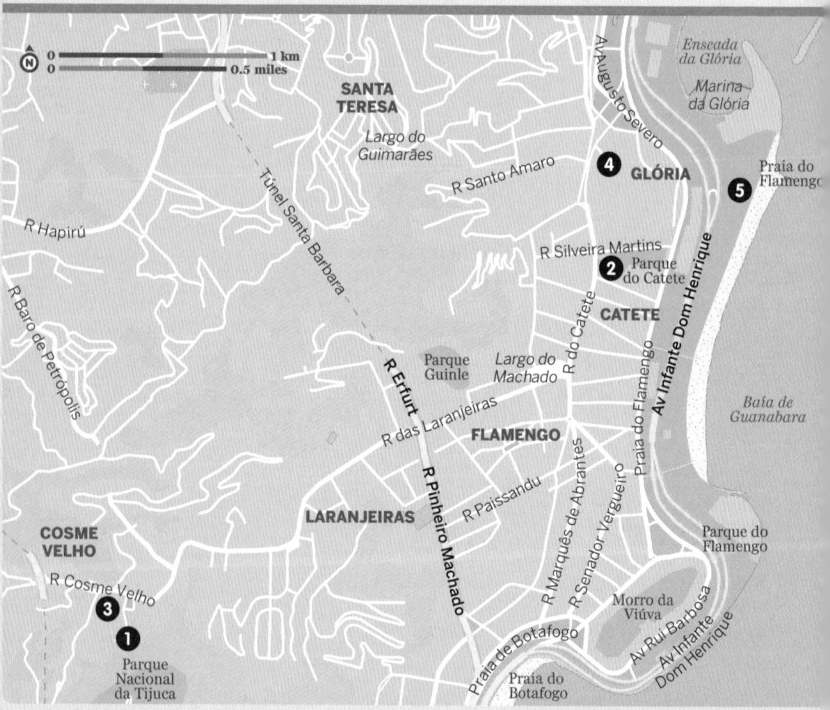

For more detail of this area see Map p242 and p241 ➡

Explore Flamengo & Around

Running east from the bay out to Corcovado, the residential neighborhoods of Flamengo, Laranjeiras, Catete, Glória and Cosme Velho have much history hidden in their old streets. The Parque do Flamengo dominates the region. Also known as the *aterro* (landfill), this beach-fronting green space is one of the world's largest urban parks, with a nationally recognized art museum, biking and running trails, sports fields, and thousands of trees and flowering plants. Inland from the park, the shaded streets of Flamengo are sprinkled with a few cafes, historic *botecos* (small neighborhood bars) and gossip-filled juice bars.

West of Flamengo, Laranjeiras is a tightly woven community with a small-town feel. Charming plazas such as the Praça São Salvador are great spots for just taking in the neighborhood. Cosme Velho lies beyond Laranjeiras and is the key access point for those heading up to the statue of Cristo Redentor by cog train.

The aging buildings of bustling Catete and Glória have seen better days. These twin districts flourished in the mid-19th century when their locations on the city outskirts made them desirable places to live. Noblemen and merchants built homes in this district, including the Barão de Novo Friburgo, who built the stately Palácio do Catete. By the end of the century, though, the wealthy began moving further out as the inner city expanded.

Local Life

➡ **Outdoors** Parque do Flamengo (p112) draws locals, especially on Sundays, when the main road through the park closes to traffic. Parque Guinle and Parque do Catete are peaceful escapes from the bustling city.

➡ **Folk Art** The Museu de Folclore Edison Carneiro (p113) has beautiful pieces from around Brazil. One-of-a-kind works of art make fine gifts at Pé de Boi (p116).

➡ **Hangouts** Centro Cultural Oi Futuro (p112) often hosts cuttiing-edge exhibits, and stages plays and concerts.

Getting There & Away

Flamengo

➡ **Bus** Leblon, Ipanema and Copacabana (571 and 573).

➡ **Metro** Flamengo, Largo do Machado, Catete, Glória.

Laranjeiras & Cosme Velho

➡ **Bus** Leblon (570 & 583), Ipanema and Copacabana (569 & 583).

➡ **Express bus** 580 from Largo do Machado metro station.

Best Places to Eat

➡ Casa da Suíça (p115)

➡ Intihuasi (p114)

➡ Luigi's (p114)

➡ Nanquim (p114)

For reviews, see 113 ➡

Best Places to Drink

➡ Belmonte (p115)

➡ Bar do Serafim (p115)

➡ Herr Brauer (p115)

➡ Devassa (p115)

For reviews, see p115 ➡

Best Live Music

➡ Casa Rosa (p115)

➡ Severyna de Laranjeiras (p116)

➡ Cariocando (p114)

For reviews, see p115 ➡

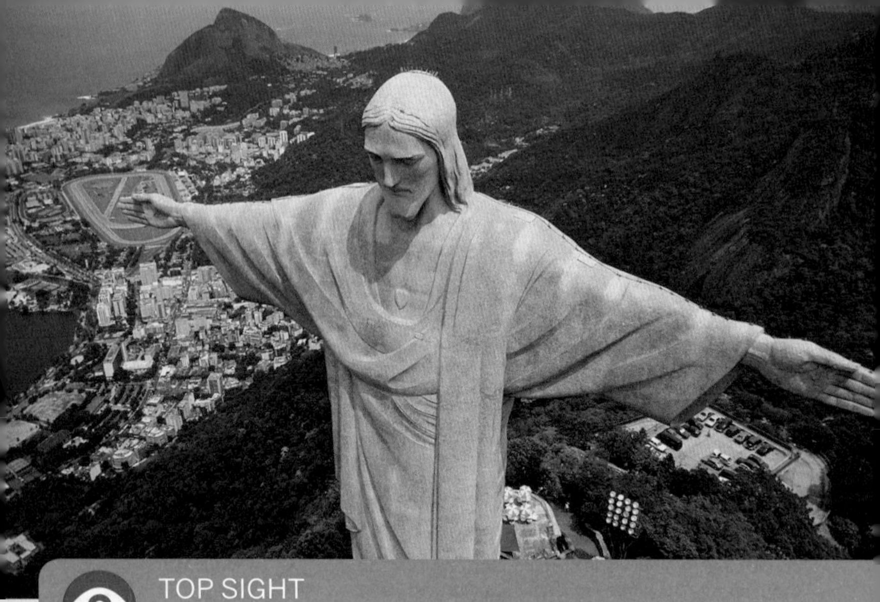

TOP SIGHT
CRISTO REDENTOR

One of Rio's most identifiable landmarks, the magnificent 38m-high Cristo Redentor (Christ the Redeemer) looms large atop the granite mountain of Corcovado. From here, the statue has stunning views over Rio, which probably explains the contented expression on his face. There are various ways to reach the statue, though the traditional way is via a steep cog train, which ascends through tropical forest and adds a touch of excitement to the experience.

The Views

Corcovado, which means 'hunchback,' rises straight up from the city to a height of 710m, and at night the brightly lit statue is visible from nearly every part of the city. When you reach the top, you'll notice the Redeemer's gaze directed at Pão de Açúcar (Sugarloaf Mountain), with his left arm pointing toward the Zona Norte, and Maracanã football stadium crowding the foreground. You can also see the international airport on Ilha do Governador just beyond and the Serra dos Órgãos mountain range in the far distance. Beneath Christ's right arm you can see Lagoa Rodrigo de Freitas, Hipódromo de Gávea, Jardim Botânico, and over to Ipanema and Leblon.

Getting to the Statue

Corcovado lies within the Floresta da Tijuca. The most popular way is from the cog station to take the red narrow-gauge train that departs every 30 minutes, and takes approximately 20 minutes to reach the top. To reach the cog station, take any 'Cosme Velho' bus: you can take bus 583 from Copacabana, Ipanema or Leblon.

DON'T MISS...

- The hike up Corcovado from Parque Lage.
- The splendid views along the way (sit on the right of the train for the best scenery).
- Other nearby sites in Cosme Velho.

PRACTICALITIES

- ☎2558-1329
- www.corcovado.com.br
- Cosme Velho 513, cog station
- adult/child R$46/23
- ⏲8am-7pm

There's also a road going up to the base of the monument. A private car or taxi will go only as far as Paineiras parking lot, from which you must transfer to an authorized van to go the 2km further to the top (R$25 per person). You can also go by van from Corcovado train station. Freelance guides and drivers linger around the train station capitalizing on the often long lines that form during peak season. A roundtrip ride costs R$25.

The most challenging way to reach the statue is on foot. You'll need a moderate level of fitness and plenty of water. It's a two-and-a-half-hour walk, with a few tough sections. The trail starts at Parque Lage near Jardim Botânico and goes through rainforest to the heights of Corcovado. At the end of the trail you'll still need to pay the admission (R$25), which includes the van ride another 1km to the site.

Historical Background

Named one of the world's Seven New Wonders in 2007, Cristo Redentor is Brazil's largest and most recognized monument. The Redeemer, which opened in 1931, is considered to be the world's largest art-deco statue. It's not a gift from the French, as is popularly believed. However, the chief sculptor, Paul Landowski, was of French-Polish origin and carried out much of the construction in France. He collaborated with the Rio architect-engineer Heitor Silva Costa (1873–1947). Many organizations helped make the statue a reality, including several individuals who went door-to-door asking for contributions.

The idea of the statue originated in 1921 when a group called Círculo Carioca held a competition for a religious monument to commemorate Brazil's upcoming 100 years of independence. Heitor's winning project, which took 10 years to build, was considered particularly ambitious at the time – naysayers doubted whether it could be accomplished at all. Heitor's original idea depicted Christ as a vertical form with a long cross held against his side but the committee wanted something recognizable from a great distance, so the crosslike outstretched arms were chosen instead. Today it's one of Brazil's most frequented attractions, welcoming more than one million visitors a year.

When to Go

Or rather when *not* to go: avoid going on weekends when the crowds are thickest. Obviously, keep an eye on the sky and don't bother going on cloudy or overcast days. Your best bet for beating the crowds is to go early.

CRISTO ON FILM

The benign savior has played a supporting role in a few Hollywood films. It has appeared in *Now, Voyager* (1942) starring Bette Davis, and Alfred Hitchcock's *Notorious* (1946) with Cary Grant and Ingrid Bergman. More recently, the disaster film *2012*, which depicted the end of the world in vivid, unadulterated glory, showed Cristo crumbling as a giant tidal wave destroys the city. As an aside, the archdiocese of Brazil didn't take kindly to the depiction and sued Columbia Pictures for copyright infringement – using the image without permission.

If you visit the statue by cog train, you can visit a couple of nearby sites that make a good add-on to the day's exploring. A short stroll west is the Museu Internacional de Arte Naïf do Brasil, with a unique collection of works from around the world (and discounted admission if you show your Corcovado ticket). A bit further along is the Largo do Boticario, a curious slice of Rio that seems straight out of the 1800s.

SIGHTS

Flamengo

PARQUE DO FLAMENGO PARK

(Parque Brigadeiro Eduardo Gomes; Map p242) Officially called Parque Brigadeiro Eduardo Gomes, Parque do Flamengo was the result of a landfill project that leveled the São Antônio hill in 1965, and now spreads all the way from downtown Rio through Glória, Catete and Flamengo, and on around to Botafogo. The 1.2 sq km of land reclaimed from the sea now stages every manner of *carioca* (resident of Rio) outdoor activity.

Cyclists and rollerbladers glide along the myriad paths, while the many football fields and sports courts are framed against the sea. On Sundays and holidays, the avenues through the park are closed (from 7am to 6pm).

Designed by famous Brazilian landscaper Burle Marx (who also landscaped Brasília), the park features some 170,000 trees of 300 different species. In addition there are three museums in the park: the Museu de Arte Moderna, the Monumento Nacional aos Mortos da II Guerra Mundial and the Museu Carmen Miranda.

MUSEU CARMEN MIRANDA MUSEUM

(Map p242; ☎2334-4293; Av Rui Barbosa 560; ⏰10am-5pm Tue-Fri, 1-5pm Sat & Sun) FREE Once the highest-paid entertainer in the USA, Carmen Miranda was the only Brazilian to leave her prints in Hollywood's Walk of Fame. Although she's largely forgotten there, the talented Brazilian singer still has her fans in Rio and has long been a cult icon among the gay community. At this tiny museum you can peek at photographs, hear music, watch a few film clips and check out some of Miranda's over-the-top platform heels.

CENTRO CULTURAL OI FUTURO ARTS CENTER

(Map p241; ☎3131-3060; www.oifuturo.org.br; Dois de Dezembro 63; ⏰galleries 11am-5pm Tue-Sun, lobby to 8pm Tue-Sun) FREE One of Rio's most visually exciting new additions is this modern arts center on the edge of Flamengo. With 2000 sq meters of exhibition space spread across six floors, the center features temporary multimedia installations that run the gamut from architecture and urban design to pop art, photo-journalism and eye-catching video art.

There's also a permanent exhibition on the history of telecommunications in Brazil. The top floor houses an auditorium where visitors can attend concerts and plays, or catch a documentary.

Cosme Velho

MUSEU INTERNACIONAL DE ARTE NAÏF DO BRASIL MUSEUM

(Map p242; ☎2205-8612; Cosme Velho 561; adult/child R$12/6; ⏰10am-6pm Tue-Fri, to 4pm Sat) A short walk west from the Corcovado cog train station, this small museum has a fascinating collection of colorful paintings made by artists often working well outside of the establishment. Also known as primitivist, *arte naïf* paintings often deal with marginalized peoples – Roma, sharecroppers, ghetto dwellers – and although small, the collection has pieces from 100 countries, giving a truly global reach to the exhibition.

Highlights here include a massive, much-reproduced painting by Lia Mittarakis, which depicts a vibrant Rio with Cristo Redentor as the focal point. Circling the room above it, 'Brasil, 5 Séculos' (Brazil, 5 Centuries), is one long canvas showing key points in Brazil's history from 1500 to the 1960s. Visitors receive a 50% discount by showing a ticket stub from the Corcovado cog train.

LARGO DO BOTICÁRIO HISTORIC SITE

(Map p242; Cosme Velho 822) The brightly painted houses on this picturesque plaza date from the early 19th century. Largo do Boticário was named in honor of the Portuguese gentleman – Joaquim Luiz da Silva Souto – who once ran a *boticário* (apothecary) utilized by the royal family. The sound of a brook coming from the nearby forest adds to the plaza's charm. Occasional art and cultural events are hosted here.

Catete

MUSEU DA REPÚBLICA MUSEUM

(Map p241; ☎3235-3693; www.museudarepublica.org.br; Rua do Catete 153; admission R$6, Wed & Sun free; ⏰10am-noon & 1-5pm Tue-Fri, 2-6pm Sat & Sun) The Museu da República, located in the Palácio do Catete, has been wonderfully restored. Built between 1858 and 1866 and easily distinguished by the bronze condors on the eaves, the palace was home to the president of Brazil from 1896 until 1954, when President Getúlio Vargas committed suicide here.

Vargas made powerful enemies in the armed forces and the political right wing, and was attacked in the press as a communist for his attempts to raise the minimum wage and increase taxes on the middle and upper classes. Tensions reached a critical level when one of Vargas' bodyguards fired shots at a journalist. Although the journalist was unharmed, an air force officer guarding him was killed, giving the armed forces the pretext they needed to demand the resignation of Vargas. In response, Vargas committed suicide, and his emotional suicide note read, 'I choose this means to be with you [the Brazilian people] always…I gave you my life; now I offer my death.' The 3rd-floor bedroom in which the suicide occurred is eerily preserved.

The museum has a good collection of art and artifacts from the Republican period, and also houses a good lunch restaurant, an art-house cinema and a bookstore.

PARQUE GUINLE PARK

(Map p241; Paulo Cesar de Andrade 407) This handsomely landscaped park is a pleasant refuge from busy Rua das Laranjeiras outside its sphinx-guarded gates. It has a small wooded area, a tiny lake with ducks and always a few *cariocas* lounging on the grass.

Designed by French landscape architect Gochet (with later flourishes by Roberto Burle Marx), the park is also home to the dramatic Palácio das Laranjeiras, the state governor's residence, and currently closed to visitors. The palace overlooks the west side of the park and is partially hidden by the thicket of trees.

MUSEU DE FOLCLORE EDISON CARNEIRO MUSEUM

(Map p241; ☎2285-0441; www.cnfcp.gov.br; Rua do Catete 179; ⏰11am-6pm Tue-Fri, 3-6pm Sat & Sun) FREE Created in 1968, the museum is an excellent introduction to Brazilian folk art, particularly from the Northeast. Its permanent collection comprises 1400 pieces, and includes Candomblé costumes, ceramic figurines and religious costumes used in festivals. The museum also features a folklore library and a small shop, selling handicrafts, books and folk music. The museum is located next door to the Palácio do Catete.

PARQUE DO CATETE PARK

(Map p241) The small landscaped park on the grounds of the Palácio do Catete provides a quiet refuge from the city. Its pond and shade-covered walks are popular with neighborhood strollers and children. Special performances in the park include concerts and plays.

Glória

IGREJA DE NOSSA SENHORA DA GLÓRIA DO OUTEIRO CHURCH

(Map p241; ☎2557-4600; www.outeirodagloria.org.br; Praça Nossa Senhora da Glória 135; ⏰9am-noon & 1-4pm Mon-Fri, 9am-noon Sat & Sun) This tiny church atop Ladeira da Glória commands lovely views out over Parque do Flamengo and the bay. Considered one of the finest examples of religious colonial architecture in Brazil, the church dates from 1739 and became the favorite of the royal family upon their arrival in 1808.

Some of the more fascinating features of the church are its octagonal design, its single tower (through which visitors enter), the elaborately carved altar (attributed to the Brazilian sculptor Mestre Valentim) and its elegant 18th-century tiles.

EATING

Flamengo has a mix of longtime local favorites and stylish newcomers. Rua Marquês de Abrantes is one of the best streets on which to see old and new vying for attention. Laranjeiras doesn't have much of a restaurant scene, but the neighborhood has several charming options for those wanting to get off the beaten path. Catete and Glória are dotted with inexpensive juice bars and lunch counters, making them good areas for those eating on a dime. Most places are along Rua do Catete, with a couple of standouts hidden along the back streets.

Flamengo

SÍRIO LIBANEZA MIDDLE EASTERN $

(Map p242; www.rotisseriasl.com.br; Largo do Machado 29, Loja 16-19, Flamengo; snacks R$7-22; ⏰8am-11pm Mon-Sat; 📶) Always packed, this bustling place serves up tasty and cheap Syrian-Lebanese cuisine and great juices. Try the hearty *kibe de forno* (oven-baked ground beef dish with spices), a hummus platter or *koftas*, followed by baklava and other sweets. It's inside the Galleria Condor on Largo do Machado.

TACACÁ DO NORTE AMAZONIAN $

(Map p242; ☎2205-7545; Barão do Flamengo 35, Flamengo; tacacá R$16; ⏲9am-11pm Mon-Sat) In the Amazonian state of Pará, people order their Tacacá late in the afternoon from their favorite street vendor. In Rio, you don't have to wait until the sun is setting. The fragrant soup of manioc paste, lip-numbing *jambu* (a Brazilian vegetable) leaves, and fresh and dried shrimp isn't for everyone. But then again, neither is the Amazon. This simple lunch counter also savory bowls of *açai*, which is how folks in the Amazon eat this berry – and quite different from the sweet juice versions served everywhere else in Rio.

RESTAURANTE KIOTO JAPANESE $$

(Map p242; ☎2225-5705; 3rd fl, Ministerio Tavares Lira 105, Flamengo; all-you-can-eat lunch/dinner R$40/50; ⏲noon-midnight) Hidden on a street behind Largo do Machado this simple, well-concealed restaurant (it's above a pool hall) is worth seeking out when craving a sushi feast that won't break the bank. There's an enormous variety of rolls at the buffet, and you can take pride in dining in a restaurant known to only a handful of *cariocas*.

INTIHUASI PERUVIAN $$

(Map p242; ☎2225-7653; Barão do Flamengo 35D, Flamengo; mains R$30-57; ⏲noon-3pm & 7-11pm Mon-Sat) Colorfully decorated with Andean tapestries and artwork, this Peruvian restaurant serves mouth-watering ceviches, *papas rellenas* (meat-filled potatoes), seafood soups and other classic dishes from the Andes. For a break from caipirinhas, try a pisco sour or a nonalcoholic *chicha morada* (a sweet concoction made from purple corn).

NANQUIM BUFFET $$

(Map p241; ☎2556-5119; Rua do Pinheiro 10, Flamengo; per kg R$70; ⏲noon-3:30pm) Hidden inside the Instituto dos Arquitetos on a quiet street, this inviting restaurant has a small but excellent self-service lunchtime buffet. Pastas, seafood, risotto, quiches, vegetarian dishes and salads are among the options. The 19th-century building is a mix of rustic and modern, with designs and sketches by Oscar Niemeyer adorning the walls. Other branches in **Jardim Botânico** (Map p234; ☎3874-0015; Rua Jardim Botânico 644, Jardim Botânico) and Ipanema offer the same mix of contemporary design and good food.

PORCÃO RIO'S BRAZILIAN, BARBECUE $$$

(Map p242; ☎3461-9020; Av Infante Dom Henrique, Flamengo; all-you-can-eat R$102; ⏲noon-midnight) Set in the Parque do Flamengo with a stunning view of Pão de Açúcar, Porcão Rio's is consistently ranked by restaurant critics as the city's best *churrascaria* (traditional barbecue restaurant). Whether you believe the hype – or simply come for the view – you're in for an eating extravaganza. Arrive early, both to score a good table and to see the view before sunset.

Laranjeiras

LUIGI'S ITALIAN $$

(Map p242; ☎2205-5331; Senador Corrêia 10, Laranjeiras; mains R$27-45; ⏲noon-midnight Tue-Sun) Well off the beaten path, Luigi's is a casual Italian restaurant set in an old villa in Laranjeiras. Join neighborhood regulars for a drink on the small covered courtyard or head to blessed air-conditioning for homemade pastas, authentic pizzas (fired up in the wood-burning oven) and good-value lunch specials (two courses for R$22).

Catete

CARIOCANDO BRAZILIAN $$

(Map p241; ☎2557-3646; http://barcariocando.com.br/site/; Silveira Martins 139, Catete; per kg R$38; ⏲noon-3pm & 7pm-midnight Mon-Sat) This atmospheric pay-by-weight restaurant serves up a good selection of Brazilian dishes by day, and transforms to a live music spot (with a mostly drinks and appetizers menu) by night (cover charge around R$20). Saturday afternoons, which feature *feijoada* and live *choro* or samba, are a great time to stop in (per person R$39).

ESTAÇÃO REPÚBLICA BUFFET $$

(Map p241; ☎2225-2650; Rua do Catete 104, Catete; per kg R$46; ⏲11am-midnight) Estação's buffet table is a neighborhood institution, featuring an extensive selection of salads, meats, pastas and vegetables. After 6pm the restaurant offers all-you-can-eat pastas, pizzas and crepes (R$20).

CATETE GRILL BUFFET **$$**

(Map p241; ☎2285-3442; Rua do Catete 239, Catete; per kg R$52; ⊙11am-11pm) The Catete Grill has an excellent buffet with a wide range of seafood (including langostinha), grilled meats, sushi, pastas, salads, appetizers and baked dishes.

Glória

TABERNA DA GLÓRIA BRAZILIAN **$$**

(Map p241; ☎2265-7835; Rua do Russel 32, Glória; mains R$32-60; ⊙noon-1am) On a small plaza in the heart of Glória, this large outdoor eatery serves decent Brazilian staples, and in abundance – most dishes here serve two. Next door is a roast chicken restaurant and both are fine spots to enjoy an ice-cold *chope* (draft beer) and open-air ambience.

CASA DA SUÍÇA SWISS **$$$**

(Map p241; ☎2252-5182; Cândido Mendes 157, Glória; mains R$44-77; ⊙noon-3pm & 7pm-midnight) Tucked inside the Swiss embassy, this cozy restaurant serves top-notch steak tartare, though it specializes in flambés and fondues. The Casa da Suíça creates an almost tangible aura of sensuality – perhaps due to those open fires flaring inside.

DRINKING & NIGHTLIFE

Few tourists visit the bars in Flamengo, which are mostly low-key neighborhood hangouts that are popular around happy hour. Rua Marquês de Abrantes is the best street to take in the scene, with bars and restaurants attracting a drinking crowd. Laranjeiras is best known for Rua Alice, which sports a couple of traditional *botecos* as well as the excellent Casa Rosa.

BELMONTE BOTECO

(Map p242; ☎2552-3349; Praia do Flamengo 300, Flamengo; ⊙9am-2am) One of the classic *botecos* in Rio, Belmonte is a vision of Rio from the '50s. Globe lights hang overhead as patrons down ice-cold drafts from the narrow bar. Meanwhile, unhurried waiters make their way across the tile floors, carrying plates of *pasteis de camarão* (shrimp pasties) or steak sandwiches. This hugely successful chain is now widespread across Rio.

BAR DO SERAFIM BAR

(Map p242; ☎2225-2843; Alice 24A; ⊙11am-11:30pm Mon-Wed, to 1am Thu-Sat, to 6pm Sun) On a lively stretch of Rua Alice, the Bar do Serafim is a simple, convivial *boteco* serving tasty Portuguese appetizers and plenty of *chope*. It's been around since 1944 and remains an institution (and popular happy-hour spot) among neighborhood regulars.

HERR BRAUER BAR

(Map p242; ☎2225-4359; Rua Barão do Flamengo 35; ⊙noon-midnight Tue-Sun, noon-4pm Mon) Dedicated to the great beers of the world, this cozy drinking den serves Belgian beers (such as Duvel and Deus), German labels (Erdinger, Warsteiner), English brew (Abbot Ale, Newcastle), plus Guinness, Brazilian microbrews and dozens of other offerings (some 80 labels in all). Stop in for happy hour (6pm to 8pm) when you can get a first-rate pint for R$14.

DEVASSA BOTECO

(Map p242; ☎2556-0618; Senador Vergueiro 2, Flamengo; ⊙noon-1am) A particularly inviting branch of the growing Devassa network, this bar is set on a shaded square, and serves the usual Devassa hits, including great drafts.

ARMAZÉM DO CHOPP BAR

(Map p242; ☎2225-1796; Marquês de Abrantes 66, Flamengo; ⊙11am-2am) On a bar-sprinkled stretch of Flamengo, this wooden barnlike bar has outdoor seating on the raised veranda in front and cooler (air-conditioned) seating inside. It's a lively local meeting spot, particularly in the early evening, and there's a good-value selection of dishes (appetizers, grilled meats) to accompany the cold beers.

ENTERTAINMENT

CASA ROSA LIVE MUSIC, CLUB

(Map p242; ☎2557-2562; www.casarosa.com.br; Alice 550, Laranjeiras; cover R$25-40; ⊙11pm-5am Fri & Sat, 5pm-1am Sun) In the first few decades of the 20th century Casa Rosa was one of the city's most famous brothels in Rio's red-light area. Times have changed somewhat and today the demure Pink

House is one of Rio's best nightspots. It has a large outdoor patio between several dance floors, where different bands play throughout the night. Saturday is the best night to go, though Casa Rosa's Sunday *feijoada* and samba party also draws its fans – go early if you plan to eat, as the *feijoada* goes fast.

MAZE INN LIVE MUSIC

(Map p241; ☎2558-5547; www.jazzrio.info; Casa 66, Tavares Bastos 414, Catete; admission before/after 10pm R$30/40; ⊙10pm-3am, 1st Fri of month) Also known as the 'Casa do Bob' after owner Bob Nadkarni, this once-a-month event is well worth attending. It's set in the guesthouse of the same name high up in Tavares Bastos (one of Rio's safest favelas). There's a fun mix of *cariocas* and expats, with live jazz and fantastic city views.

SEVERYNA DE LARANJEIRAS LIVE MUSIC

(Map p242; ☎2556-9398; www.severyna.com.br; Ipiranga 54, Laranjeiras; admission R$15; ⊙11:30am-1am) At night this broad, rustically decorated dining hall serves Northeastern fare to a backdrop of Brazilian rhythms. Large percussive groups perform samba, MPB (Música Popular Brasileira) and *forró* (popular music of the Northeast), among other styles, to a sometimes packed house. Shows begin either at 7pm or 9pm.

CENTRO CULTURAL OI FUTURO PERFORMING ARTS

(Map p241; ☎3131-3060; www.oifuturo.org.br; Dois de Dezembro 63, Catete) This hypermodern cultural center and gallery space also stages dance performances and concerts. The fare is generally not mainstream.

ESPAÇO MUSEU DA REPÚBLICA CINEMA

(Map p241; ☎3826-7984; Museu da República, Rua do Catete 153, Catete) The screening room located behind the dramatic Museu da República shows contemporary and vintage films of indie and world-cinema. Entrance is via the Parque do Catete.

SHOPPING

While not a traditional shopping destination, this area offers some worthwhile exploring, particularly if you stop in at the whimsical vintage shop on Rua Alice and the art gallery-handicrafts emporium known as Pé de Boi in Laranjeiras.

PÉ DE BOI HANDICRAFTS

(Map p242; ☎2285-4395; Ipiranga 55, Laranjeiras; ⊙10am-7pm Mon-Fri, 9am-1pm Sat) Although everything is for sale here, Pé de Boi feels more like an art gallery than a handicrafts shop, owing to the high quality of the wood and ceramic works, and the tapestries, sculptures and weavings. This is perhaps Rio's best place to see one-of-a-kind pieces by artists from Bahia, Amazonia, Minas Gerais and other parts of Brazil. Don't miss the upstairs area (with photos of some of the artists whose work is here).

MARACATU BRASIL MUSICAL INSTRUMENTS

(Map p242; ☎2557-4754; www.maracatubrasil.com.br; Ipiranga 49, Laranjeiras; ⊙10am-6pm Mon-Sat) You can't miss the lime-green building that houses this small percussion store and workshop. Inside, you can buy an *afoxê* (a gourd shaker with beads strung around it), conga and bongo drums, tambourines and other Brazilian percussion instruments. Upstairs is a drum clinic, where you can study with local instructors.

SPORTS & ACTIVITIES

MAR DO RIO DIVING

(Map p241; ☎2225-7508; www.mardorio.com.br; Shop 16, Marina da Glória, Av Infante Dom Henrique, Glória) One of several dive operators in the Marina da Glória, Mar do Rio offers two-tank dives for around R$200 on Saturday and Sunday, departing at 8:30am and returning at 2:30pm. It also offers night dives twice a month. Less-experienced divers can opt for one of the courses, including a five-day PADI-certified basic course.

MARLIN YACHT TOURS FISHING

(Map p241; ☎2225-7434; www.marlimyacht.com.br; Marina da Glória, Av Infante Dom Henrique, Glória) The Marina da Glória has a number of boating outfits, although Marlin Yacht Tours has one of the best reputations. It offers several excursions: 2-hour Baía de Guanabara (Guanabara Bay) tours (R$60 per person), four-hour cruises around the Cagarras Islands (R$95 per person) and 3-hour sailboat excursions (R$180 per person). If your pockets are deep, Marlin also hires out schooners, sailboats and motorboats, allowing you to create your own itinerary.

Centro & Cinelândia

CENTRO | CINELÂNDIA

Neighborhood Top Five

❶ Peering back through hundreds of years of Brazilian history at the interactive **Museu Histórico Nacional** (p119), one of Rio's best museums.

❷ Taking in the fascinating exhibitions at the **Centro Cultural Banco do Brasil** (p120).

❸ Getting an eyeful of ornate, gilded splendor of the magnificent 17th-century **Mosteiro de São Bento** (p121).

❹ Watching a show inside the beautifully restored **Theatro Municipal** (p120).

❺ Sipping coffee and munching on pastries inside the decadent **Confeitaria Colombo** (p127).

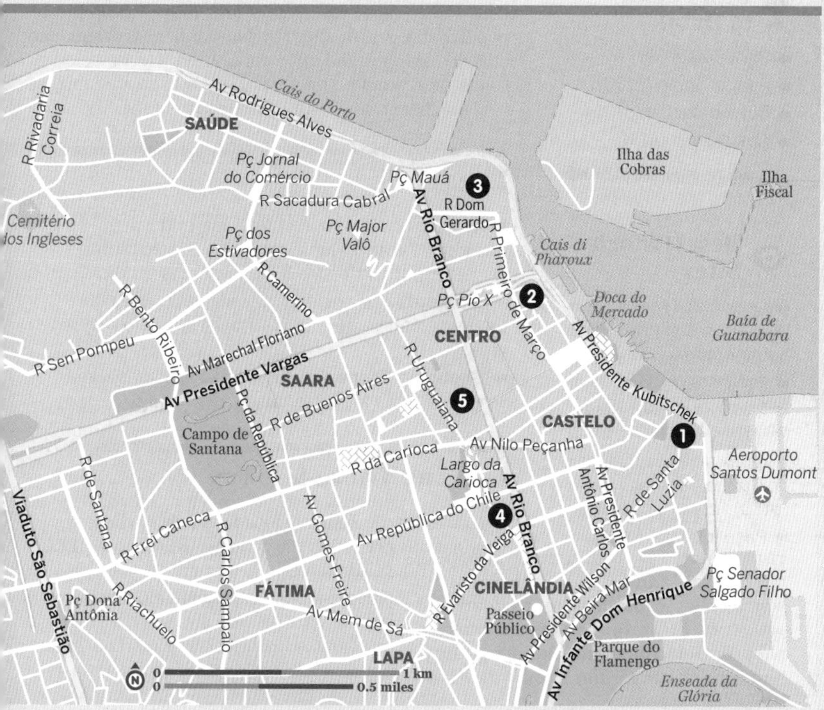

For more detail of this area see Map p246 ➡

Lonely Planet's Top Tip

Centro provides good value for money. There are lots of good museums in the area that have free admission, and stiff competition helps keep lunch prices down – particularly at the many decent pay-by-weight restaurants. For an inexpensive cruise on the bay, hop on the ferry to Niterói.

Best Places to Eat

- Cais do Oriente (p129)
- AlbaMar (p129)
- Brasserie Rosário (p128)
- Rancho Inn (p128)
- Govinda (p128)

For reviews, see p127

Best Places to Drink

- Bar Luiz (p128)
- Adega Timão (p130)
- Boteco Casual (p130)
- Amarelinho (p130)

For reviews, see p129

Best Historic Sites

- Igreja São Francisco da Penitência & Convento de Santo Antônio (p120)
- Ilha Fiscal (p127)
- Mosteiro de São Bento (p121)
- Igreja de Nossa Senhora do Carmo da Antiga Sé (p120)
- Paço Imperial (p121)

For reviews, see p120

Explore Centro & Cinelândia

Rio's business and financial hub is a wild architectural medley of old and new, with striking baroque churches and narrow colonial streets juxtaposed with looming office towers and wide, traffic-filled boulevards. During the week, it's all fuss and hurry as Rio's lawyers, secretaries and clerks jostle among the crowded streets. But despite the pace, it's well worth joining the fray as Centro has some of the city's best museums and its most intriguing historical sights, with avant-garde art galleries, 18th-century cathedrals and sprawling royal collections in former imperial buildings.

Many pedestrian-only areas crisscross Centro, and for the urban wanderer, there's no better destination in Rio. The most famous sub-district is known as Saara, a giant street bazaar crammed with discount stores and sprinkled with Lebanese restaurants.

Speaking of eating, Centro's restaurants suit every taste and budget, from greasy diners to elegant French bistros, with excellent per-kilo spots, art-nouveau cafes and old-fashioned pubs. After lunch, *cariocas* (residents of Rio) browse the bookstores, music shops, galleries and curio shops. By workday's end, the bars and streetside cafes buzz with life as *cariocas* unwind over ice-cold *chope* (draft beer).

At the southern edge of the business district, Cinelândia's shops, bars, restaurants and movie theaters are popular day and night. The bars and restaurants get crowded at lunch and after work, when street musicians sometimes wander the area. There's a greater mix of *cariocas* here than in any other section of the city.

Local Life

- **Arts** Several key concert halls are in the area, including Theatro Municipal (p120), Teatro Carlos Gomes (p131) and Teatro Rival Petrobras (p131).
- **Hangouts** The open-air bars along Travessa do Comercio and nearby streets draw festive after-work crowds.
- **Shopping Strips** The narrow, pedestrian-packed streets of Saara are intriguing for browsing.

Getting There & Away

- **Bus** From the Zona Sul look for the following destinations printed in the window: 'Rio Branco,' 'Praça XV' and 'Praça Tiradentes'.
- **Metro** Cinelândia, Carioca, Uruguaiana, Presidente Vargas.

TOP SIGHT

MUSEU HISTÓRICO NACIONAL

Home to one of the most important collections in Brazil, the National History Museum has a treasure trove of artifacts dating back to the early days of the Portuguese presence in the New World. The extensive collection, containing over 250,000 items, is set inside a sprawling 18th-century complex that was once part of the Forte de Santiago, a strategic point for the city's defense.

The collection begins with a survey of Brazil's pre-Columbian cultures in the hall titled 'Oreretama', meaning 'our land' in Tupi. From there, it continues to the Portuguese maritime empire of the 15th century, with exquisite porcelain and objects from trading in the Far East, and moves on to the colonization of Brazil. Exhibits depict early life through models (such as the curious mechanized model of a sugar mill), and don't shy away from the horrors of slavery.

There are also some fine pieces documenting the presence of the Portuguese royal family (when the entire court packed up and sailed to Rio, ahead of Napoleon's invasion), displays from the bloody war of the Triple Alliance, a reconstructed 1840s pharmacy and a fascinating collection of imperial carriages.

The 20th century receives less attention, and for an understanding of the Vargas period, you'll have to pay a visit to the former presidential palace, the Museu da República (p112), in Catete.

The best way to get there is by metro to Cinelândia station and walking 15 minutes northeast to the museum. Allow about two hours to view the whole collection.

DON'T MISS...

- Pre-Columbian exhibits portraying indigenous culture, myths and everyday tools.
- The full-size recreation of a 19th century pharmacy.
- The gilded imperial carriages.

PRACTICALITIES

- Map p246
- ☎2550-9224
- www.museuhistoriconacional.com.br
- off General Justo near Praça Marechal Âncora
- admission R$8, Sun free
- ⏲10am-5:30pm Tue-Fri, 2-6pm Sat & Sun

SIGHTS

Centro

CENTRO CULTURAL BANCO DO BRASIL — CULTURAL CENTER

(CCBB; Map p246; ☎3808-2338; Primeiro de Março 66; ⊙9am-9pm Tue-Sun) FREE Housed in a beautifully restored 1906 building, the Centro Cultural Banco do Brasil (CCBB) hosts some of Brazil's best exhibitions. Facilities include a cinema, two theaters and a permanent display of the evolution of currency in Brazil. There is always something going on, from exhibitions, lunchtime and evening concerts, to film screenings, so look at *O Globo*'s entertainment listings before you go.

THEATRO MUNICIPAL — THEATER

(Map p246; ☎2332-9220; www.theatromunicipal.rj.gov.br; Av 13 de Maio, Praça Floriano; guided tour R$10) Built in 1905 in the style of the Paris Opera, the magnificent Municipal Theater is the home of Rio's opera, orchestra and ballet. Its lavish interior contains many beautiful details – including the stage curtain painted by Italian artist Eliseu Visconti, which contains portraits of 75 major figures from the arts including Carlos Gomes, Wagner and Rembrandt. Hour-long guided tours are offered from Tuesday to Friday (at 12pm, 2pm, 3pm and 4pm) and Saturday (at 12pm and 2pm). It's also well worth coming for a performance.

MUSEU NACIONAL DE BELAS ARTES — MUSEUM

(Map p246; ☎2219-8474; www.mnba.gov.br; Rio Branco 199, Centro; adult/student R$8/4; ⊙10am-6pm Tue-Fri, noon-5pm Sat & Sun) Rio's fine arts museum houses more than 18,000 original paintings and sculptures, some of which date back to works brought over from Portugal by Dom João VI in 1808. One of its most important galleries is the **Galeria de Arte Brasileira**, with 20th-century classics such as Cândido Portinari's *Café*. Other galleries display Brazilian folk art, African art and furniture, as well as contemporary exhibits. Guided tours are available in English (call ahead).

IGREJA DE NOSSA SENHORA DO CARMO DA ANTIGA SÉ — CHURCH

(Map p246; Sete de Setembro 14; ⊙10am-4pm Tue-Sun) This beautifully restored church and former cathedral dates back to the 1770s, and it played an important role in the imperial days of Rio. The elaborately gilded rococo-style interior witnessed royal baptisms, weddings and funereal rites, and several kings were crowned here – including Pedro I (in 1822) and his son Pedro II (1841); it is the only place in the New World where this occurred. The royal family used to sit in the balcony boxes overlooking the altar.

IGREJA SÃO FRANCISCO DA PENITÊNCIA & CONVENTO DE SANTO ANTÔNIO — CHURCH

(Map p246; ☎2262-0197; Largo da Carioca 5; admission R$2; ⊙church 8am-7pm Mon-Fri, to 11am Sat, 9-11am Sun) Overlooking the Largo da Carioca is the baroque Igreja São Francisco da Penitência, dating from 1726. Restored to its former glory, the church's sacristy, which dates from 1745, has blue Portuguese tiles and an elaborately carved altar made out of jacaranda wood. It also has a roof panel by José Oliveira Rosa depicting St Francis receiving the stigmata.

The church's **statue of Santo Antônio** is an object of great devotion to many *cariocas* in search of a husband or wife.

PORTO MARAVILHA

Rio's docklands, located north of Centro in the neighborhoods of Gamboa and Barrio Saúde (as well as stretching into Centro, São Cristóvão and Cidade Nova), will be transformed into the Porto Maravilha (Marvelous Port; www.portomaravilha.com.br), the most exciting and ambitious of the city's transformation for the Olympic stage. The massive urban waterfront revitalization project, clocking in at an area of 5 million sq m and a projected tally of R$8 billion over 15 years, will turn a historic but underused and dilapidated port into one of Rio's showcase attractions, including new cultural attractions like the Art Museum of Rio de Janeiro (MAR), the Museu da Amanha and the Jardim do Valongo hanging gardens; and 17km of bike paths, numerous parks, and squares dotted with 15,000 new trees. As the traditional birthplace for samba and *choro*, Rio's port will indeed be singing again by 2016.

A garden on the church grounds leads to the catacombs, used until 1850. Visits must be arranged in advance.

Next door, the Convento de Santo Antônio was built between 1608 and 1615. It contains the chapel of Nossa Senhora das Dores da Imaculada Conceição. Fabiano de Cristo, a miracle-working priest who died in 1947, is entombed here.

MOSTEIRO DE SÃO BENTO CHURCH

(Map p246; ☎2206-8100; Dom Gerardo 68; ⏱7am-6pm) This is one of the finest colonial churches in Brazil. Built between 1617 and 1641 on Morro de São Bento, the monastery has a superb view over the city. The simple facade hides a baroque interior richly decorated in gold. Among its historic treasures are wood carvings designed by Frei Domingos da Conceição (and made by Alexandre Machado) and paintings by José de Oliveira Rosa.

On Sunday, the High Mass at 10am includes a choir of Benedictine monks singing Gregorian chants; early risers can also hear mass on weekdays at 7:30am. To reach the monastery from Rua Dom Gerardo, go to No 40 and take the elevator to the 5th floor.

REAL GABINETE PORTUGUÊS DE LEITURA HISTORIC BUILDING

(Map p246; ☎2221-3138; Luís de Camões 30; ⏱9am-6pm Mon-Fri) FREE Built in the Portuguese manueline style in 1837, the gorgeous Portuguese Reading Room houses over 350,000 works, many dating from the 16th, 17th and 18th centuries. It also has a small collection of paintings, sculptures and ancient coins.

PAÇO IMPERIAL HISTORIC BUILDING

(Map p246; ☎2215-2622; Praça XV (Quinze) de Novembro 48; ⏱noon-6pm Tue-Sun) FREE The former imperial palace was originally built in 1743 as a governor's residence. Later it became the home of Dom João and his family when the Portuguese throne transferred the royal seat of power to the colony. In 1888 Princesa Isabel proclaimed the Freedom from Slavery Act from the palace's steps. The building was neglected for many years but has been restored and is used for exhibitions and concerts; its cinema frequently screens foreign and art-house films.

MUSEU DE ARTE MODERNA MUSEUM

(MAM; Map p246; ☎2240-4944; www.mamrio.org.br; Av Infante Dom Henrique 85; admission R$12; ⏱noon-6pm Tue-Fri, to 7pm Sat & Sun) At the northern end of Parque do Flamengo, MAM is immediately recognizable by the striking postmodern edifice designed by Alfonso Eduardo Reidy. The landscaping of Burle Marx is no less impressive.

After a devastating fire in 1978 that consumed 90% of its collection, the Museu de Arte Moderna is finally back on its feet, and now houses 11,000 permanent works, including pieces by Brazilian artists Bruno Giorgi, Di Cavalcanti and Maria Martins. Curators often bring excellent photography and design exhibits to the museum, and the cinema hosts regular film festivals throughout the year.

CENTRO DE ARTE HÉLIO OITICICA MUSEUM

(Map p246; ☎2242-1012; Luis de Camões 68; ⏱11am-6pm Tue-Fri, to 5pm Sat & Sun) FREE This avant-garde museum is set in a 19th-century neoclassical building that originally housed the Conservatory of Music and Dramatic Arts. Today the center displays permanent works by the artist, theoretician and poet Hélio Oiticica, as well as bold contemporary art exhibitions, well-tuned to Oiticica's forward-leaning aesthetics.

MUSEU NAVAL MUSEUM

(Map p246; ☎2104-6851; Dom Manuel 15, Praça XV (Quinze) de Novembro; ⏱noon-5pm Tue-Sun) FREE Chronicling the history of the Brazilian navy from the 16th century to the present, the museum also has exhibitions of model warships, maps and navigational instruments.

Naval enthusiasts should also visit the nearby Espaço Cultural da Marinha, on the waterfront near the eastern end of Av Presidente Vargas. It contains the Riachuelo submarine, which you can wander through, the Bauru (a WWII torpedo boat) and the royal family's large rowboat. The boat tour to Ilha Fiscal leaves from the docks here.

MUSEU HISTÓRICO E DIPLOMÁTICO MUSEUM

(Map p246; ☎2253-2828; Av Marechal Floriano 196; ⏱tours 2pm, 3pm & 4pm Mon, Wed & Fri) FREE Housed in the neoclassical Palácio Itamaraty, the Museum of History and Diplomacy served as the private presidential home from 1889 until 1897. The museum has an impressive collection of art, antiques and maps. Visits are by guided 45-minute tours. Call ahead to ensure an English-speaking guide. The museum is just a short walk northwest of Presidente Vargas metro station.

BARBEARIA
ZE DO CARMO
PRAÇA CANTÃO
TAMOS EM LUTO!

PEETER VIISIMAA / GETTY IMAGES ©

1. Santa Marta favela 2. Hillside favela 3. Child painting a mural

Favelas

In recent years, many of Rio's favelas have been transformed. Although controversial, the pacification plan – police invasions to drive out drug traffickers followed by the installation of security posts – has been largely successful. Public investment has poured into these safe harbors, helping to unite them with the rest of the city.

Traveling in Style

New transportation has been installed at some favelas, including cable cars at sprawling Complexo do Alemão (p148), elevators whisking residents up to Cantagalo (p59) and Pavão/Pavãozinho, and a tram to the top of Santa Marta. As part of the port beautification (Porto Maravilha), plans are underway to add a cable car to Morro da Providência, considered Rio's oldest favela, and one of its most crime-ridden until recently.

Artful Intentions

Favelas have attracted artists. The rainbow-colored hues painted across residences overlooking Praça Cantão in Santa Marta have helped show the world that a favela is more than a backdrop of poverty and hopelessness. The giant photographs by French artist JR have raised awareness of marginalized communities. In Morro da Providência, his oversized portraits plastered on homes, show the human, individual face of the favela rather than the faceless million-plus who live in Rio's shanty towns.

FAVELA EXPERIENCES

- ➡ Marcelo Armstrong and Paulo Amendoim lead recommended tours around Rocinha.
- ➡ Take in the aerial views over Complexo do Alemão or Morro do Cantagalo in Ipanema.
- ➡ Spend the night in a favela guesthouse; it's a great way to see beyond the stereotypes.

IGREJA DE NOSSA SENHORA DE CANDELÁRIA CHURCH

(Map p246; ☎2233-2324; Praça Pio X; ⏱8am-4pm Mon-Fri, to noon Sat, 9am-1pm Sun) The construction of the original church (dating from the late 16th century) on the present site was credited to a ship's captain who was nearly shipwrecked at sea. Upon his safe return he vowed to build a church to NS de Candelária. A later design led to its present-day grandeur.

Built between 1775 and 1894, NS de Candelária was the largest and wealthiest church of imperial Brazil. The interior is a combination of baroque and Renaissance styles. The ceiling above the nave reveals the origin of the church. The cupola, fabricated entirely from limestone shipped from Lisbon, is one of its most striking features. Mass is said at 7am daily except Monday and Saturday, and at 9am and 11am on Sunday. But be sure to watch out for traffic as you cross to the church.

IGREJA DE NOSSA SENHORA DO ROSÁRIO E SÃO BENEDITO CHURCH

(Map p246; Uruguaiana 77; ⏱7am-5pm Mon-Fri, to 1pm Sat) Sadly, a fire in 1967 destroyed much of the elaborate interior of this historic church, leaving only the unadorned walls that date back to the early 1700s. Dedicated to our Lady of the Rosary as well as the black St Benedict, the church has been an important icon for Afro-Brazilians, serving a congregation of mostly black and mulatto Catholics over the years. Penitents leave offerings to the black martyr Anastasia (venerated as a saint, but not recognized officially by the Catholic church) in a candle-lit room next to the entrance. A huge crowd gathers every May 13, to commemorate the end of slavery.

PRAÇA XV (QUINZE) DE NOVEMBRO HISTORIC SITE

(Near Rua Primeiro de Março) The first residents on this historic site were Carmelite fathers who built a convent here in 1590. It later came under the property of the Portuguese crown and became Largo do Paço, which surrounded the royal palace (Paço Imperial). The square was later renamed Praça XV (Quinze) de Novembro after Brazil declared itself a republic on November 15, 1822. A number of historic events took place here: the coronation of Brazil's two Emperors (Pedro I and Pedro II), the abolition of slavery and the overthrow (deposition) of Emperor Dom Pedro II in 1889.

CENTRO CULTURAL JUSTIÇA FEDERAL CULTURAL CENTER

(Map p246; ☎3261-2550; Av Rio Branco 241; ⏱noon-7pm Tue-Sun) FREE The stately building overlooking the Praça Floriano served as the headquarters of the Supreme Court (Supremo Tribunal Federal) from 1909 to 1960. Following a restoration project completed in 2001, it opened as a cultural center, featuring exhibitions on photography and Brazilian art, though some fascinating shows from abroad sometimes make their way here.

CENTRO CULTURAL CORREIOS CULTURAL CENTER

(Map p246; ☎2253-1580; Visconde de Itaboraí 20; ⏱noon-7pm Tue-Sun) FREE In a grand edifice dating from the 1920s, this cultural center houses three spacious floors that host a creative line-up of changing exhibitions – mostly focusing on Brazilian artists, writers and architects. Take the old-fashioned elevator to the top floor and work your way down.

TRAVESSA DO COMÉRCIO STREET

(Map p246; Near Praça XV (Quinze) de Novembro) Beautiful two-story colonial townhouses line this narrow cobblestone street leading off Praça XV (Quinze) de Novembro. The archway, called Arco de Teles, leading into the area was once part of an old viaduct running between two buildings. Today, Travessa do Comércio contains half a dozen restaurants and drinking spots that open onto the streets. It's a favorite spot for *cariocas* after work.

CASA FRANÇA-BRASIL CULTURAL BUILDING

(Map p246; ☎2332-5120; www.casafrancabrasil.rj.gov.br; Visconde de Itaboraí 78; ⏱10am-8pm Tue-Sun) FREE In a neoclassical building dating from 1820, the Casa França-Brasil sponsors changing exhibitions often dealing with political and cultural facets of *carioca* society. The classical revival building once served as a customs house. There's a restaurant attached.

BIBLIOTECA NACIONAL HISTORIC BUILDING

(Map p246; ☎2220-9484; Av Rio Branco 219; admission R$2; ⏱10am-5pm Mon-Fri, 12:30pm-4:30pm Sat & Sun) Inaugurated in 1910, the neoclassical national library is the largest in Latin America, with more than nine million volumes, including many rare books and manuscripts. Among the treasure trove are original letters written by Princess Isabel, the first newspapers printed in the country and two copies of the precious Mainz Psalter Bible, printed in 1492. Call ahead to arrange a free guided tour (available in English, Spanish or Portuguese).

PALÁCIO TIRADENTES HISTORIC BUILDING

(Map p246; ☎2588-1251; Primeiro de Março; ⏲10am-5pm Mon-Sat, noon-5pm Sun) FREE The stately Tiradentes Palace houses the seat of the legislative assembly. Exhibits on the 1st and 2nd floors relate the events that took place there between 1926 and the present. One of its darkest hours was when the National Assembly was shut down in 1937 under the Vargas dictatorship; it later served as his Department of Press and Propaganda. Most information is in Portuguese, though you can listen to a rundown of history in English at the interactive machine in the foyer. The statue in front, incidentally, is not a likeness of Russian mystic Rasputin, but rather that of martyr Tiradentes, who led the drive toward Brazilian independence in the 18th century.

CENTRO DE REFERÊNCIA DO ARTESANATO BRASILEIRO GALLERY

(Map p246; ☎3380-1850; Praça Tiradentes 71; ⏲9am-6pm Mon-Fri) FREE This tiny museum showcases the craft-making traditions across Brazil. Changing exhibits feature woodcarvings, ceramics, textiles, jewelry, metal work, basket weaving and even recycled materials in the creation of both popular and sacred art. Although nothing here is for sale, if you're interested in a particular piece, the staff can provide contact information for any of the artists represented.

CAMPO DE SANTANA PARK

(Map p246; Praça da República & Rua Frei Caneca) Campo de Santana is a pleasant park that, on September 7, 1822, was the scene of the proclamation of Brazil's independence from Portugal by Emperor Dom Pedro I of Portugal. The landscaped park with an artificial lake and swans is a fine place for a respite from the chaotic streets, and you're liable to see a few *agoutis* (a hamsterlike rodent native to Brazil) running wild here.

PASSEIO PÚBLICO PARK

(Map p246; Rua do Passeio; ⏲9am-5pm) FREE The oldest park in Rio, the Passeio Público was built in 1783 by Mestre Valentim, a famous Brazilian sculptor, who designed it

WORTH A DETOUR

NITERÓI

Niterói's principal attraction is the famous **Museu do Arte Contemporânea** (MAC; ☎2620-2400; www.macniteroi.com.br; Mirante da Boa Viagem, Niterói; admission R$6; ⏲10am-6pm Tue-Sun). Designed by Brazil's most famous architect, Oscar Niemeyer, the MAC has a wild curvilinear design that blooms like a flower (or more prosaically, a flying saucer) against sweeping bay views. Unfortunately, the exhibits inside the museum are less inspiring. To get to the MAC from the Niterói ferry terminal, turn right as you leave and walk about 50m across to the bus terminal in the middle of the road; a 47B minibus will drop you at the museum door.

The cruise from MAC across the bay, however, is perhaps just as valid a reason for leaving Rio. Out on the water, you'll have impressive views of downtown, Pão de Açúcar (p99) and the other green mountains rising up out of the city; you'll also see planes (quite close) landing and taking off at Aeroporto Santos Dumont. Try to be on the water at sunset when Centro glows with golden light. The **ferry** (☎0800-721-1012; www.grupoccr.com.br/barcas) costs R$9 return and leaves from Praça XV (Quinze) de Novembro in Centro every 20 minutes; it's usually packed with commuters. Once you reach the dock, there isn't much to see in the immediate area. From here catch a bus to the MAC or to one of the beaches – or just turn around and return by ferry.

The **Ponte Rio-Niterói** (Ponte Pres Costa E Silva) bridge offers spectacular views of the Baía de Guanabara (Guanabara Bay). It is 15.5km long, 60m high and 26.6m wide, with two three-lane roads. There's a tollbooth 3km from the Niterói city center.

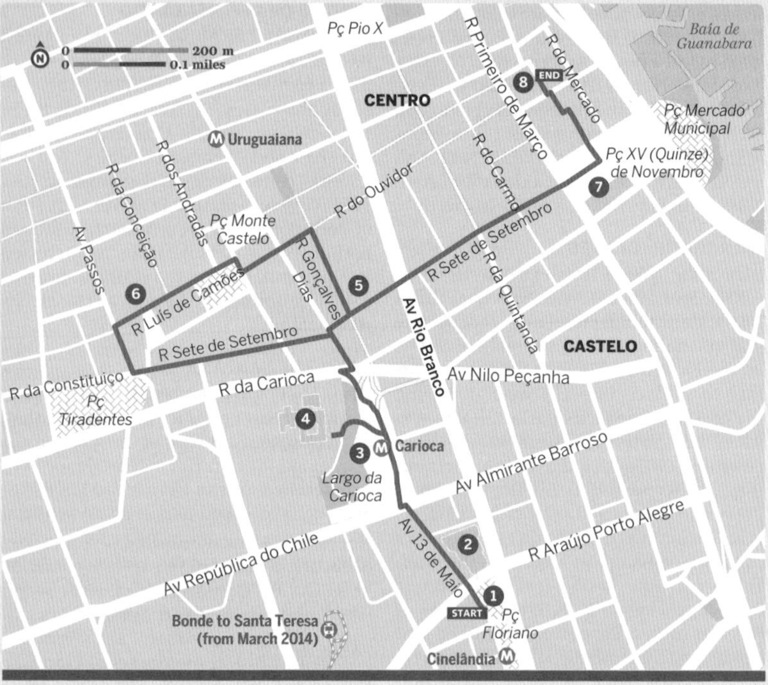

Neighborhood Walk
Historic Centro

START PRAÇA FLORIANO
END TRAVESSA DO COMÉRCIO
DISTANCE 3KM
DURATION FOUR HOURS

A mélange of historic buildings and skyscrapers, Centro is a fine place to experience the city away from its beaches and mountains. Do this tour during the week, as it's deserted (and unsafe) on weekends.

Start at the 1 **Praça Floriano**, a scenic plaza set with several outdoor cafes. On the north side, the neoclassical 2 **Theatro Municipal** (p120) is one of Rio's finest buildings, particularly after its recent R$65 million renovation. If you time it right, take a guided tour.

Stroll north along Av 13 de Maio. You'll pass through the 3 **Largo da Carioca**, a bustling area with a small market. On the hill is 4 **Igreja São Francisco da Penitência** (p120), a 17th-century church with a jaw-dropping gilded interior. Reach the church via stairs or elevator near the Carioca metro station.

After taking in the views, walk over to narrow Rua Gonçalves Dias to reach 5 **Confeitaria Colombo** for caffeine, pastries and art nouveau.

From Rua Gonçalves Dias, turn left on Rua do Ouvidor, following it to Largo de San Francisco de Paula. One block further is the 6 **Real Gabinete Português de Leitura** (p121), a historic reading room that seems straight out of 19th-century Portugal.

Turn right when exiting and pass Praça Tiradentes, before heading left over to Rua Sete de Setembro. Follow it until it ends near the 7 **Paço Imperial** (p121). Once the seat of the Portuguese rulers in Brazil, the building today houses intriguing art exhibitions, and cafes.

Leaving the Paço, cross Praça XV de Novembro and take the narrow lane beneath the arch. You'll walk along one of Centro's oldest lanes, through 8 **Travessa do Comércio** (p124), with open-air restaurants and bars. It's a fitting ending to the day's wander.

after Lisbon's botanical gardens. In 1860 the park was remodeled by French landscaper, Glaziou. The park features some large trees, a pond with islands and an interesting crocodile-shaped fountain. The entrance gate was built by Valentim. Before the Parque do Flamengo landfill, the sea came right up to the edge of this park.

CENTRO CULTURAL CARIOCA CULTURAL CENTER
(Map p246; ☎2242-9642; www.centroculturalcarioca.com.br; Rua do Teatro 37) This restored theater near Praça Tiradentes is once again a major contributor to the arts in downtown Rio. Its exposed brick walls and large wood-framed windows form the backdrop to superb musical groups – often samba – performing throughout the week, and there are dance recitals, book releases and ongoing exhibitions. Dance classes are also offered here.

Cinelândia

PRAÇA FLORIANO PLAZA
(Map p246; Av Rio Branco) The heart of modern Rio, the Praça Floriano comes to life at lunchtime and after work when the outdoor cafes are filled with beer drinkers, samba musicians and political debate. The square is also Rio's political marketplace and is the site of daily speechmaking, literature sales and street theater.

Most city marches and rallies culminate here on the steps of the old Câmara Municipal in the northwestern corner of the plaza.

MONUMENTO NACIONAL AOS MORTOS DA II GUERRA MUNDIAL MONUMENT
(☎2240-1283; Av Infante Dom Henrique 75; ⏲10am-4pm Tue-Sun) FREE This elegant monument to the soldiers who perished in WWII contains a **museum**, a **mausoleum** and the **Tomb of the Unknown Soldier**. The museum exhibits uniforms, medals and documents from Brazil's Italian campaign. There's also a small lake and **sculptures** by Ceschiatti and Anísio Araújo de Medeiros.

ILHA FISCAL HISTORIC BUILDING
(☎2233-9165; admission R$15; ⏲tours 12:30pm, 2pm & 3:30pm Thu-Sun) This eye-catching lime-green, neo-Gothic palace sitting in the Baía de Guanabara looks like something out of a child's fairytale book. It was designed by engineer Adolfo del Vecchio and completed in 1889. Originally used to supervise port operations, the palace is famous as the location of the last Imperial Ball on November 9, 1889. Today it's open for guided tours three times a day from Thursday to Sunday; tours leave from the dock near Praça XV (Quinze) de Novembro (usually by boat, but sometimes by van).

EATING

Rio's busiest neighborhood has everything from greasy lunch counters to French bistros. Most restaurants open only for lunch on weekdays. Many pedestrian-only areas throughout Centro (such as Rua do Rosário) are full of restaurants, some spilling onto the sidewalk, others hidden on upstairs floors – restaurant hunting is something of an art. Areas worth exploring include Travessa do Comércio just after work, when the restaurants and cafes fill with chatter; another early-evening gathering spot is Av Marechal Floriano, full of snack bars specializing in fried sardines and beer. Cinelândia, behind Praça Floriano, features a number of open-air cafes and restaurants.

CONFEITARIA COLOMBO CAFE $
(Map p246; ☎2505-1500; www.confeitariacolombo.com.br; Gonçalves Dias 34, Centro; pastries around R$7; ⏲9am-8pm Mon-Fri, to 5pm Sat) Stained-glass windows, brocaded mirrors and marble countertops create a lavish setting for coffee or a meal. Dating from the late 1800s, the Confeitaria Colombo serves desserts – including a good *pastel de nata* (custard tart) – befitting the elegant decor. The restaurant overhead, **Cristóvão** (Map p246; buffet R$50; ⏲noon-4pm), spreads an extensive buffet (R$70 per person) of Brazilian dishes for those wanting to further soak up the splendor.

BISTRÔ DO PAÇO CAFE $
(Map p246; ☎2262-3613; Praça XV (Quinze) de Novembro 48, Paço Imperial, Centro; mains R$14-30; ⏲noon-7pm) On the ground floor of the Paço Imperial, this informal restaurant offers a tasty assortment of quiches, salads, soups and other light fare. Save room for the delicious pies and cakes.

GOVINDA VEGETARIAN $

(Map p246; ☎3549-9108; 2nd fl, Rodrigo Silva 6, Centro; lunch R$26; ⏰11:30am-3pm Mon-Fri) Amid artwork and decorations from India, the always welcoming Hare Krishnas whip up tasty vegetarian dishes made with care. It's tucked down a narrow lane just off Rua São José and is always packed, so arrive early to get a seat.

CASA CAVÉ PATISSERIE $

(Map p246; ☎2222-2358; Sete de Setembro 137, Centro; pastries R$5-7; ⏰8:30am-7:30pm Mon-Fri, to 1pm Sat) Set with attractive tile floors and marble tabletops, this simple, historic coffeehouse (c 1860) lures in passersby with its shop windows full of tempting desserts. Try Portuguese classics like the *pastel de belém* (custard tart) or *pastel de Santa Clara* (made from eggs and almonds).

CAFÉ DO BOM CACHAÇA DA BOA CAFE $

(Map p246; ☎2509-1018; Rua da Carioca 10, Centro; sandwiches R$12-18; ⏰10am-8pm Mon-Fri, to 2pm Sat) With a vaguely professorial air, this wood-lined cafe and bookshop doles out sandwiches, coffees and ice cream, but it's best known for its *cachaça* (potent cane spirit) menu – with over 100 varieties available.

BRASSERIE ROSÁRIO FRENCH $$

(Map p246; ☎2518-3033; Rua do Rosário 34, Centro; mains R$21-58; ⏰11am-9pm Mon-Fri, to 6pm Sat) Set in a handsomely restored 1860s building, this atmospheric bistro has a hint of Paris about it. The front counters are full of croissants, *pain au chocolat* (chocolate croissant) and other baked items, while the restaurant menu features roast meats and fish, soups, baguette sandwiches and the like.

RANCHO INN CONTEMPORARY $$

(Map p246; ☎2233-6144; 2nd fl, Rua do Rosário 74, Centro; mains R$28-42; ⏰11:30am-3pm Mon-Fri) Exposed brick and tall windows lend a vaguely Parisian air to this charming lunchtime spot. You can opt for the fixed-price buffet (R$27) or order more complicated dishes off the menu: goat's milk cheese and sundried tomato salad, risotto with duck and shiitake mushrooms, followed by profiteroles, chocolate brownie à la mode or other decadent desserts.

BAR LUIZ GERMAN $$

(Map p246; ☎2262-6900; Rua da Carioca 39, Centro; mains R$26-52; ⏰11am-10pm Mon-Sat) Bar Luiz first opened in 1887, making it one of the city's oldest *cervejarias* (pubs). A festive air fills the old saloon as diners get their fill of traditional German cooking (potato salad and smoked meats), along with ice-cold drafts – including dark beer – on tap.

CAFÉ ARLEQUIM CAFE $$

(Map p246; ☎2220-8471; Praça XV (Quinze) de Novembro 48, Paço Imperial, Centro; mains R$18-36; ⏰9am-8pm Mon-Fri, 10am-6pm Sat) In the middle of a shop selling books and CDs, this small, lively, pleasantly air-conditioned cafe is a fine spot to refuel, with Italian (Illy) coffee, sandwiches, salads, quiches, lasagna and desserts.

ATELIÊ CULINÂRIO BRAZILIAN $$

(Map p246; ☎2240-2573; Praça Floriano, Cinelândia; mains R$20-40; ⏰noon-10pm Mon-Fri) Next to the art-house cinema Odeon Petrobras, this place serves up decent Brazilian fare on its open-air terrace to a festive crowd. Ateliê opens onto the Praça Floriano, which is a lively gathering spot on weekday evenings. On weekends, it stays opens during film screenings next door.

BEDUÍNO MIDDLE EASTERN $$

(Map p246; ☎2524-5142; Av Presidente Wilson 123, Centro; mains R$25-34; ⏰7am-11pm Mon-Fri, 7am-5pm Sat) Good food and fair prices are Beduíno's keys to success, with 30 different traditional Middle Eastern dishes to choose from, and a popular all-you-can-eat lunch buffet (R$42). If you're around on Tuesdays, you can stop in for a belly dancing show at 7pm.

THE LINE BRAZILIAN $$

(Map p246; ☎2224-6438; Travessa do Comércio 9; per kg R$36; ⏰11:30am-3:30pm Mon-Sat) In an atmospheric building on one of Centro's oldest streets, The Line spreads a good and reasonably priced lunch buffet. Stop in Saturday for all-you-can-eat *feijoada* (R$30 per person).

BISTRÔ THE LINE BISTRO $$

(Map p246; ☎2233-3571; Visconde de Itaboraí 78, Casa França-Brasil, Centro; mains R$30-42; ⏰10am-8pm) Inside the Casa França-Brasil, this charming restaurant serves bistro fare (risottos, grilled salmon, filet mignon) at lunchtime as well as coffee, cocktails and desserts. The veranda has a fine view of Igreja da Candelária.

WORTH A DETOUR

ILHA DE PAQUETÁ

This **tropical island** (☎ferry 0800-721-1012; www.grupoccr.com.br/barcas) in the Baía de Guanabara was once a very popular tourist spot and is now frequented mostly by families from the Zona Norte. There's a certain dirty, decadent charm to the colonial buildings, unassuming beaches and businesses catering to local tourism. The place gets crowded on weekends.

There are no cars on the island. Transport is by foot, bicycle (with literally hundreds for rent) or horse-drawn cart.

Go to Paquetá for the boat ride through Rio's famous bay and to see *cariocas* at play – especially during the Festa de São Roque, which is celebrated with fireworks, a procession and music on the weekend following 16 August.

Boats leave from near the Praça XV (Quinze) de Novembro in Centro. The ferry takes 70 minutes and will cost you R$9 for a return trip. There are nine departures daily, the most useful being 7:10am, 10:30am and 1:30pm.

CEDRO DO LÍBANO LEBANESE **$$**

(Map p246; ☎2224-0163; Senhor dos Passos 231, Centro; mains R$34-55; ⊙11am-5pm) If you can get past the wedding reception-like decor – white tablecloths and plastic chairs and tables – you can enjoy some excellent traditional Lebanese cooking at this 70-plus-year-old institution. Kibbe, *koftas* and lamb are served tender and cooked to perfection.

RIO BRASA BUFFET **$$**

(Map p246; ☎2199-9191; Ave Rio Branco 277, Centro; per kg R$63; ⊙11am-4pm Mon-Sat) Handily located near the Praça Floriana, this shiny per-kilo restaurant prepares a high-quality lunch buffet with separate counters for salads, sushi, baked dishes and grilled meats (the restaurant's specialty). Prices are lower after 2pm (per kg R$54).

DA SILVA PORTUGUESE **$$**

(Map p246; ☎2524-1010; 4th fl, Av Graça Aranha 187, Centro; all-you-can-eat R$50, after 2pm R$40; ⊙noon-4pm Tue-Sat) Hidden inside the Clube Ginástico Português, this large, simply decorated restaurant spreads one of Rio's best lunch buffets. Portuguese in flavor, Da Silva has delicious salads, steaks and seafood, along with an enormous variety of addictive *bacalhau* dishes and dozens of other dishes.

CAIS DO ORIENTE CONTEMPORARY **$$$**

(Map p246; ☎2233-2531; www.caisdooriente.com.br; Visconde de Itaboraí 8, Centro; mains R$45-60; ⊙noon-4pm Sun & Mon, to midnight Tue-Sat) Brick walls lined with tapestries stretch high to the ceiling in this almost-cinematic 1870s mansion. Set on a brick-lined street, hidden from the masses, Cais do Oriente blends elements of Brazilian and Mediterranean cooking, including a recommended *cherne* (grouper) with prawns, Brazil nuts and roasted potatoes. There's a back courtyard and an upstairs concert space that hosts periodic concerts.

ALBAMAR SEAFOOD **$$$**

(Map p246; ☎2240-8378; Praça Marechal Âncora 186; mains R$60-80; ⊙noon-5pm) AlbaMar has long been one of Rio's best seafood destinations. Top picks are fresh oysters, grilled seafood with vegetables and *moqueca* (seafood stew cooked in coconut milk) dishes. The old-fashioned green gazebolike structure offers excellent views of the Baía de Guanabara and Niterói.

DRINKING & NIGHTLIFE

Rio's working folk have some fine choices when it comes to joining the happy-hour fray. One of the most magical settings for a sundowner is along the historic Travessa do Comércio. The sidewalk tables on this narrow, cobbled lane are packed on weekday nights, particularly as the weekend nears (Thursday is always a good bet). These places see a bit of action during the day on Saturday (several restaurants along Rua do Rosario serve *feijoada* – black bean and pork stew), but close the rest of the weekend. Another choice after-work spot is Praça Floriano, with its handful of bars.

ADEGA TIMÃO BOTECO

(Map p246; ☎2516-1065; Visconde de Itaboraí 10; ⏲noon-midnight Tue-Sun) This open-sided nautical-themed bar has been around since the 1950s, serving cold beer and appetizers to those stepping in off the cobblestones. It's a great stop before or after catching an exhibit at the CCBB.

BOTECO CASUAL BAR

(Map p246; ☎2232-0250; Travessa do Comércio 26, Centro; ⏲noon-midnight Mon-Fri, to 6pm Sat) Hidden in a narrow lane leading off Praça XV (Quinze) de Novembro, Boteco Casual is one of several photogenic open-air bars on Travessa do Comércio. The narrow pedestrian lane is a popular meeting spot and a festive air arrives at workday's end as *cariocas* fill the tables spilling onto the street.

AMARELINHO BOTECO

(Map p246; ☎2240-8434; Praça Floriano 55, Cinelândia; ⏲11am-2am Mon-Sat, to midnight Sun) Easy to spot by its bright *amarelo* (yellow) awning, Amarelinho has a splendid setting on the Praça Floriano. Waiters serve plenty of *chope* (draft beer) here, wandering among the crowded tables, with the Theatro Municipal in the background. Amarelinho is a popular lunch spot but packs in even bigger crowds for that ever-important after-work brew.

ATELIÊ CULINÂRIO BAR

(Map p246; ☎2240-2573; Praça Floriano, Cinelândia; ⏲noon-10pm Mon-Fri) A lunch and after-work crowd gathers at this pleasant open-air bistro on the edge of Praça Floriano.

ESCH CAFÉ BAR

(Map p246; ☎2507-5866; Rua do Rosário 107, Centro; ⏲noon-10pm Mon-Fri) The smoky twin of the Leblon Esch Café (p71), this Esch offers the same selection of Cuban cigars from its humidor. Its dark-wood interior has stuffed leather chairs and there's a decent food-and-cocktail menu.

☆ ENTERTAINMENT

ODEON PETROBRAS CINEMA

(Map p246; ☎2240-1093; Praça Floriano 7, Cinelândia) Rio de Janeiro's landmark cinema is a remnant of the once flourishing movie-house scene that gave rise to the name Cinelândia. The restored 1920s film palace shows independent films, documentaries and foreign films, and sometimes hosts the gala for prominent film festivals.

TRAPICHE GAMBOA SAMBA

(Map p246; ☎2516-0868; Sacadura Cabral 155, Gamboa; admission R$15-20; ⏲7pm-midnight Tue & Wed, to 4am Thu-Sat) Another charming live samba joint, Trapiche Gamboa is set in a multistory colonial edifice in Gamboa (just north of Centro) and has a friendly mixed crowd and decent appetizers. It's a casual affair, with samba musicians gathering around a table on the ground floor, and dancers spilling out in front of them. It's best reached by taxi (R$35 or so from the Zona Sul).

CENTRO CULTURAL CARIOCA SAMBA

(Map p246; ☎2252-6468; www.centroculturalcarioca.com.br; Rua do Teatro 37, Centro; admission R$30-40; ⏲7pm-1am Mon-Thu, 8:30pm-2am Fri & Sat) This carefully restored 19th-century building hosts an excellent musical line-up throughout the week, and it is a good option for those wanting to escape the Lapa crowds. The scene here is slightly more staid, which makes it a good choice for couples.

PEDRA DO SAL SAMBA

(Map p246; Largo João da Baiana; ⏲7:30pm-midnight Mon) FREE The Monday-night street party is a major draw for lovers of samba, whether they be Brazilian or foreign, rich or poor. The lively *samba da mesa* (samba of the table) features a handful of changing players who belt out well-known songs to swaying, joyful crowds surrounding the tiny plaza.

The atmospheric but run-down setting is rich in history – samba in fact was born in the Bahian community that once flourished here. Because the action happens outdoors, the music is cancelled on heavy rain days. It's not safe to walk around here; take a taxi (around R$40 from the Zona Sul).

ESTUDANTINA MUSICAL SAMBA

(Map p246; ☎2232-1149; www.estudantinamusical.com.br; Praça Tiradentes 79, Centro; admission R$10-25; ⏲10pm-3:30am Thu-Sat) This old dance hall packs large, older crowds on the weekend, there to enjoy the excellent samba bands. Occasional big-name artists perform here. The open-air veranda provides a nice spot to cool off if you've danced yourself into a sweat.

TEATRO RIVAL PETROBRAS LIVE MUSIC

(Map p246; ☎2240-4469; www.rivalpetrobras.com.br; Álvaro Alvim 33, Cinelândia; admission R$30-80; ⏰box office 3-9pm Mon-Fri, 4-9pm Sat) Near Praça Floriano, this modern 450-seat hall has become a popular spot for some of the city's up-and-coming groups as well as veteran musicians well known in Brazil (Tania Alves, Mart'nalia). Four or five nights a week, Teatro Rival hosts MPB (Música Popular Brasileira), samba, *chorinho* and *forró* groups.

ESPAÇO BNDES PERFORMING ARTS

(Map p246; ☎2172-7447; Av República do Chile 100, Centro; ⏰10am-8pm Mon-Fri) Weekly concerts are held at this Centro venue throughout the year. Featuring a mix of popular and classical music, BNDES in the past has featured musicians exploring symphonic pop, and experimental groups playing samba-jazz.

TEATRO CARLOS GOMES PERFORMING ARTS

(Map p246; ☎2232-8701; www.teatrocarlosgomes.com.br; Pedro I, 22, Centro; admission R$20-80) Facing the Praça Tiradentes, the large Teatro Carlos Gomes stages avant-garde dance shows and experimental theater. The theater seats 600.

TEATRO DO CENTRO CULTURAL BANCO DO BRASIL PERFORMING ARTS

(Map p246; ☎3808-2020; www.bb.com.br; Primeiro de Março 66, Centro) In addition to its exhibitions, this large cultural center in downtown Rio has two stages and a cinema. Film, dance and musical events are often coordinated with current exhibits.

TEATRO NELSON RODRIGUES PERFORMING ARTS

(Map p250; ☎2262-5483; Av República do Chile 230, Centro) Inside the wildly modernist 1970s-era Caixa Cultural complex, you'll find one of Brazil's best stages for dance and theater. Also on-site are several art galleries, a lunchtime bistro, gardens and a koi pond.

THEATRO MUNICIPAL THEATER

(Map p246; ☎021 2332 9195; www.theatromunicipal.rj.gov.br; Manuel de Carvalho) This gorgeous art-nouveau theater provides the setting for Rio's best opera, ballet and symphonic concerts. The theater seats 2400, and sight lines are generally quite good.

THE WEEK GAY CLUB

(Map p246; ☎2253-1020; www.theweek.com.br; Rua Sacadura Cabral 154, Centro) Rio's best gay dance club has a spacious dance floor, excellent DJs and lots of go-go dancers. Plans are underway to move to a new location; check the website for details.

CLUB SIX CLUB

(Map p246; ☎2510-3230; www.clubsix.com.br; Rua das Marrecas 38, Lapa; admission R$10-50; ⏰11pm-6am Fri & Sat) Near the Arcos da Lapa, Club Six is a huge industrial space housing three dance floors, five bars and a number of spots for lounging. It's a top pick for dancing, with DJs spinning house, hip-hop, trance and MPB till daybreak.

SHOPPING

For a break from the chrome and glass of the Zona Sul, check out the old-school shops of historic Centro. Bargains abound in the narrow pedestrian streets around Saara, where shops peddle everything from clothes and cosmetics to toys, jerseys and all the fabric and sequins you'd ever need to make your own Carnaval costume. Nearby streets offer a little of everything, including discounted record stores, used bookshops and percussion stores often set behind century-old shopfronts.

GRANADO BEAUTY

(☎3231-6747; Primeiro de Março 14, Centro; ⏰8am-8pm Mon-Fri, to 2pm Sat) A classic-looking apothecary, Granado (since 1870) incorporates Brazilian ingredients in its all-natural products. Favorites include the Castanha do Brasil (made from chestnuts from the Amazon) line of moisturizers, shampoos and conditioners. You'll also find bright, sweet-smelling soaps and bath gels (even for pets and babies), scented candles, perfumes, shaving products and retro-looking bags. Other locations are in Lapa and Leblon.

NOVA LIVRARIA LEONARDO DA VINCI BOOKS

(Map p246; www.leonardodavinci.com.br; Rio Branco 185, Edifício Marquês de Herval, Centro; ⏰9am-7pm Mon-Fri, to 1pm Sat) Boasting one of Rio's best foreign-language book collections, da Vinci also has a wide range of art and photography books, as well as coffee-table books covering Rio's history and architecture.

It's one floor down; follow the spiral ramp. There's a decent coffee shop nearby.

ARLEQUIM BOOKS, MUSIC

(Map p246; ☎2220-8471; Praça XV (Quinze) de Novembro 48, Paço Imperial, Centro; ⏲9am-8pm Mon-Fri, 10am-6pm Sat) Bossa nova plays overhead at this charming cafe (mains R$18 to R$34), bookstore and music shop. As well as new books (including foreign-language titles), Arlequim sells CDs covering bossa, samba and other styles. The menu features salads, sandwiches and, uh, chop suey.

LIVRARIA DA TRAVESSA BOOKS, MUSIC

(Map p246; ☎3231-8015; Sete de Setembro 54, Centro; ⏲9am-8pm Mon-Fri, to 2pm Sat) Livraria da Travessa makes a peaceful refuge from the people-packed sidewalks out front. There are some books in English, and an array of colorful (but pricey) coffee-table books. There's another **branch** (Map p246; Travessa de Ouvidor 17) around the corner and a third **Centro branch** (Av Rio Branco 44), all with in-store cafe-restaurants.

L'ESCALIER ANTIQUES

(Map p246; ☎8106-6082; 2nd fl, Rua do Rosário 38; ⏲10am-6pm Tue-Fri, to 2pm Sat) One of a handful of new galleries on this colonial street, L'Escalier sells a mix of antiques, craft-like decorations from the Northeast and artwork (including works by indigenous painters as well as reproductions from famous 19th-century landscapes).

LOJA NOVO DESENHO HOMEWARES

(Map p246; ☎2524-2290; Av Infante Dom Henrique 85, Centro; ⏲noon-6pm Tue-Fri, to 7pm Sat & Sun) Inside Museu de Arte Moderna (p121), this 'Store of New Design' sells fanciful objects that are pure eye candy. Some of Rio's best modern designs are here (created by some of the country's best industrial designers). And you'll find whimsical two-dimensional vases, surreal clock faces and other clever works.

LIDADOR DRINK, FOOD

(Map p246; ☎2533-4988; Rua da Assembléia 65, Centro; ⏲9am-8pm Mon-Fri, to 1pm Sat) Gleaming bottles stretch high to the ceiling of this well-stocked liquor cabinet. Founded in 1924, Lidador also sells smoked meats, cheeses, chocolates and imported goods.

CASA OLIVEIRA MUSICAL INSTRUMENTS

(Map p246; ☎2508-8539; Rua da Carioca 70, Centro; ⏲9am-7pm Mon-Fri, to 2pm Sat) One of several excellent music shops on Rua da Carioca, Casa Oliveira sells all the pieces that make up the rhythm section of Carnaval *baterias* (percussion sections). Unique souvenirs for the musically minded include *cavaquinos* (ukulele-sized guitars), which start at around R$180, and *pandeiros* (tambourines), starting at R$45.

BERINJELA MUSIC, BOOKS

(Map p246; ☎2532-3646; Av Rio Branco 185, Centro; ⏲9am-7pm Mon-Fri, 10am-1pm Sat) Berinjela is a fine place to hunt for old records and classic samba CDs, and there's also a selection of used books (though only a handful in English). It's hidden in a small shopping center, down a spiral ramp and just past Leonardo da Vinci bookshop.

TABACARIA AFRICANA CIGARS, TOBACCO

(Map p246; ☎2509-5333; Praça XV (Quinze) de Novembro, Centro; ⏲9am-5pm Mon-Fri) The sweet fragrance of pipe tobacco is embedded in the walls and furniture of this shop facing the Praça Quinze. Regulars sit at the table in front slowly drawing on the pick of the day while the afternoon drifts by, smokelike. In the back, the glass jars contain a variety of flavors and aromas. Let the shopkeeper put a mix together for you.

SPORTS & ACTIVITIES

CENTRO EXCURSIONISTA BRASILEIRA ROCK CLIMBING

(CEB; Map p246; ☎2252-9844; www.ceb.org.br; 8th fl, Av Almirante Barroso 2, Centro; ⏲office 2-6pm Mon-Fri, meetings 7pm Thu) Founded in 1919, CEB sponsors day hikes and weekend treks (with camping). The club plans activities at its weekly meeting, a good spot to have a chat with the laid-back enthusiasts. The office is open during the week and provides info on upcoming excursions.

CENTRO CULTURAL CARIOCA DANCE

(Map p246; ☎2252-6468; www.centrocultural carioca.com.br; Sete de Setembro 237, Centro; ⏲11am-8pm Mon-Fri) The cultural center offers one-hour classes in samba, ballroom dancing and the sensual lambada. Most classes meet twice a week and cost around R$90 for a month-long course. The large dance hall hosts parties on Friday at which samba bands perform.

Santa Teresa & Lapa

SANTA TERESA | LAPA

Neighborhood Top Five

❶ Photographing the **Escadaria Selarón** (p135), a moving work of art created by an artist who made the mosaic-covered staircase his life's work.

❷ Watching sunlight play through the dazzling stained-glass windows at the **Catedral Metropolitana** (p136).

❸ Surveying the exquisite collection at **Museu Chácara do Céu** (p136).

❹ Taking in the fine views over Rio and Baía de Guanabara from the **Parque das Ruínas** (p136).

❺ Strolling through the picturesque streets of village-like Santa Teresa.

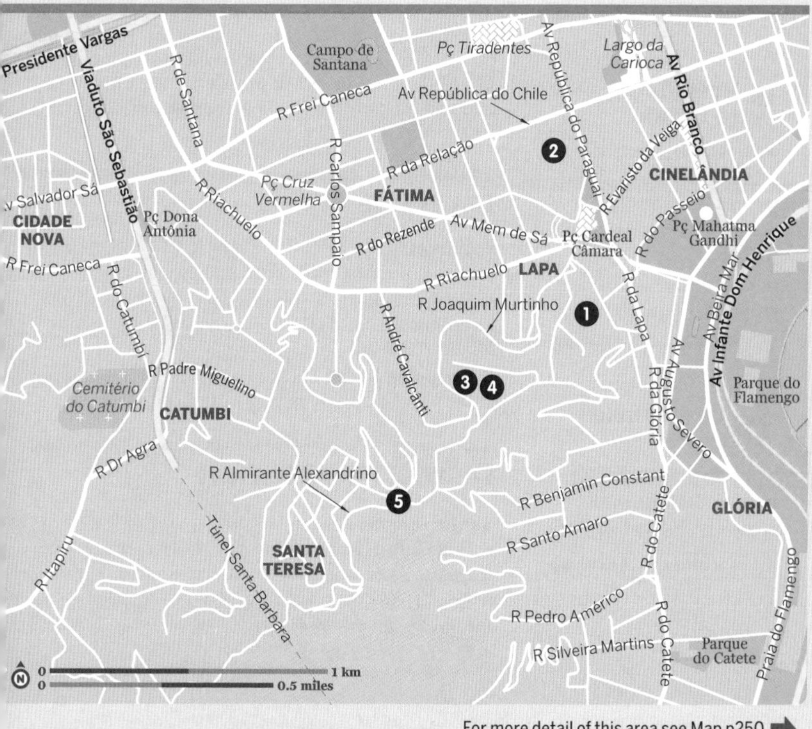

For more detail of this area see Map p250

Lonely Planet's Top Tip

Santa Teresa is fringed by favelas. Be cautious when walking around, and avoid deserted streets. The best time to explore is on Saturday or Sunday when the neighborhood is at its liveliest.

Despite signs of renewal, Lapa still has its share of crime. Take care when strolling around the neighborhood, and be mindful of pickpockets on busy weekend nights.

Best Places to Eat

- Espírito Santa (p138)
- Sobrenatural (p138)
- Aprazível (p138)
- Térèze (p138)
- Nova Capela (p137)

For reviews, see p137

Best Places to Drink

- Bar dos Descasados (p139)
- Lapa 40 Graus (p141)
- Choperia Brazooka (p139)
- Leviano Bar (p141)
- Antônio's (p139)

For reviews, see p139

Best Samba Clubs

- Rio Scenarium (p140)
- Democráticus (p140)
- Carioca da Gema (p141)

For reviews, see p140

Explore Santa Teresa & Lapa

Icons of bohemian Rio, Santa Teresa and Lapa are two rough-and-tumble neighborhoods that have contributed considerably to the city's artistic and musical heritage. On a hill overlooking the city, Santa Teresa has an impressive collection of 19th-century mansions set along winding lanes. Many beautiful colonial homes stretch skyward, their manicured gardens hidden behind gabled fences.

Today, Santa Teresa is a buzzword for a vibrant arts scene. Throughout the year, impromptu festivals and street parties fill the air, ranging from *maracatu* drumming along Rua Joaquim Murtinho to live jazz at the Parque das Ruínas, to the annual Portas Abertas event, where dozens of artists open their studios and cover the streets with living installations.

The streets of Lapa lie down the hill from Santa Teresa and south of Cinelândia. Formerly a residential neighborhood of the wealthy, Lapa became a red-light district in the 1930s. Although it is still a derelict area, it's also one of the music capitals of Brazil. At night, revelers from all over the city mingle among its samba clubs and music-filled bars. The music scene has brought some gentrification to the area, including new restaurants and hostels.

Lapa's landmark aqueduct, Arcos da Lapa, is one of the neighborhood's most prominent features. Coursing over the 64m-high structure are narrow tracks that once carried the *bonde* (tram; p136) to and from Santa Teresa. Although out of service at press time, according to government officials the *bonde* will reopen before the 2014 World Cup.

Local Life

- **Markets** Lapa's excellent Feira do Rio Antigo (p143) features antiques, crafts, food and live music.
- **Hangouts** Santa Teresa has some fine local haunts, including the Bar do Gomes (p139) and the Bar do Mineiro (p138).
- **Shopping Strips** The Rua do Lavradio is dotted with antique shops and cafes, plus samba clubs by night.

Getting There & Away

Santa Teresa

- **Bus** Centro (206 & 214) from Carioca metro station

Lapa

- **Bus** Leblon, Ipanema & Copacabana (161); Gávea & Jardim Botânico (158 & 161)
- **Metro** Cinelândia

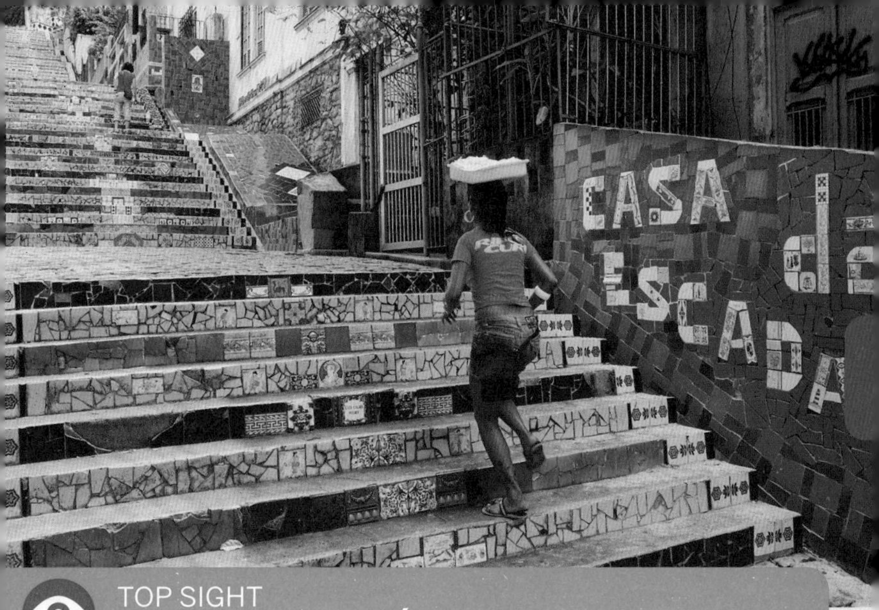

TOP SIGHT
ESCADARIA SELARÓN

Created by the Chilean-born artist Selarón, the staircase bearing his name boasts colorful mosaics that cover the 215 steps leading up into the hilltop enclave of Santa Teresa. Situated in the heart of Rio's vibrant samba district, the *escadaria* has come to symbolize Lapa's creative and bohemian spirit, and its rebirth from a worn and battered former red-light district to a musical powerhouse.

Sadly, Selaron died at the age of 65 in early 2013 – his body was found on the same steps to which he'd devoted the last 20 years of his life. Selaron was a well-known figure in the neighborhood, having moved to Rio in 1983 and settling in a house right off the stairway. What started out as a whim in 1990 evolved into an obsession; he was often spotted at work in Lapa and rarely left the neighborhood.

The mosaics started out as a homage to the Brazilian people utilizing green, yellow and blue. Later he added mirrors and unusual colors and patterns to brilliant effect. As the media began to cover his unusual contribution to the urban landscape, his fame spread, and soon travelers began arriving with ceramics from their own countries to donate. These donations he later incorporated into his ever-evolving installation (tiles hail from more than 60 countries). After he completed the stairs, he began covering other surfaces in need of cosmetic attention, including mosaics near the Arcos da Lapa.

The stairs have been named a city landmark, and have been featured in numerous magazines and photo and film shoots. Snoop Dogg's 'Beautiful' features the steps as well as U2's 'Walk On'. Rio's stirring bid for the Olympics 'The Passion That Unites Us' also showcases the steps.

A hand-painted sign in English and Portuguese explains Selarón's vision.

DON'T MISS...

- The plaque describing Selaron's work.
- Mosaics of pregnant women, including one with Selaron's own face!
- Depictions of the steps in music videos.

PRACTICALITIES

- Map p250
- stairway btwn Joaquim Silva in Lapa & Pinto Martins in Santa Teresa

SIGHTS

Santa Teresa

MUSEU CHÁCARA DO CÉU MUSEUM

(Map p250; ☎3970-1126; www.museuscastromaya.com.br; Murtinho Nobre 93, Lapa; admission R$2, free Wed; ⏲noon-5pm Wed-Mon) The former mansion of art patron and industrialist Raymundo Ottoni de Castro Maya contains a small but diverse collection of modern art – formerly Ottoni's private collection, which he bequeathed to the nation. In addition to works by Portinari, Di Cavalcanti and Lygia Clark, the museum displays furniture and Brazilian maps dating from the 17th and 18th centuries. Beautiful gardens surround the building, and a panoramic view of Centro and Baía de Guanabara awaits visitors.

PARQUE DAS RUÍNAS VIEWPOINT

(Map p250; ☎2215-0621; Murtinho Nobre 169; ⏲10am-8pm Tue-Sun) FREE This park contains the ruins – exterior brick walls and a newly built staircase – of the mansion belonging to Brazilian heiress Laurinda Santos Lobo. Her house was a meeting point for Rio's artists and intellectuals for many years until her death in 1946. There's a small gallery on the ground floor, but the real reason to come here is for the excellent view from the viewing platform up top. There's also a small outdoor cafe-kiosk and terrace where open-air concerts are sometimes held.

CASA DE BENJAMIN CONSTANT HISTORIC BUILDING

(Map p250; ☎3970-1177; Monte Alegre 255; admission R$2, Sun free; ⏲10am-5pm Wed-Sun) This estate served as the residence for one of Brazil's most influential politicians in the founding of the young republic. Benjamin Constant (1837–91) was an engineer, military officer and professor before taking an active role in the Provisional Government. He is also remembered for founding a school for blind children. Painstakingly preserved, his house provides a window into his life and times. The lush gardens surrounding his estate provide a fine view over Centro and the western side of Santa Teresa.

CENTRO CULTURAL LAURINDA SANTOS LOBO CULTURAL CENTER

(Map p250; ☎2242-9741; Monte Alegre 306; ⏲9am-8pm Tue-Sun) FREE Built in 1907, this large mansion once served as a salon for artists from Brazil and abroad as socialite Laurinda Santos Lobo hosted her parties here. Guests included Villa-Lobos and Isadora Duncan. Today, as a cultural center, the building still plays an active role in the neighborhood by hosting exhibitions and open-air concerts throughout the year.

LARGO DAS NEVES SQUARE

(Map p250; End of Rua Progresso) A slice of small-town life in the city, this small plaza is the gathering point for neighborhood children and families, who lounge on the benches by day. At night, the bars surrounding the square come alive with revelers crowding the walkways. At times, MPB (popular Brazilian music) bands perform to a young crowd here. Largo das Neves is the terminus of the Paula Matos *bonde* line.

LARGO DO GUIMARÃES SQUARE

(Map p250; Almirante Alexandrino) The plaza named after Joaquim Fonseca Guimarães (a local resident whose house became Hotel Santa Teresa just up the road) now forms the center of bohemian Santa Teresa. A festive Carnaval street party originates here, and a number of restaurants, handicrafts and thrift shops lie within a short distance.

Lapa

ARCOS DA LAPA AQUEDUCT

(Map p250; Near Av Mem de Sá) The landmark aqueduct dates from the mid-1700s when it was built to carry water from the Carioca River to downtown Rio. In a style reminiscent of ancient Rome, the 42 arches stand 64m high. It carried the *bonde* on its way to and from Santa Teresa until an accident in 2011, after which the *bonde* was closed (it is expected to reopen in March 2014).

CATEDRAL METROPOLITANA CHURCH

(Map p250; ☎2240-2669; www.catedral.com.br; Av República do Chile 24; ⏲7am-6pm) The enormous cone-shaped cathedral was inaugurated in 1976 after 12 years of construction. Among its sculptures, murals and other works of art, the four vivid stained-glass windows, which stretch 60m to the ceiling, are breathtaking. The **Museu de Arte Sacra** (Museum of Sacred Art; Map p250; ☎2240-2669; admission R$2; ⏲9am-noon & 1-4pm Wed, 9am-noon Sat & Sun) in the basement contains a number of historical items, including the baptismal font used at the christening of royal princes and the throne of Dom Pedro II. The cathedral can accommodate up to 20,000 worshippers.

FUNDIÇÃO PROGRESSO ARTS CENTER
(Map p250; ☑2220-5070; www.fundicaoprogresso.com.br; Rua dos Arcos 24; ⊗9am-6pm Mon-Fri) `FREE` Once a foundry for the manufacturing of safes and ovens, the building today hosts avant-garde exhibitions, concerts and excellent samba performances throughout the year. It is one of the few buildings in the area that survived the 1950s neighborhood redistricting project to widen the avenue.

 EATING

Great views, a diverse crowd and a scenic atmosphere among late 19th-century buildings all set the stage for a great night out in bohemian Santa Teresa. Most restaurants are within a short stroll of Largo do Guimarães. Although Lapa is known more for its samba than its cuisine, more and more restaurants are opening in the area, catering to the young crowds heading to the dance halls.

LARGO DAS LETRAS CAFE $
(Map p250; ☑2221-8992; Almirante Alexandrino 501, Santa Teresa; snacks R$3-6; ⊗2-10pm Tue-Sat, 2-8pm Sun) Directly above the Largo do Guimarães *bonde* stop, this bookstore and cafe has shaded outdoor tables that make a fine break when exploring. The cafe is up a flight of steps, and is set back from the street.

NEGA TERESA BRAZILIAN $
(Map p250; Monte Alegre; mains R$16-26; ⊗noon-midnight Tue-Sun) This no-nonsense place serves up tasty and filling plates amid the banter of a mostly neighborhood crowd. The menu is as straightforward as the open-sided, thick-walled interior: salmon, *bife a cavalo* (steak with fried egg), fish fillet or ribs and potatoes.

CAFECITO CAFE $
(Map p250; ☑2221-9439; www.cafecito.com.br; Paschoal Carlos Magno 121, Santa Teresa; sandwiches R$11-21; ⊗10am-10pm) A few steps above street level, this open-air cafe attracts a mix of foreigners and neighbor-

hood regulars (the Argentine owner is a longtime Santa Teresa resident). You'll find imported beers, desserts, cocktails (caiprinhas and mojitos), tapas plates and gourmet sandwiches (with ingredients like smoked trout, artichoke hearts and prosciutto).

ESPAÇO LAPA CAFE CAFE $
(Map p250; ☑3971-6812; www.espacolapacafe.com.br; Gomes Freire 457; mains R$13-28; ⊗11am-midnight Mon-Sat) This creative eat, drink and live-music space serves up good three-course lunch specials, plus sandwiches, snacks and a huge beer selection – over 300 varieties (though not always available) – from across the globe. Several nights a week, live bands playing rock, pop and salsa take to the small stage out the back.

NOVA CAPELA PORTUGUESE $$
(Map p250; ☑2552-6228; Av Mem de Sá 96, Lapa; mains for 2 R$60-90; ⊗11am-4am) This classic, old-time eating and drinking spot opened in 1967 and is a well-known draw for neighborhood bohemians – a noisy mix of artists, musicians and party kids who fill the place until early in the morning. Legendarily bad-tempered waiters serve up big plates of traditional Portuguese cuisine. The *cabrito* (goat) dish is the most famous.

BAR BRASIL GERMAN $$
(Map p250; ☑2509-5943; Av Mem de Sá 90, Lapa; mains for 2 R$45-60; ⊗11:30am-midnight Mon-Sat) According to legend, this German restaurant went by the name Bar Adolf until WWII. Although the name has been Brazilianized, the cuisine is still prepared according to the same pre-war tradition. Sauerkraut, wursts, lentils and an ever-flowing tap quench the appetites and thirsts of the sometimes-rowdy Lapa crowd.

ERNESTO GERMAN $$
(Map p250; ☑2509-6455; Largo da Lapa 41, Lapa; mains R$20-43; ⊗11am-midnight Mon-Sat) With high ceilings and exposed brick walls, there's an old-time feel to this restaurant and drinking spot just a short stroll from the samba clubs in Lapa. Ernesto has an extensive menu, though its grilled meats, codfish dishes and German-inspired plates (sausage with lentils) are standouts. There's live music – MPB or samba – on Wednesday (from 8pm; R$7) and Friday (from 10pm; R$13).

MIKE'S HAUS GERMAN $$

(Map p250; ☎2509-5248; Almirante Alexandrino 1458A, Santa Teresa; mains R$30-50; ⏲noon-midnight Tue-Sun) Mike's Haus has a pub-like atmosphere with traditional German cooking and cold glasses of imported Weizenbier. The only downside is that it's a long way from the center of Santa Teresa. It has a smaller, better located branch (but with a simplified menu) closer to Largo do Guimarães.

BAR DO MINEIRO BRAZILIAN $$

(Map p250; ☎2221-9227; Paschoal Carlos Magno 99, Santa Teresa; mains R$32-47; ⏲noon-2am Tue-Sat, to midnight Sun) Black-and-white photographs of legendary singers cover the walls of this old-school *boteco* in the heart of Santa Teresa. Lively crowds have been filling this spot for years to enjoy traditional Minas Gerais dishes. *Feijoada* (black bean and pork stew) is tops (and good value at R$33 for one), and served every day, along with appetizers, including *pasteis* (savory pastries). Strong caipirinhas will help get you in the mood.

CANTINHO DO SENADO BRAZILIAN $$

(Map p250; ☎2509-0535; Rua do Lavradio 50, Lapa; mains R$27-56; ⏲11am-11pm Tue-Sat) This nondescript restaurant on antique row serves an excellent *feijoada*, which is enough to feed two. The chalkboard menu out front lists other daily specials, usually grilled plates of steak, trout, chicken or fillet of salmon, You can dine in the casual open-sided bar on the ground floor or upstairs amid air-conditioning.

SANSUSHI JAPANESE $$

(Map p250; ☎2252-0581; Almirante Alexandrino 382, Santa Teresa; sushi combo for 2 R$60; ⏲6-10pm Tue-Thu, 2-11pm Fri-Sun) This tiny sushi spot on Santa Teresa's main strip attracts a loyal local following with its delectable sushi and sashimi (36 varieties) as well as teriyaki and other hot dishes. You can also opt for all-you-can-eat sushi (R$42 to R$55).

SANTA SCENARIUM BRAZILIAN $$

(Map p250; ☎3147-9007; www.santoscenarium.blogspot.com; Rua do Lavradio 36; mains R$20-36; ⏲11:30am-midnight Tue-Sat, to 5pm Mon) Angels, saints and other sacred images adorn the exposed brick walls of this marvelously atmospheric restaurant on Lapa's antique row. Grilled meats and other Brazilian staples are on offer at lunchtime, while at night *cariocas* gather for cold beer, appetizers and sandwiches (like the popular filet mignon with mozzarella and sliced pineapple). There's live music most nights.

MANGUE SECO CACHAÇARIA BAHIAN $$

(Map p246; ☎3852-1947; Rua do Lavradio 23, Lapa; mains for 2 R$56-79; ⏲11am-midnight Mon-Thu, 11am-2am Fri & Sat) Mangue Seco serves a mix of seafood and Bahian fare, with hearty *moquecas* (seafood stews cooked in coconut milk) and *caldeirada de frutos do mar* (also a seafood stew). Upstairs, there's a bar with over 100 types of *cachaça* (cane liquor) and live samba Friday (from 9pm) and Saturday (from 10pm).

★ESPÍRITO SANTA AMAZONIAN $$$

(Map p250; ☎2507-4840; Almirante Alexandrino 264, Santa Teresa; mains R$42-60; ⏲noon-midnight Wed-Mon) Espírito Santa is set in a beautifully restored mansion in Santa Teresa. Take a seat on the back terrace with its sweeping views or inside the charming, airy dining room, and feast on rich, expertly prepared meat and seafood dishes from the Amazon and the Northeast.

SOBRENATURAL SEAFOOD $$$

(Map p250; ☎2224-1003; Almirante Alexandrino 432, Santa Teresa; mains for 2 around R$110; ⏲noon-midnight Mon-Sat, noon-10pm Sun) The exposed brick and old hardwood ceiling set the stage for feasting on the *frutas do mar* (seafood). Lines gather on weekends for crabmeat appetizers, fresh grilled fish and flavorful platters of *moqueca*. During the week, stop by for tasty lunchtime specials. There's live music Monday, Wednesday, Friday and Saturday nights.

★APRAZÍVEL BRAZILIAN $$$

(Map p250; ☎2508-9174; Aprazível 62, Santa Teresa; mains around R$70; ⏲7-11pm Tue-Sun) Hidden on a windy road high up in Santa Teresa, Aprazível offers beautiful views and a lush garden setting. Grilled fish and roasted dishes showcase the country's culinary highlights of land and sea (standouts include grilled orange-infused tropical fish with coconut rice and roasted plantains).

This place is a bit out of the way, so call ahead (sometimes, the restaurant is booked up by groups), take a taxi and have your map handy, as drivers don't always know this place.

TÉRÈZE FUSION $$$

(Map p250; ☎3380-0220; Felicio dos Santos, Hotel Santa Teresa, Santa Teresa; mains R$70;

noon-3:30pm & 7:30am-11pm) Under the command of French chef Damien Montecer, Térèze provides a memorable dining experience. All the elements are there, from the inventive menu (char-grilled octopus with couscous salad, black risotto with seafood, macadamia-crusted veal tenderloin) to the suggested wine pairings and the superb views over the city. Even the design is green – tables and artwork are made from reclaimed lumber and recycled materials.

DRINKING & NIGHTLIFE

Santa Teresa and Lapa are two of Rio's most atmospheric neighborhoods, but they are still rough around the edges, so take care when visiting. Lapa is at its wildest during the weekends, with *cariocas* from all over the city heading to the neighborhood's samba clubs. Santa Teresa's bar scene is sprinkled along the main street near Largo do Guimarães, though Largo das Neves, with its tiny plaza and open-sided bars, is also a draw. Take a taxi when visiting these neighborhoods at night.

BAR DOS DESCASADOS — LOUNGE

(Map p250; 3380-0200; Almirante Alexandrino 660, Santa Teresa; noon-midnight) Inside Hotel Santa Teresa, this stylish bar with outdoor seating has lovely views over the city (looking north). You can enjoy decadent cocktails (including a caipirinha made with tangerines grown on the property) and savory snacks (such as salmon tartare) while pondering the A-list crowd and the intriguing history that surrounds you – the building was once a hotel for the recently divorced, and before that the bar functioned as the slave quarters of a working coffee plantation. The bar is fairly empty during the week but becomes a livelier destination, mostly for couples, on weekends.

CHOPERIA BRAZOOKA — BAR

(Map p250; 2224-3235; Av Mem de Sá 70, Lapa; 6pm-2am Tue-Wed, 6pm-5am Thu-Sat) This popular four-story beer house has lots of nooks and crannies where you can while away the night over ice-cold drafts and tasty appetizers. The 20- and 30-something crowd packs this place, so arrive early to score a table.

ANTÔNIO'S — BOTECO

(Map p250; 2224-4197; Av Mem de Sá 88, Lapa; 4pm-3am Mon-Fri, from noon Sat & Sun) Antônio's in Lapa has lots of old-school charm with its hanging lamps, wrought-iron trimwork and simple wooden tables (with a few seats on the sidewalk for taking in the pulsing street scene). Plenty of other drinking spots are nearby, if you feel like wandering.

ADEGA FLOR DE COIMBRA — BAR

(Map p250; 2224-4582; Teotônio Regadas 34, Lapa; noon-midnight) In the same building that was once the home of Brazilian painter Cândido Portinari, the Adega Flor de Coimbra has been a bohemian haunt since it opened in 1938. Back in its early days, leftists, artists and intellectuals drank copiously at the slim old bar looking out on Lapa. Today, the bar-restaurant draws a mix of similar types, who drink wine and sangria with Adega's tasty *bolinhos de bacalhau* (codfish croquettes) or *feijoada* (R$50 for two).

GOYA-BEIRA — BAR

(Map p250; 2232-5751; Largo das Neves 13, Santa Teresa; 6pm-midnight Sun-Thu, to 2am Fri & Sat) Small but charming Goya-Beira is one of Santa Teresa's gems, with a peaceful view onto Largo das Neves. Owner Rose Guerra prepares intriguing *cachaça* infusions as well as pizzas and appetizers. Things are liveliest on weekends.

BAR DO GOMES — BOTECO

(Map p250; 2232-0822; Áurea 26, Santa Teresa; noon-midnight Mon-Sat, to 10pm Sun) Although the sign says 'Armazém do São Thiago', everyone calls the place the Bar do Gomes. Regardless, this simple hole-in-the-wall has long been a favorite gathering spot, particularly on weekends, when young and old pack the few stand-up tables and bar front, spilling onto the sidewalk.

BOTECO DO GOMES — BOTECO

(Map p250; 2531-9717; Rua do Riachuelo 62, Lapa; 7am-1am) In Lapa, the Boteco do Gomes has the classical look of an old-time bar with brick walls, art-deco light fixtures, and tile floors. Patrons are a mix of musicians, students and Lapa hangabouts, who gather for a quick drink at stand-up tables in front or the roomier dining area out the back.

LOCAL KNOWLEDGE

THE DANCE HALLS OF OLD *CARMEN MICHAEL*

If you're interested in Brazilian music and dance, shine up your dancing shoes and head for some of Rio's old-school-style dance halls, known as *gafieiras*. Originally established in the 1920s as dance halls for Rio's urban working class, *gafieiras* nowadays attract an eclectic combination of musicians, dancers, *malandros* (con men) and, of course, the radical chic from Zona Sul. Modern and sleek they are not. Typically held in the ballrooms of old colonial buildings in Lapa, the locations are magnificently Old World. Bow-tied waiters serve ice-cold *cerveja* (beer) under low, yellow lights and, while the setup initially looks formal, give it a few rounds and it will dissolve into a typically raucous Brazilian evening.

Before *gafieiras* were established Rio's different communities were polarized by their places of social interaction, whether it was opera and tango for the Europeans or street *choro* (romantic, intimate samba) for the Africans. Responding to a social need, and in tandem with the politics of the time, *gafieiras* quickly became places where musicians and audiences of black and white backgrounds alike could mix and create new sounds. Through the *gafieiras* the street-improvised *choro* formations became big-band songs and a new Brazilian sound was born. The best and oldest dance halls are Democráticus (p140), attracting a young yet fashionably bohemian crowd on Wednesday, and Estudantina Musical (p130) on Praça Tiradentes, which operates from Friday to Sunday.

The standard of dancing is outstanding in Brazil, so expect to see couples who would be considered professional in Europe or the US dancing unnoticed across the polished floors. While just about anything goes in Rio, it's an opportunity for the *cariocas* to dress up a little, so you will see quite a few dresses and smart shoes. Don't be intimidated by the other dancers. Unlike in Buenos Aires, where the tango is for experts only, Brazilians are pretty relaxed about newcomers dancing. For those traveling solo, *gafieiras* are fantastic places to meet some intriguing locals and learn a few steps. Dance around the edge of the dance floor with the rest of the dancers to get a closer look at how the dance works – if you are a woman, you won't wait long before someone asks you to dance. Alternatively you can take a lesson and perhaps meet some fellow beginners to dance with. There are a number of places where you can sign up for a group or private lesson.

BOTEKO DO JUCA BOTECO

(Map p250; ☎2242-5372; Av Mem de Sá 95, Lapa; ⊙noon-2am) A staple of Lapa's hard-drinking scene, this classic-looking spot attracts a diverse bunch – old artists, shop owners, musicians, prostitutes and the odd ones you can't pin down – and the crowd tends to get more colorful as the night progresses.

☆ ENTERTAINMENT

CIRCO VOADOR CONCERT VENUE

(Map p250; ☎2533-0354; www.circovoador.com.br; Rua dos Arcos, Lapa; admission R$50-80) In a curvilinear building behind the Arcos da Lapa, Circo Voador hosts big-name Brazilian and international artists. The acoustics are excellent, and after a show you'll find plenty of other musical options in the area. Check the website to see what's on. You can also take classes in capoeira (Afro-Brazilian martial arts), dance, percussion and yoga.

RIO SCENARIUM SAMBA

(Map p250; www.rioscenarium.com.br; Rua do Lavradio 20, Lapa; cover R$20-40; ⊙Tue-Sat 7pm-4am) One of the city's most photogenic nightspots, Rio Scenarium has three floors, each lavishly decorated with antiques. Balconies overlook the stage on the 1st floor, with dancers keeping time to the jazz-infused samba, *choro* or *pagode* filling the air. Rio Scenarium receives much press outside of Brazil, and attracts at least as many foreigners as locals.

DEMOCRÁTICUS SAMBA

(Map p250; ☎2252-4611; Rua do Riachuelo 93, Lapa; admission R$25-50; ⊙10pm-3am Wed-Sat) Murals line the foyer of this 1867 mansion. The rhythms filter down from above.

Follow the sound up the marble staircase and out into a large hall filled with tables, an enormous dance floor and a long stage covered with musicians. A wide mix of *cariocas* gathers here to dance, revel in the music and soak up the splendor of the samba-infused setting. If you come to just one *gafieira* in Lapa, Democráticus is a good choice.

CARIOCA DA GEMA SAMBA

(Map p250; www.barcariocadagema.com.br; Av Mem de Sá 79, Lapa; cover R$21-25; 7pm-1:30am Mon-Thu, 9pm-3:30am Fri-Sun) Although it's now surrounded by clubs, Carioca da Gema was one of Lapa's pioneers when it opened in 2000. This small, warmly lit club still attracts some of the city's best samba bands, and you'll find a festive, mixed crowd filling the dance floor most nights.

LAPA 40 GRAUS LIVE MUSIC

(Map p250; 3970-1338; Riachuelo 97, Lapa; admission R$5-30; 6pm-5am Tue-Sat) This impressive multistory music venue and pool hall has tables for lounging on the 1st floor, over a dozen pool tables on the 2nd floor, and a small stage and dancing couples on the top floor. There are usually two shows nightly. Pop, rock, samba and *choro* kick off around 7pm and 11pm.

SEMENTE SAMBA

(Map p250; 9781-2451; Joaquim Silva 138, Lapa; admission R$20-30; 8pm-2am Sat-Thu) One of the few venues in Lapa that holds court on Sunday and Monday nights, Semente has longevity. Although it has closed and reopened a few times, it was one of the first places in Lapa to bring samba back to the city. Its current incarnation is small and intimate, with good bands and a crowd that comes for the music rather than the Lapa mayhem.

BARZINHO CLUB

(Map p250; 2221-4709; Rua do Lavradio 170, Lapa; admission R$15-40; 6pm-2am Tue-Thu, to 4am Fri & Sat) A new venue, Barzinho brings a touch more glamour to Lapa, courtesy of the celebrated DJ (and part owner) Rodrigo Penna who spins here one night a week and draws a dance-loving mostly Zona Sul crowd. Glittering chandeliers, colored wall-mounted light panels and artfully displayed kitsch (dolls, action figures, old-fashioned toys) lend a creative vibe, and you can head to a table on the upper level for a view over the long space.

LEVIANO BAR BAR, CLUB

(Map p250; 2507-5967; Av Mem de Sá 49; 6pm-late) Near the entrance to Mem de Sá, the Leviano Bar is part of new crop of slightly more upscale drinking and dance spots. Watch the passing people parade – and take in the great view of the Arcos da Lapa – from outdoors in front before heading to the upstairs dance floor where DJs mix house, electro-samba, soul and reggae.

TRIBOZ JAZZ

(Map p250; 2210-0366; www.triboz-rio.com; Conde de Lages 19, Lapa; cover R$20-30; 6-8pm & 9pm-1am Thu-Sat) Not for lazy ears, this avant-garde jazz house, a little hidden gem among the sonic cognoscenti, is unique in Rio for its serious approach to performances. Run by an Australian ethnomusicologist, it sits in a shadier part of old Lapa in a signless mansion, which transforms into a beautiful showcase space for Brazil's most cutting-edge artists. It attracts 30+ and/or music aficionado, who come for the evening's three 45-minute sets and good-value Australian-inspired grub. Reservations are essential two days in advance by phone only.

FAVELLAS SAMBA

(Map p250; 2507-0580; www.favellaslapa.com.br; Mem de Sá 59; admission around R$30; 7pm-3am Tue-Sat) Decorated with colorfully painted walls, kites, laundry lines and other kitschy elements, this eye-catching new places brings a taste of the favela to Lapa. Like other spots on the street, Favellas features a solid samba line-up with shows kicking off around 11pm.

BECO DO RATO LIVE MUSIC

(Map p250; 2508-5600; http://becodorato.com.br; Joaquim Silva 11, Lapa; 8pm-3am Tue-Fri) FREE One of Lapa's classic spots, this tiny bar has excellent live groups playing to a samba-loving crowd. The outdoor seating and informal setting are an unbeatable mix. Marcio, the friendly owner, hails from Minas Gerais; to get the night started, ask him for a tasty *cachaça* from his home state. Friday night is one of the best nights to go, though there's also live music on Tuesday and Thursday.

MANGUE SECO CACHAÇARIA SAMBA

(Map p246; ☎3852-1947; Rua do Lavradio 23, Lapa; admission R$15-30; ⏰11am-midnight Mon-Thu, to 2am Fri & Sat) Set in a street lined with a mix of antique shops and bars, the two-story Mangue Seco has a casual bar and restaurant on the 1st floor and a *cachaçaria* (*cachaça* bar) on the 2nd floor. Sample over 100 different brands of the fiery stuff while listening to live *choro,* bossa nova or samba bands (starting at 6pm Monday to Thursday, and 9pm or 10pm Friday and Saturday).

MAS SERÁ O BENEDITO SAMBA

(Map p250; ☎2232-9000; Av Gomes Freire 599, Lapa; admission R$15-30; ⏰noon-4pm & 5pm-3am Mon-Sat) This beautifully restored space (occupying a 19th-century mansion) opened in 2009 and immediately attracted a following. It has a restaurant on the ground floor, two pool tables on the 2nd floor and a concert space with live samba on the 3rd floor, where bands play nightly.

MISTURA CARIOCA SAMBA

(Map p250; ☎7830-6098; Av Gomes Freire 791, Lapa; admission R$12-18; ⏰8pm-3am Wed-Sat) A classic but less popular samba club in Lapa, Mistura Carioca has two levels, with the band playing on the 1st floor, and a quiet upper level, where you can look down on the scene below. Big glass chandeliers add to the old-time charm.

SACRILÉGIO SAMBA

(Map p250; ☎3970-1461; Av Mem de Sá 81, Lapa; admission R$20-30; ⏰7pm-1am Tue, to 3am Wed-Fri, 9pm-3am Sat) Next door to Carioca da Gema, Sacrilégio is another major spot for catching live bands in an intimate setting. The outdoor garden makes a fine spot for imbibing a few cold *chopes* while the music filters through the windows. In addition to samba, Sacrilégio hosts *choro, forró* and MPB bands.

PARADA DA LAPA LIVE MUSIC

(Map p250; ☎2524-2950; www.paradadalapa.com.br; Rua dos Arcos 10, Lapa; admission R$20-60; ⏰10pm-4am Fri-Sun) In an annex next to Fundição Progresso, this multilevel bar and live-music venue has an upstairs open-air terrace with magical views of the Lapa Arches. The stage inside hosts an eclectic line-up of live samba, MPB, jazz, rock and cabaret performances.

TEATRO ODISSÉIA SAMBA

(Map p250; ☎2224-6367; Av Mem de Sá 66, Lapa; admission R$25-35; ⏰10pm-5am Fri-Sun) This spacious three-story Lapa club features live-music shows and DJs, with a relaxed area upstairs if you need a break from the sounds. There's also a terrace with views of the Lapa Arches. You'll find plenty of samba, while MPB and rock make an occasional appearance at the club.

FUNDIÇÃO PROGRESSO CONCERT VENUE

(Map p250; ☎2220-5070; www.fundicao.org; Rua dos Arcos 24, Lapa; admission R$25-40) This former foundry in Lapa hides one of Rio's top music and theater spaces. A diverse range of shows is staged here, which include big-name acts like Manu Chao and Caetano Veloso, as well as theater, video arts and ballet. The foundation is one of Lapa's premier arts institutions, and you can study dance, capoeira and circus arts here.

SALA CECÍLIA MEIRELES PERFORMING ARTS

(Map p250; ☎2332-9223; www.salaceciliameireles.com.br; Largo da Lapa 47, Lapa) Lapa's splendid early-20th-century gem hosts orchestral concerts throughout the year. Lately, the repertoire has included contemporary groups, playing both *choro* (romantic, intimate samba) and classical music. At research time the concert hall was closed for renovations.

CINE SANTA TERESA CINEMA

(Map p250; ☎2222-0203; www.cinesanta.com.br; Paschoal Carlos Magno 136, Santa Teresa) This small, single-screen theater is well located on Largo do Guimarães. Befitting the art-loving 'hood, the cinema screens a selection of independent and Brazilian films.

SHOPPING

Stomping ground for Rio's bohemian crowd, Santa Teresa has a growing number of handicraft shops and vintage stores with some enticing restaurants and cafes that add to the appeal. In Lapa, you'll find Rua do Lavradio, the city's best antiques street. It's at its liveliest on the first Saturday of the month.

SCENARIUM ANTIQUE ANTIQUES

(Map p250; ☎3147-9014; Rua do Lavradio 28, Lapa; ⏰9am-6pm Mon-Fri, to 2pm Sat) One of

Lavradio's best antique shops, this place is packed with glass and ceramic wares, furniture, iron kettles, lamps, oil paintings and a wide variety of other displays that make for a curious glimpse into the past.

FLANAR ANTIQUES

(Map p250; ☎2507-2751; Rua do Lavradio 60, Lapa; ⏰9am-6pm Mon-Fri, to 2pm Sat) The old colonial edifice hides an intriguing selection of antiques – from tables and chairs to chandeliers, glassware, ceramics and old oil paintings. Although many objects for sale here won't fit in your suitcase, it's still a fun place to browse.

LA VEREDA HANDICRAFTS HANDICRAFTS

(Map p250; ☎2507-0317; Almirante Alexandrino 428, Santa Teresa; ⏰10am-8pm) Near Largo do Guimarães, La Vareda stocks a colorful selection of handicrafts from local artists and artisans. Hand-painted clay figurines by Pernambuco artists, heavy Minas ceramics, delicate sterling silver jewelry and loosely woven tapestries cover the interior of the old store. Other cool gift ideas: T-shirts bearing a *bonde* image, block prints by local artist Erivaldo and vibrant art-naïf canvases by various Santa artists. There are several other handicraft shops and galleries also on this street.

PLANO B MUSIC, TATTOOS

(Map p250; ☎2509-3266; www.planob.net; Francisco Muratori 2A, Lapa; ⏰noon-8pm Mon-Fri, to 6pm Sat) Only in Lapa will you encounter a place where you can pick through bins of old jazz records and new electronic mixes before stepping into the back room to get a tattoo, inspired perhaps by that old Elza Soares song playing overhead. Plano B also has a decent selection of CDs, and the young staff can advise – if samba-funk eludes you. It also hosts DJ spin sessions some weekend nights; check the website.

FEIRA DO RIO ANTIGO MARKET

(Map p250; ☎2224-6693; Rua do Lavradio, Lapa; ⏰10am-6pm 1st Sat of month) Although the Rio Antiques Fair happens just once a month, don't miss it if you're in town. The colonial buildings become a living installation as the whole street fills with antiques, and samba bands add to the ambience.

SPORTS & ACTIVITIES

FUNDIÇÃO PROGRESSO DANCING

(Map p250; ☎2220-5070; www.fundicaoprogresso.org; Rua dos Arcos 24) This cultural center offers a wide range of courses, including classes in dancing (African styles, as well as salsa, tango and samba). Those seeking something different can sign up for classes in percussion, acrobatics (run by the respected dance-theater-circus outfit Intrépida Trupe) or capoeira (Afro-Brazilian martial arts). Courses are typically around R$200 for the month.

NÚCLEO DE DANÇA RENATA PEÇANHA DANCING

(Map p250; ☎2221-1011; www.renatapecanha.com.br; Rua dos Inválidos 129, Lapa) A large upstairs studio on the edge of Lapa, this dance academy offers classes in *forró,* salsa, zouk (a slow and sensual dance derived from the lambada) and samba. Twice-weekly classes cost about R$90 per month.

Zona Norte

Neighborhood Top Five

❶ Hearing the roar of the crowds as some of the world's best players take to the field inside hallowed **Maracanã Football Stadium** (p146).

❷ Browsing handicrafts, snacking on Northeastern dishes and partner-dancing to live *forró* inside the sprawling **Feira Nordestina** (p148).

❸ Exploring relics from Brazil's early 19th-century past at the neoclassical **Museu do Primeiro Reinado** (p148).

❹ Taking a stroll amid the greenery of the once imperial **Quinta da Boa Vista** (p148).

❺ Perusing pre-Columbian artifacts inside the **Museu Nacional** (p148), a former royal palace.

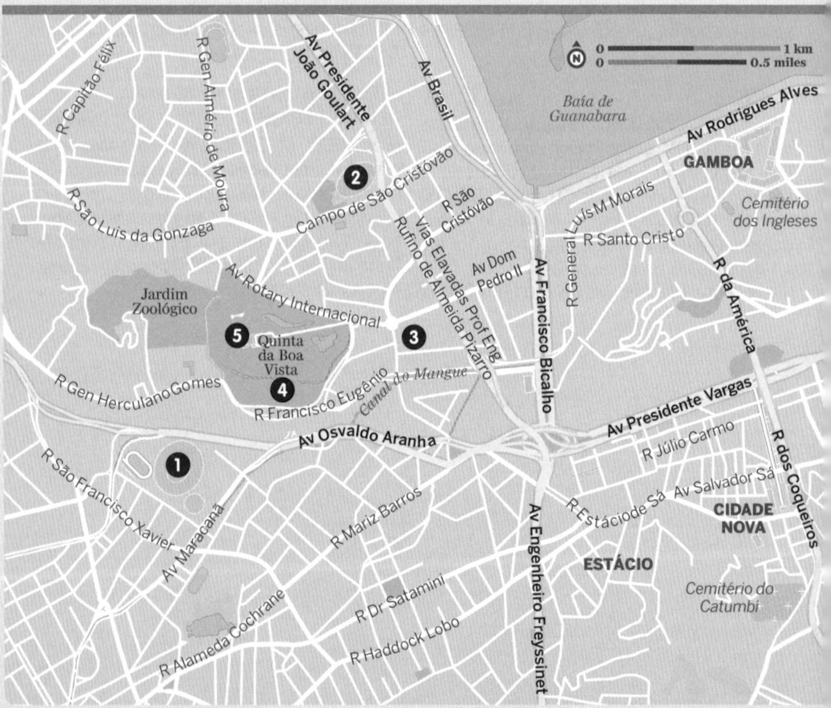

For more detail of this area see Map p254 ➡

Explore Zona Norte

Vast Zona Norte sprawls many kilometers toward the Baixada Fluminense. It boasts fewer attractions than the Zona Sul and Centro, but there are still excellent reasons to visit, including soccer rowdiness at Maracanã, great views from little-visited landmarks and historical intrigue at former palaces.

The Zona Norte is home to many distinct neighborhoods and favelas, including several with pivotal roles in the competitive Carnaval parade. Rehearsals at samba schools (p46) are a worthwhile draw, and attract huge crowds as Carnaval draws nearer. Some favelas are receiving dramatic makeovers, including Complexo do Alemão, a collection of communities that is slowly becoming a tourist attraction, courtesy of an aerial cable-car system that glides over the favela hillsides.

In the 19th century the Zona Norte was the home of the nobility, including Dom João VI. The area saw dramatic transformation as mangrove swamps were cleared to make way for stately homes. In the 20th century, the wealthy moved out and exploding urbanism transformed the landscape into a gritty, heavily populated, working-class suburb. A visit is recommended for those who want to see how the rest of Rio lives. You'll escape the tourist crowds and experience an authentic slice of Rio far removed from the picture-postcard sights of the Zona Sul.

Although the area is spread out, several sites are fairly close together and are easily reached by metro, lying just west of Centro. Other places are best reached by taxi.

Local Life

- **Nightlife** Dusting off your dance shoes and joining *forró*-loving crowds at a long night of live music and dancing in the Feira Nordestina.
- **Markets** Cadeg is Rio's largest market and a fine place to browse the endless rows of produce, meats and fish; it's also home to great-value restaurants, with a festive air (and live music) on weekends.

Getting There & Away

Maracanã

- **Bus** From Copacabana, Ipanema & Leblon (464); to Copacabana and Ipanema (456 & 457), to Leblon (464)
- **Metro** Maracanã

Quinta da Boa Vista

- **Bus** Copacabana, Ipanema and Leblon (474)
- **Metro** São Cristóvão (for Museu Nacional and Jardim Zoológico)

Lonely Planet's Top Tip

The best time to visit this area is on weekends, when you'll find the markets, parks and other attractions at their liveliest.

Best Places to Eat

- Aconchego Carioca (p149)
- Barsa (p149)
- Da Gema (p149)

For reviews, see p149

Best Views

- Sambódromo (p149)
- Complexo do Alemão (p148)
- Igreja da Penha (p149)

For reviews, see p148

Best Shopping

- Sports Museum (p149)
- Feira Nordestina (p148)
- CADEG (p149)

For reviews, see p148

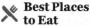

TOP SIGHT
MARACANÃ FOOTBALL STADIUM

Rio's Maracanã stadium is hallowed ground among football lovers. The massive arena has been the site of legendary victories and crushing defeats (like Brazil's gut-wrenching loss in the final game of the 1950 World Cup to Uruguay). However, Maracanã's best days may be yet to come, with the stadium playing a starring role in both the 2014 World Cup and the 2016 Summer Olympics. But no matter who takes the field, the 80,000-seat open-air arena comes to life in spectacular fashion on game day.

The Spectacle

A game at Maracanã is a must-see. Matches here rate among the most exciting in the world, and the fans some of the most colorful. The devoted pound huge samba drums, spread vast flags across great swaths of the stadium, dance in the aisles and detonate smoke bombs in team colors. You'll hear – and feel – the deafening roar when the home team takes the field, and the wall of sound and palpable air of near hysteria will surround you when a player pounds the ball into the back of the net. Things are only slightly calmer since alcohol was banned inside the stadium back in 2003 (though with pressure from FIFA, an exception to the law has been put in place for the 2014 World Cup).

DON'T MISS...

- A match-up between any of Rio's hometown rivals.
- A walk through a half-century of football lore inside the Sports Museum.

PRACTICALITIES

- Map p254
- ☎8871-3950
- www.suderj.rj.gov.br/maracana.asp
- Av Maracanã, São Cristóvão
- admission R$15-100
- 🕘9am-7pm
- Maracanã metro station

Going to a Game

Games take place year-round and generally happen on Saturday or Sunday (starting at 4pm or 6pm) or on Wednesday and Thursday (around 8:30pm). Although buses run to and from the stadium, on game days the metro is generally faster and less crowded. The stadium has color-coded seating, with tourists and more sedate folk generally sitting in the somewhat isolated white section, and rowdier flans flocking to the green and yellow sections or the wildest fans to the blue section on the lowest level. Those who want the best views at any price opt for the special seats (which cost upwards of R$150). The ticket price is R$25 to R$50 for most games.

If you prefer to go in a group, a number of English-speaking tour operators organize game-day outings, including round-trip transportation. Leading big-group tours are Brazil Expedition (p203) and Be A Local (p204). For something more small-scale, independent guide Sergio Manhães (p50) takes up to four guests with him on game day. All have been recommended by readers.

Renovations & Olympic Preparations

Maracanã, which has undergone a massive R$800 million renovation before the 2014 World Cup, remains Brazil's largest sport's arena – though it no longer holds as many fans in years past. Renovations include replacing all seats in the arena, demolishing the lower level to improve visibility, expanding access ramps and fitting the stadium with a new roof, which will now cover all seats, and also be sustainably designed – complete with a rainwater collection system. The facade, which is a protected landmark under the National Institute of Historical and Artistic Heritage, will remain unchanged.

For the World Cup it is slated to host seven games – more than any of the other 11 venues in Brazil. And it will host the finals on 13 July. After the World Cup, Maracanã will continue serving as the staging post for matches between Rio's league teams – Flamengo, Fluminense, Vasco da Gama and Botafogo. Come 2016, the stadium is expected to take the spotlight once again as the setting for the opening and closing ceremonies of the Summer Olympics and Paralympic Games, as well as serving as the main venue for football matches during the games.

Resources

For more information on the big events happening in Maracanã, visit the following sites:

FIFA (www.fifa.com/worldcup) The latest World Cup news: venues, matches, team standings, tickets.

Summer Olympics (www.olympic.org) Events, venues, tickets and results.

Samba Foot (www.sambafoot.com) Good all-around site for info on Brazilian club games.

World Cup Blog (http://brazil.worldcupblog.org) Readable site with all the latest on players, teams, coaches.

MARACANAÇO

The last time Brazil hosted the World Cup was in 1950, when the final game played inside Maracanã stadium, which had been built in preparation for the big tournament. Brazil made it all the way to the finals, and more than 170,000 fans packed the stadium to watch the last match against Uruguay. With the match tied at 1-1, Uruguay scored a goal with just 11 minutes left to play. The victory stunned the crowd and left a deep scar on the nation's psyche – this crippling defeat on home soil is still in parlance today and referred to as the *maracanaço*, roughly translated as – *that God-awful thing that happened in Maracanã!*

Inside the stadium, there's a sports museum (p149) – opening hours vary on game days, when it closes five hours before the match. It has photographs, posters, cups and the uniforms of Brazilian sporting greats, including Pelé's famous No 10 shirt. There's also a store where you can buy soccer shirts. Enter by the north entrance, through gate 15 off Rua Mata Machado.

SIGHTS

FEIRA NORDESTINA MARKET

(Map p254; ☎2580-5335; www.feiradesaocristovao.org.br; Campo de São Cristóvão; admission R$3; ⏰10am-6pm Tue-Thu, 10am Fri to 9pm Sun) This enormous fair (32,000 sq meters with over 600 stalls) is not to be missed. It showcases the culture from the Northeast, with *barracas* (food stalls) selling Bahian dishes as well as beer and *cachaça* (cane liquor), which flows in great abundance here. The best time to go is on weekends, when you can catch live bands playing *forró,* plus samba groups and comedy troupes, MPB (Música Popular Brasileria) and *rodas de capoeira* (capoeira circles). The vibrant scene runs nonstop from Friday morning through to Sunday evening. In addition to food and drink, you can browse music CDs (*forró,* of course), hammocks and a wide assortment of handicrafts.

QUINTA DA BOA VISTA PARK

(Map p254; ☎2562-6900; ⏰9am-5pm) Quinta da Boa Vista was the residence of the Portuguese imperial family until the Republic was proclaimed. Today, it's a large and busy park with gardens and lakes. At weekends it's crowded with football games and families from Zona Norte. The former imperial mansion houses the **Museu Nacional** and **Museu da Fauna**. The **Jardim Zoológico**, Rio's zoo, is 200m away.

MUSEU NACIONAL MUSEUM

(Map p254; ☎2562-6900; Quinta da Boa Vista; admission R$3; ⏰10am-4pm Tue-Sun) There are many interesting exhibits: dinosaur fossils, saber-toothed tiger skeletons, beautiful pieces of pre-Columbian ceramics from the littoral and high plains of Peru, a huge meteorite, hundreds of stuffed birds, mammals and fish, gruesome displays of tropical diseases, and exhibits on the peoples of Brazil.

This museum and its imperial entrance are still stately and imposing, and the view from the balcony to the royal palms is majestic. However, the weathered buildings and unkempt grounds have clearly declined since the fall of the monarchy.

MUSEU DO PRIMEIRO REINADO NOTABLE BUILDING, MUSEUM

(Map p254; ☎2332-4513; Av Dom Pedro II 293; ⏰11am-5pm Tue-Fri) FREE A 10-minute walk east of the Quinta da Boa Vista, this former mansion of the Marquesa de Santos depicts the history of the First Reign (the reign of bumbling Dom Pedro I before he was driven out of the country). The collection includes documents, furniture and paintings, but the main attraction is the building and its interior, with striking murals by Francisco Pedro do Amaral.

JARDIM ZOOLÓGICO ZOO

(Map p254; ☎3878-4200; Quinta da Boa Vista; admission R$6; ⏰9am-4:30pm Tue-Sun) Covering more than 12 hectares, the zoo at Quinta da Boa Vista has a wide variety of reptiles, mammals and birds – mostly indigenous to Brazil. Special attractions include the large walk-through aviary and the night house, which features nocturnal animals. The monkey house is also a crowd favorite. Some animal enclosures are cramped, though overall the reproduced habitats are fairly well done.

COMPLEXO DO ALEMÃO FAVELA

(aerial tram R$1) This sprawling collection of makeshift communities has gotten a new lease on life since the inauguration of a *teleférico* (cable car) in 2011. With five stations set on the hills of this 70,000-strong community, the once arduous journey in and out of the favela is now a breeze. Tourists are slowly discovering one of Rio's newest unsung attractions, which has splendid views over the hillsides.

Disembark at Palmeiras (the upper-most station) for a poke around, there are snack stands and occasional live music on weekends. The easiest way to get there is by taxi (to Bonsucesso, the lowest gondola station), though if you're confident moving about Rio, you can take a commuter train from Central Station to Bonsucesso, which connects to the *teleférico* (and save yourself R$40 one-way taxi fare). Be aware, that although security has improved dramatically in the last few years, there are still ocassional outbreaks of violence, with the rare shootout between police and drug traffickers every now and again.

CIDADE DO SAMBA CULTURAL CENTER

(Samba City; Map p254; ☎2213-2503; www.cidadedosambarj.globo.com; Rivadávia Correa 60, Gamboa; ⏰10am-5pm Tue-Sat) One of the biggest developments in Rio's Carnaval world is Cidade do Samba, which opened in 2006. Located north of Centro near the port, the 'city' is actually made up of 14 large build-

WORTH A DETOUR

BEACHES OF EAST RIO

A number of beaches lie just east of Niterói. The ones closest to town are too polluted for swimming, but as you continue out you'll reach some pristine beaches – **Piratininga**, **Camboinhas**, **Itaipu** and finally **Itacoatiara**, the most fabulous of the bunch. Framed by two looming hills on either side of the shore and backed by vegetation, the white sands of Itacoatiara seem a world away from the urban beaches of Rio. *Barracas* (food stalls) sell scrumptious plates of fish, and there are also food stands overlooking the beach. The surf is strong here – evidenced by the many surfers jockeying for position – so swim with caution. To get there, you can take bus 38 or any bus labeled 'Itacoatiara' from the ferry terminal (R$4, 50 minutes). If you're traveling in a group, you can negotiate a return fare with a taxi driver.

ings in which the top schools assemble the Carnaval floats.

CADEG MARKET

(Map p254; www.cadeg.com.br; Capitão Félix 110, Benfica; ⏲1am-5pm Mon-Sat, to 2pm Sun) While the Centro de Abastecimento do Estado da Guanabara (Supply Center of Guanabara State) doesn't have quite the same cachet as Ipanema beach, this voluminous market packs a treasure trove of fruits, vegetables, meats, fish, cheeses, flowers and spices. And while the 350-plus shops are mostly a wholesale affair (hence the 1am opening time), the real reason to come here is for lunch, with a number of good and decidedly unfussy restaurants spread around the four-story building.

IGREJA DA PENHA CHURCH

(☎3887-5115; Largo da Penha, Penha; ⏲7am-6pm) Rio's most dramatically set church is a 17th-century double-steepled confection that offers dramatic 360-degree views from its clifftop perch. A recently renovated tram whisks visitors up to the top (free of charge), though the faithful prefer to ascend those 382 steps on their own power – and some even do it on their knees. The church is surrounded by favelas and best reached by taxi.

SAMBÓDROMO ARENA

(Map p254; Marques do Sapuçai) The epicenter of Rio's Carnaval, the Sambódromo was designed by Oscar Niemeyer and completed in 1984. During the big parades, come for the fantastic views from the stands across elaborate floats, whirling dancers and pounding drum corps.

SPORTS MUSEUM MUSEUM

(Map p254; admission R$20; ⏲9am-5pm Mon-Fri) Inside the Maracanã Football Stadium, the sports museum has photographs, posters, cups and the uniforms of Brazilian sporting greats, including Pelé's famous No 10 shirt. There's also a store where you can buy football shirts. At research time, the museum was closed as ongoing renovations on the stadium continued in preparation for the World Cup.

EATING

ACONCHEGO CARIOCA BRAZILIAN $$

(Map p254; ☎2273-1035; Barão de Iguatemi 379, Praça da Bandeira; mains for two R$65-90; ⏲noon-11pm Tue-Sat, to 5pm Sun) Aconchega Carioca consistently ranks as one of the best places in town to eat traditional Brazilian cuisine. The setting, cozy and welcoming, has a casual neighborhood vibe, but attracts diners from across the city who come for *bobó de camarão* (shrimp and coconut milk stew), pork ribs with guava sauce and a *cachaça*-tinged flan for dessert.

BARSA PORTUGUESE $$

(Map p254; ☎2585-3743; 4th fl, Capitão Félix 110, Benfica; mains for two around R$70-150; ⏲noon-4pm Mon-Thu, to 5pm Fri-Sun) Inside the massive CADEG market, Barsa serves mouth-watering dishes using the freshest ingedients imaginable (not surprising, since Rio's largest produce market surrounds the place).The most famous dish is their roast suckling pig and all the fixings, which serves four and costs R$280 – though half servings are also available. On Sundays, there's live *chorinho* (a kind of instrumental music).

DA GEMA BRAZILIAN $$

(☎2208-9414; Barão de Mesquita 615, Tijuca; snacks R$4-24; ⏲5pm-midnight Tue-Fri, noon-2am

Sat, to 8pm Sun) Well off the beaten path, this humble-looking *botequim* (bar with table service) serves up mouth-watering *petiscos* (appetizers). It was begun by three culinary graduates who have elevated simple bar ingredients into high art in dishes like *pastel de feijao-preto* (black bean pasties), house-made *linguiça* (sausage) and *fondue da gema*, which is a polenta with crunchy pork rinds, sweet peppers, served with pork ribs and sausage. It's location near Salgueiro samba school (400m away), makes it a good pre-party spot on Saturday nights.

RESTAURANTE QUINTA DA BOA VISTA PORTUGUESE **$$**

(Map p254; ☎2589-4279; www.restaurantequintaboavista.com.br; Parque da Quinta da Boa Vista, São Cristóvão; mains R$40-60; ⏰10am-6pm) Inside the 1822 chapel of the former royal palace, this place serves up excellent *bacalhau ao forno* (oven-baked codfish), *caldeirada de frutos de mar* (seafood stew) and other Portuguese classics – the *picanha* (rumpsteak) is also top-notch. The servers, dressed in period costume, add a whimsical touch to the proceedings.

Barra da Tijuca & Western Rio

Neighborhood Top Five

❶ Hiking through tropical rainforest, enjoying stunning views from rocky lookouts and recovering beneath cool waterfalls in the **Floresta da Tijuca** (p156).

❷ Basking on the wide golden sands of **Praia da Barra da Tijuca** (p153).

❸ Exploring the lushly decadent gardens of **Sítio Burle Marx** (p153).

❹ Delving into Brazil's rich folk art traditions at the impressive **Casa do Pontal** (p153).

❺ Looking for wildlife walking the peaceful trails of the **Parque Ecológico Chico Mendes** (p153).

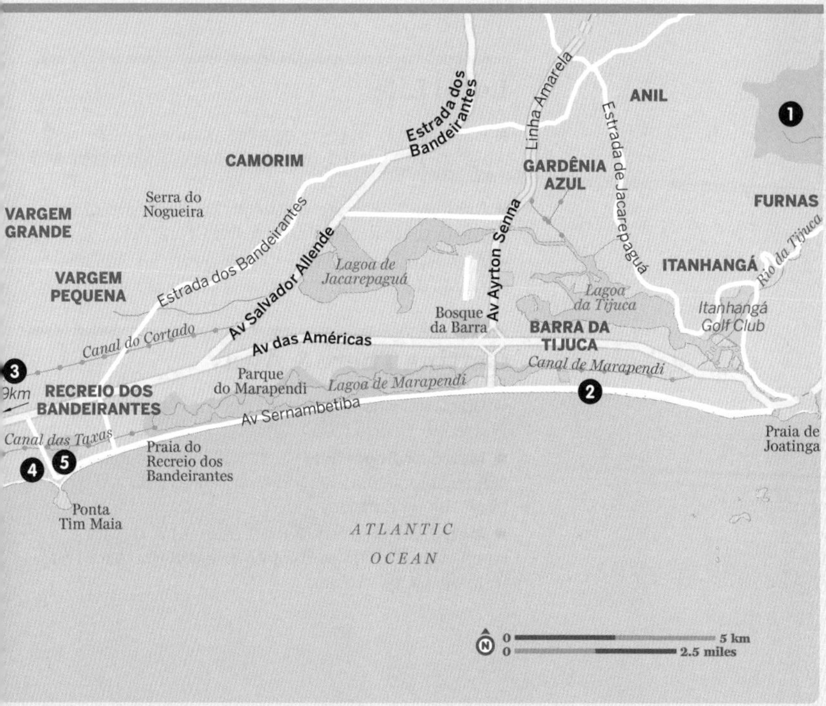

For more detail of this area see Map p252

Best Places to Eat

- Don Pascual (p156)
- Barreado (p157)
- Bira (p157)

For reviews, see p156

Best Places to Walk

- Floresta da Tijuca (p156)
- Bosque da Barra (p153)
- Parque Ecológico Chico Mendes (p153)

For reviews, see p153

Best Places to Shop

- The Village (p157)
- Fashion Mall (p157)
- Barra Shopping (p157)

For reviews, see p157

Explore Barra da Tijuca & Western Rio

The Miami of Rio, Barra – as it's known locally – is a sprawling suburb with huge malls and entertainment complexes, long traffic corridors and very little pedestrian movement. The beach here is the real attraction, a wide and lovely 15km-long stretch of shoreline.

The commercial area feels quite different from other parts of Rio, as Barra's development happened relatively recently. The middle classes first began moving here in the 1970s, when *cariocas* (residents of Rio) fled crowded, crime-ridden streets to live on an unpopulated stretch of beachfront. Today, the influx of new residents has created crowded, problematic conditions once again.

While first-time visitors to Rio don't always make it to Barra da Tijuca, there are some intriguing sights here aside from the beach. The Sítio Burle Marx (p153) contains some of the city's most picturesque gardens, while the Casa do Pontal (p153) houses a fascinating collection of folk art.

Once you get beyond the development of Barra, the region gets less and less urban, and you'll soon feel like you're deep in the tropics. Some of Rio's best beaches lie out this way. There are also some great restaurants in idyllic settings – feast on seafood while watching crashing waves – all of which seems a far cry from busy downtown Rio.

Local Life

- **Hangouts** Even party people from the Zona Sul will make the trip out to Nuth (p157), one of Rio's loveliest nightclubs.
- **Beaches** The western beaches are quite stunning, particularly Joatinga, Prainha and Grumari.
- **Arts** Barra's brand-new Cidade das Artes (p157) is the go-to destination for concerts and performances.

Getting There & Away

- **Bus** Copacabana, Ipanema and Leblon (308 & 523); Flamengo, Centro (308 & 309)
- **Metrô na Superfície**The Barra Expresso metro bus connects Ipanema/General Osório metro station with points along Barra.
- **Metrô** The planned Linha 4 expansion, due for completion by 2016, will finally connect Barra da Tijuca to Ipanema and Leblon.

SIGHTS

PRAIA DA BARRA DA TIJUCA BEACH

(Map p252; Av Sernambetiba, Recreio dos Bandeirantes) The best thing about Barra is the beach. It stretches for 12km, with the lovely blue sea lapping at the shore. The first few kilometers of the eastern end of the beach are filled with bars and seafood restaurants.

The young and hip hang out in front of *barraca* (stall) No 1 – in an area known as *Praia do Pepê,* after the famous *carioca* hang-gliding champion who died during a competition in Japan in 1991.

SÍTIO BURLE MARX GARDENS

(2410-1412; visitas.srbm@iphan.gov.br; Estrada da Barra de Guaratiba 2019, Guaratiba; admission R$10; tours 9:30am & 1:30pm Tue-Sat, by advance appointment only) This 35-hectare estate was once the home of Brazil's most famous landscape architect, Roberto Burle Marx. The estate's lush vegetation includes thousands of plant species, some of which are rare varieties from different corners of the globe. A 17th-century **Benedictine chapel** also lies on the estate, along with Burle Marx's original farmhouse and studio, where you can see displays of paintings, furniture and sculptures by the talented designer.

PARQUE ECOLÓGICO CHICO MENDES PARK

(Map p252; 2437-6400; Km 17, Av Jarbas de Carvalho 679, Recreio dos Bandeirantes; 8am-5pm) This 40-hectare park was created in 1989 and named after the Brazilian ecological activist who was murdered for his work. The park protects the remaining sand-spit vegetation from real estate speculators. The facilities include a visitors center and ecological trails leading to a small lake.

CASA DO PONTAL MUSEUM

(Map p252; 2490-3278; www.museucasadopontal.com.br; Estrada do Pontal 3295, Recreio dos Bandeirantes; admission permanent collection/temporary exhibits R$10/4; 9:30am-5pm Tue-Sun) Owned by French designer Jacques Van de Beuque, this impressive collection of more than 5000 pieces is one of the best folk-art collections in Brazil. The assorted artifacts are grouped according to themes, including music, Carnaval, religion and folklore. The grounds of the museum are surrounded by lush vegetation.

BOSQUE DA BARRA PARK

(Map p252; 3151-3428; Av das Américas 6000, intersection of Av Ayrton Senna, Barra da Tijuca; 8am-6pm Tue-Sun) Covering 50 hectares of salt-marsh vegetation, this park is a refuge and breeding area for many small birds and

WORTH A DETOUR

BEACHES WEST OF RIO

Although Copacabana and Ipanema are Rio's most famous stretches of sand, there are many stunning beaches in the area, some in spectacular natural settings.

The first major beach you'll reach heading west of Leblon is **Praia do Pepino** in São Conrado. It's close to where the hang gliders land, but not the cleanest beach around. Further west is the small, lovely but well-concealed **Praia da Joatinga**, reachable by a steep path down a rocky hillside. Be aware of the tides, so you don't get stranded.

Although it gets crowded on weekends, **Praia do Recreio dos Bandeirantes** is almost deserted during the week. The large rock acts as a natural breakwater, creating a calm bay. The 2km-long stretch of sand is popular with families.

The secluded 700m-long **Praia da Prainha** lies just past Recreio. It's one of the best surfing beaches in Rio, so it's always full of surfers. Waves come highly recommended here.

The most isolated and unspoiled beach close to the city, **Praia de Grumari** is quiet during the week and packed on weekends with *cariocas* looking to get away from city beaches. It is in a gorgeous setting, surrounded by mountains and lush vegetation.

From Grumari, a narrow road climbs over a jungle-covered hillside toward **Praia de Guaratiba**. West of here is a good view of the **Restinga da Marambaia** (the vegetation-rich strip between the beach and the mainland), closed off to the public by a naval base. *Cariocas* enjoy eating lunch at several of the seafood restaurants in the area.

It's very difficult to reach these beaches by public transport. It's best to go by private car or taxi.

1

2

1. Jardim Botânico (p79) 2. *Maracujá* (passion fruit) flower
3. Floresta da Tijuca (p156)

Green Spaces

No matter where you are in the city, you won't have to travel far to get a dose of nature. Rio has abundant parks and green spaces, some quite small and manicured (Parque do Catete) and others veritable wildernesses (Floresta da Tijuca).

Floresta da Tijuca

Rio's wide rainforest-covered expanse (p156) is teeming with plant and animal life. You can take scenic or challenging walks, including rewarding scrambles up its 900m-high peaks.

Sítio Burle Marx

Far west of town, but worth the trip, the gardens (p153) of Rio's famous landscape architect bloom with thousands of plant species. The lush estate is full of history, which you'll discover on a guided tour.

Parque do Flamengo

The landfill-turned-green space (p112) is best on Sunday when through-streets close to traffic, and runners and cyclists claim the long curving paths skirting the bay.

Jardim Botânico

These stately royal gardens (p79) make for a fine break from the beach. Here you can take in rare orchids, see massive Vitória Régia lilies and other Amazonian flora and admire the royal palms planted when the Portuguese royals ruled from Rio.

Parque do Catete

Behind the former presidential palace, this small but elegant park (p113) is complete with a swan-filled pond and a gallery (and cinema) adjoining the green space.

WORTH A DETOUR

FLORESTA DA TIJUCA – PARQUE NACIONAL DA TIJUCA

The Tijuca is all that's left of the Atlantic rainforest that once surrounded Rio de Janeiro. In just 15 minutes you can go from the concrete jungle of Copacabana to the 120-sq-km tropical jungle of the **Floresta da Tijuca** (www.parquedatijuca.com.br; 8am-5pm) FREE. A more rapid and dramatic contrast is hard to imagine. The forest is an exuberant green, with beautiful trees, creeks and waterfalls, mountainous terrain and high peaks. It has an excellent, well-marked trail system. Candomblistas (practitioners of the Afro-Brazilian religion of Candomblé) leave offerings by the roadside, families have picnics and serious hikers climb the 1012m to the summit of **Pico da Tijuca**.

The heart of the forest is the **Alto da Boa Vista** area in the **Floresta (Forest) da Tijuca**, with many lovely natural and man-made features. Among the highlights of this beautiful park are several waterfalls (**Cascatinha de Taunay**, **Cascata Gabriela** and **Cascata Diamantina**), a 19th-century chapel (**Capela Mayrink**) and numerous caves (**Gruta Luís Fernandes**, **Gruta Belmiro** and **Gruta Paulo e Virgínia**). Also in the park is a lovely picnic spot (**Bom Retiro**) and two restaurants – the elegant **Restaurante Os Esquilos** (2492-2197; Estrada Barão d'Escragnolle; mains R$42-55; noon-6pm Tue-Sun) and **Restaurante a Floresta** near the ruins of Major Archer's house (**Ruínas do Archer**).

The park is home to many different bird and animal species, including iguanas and monkeys, which you might encounter on one of the excellent day hikes you can make here (the trails are well signed). Good free trail maps are given out at the park entrance.

The entire park closes at sunset. It's best to go by car, though if you don't have a vehicle, numerous outfits lead hiking tours including **Jungle Me** (p204), **Rio Adventures** (p49) and **Rio Hiking** (p49).

The best route by car is to take Rua Jardim Botânico two blocks past the Jardim Botânico (heading east from Gávea). Turn left on Rua Lopes Quintas and then follow the Tijuca or Corcovado signs for two quick left turns until you reach the back of the Jardim Botânico, where you turn right. Then follow the signs for a quick ascent into the forest and past the picturesque lookout points of **Vista Chinesa** and **Mesa do Imperador**. As soon as you seem to come out of the forest, turn right onto the main road and you'll see the stone columns to the entrance of Alto da Boa Vista on your left after a couple of kilometers. You can also drive up to Alto da Boa Vista by heading out to São Conrado and turning right up the hill at the Parque Nacional da Tijuca signs. Coming from Barra da Tijuca, take Estrada da Barra da Tijuca north, which eventually turns into Rua da Boa Vista, from which there are entrances into the park.

animals. The woods have a jogging track and cycle path.

PARQUE DO MARAPENDI PARK

(Map p252; Av Sernambetiba, Recreio dos Bandeirantes; 8am-5pm) At the end of Av Sernambetiba in Recreio dos Bandeirantes, this biological reserve sets aside 70 hectares for study and has a small area for leisure, with workout stations and games areas.

EATING

Other parts of Rio offer some of the city's more rustic dining experiences. Far from the bustling streets of central Rio, one can find open-air spots overlooking the coast – beautiful views complemented by fresh seafood. The following places are best reached by private transport.

DON PASCUAL CONTEMPORARY $$$

(2428-6237; www.donpascual.com.br; Estrada do Sacarrão 867, Vargem Grande; mains R$46-65; noon-1am) Amid lush scenery, Don Pascual has undeniable charm, with dining on open-sided wooden decks, listening to the sounds of birdsong – and perhaps spying a toucan flitting past. Not surprisingly, by night, it's all couples at the candlelit tables. The food is good – juicy *picanha*, *feijoado do mar* (seafood and white-bean stew) and *ravioli de cordeiro* (lamb ravioli) – but not quite as dazzling as the ambience.

The only problem is it's hard to get to; call ahead for specific directions. You can also spend the night – or simply arrive early and go for a dip in the pool.

BARREADO SEAFOOD **$$$**

(Map p252; ☎2442-2023; Estrada dos Bandeirantes 21295, Vargem Grande; mains for 2 around R$100; ⌚noon-11pm Thu-Sat, to 8pm Sun) In a lush setting west of Barra, this rustic spot serves Brazilian seafood with a twist – such as shrimp served in pumpkin with rice, and trout with Brazil nuts. It's located about 35km west of Leblon.

BIRA SEAFOOD **$$$**

(☎2410-8304; Estrada da Vendinha 68A, Barra de Guaratiba; mains for 3 around R$215; ⌚noon-5pm Thu-Sun) Splendid views await diners who make the trek to Bira, about 45 minutes west of the city. On a breezy wooden deck, diners can partake in the flavorful, rich seafood served in huge portions – big enough for three. It's located about 35km west of Rio in the marvelous seaside setting of Barra da Guaratiba.

DRINKING & NIGHTLIFE

NUTH CLUB

(Map p252; ☎3575-6850; www.nuth.com.br; admission men R$40-70, women R$20-30; ⌚9pm-4am) This club (pronounced 'Nooch') is one of the city's favorite dance spots, despite its location in Barra. Expect a friendly, well-dressed crowd grooving to DJs spinning electro-samba, house and hip-hop. If you don't like the venue, or the price tag, there are other bars and restaurants nearby.

ENTERTAINMENT

CIDADE DAS ARTES PERFORMING ARTS

(Map p252; Av das Americas 5300, Barra da Tijuca) After years of cost overruns and construction delays, this stunning new concert hall finally opened in 2013. The R$500 million venture (originally slated to cost R$80 million) houses a grand 1800-seat concert hall, as well as theaters, a chamber music hall, a cinema and a restaurant. It's home to the Brazilian Symphony Orchestra, and a wide-ranging repertoire is planned for the future.

CITIBANK HALL CONCERT VENUE

(Map p252; Av Ayrton Senna 3000, Barra da Tijuca) Rio's largest (6000-seat) concert house tends to change names every few years, but continues to host top international and Brazilian bands, as well as ballet, opera and Broadway shows. The hall is in the Via Parque Shopping Center. Purchase tickets through **Tickets for Fun** (www.ticketsforfun.com.br).

UCI – NEW YORK CITY CENTER CINEMA

(Map p252; ☎2461-1818; Av das Americas 5000, New York City Center, Barra da Tijuca) UCI – New York City Center is Brazil's largest megaplex, featuring 18 different screening rooms complete with large, comfortable chairs and stadium seating. Films are screened constantly (every 10 minutes on weekends).

SHOPPING

Barra da Tijuca is the kingdom of shopping malls, each offering something slightly different than the one next door.

THE VILLAGE MALL

(Map p252; ☎3252-2999; www.shoppingvillage.com.br; Av das Américas 3900, Barra da Tijuca; ⌚11am-11pm Mon-Sat, 1pm-9pm Sun) This brand new shopping behemoth is Rio's most extravagant mall, with high-end retailers like Prada, Louis Vuitton, Cartier, Tiffany, Miu Miu and others.

FASHION MALL MALL

(☎2111-4427; Estrada da Gávea 899, São Conrado; ⌚10am-10pm Mon-Sat, noon-9pm Sun) This is not only Rio's most beautiful mall but it also features all the big international names – Armani, Versace, Louis Vuitton and others – plus all of Brazil's most recognizable designers. It's located in the posh neighborhood of São Conrado, near the Hotel Intercontinental.

BARRA SHOPPING MALL

(Map p252; ☎4003-4131; Av das Américas 4666, Barra da Tijuca; ⌚10am-10pm Mon-Sat, 1-9pm Sun) Rio's largest mall (one of the biggest on the continent) is an easy place to shop away a few hours or days as do 30 million shoppers each year. Over 500 stores clutter this 4km-long stretch, plus five movie screens, a kids' parkland and a wealth of dining options.

RIO DESIGN CENTER SHOPPING CENTER

(Map p232; ☎2430-3024; www.riodesign.com.br; Av das Américas 7777, Barra da Tijuca; ⏰10am-10pm Mon-Sat, 1-9pm Sun) This architecturally rich center features a number of excellent home-furnishing stores selling designer lamps, vases, decorative pieces and furniture. It also has some very good restaurants and a few art galleries.

VIA PARQUE SHOPPING SHOPPING CENTER

(Map p252; ☎2430-5100; www.shoppingviaparque.com.br; Av Ayrton Senna 3000, Barra da Tijuca; ⏰10am-10pm Mon-Sat, 1-9pm Sun) With 280 stores, six movie theaters and an abundance of restaurants, this shopping center is the heart of Rio's thriving consumer culture. The center also houses one of the city's big, busy and diverse concert arenas, Citibank Hall.

Sleeping

Rio has a wide range of lodging options, including boutique B&Bs, trendy hostels and bohemian guesthouses. There are scores of luxury hotels, particularly in Copacabana. Unfortunately, prices are high, and the value-for-money ratio is poor – in 2012, Rio earned the dubious honor of being the world's most expensive major city for a hotel stay.

Hotels

Despite Rio's growing popularity, the city's hotel scene is lackluster. The majority of hotels are glass and steel high-rises, with marble- and chrome-filled lobbies, and comfortable but uninspiring rooms. The best feature will be the view (if any) and the door by which to exit the room and explore this fascinating city. Other amenities to look for include pools, wi-fi (standard in most hotels, but not always free) and perhaps beach service (towels, chairs, attendants).

Hostels

With over 100 hostels scattered around the city, Rio does not lack for budget lodgings. These hostels are great settings to meet other travelers. With the booming economy, more and more Brazilians are traveling, so your dorm mate is just as likely to be from Porto Alegre as he or she is from Perth. Rio's hostels range in price and style, and subcultures dominate. For a bohemian vibe, try Santa Teresa, for the nightclub scene, look in Ipanema and Leblon. And for something totally different, stay in a hostel located in a favela.

Apartment Rentals

The best way to save money in Rio is to hire an apartment. There are numerous rental outfits in Ipanema and Copacabana, though you can just as easily go through Air BnB (www.airbnb.com), which usually has better deals – you can rent a whole apartment or simply a room in a shared flat, making it a good way to meet *cariocas* (Rio residents).

If you go through an agency, nightly rates start around R$200 for a studio apartment in Copacabana or R$350 in Ipanema. Typically, you'll need to pay 30% to 50% up front (some agencies accept credit cards, others use Paypal). Make sure you ask whether utilities and cleaning fees are included in the price. See Apartment Agencies (p166) for a list of reputable outfits.

Prices & Reservations

Rooms with an ocean view cost about 30% to 50% more than rooms without. During the summer (December through March), hotel rates typically rise by about 30% and many places book up well in advance, so it's wise to reserve ahead. There's no getting around it: prices double or triple for New Year's Eve and Carnaval, and most accommodations, including hostels, will only book in four-day blocks around these holidays. For the Summer Olympics, prepare for exorbitant price hikes. It's never too early to book for Carnaval, with better places filling up to a year in advance.

Breakfast

Nearly every guesthouse, hostel and hotel serves some form of *café da manha* (breakfast). At cheaper places, this may only be a roll with bread and some instant coffee; better places serve fresh fruits, juices, strong coffee, yogurt, cheese and cured meats, fresh breads and perhaps cooked eggs. Oddly, Rio's most expensive lodgings now charge for breakfast.

NEED TO KNOW

Price Ranges

Prices are for double rooms, except for hostels with only dorm beds, in which case the price is for one person.

$	less than R$200
$$	R$200 to R$500
$$$	more than R$500

Room Tax

Keep in mind that many hotels add between 5% and 15% in taxes and service charges. The cheaper places don't generally bother with this. Be sure to read the fine print when booking.

Websites

- Air Bnb (www.airbnb.com) The best site for apartment rentals.
- Couchsurfing (www.couchsurfing.com) Over 10,000 hosts in Rio, and an active meet-up community.
- Booking (www.booking.com) Generally the best deals for hotels and guesthouses.
- Lonely Planet (www.lonelyplanet.com/hotels) Extensive hotel reviews and online booking.

Lonely Planet's Top Choices

Maze Inn (p170) A unique place with striking views in Tavares Bastos, one of Rio's safest favelas.

Casa Mosquito (p164) Beautifully designed boutique guesthouse above Ipanema.

Don Pascual (p172) Incredible setting amid tropical rainforest, lovely pool and restaurant.

Casa Beleza (p171) One of many unique and charming small-scale guesthouses in Santa Teresa.

Hotel Santa Teres (p172) Rio's finest boutique hotel, with a great restaurant and bar.

Best Guesthouses

Casa Cool Beans (p172)

Casa da Carmen e do Fernando (p171)

Bonita (p163)

Casalegre (p171)

Casa Áurea (p171)

Margarida's Pousada (p163)

Best Boutique Lodging

Hotel Fasano (p165)

Le Relais Marambaia (p172)

Villa Laurinda (p172)

Castelinho 38 (p172)

Best Unusual Stays

Le Relais Marambaia (p172)

Rio Surf 'N Stay (p172)

Pousada Favelinha (p170)

Cama e Café (p171)

Best by Budget

$

Rio Hostel (p170)

Cabana Copa (p166)

Oztel (p169)

Z.Bra Hostel (p163)

$$

Casa Cool Beans (p172)

Casa da Carmen e do Fernando (p171)

Villa Laurinda (p172)

Casalegre (p171)

Rio Guesthouse (p167)

$$$

Marina All Suites (p165)

Copacabana Palace (p168)

Hotel Fasano (p165)

Where to Stay

Neighborhood	For	Against
Ipanema & Leblon	Great location near the beach and the lake, with Rio's best restaurants and bars surrounding you. Great views possible – ocean, lake or possibly Corcovado.	Pricier than any other location. Not as many options as Copacabana.
Copacabana & Leme	A wealth of lodging possibilities packed into a long narrow high-rise-lined neighborhood. Proximity to the beach. Good transport connections to other parts of the city. A handful of good restaurants and bars.	Nightlife is more limited than Ipanema or even Botafogo. It's very touristy and some *cariocas* avoid going there. Sex tourism in some parts; tourist-trap restaurants along Av Atlantica.
Botofogo & Urca	Good neighborhood, with restaurants, bars and nightclubs that attract a local crowd.	Not being within walking distance of the beach. Noisy streets. Few attractions.
Flamengo & Around	Better prices than the beachside districts.	Few options, mostly budget. Very few restaurants and bars, not much nightlife.
Santa Teresa & Lapa	Santa Teresa: Charming bohemian district with great architecture and alternative, art-minded residents. A handful of good restaurants and drinking spots. Lapa: The epicenter of Rio's samba-fueled nightlife.	Santa Teresa: Far from the beaches, poor transportation links. Lapa: Unappealing and grubby by day.
Barra da Tijuca & Western Rio	Great beaches, laid-back vibe.	Long commutes into town. No neighborhood vibe – you'll need a car to get around.

Ipanema & Leblon

RIO HOSTEL – IPANEMA HOSTEL $

(Map p228; ☎2287-2928; www.riohostelipanema.com; Casa 1, Canning 18, Ipanema; dm/d from R$45/150; @ wi-fi) This friendly hostel is in a small villa on a peaceful stretch of Ipanema. A mix of travelers stay here, enjoying the clean rooms, the airy top-floor deck with hammocks and the small front veranda. The same owners operate the respected Santa Teresa hostel of the same name.

HOSTEL HARMONIA HOSTEL $

(Map p228; ☎2523-4905; www.casadaharmonia.com; Casa 18, Barão da Torre 175, Ipanema; dm/d without bathroom R$60/130; @ wi-fi) Run by a Swede and a Californian, Hostel Harmonia is one of the best hostels in Ipanema, with a good traveler vibe. The lounge and rooms have two-toned wood floors, and quarters are clean and well maintained with four to six beds in each room.

LEMON SPIRIT HOSTEL HOSTEL $

(Map p232; ☎2294-1853; www.lemonspirit.com; Cupertino Durão 56, Leblon; dm R$70-80; air-con @ wi-fi) Leblon's first hostel boasts an excellent spot one block from the beach. The dorm rooms (four to six beds in each) are clean and simple without much decor. There's also a tiny courtyard in front, and the attractive lobby bar is a good place to meet other travelers over caipirinhas.

CHE LAGARTO IPANEMA HOSTEL $

(Map p228; ☎2512-8076; www.chelagarto.com; Paul Redfern 48; dm/d from R$60/180; air-con @ wi-fi)

LOVE AMONG THE CARIOCAS

Living in such a crowded city, *cariocas* (residents of Rio) sometimes have a difficult time snatching a few moments of privacy. For those living with their parents or sharing a tiny apartment with roommates, an empty stretch of beach, a park bench or a seat in the back of a cafe are all fine spots to steal a few kisses, but for more...progressive action, *cariocas* take things elsewhere – to the motel, aka the *love* motel.

Love motels aren't so much a *carioca* oddity as they are a Brazilian institution. They're found in every part of the country, usually sprouting along the outskirts of cities and towns. Some are designed with lavish facades – decked out to resemble medieval castles, Roman temples or ancient pyramids – while others blend in discreetly. Regardless of the exteriors, the interiors are far removed from the 'less is more' design philosophy. Mirrors cover the ceiling while heart-shaped, vibrating beds stretch beneath them. Rose-tinted mood lights, Jacuzzis, televisions loaded with porn channels, dual-headed showers and a room-service menu on the bedside table featuring sex toys – all these come standard in most love motels. Such places scream seediness in the West. In Brazil, however, they're nothing out of the ordinary. People need a place for their liaisons – they might as well have a laugh and a bit of fun while they're at it. The motels are used by young lovers who want to get away from their parents, parents who want to get away from their kids and couples who want to get away from their spouses. They are an integral part of the nation's social fabric, and it's not uncommon for *cariocas* to host parties in them.

The quality of the motels varies. The most lavish are three-story suites with a hot tub beneath a skylight on the top floor, a sauna and bathroom on the 2nd floor, and the garage underneath (allowing anonymity). They come standard with all the other mood-enhancement features. For the best suites, expect to pay upwards of R$500 for eight hours, and more on weekends. *Cariocas* claim that an equally fine time can be had at standard rooms.

If you wish to check out this cultural institution, here are some options:

Shalimar (☎3322-3392; www.hotelshalimar.com.br; Av Niemeyer 218, Vidigal; r for 6hr from R$78)

VIPs (☎3322-1662; www.vipsmotel.com.br; Av Niemeyer 418, Vidigal; ste for 8hr R$155-580)

Love Time (Map p241; ☎7128-8054; www.lovetimehotel.com.br; Rua do Catete 63; r for 4hr R$82-194)

Part of a small empire of hostels in South America, Che Lagarto's Ipanema branch is a popular budget spot for those young travelers who want to be close to the beach. It's a five-story hostel, with basic rooms and not much common space – aside from a bar on the ground floor.

LIGHTHOUSE HOSTEL HOSTEL $

(Map p228; ☎2522-1353; www.thelighthouse.com.br; No 20, Rua Barão da Torre 175, Ipanema; dm/d without bathroom R$60/160; ❄@📶) Along with a handful of other budget spots on this quiet lane, the Lighthouse has an easygoing vibe and clean, simple rooms that attract a good mix of backpackers. Accommodations consist of eight-bed dorm rooms and one private double (with a foldout sofa to sleep three).

Z.BRA HOSTEL HOSTEL $$

(Map p232; ☎3596-2386; www.zbrahostel.com; General San Martin 1212, Ipanema; dm R$90, d with without/with bathroom from R$240/295; ❄@📶) One of Rio's most stylish hostels, Z.Bra has customized ultramodern dorm beds, with top-quality mattresses and thoughtful details (low lighting, reading lamps, big lockers). The small ground-floor bar aims for retro cool, with mid-century furnishings and a tiny stage that hosts occasional bands and arts events. The owners have inside tips on great parties around Rio (and can help you beat the lines).

MANGO TREE HOSTEL $$

(Map p228; ☎2287-9255; www.mangotreehostel.com; Prudente de Morais 594, Ipanema; dm from R$55, d without/with bathroom from R$170/190; ❄@📶) In a handsome villa in Ipanema, this popular hostel offers rooms with two-toned wood floors and a welcoming atmosphere. The front porch provides open-air space for unwinding, and there's also a lounge/TV room. Bedbugs have been an issue in the past.

IPANEMA BEACH HOUSE HOSTEL $$

(Map p228; ☎3202-2693; www.ipanemahouse.com; Barão da Torre 485, Ipanema; dm R$60, d without/with bathroom from R$180/200; @📶🏊) This is one of Rio's best-looking hostels. It's set in a converted two-story house with six- and nine-bed dorms (in the form of three-tiered bunk beds). There are private rooms, indoor and outdoor lounge spaces, a small bar and an attractive pool. Prices are higher on weekends.

MARGARIDA'S POUSADA INN $$

(Map p228; ☎2239-1840; www.margaridaspousada.com; Barão da Torre 600, Ipanema; s/d/tr R$200/250/320; ❄@) For those seeking something smaller and cozier than a high-rise hotel, try this superbly located Ipanema guesthouse (pousada). You'll find 11 pleasant, simply furnished rooms scattered about the low-rise building. Margarida also operates a secluded pousada for long-term guests in Jardim Botânico; contact her in Ipanema for details.

BONITA HOSTEL $$

(Map p228; ☎2227-1703; www.bonitaipanema.com; Barão da Torre 107, Ipanema; dm from R$60, d without/with bathroom R$220/250; ❄@📶🏊) This peacefully set converted house has history: it's where bossa nova legend Tom Jobim lived (1962–65), writing some of his most famous songs. Rooms are clean but simply furnished, and most open onto a shared deck overlooking a small pool and patio.

IPANEMA HOTEL RESIDÊNCIA SERVICED APARTMENTS $$

(Map p228; ☎3125-5000; www.ipanemahotel.com.br; Rua Barão da Torre 192, Ipanema; d from R$450; ❄🏊) Set on one of Ipanema's lovely tree-lined streets, this high-rise has large apartments, with kitchen units, lounge areas and pleasant bedrooms. Each apartment is furnished differently, so look at a few before committing.

LEBLON OCEAN HOTEL RESIDÊNCIA SERVICED APARTMENTS $$

(Map p232; ☎2158-8282; Rainha Guilhermina 117, Leblon; apt from R$450; ❄📶🏊) This all-suites hotel has a range of spacious, simply furnished suites, all with kitchen units and small balconies. There's also a small indoor pool and sauna, and Rio's best restaurants (and a handful of bars) are just outside the door. The only catch is that you have to book a minimum of five days.

IPANEMA INN HOTEL $$

(Map p228; ☎2523-6092; www.ipanemainn.com.br; Maria Quitéria 27, Ipanema; d R$346-531; ❄) Ipanema Inn is a simple hotel whose rooms have off-white ceramic tile floors and simple wood furnishings; some are disappointingly small. *Superiores* (front-facing rooms) don't have ocean views, but if you lean far enough out the window, you get a glimpse of the beachfront.

HOTEL SAN MARCO HOTEL **$$**

(Map p228; ☎2540-5032; www.sanmarcohotel.net; Visconde de Pirajá 524 , Ipanema; s/d R$260/275; ❄@📶) It's all about location at this midrange Ipanema hotel. A tiny elevator carries you up to the rooms, which are small but clean with tile floors and a mint-green color scheme. There are also a couple of coffin-sized 'economy' rooms that run R$205/225 for a single/double.

HOTEL VERMONT HOTEL **$$**

(Map p228; ☎3202-5500; www.hotelvermont.com.br; Visconde de Pirajá 254, Ipanema; s/d from R$310/350; ❄) The Hotel Vermont offers no-frills accommodations at a good location. Although the place received a makeover in recent years, the rooms are nothing fancy – small and clean, with tile floors, striped duvets and tiny, modern bathrooms. Light sleepers should avoid rooms facing noisy Visconde de Pirajá.

ARPOADOR INN HOTEL **$$**

(☎2523-0060; www.arpoadorinn.com.br; Francisco Otaviano 177, Ipanema; r R$345, with view R$621; ❄📶) Overlooking Praia do Arpoador (Arpoador beach), this six-story hotel is the only one in Ipanema or Copacabana that doesn't have a busy street between it and the beach. The rooms are small and basic, but the brighter, prettier 'deluxe' rooms have glorious ocean views.

★**CASA MOSQUITO** GUESTHOUSE **$$$**

(Map p228; ☎3586-5042; www.casamosquito.com; Saint Roman 222, Ipanema; r R$660-1200) Opened by two French expats, the Casa Mosquito is a beautifully designed boutique guesthouse with luxuriously appointed rooms. The converted all-white 1940s mansion sits on a tranquil garden-filled property with scenic views of Pão de Açúcar and the Pavão-Pavãozinho favela. Meals available by request. More rooms and a pool are planned for the future. Casa Mosquito is located on a steep winding street about 10 minutes' walk from Praça General Osório.

MERCURE RIO DE JANEIRO HOTEL **$$$**

(Map p228; ☎2114-8100; www.mercure.com; Av Rainha Elizabeth 440, Ipanema; d from R$650; ❄@📶🏊) Not to be confused with the slightly fancier Mercure Arpoador, this hotel offers trim and tidy suites, with pressed-wood floors, big windows and light, muted colors. Some rooms have balconies, and the upper two floors (eight and nine) have slightly better views (though you still won't see the ocean). There's also a pool, which is surrounded by tall buildings.

MAR IPANEMA HOTEL **$$$**

(Map p228; ☎3875-9190; www.maripanema.com.br; Visconde de Pirajá 539, Ipanema; d R$575-750; ❄) This reliable hotel in Ipanema has trim, modern rooms with decent beds, good lighting and an inviting color scheme. It's also in a great location, on Ipanema's lively shopping strip, just two blocks from the beach. The downside is the lack of a view, which is a small loss if you plan to spend your day out enjoying the city.

MONSIEUR LE BLOND SERVICED APARTMENTS **$$$**

(Map p232; ☎3722-5000; gerenciamlblond@hotmail.com; Av Bartolomeu Mitre 455, Leblon; ste from R$650; ❄🏊) A five-minute walk from Praia do Leblon (Leblon beach), this spot combines the service of a hotel with the convenience of an apartment. The colorful accommodations are all comfortably furnished with small kitchens, combined living-dining areas and balconies – some with fine views. The pool, which gets direct sunlight only part of the day, makes a fine place for sunbathing and mingling.

VISCONTI SERVICED APARTMENTS **$$$**

(Map p228; ☎2111-8600; www.promenade.com.br; Prudente de Morais 1050, Ipanema; ste from R$615; ❄) The Visconti has stylish modern suites (wood floors, stuffed leather furniture, modular lamps) with living-dining rooms, balconies and bedrooms. It's on a residential, tree-lined street a block from the beach.

SHERATON HOTEL **$$$**

(☎2274-1122; www.sheraton-rio.com; Av Niemeyer 121, Vidigal; d from R$450; ❄@🏊) The Sheraton is a true resort hotel, with large, peaceful grounds. Every room has a balcony, facing either Leblon and Ipanema or verdant greenery. The rooms are nicely furnished in a cozy, contemporary style, and if you stay out here you'll enjoy a nearly private beach in front, tennis courts, swimming pools and a good health club. The main drawback is that it's a bit far from the action.

EVEREST RIO HOTEL **$$$**

(Map p228; ☎2525-2200; www.everest.com.br; Prudente de Morais 1117, Ipanema; d R$520-750; ❄📶) Another of Ipanema's pricey high-rise hotels, the Everest Rio features a range of rooms, from small dated rooms to more recently renovated quarters with a bright, spacious contemporary look. All rooms have large windows and modern bathrooms; the best have a view of the lake.

IPANEMA TOWER HOTEL $$$
(Map p228; ☑2247-7033; www.ipanematower.com; Prudente de Morais 1008, Ipanema; ste from R$664; ❄ ✻) Along one of Ipanema's main thoroughfares, the all-suites Ipanema Tower has large, fully furnished apartments with pressed-wood floors, a balcony (some with ocean views), small kitchen, living room and bedroom. While the furnishings are far from opulent, they're cozy enough, with a decent kitchen table and a few pieces of modern artwork on the walls.

GOLDEN TULIP IPANEMA PLAZA HOTEL $$$
(Map p228; ☑3687-2000; www.goldentulip ipanemaplaza.com; Farme de Amoedo 34, Ipanema; d from R$652; ❄ ✻) A top choice, the 18-story Plaza features nicely decorated rooms with tile floors, a muted color scheme and sizable windows to let in the tropical rays. You'll also find broad, comfortable beds, spacious bathrooms (with bathtubs) and a lovely rooftop pool. Some rooms overlook the ocean; others face the outstretched arms of Cristo Redentor.

SOL IPANEMA HOTEL $$$
(Map p228; ☑2525-2020; www.solipanema.com.br; Av Vieira Souto 320, Ipanema; s/d R$505/560, with ocean view R$635/705; ❄ ⎙ ✻) Occupying prime real estate facing Ipanema beach, the tall, slender Sol Ipanema features rooms decorated in creams and earth tones with dark-wood furnishings and good lighting. Pricier rooms have magnificent, unobstructed ocean views but are otherwise identical to the standard rooms.

CAESAR PARK HOTEL $$$
(Map p228; ☑2525-2525; www.sofitel.com; Av Vieira Souto 460, Ipanema; d from R$690; ❄ @ ✻) Popular with business travelers, this well-located beachfront option has sizable rooms with a warm, inviting feel, artwork on the walls, and flat-screen TVs. The best rooms have ocean views.

HOTEL PRAIA IPANEMA HOTEL $$$
(Map p228; ☑2141-4949; www.praiaipanema.com; Av Vieira Souto 706, Ipanema; d from R$730; ⊜ ❄ @ ✻) With a view of Ipanema beach, this popular 16-story hotel offers trim, comfortable rooms, each with a balcony. The design is sleek and modern, with off-white tile floors, recessed lighting and artwork on the walls. Stretch out on the molded white lounge chairs next to the rooftop pool. The bar has a view, and there's a small fitness center.

RITZ PLAZA HOTEL SERVICED APARTMENTS $$$
(Map p232; ☑2540-4940; www.ritzhotel.com.br; Av Ataúlfo de Paiva 1280, Leblon; r from R$505; ❄ ⎙ ✻) In one of Rio's most desirable areas, this stylish low-key hotel has attractive, uniquely designed rooms and common areas that give the Ritz a boutique feel. The best rooms have kitchen units and balconies – some with partial ocean views – and all are trimmed with artwork, good lighting and spotless bedrooms. Amenities include an elegant (if often empty) bar, a sauna, pool and a spa.

MARINA PALACE HOTEL $$$
(Map p232; ☑2172-1000; www.hotelmarina.com.br; Av Delfim Moreira 630, Leblon; r from R$490; ❄ @ ⎙ ✻) Occupying a privileged position overlooking Praia do Leblon, this 26-story hotel has contemporary rooms with artwork, sizable beds, flat-screen TVs and DVD and CD players. Spacious deluxe rooms face the ocean. The Marina has top-notch service and a top-floor bar and restaurant with 360-degree views.

MARINA ALL SUITES BOUTIQUE HOTEL $$$
(Map p232; ☑2172-1100; www.marinaallsuites.com.br; Av Delfim Moreira 696, Leblon; ste from R$865; ❄ @ ✻) Here you'll find beautifully decorated rooms, doting service and all the creature comforts. As per the name, it's all suites here, meaning that, between the comfy bedroom and living room, you'll have 39 to 75 sq meters in which to stretch out. The best rooms in the oceanfront hotel have splendid views of the shoreline; other attractions are the trendy Bar D'Hotel, the lovely top-floor pool and the spa with a full range of treatments.

HOTEL FASANO HOTEL $$$
(Map p228; ☑3202-4000; www.fasano.com.br; Av Vieira Souto 80, Ipanema; d from R$1620; ❄ @ ⎙ ✻) Designed by Philippe Starck, the Fasano has 91 sleek rooms set with Egyptian cotton sheets, goose-down pillows and high-tech fittings. The best rooms have balconies overlooking the crashing waves of Ipanema beach, which lies just across the

road. Rooms without a view simply don't justify the price. The lovely rooftop pool (open to guests only) is truly breathtaking – as are the room rates.

With stylish rooms, a great location and a much-touted seafood restaurant and bar, this is the top destination for the style set and celebutantes (Beyoncé and Madonna both stayed here in 2010).

Copacabana & Leme

CABANA COPA HOSTEL $

(Map p236; ☎3988-9912; www.cabanacopa.com.br; Travessa Guimarães Natal 12, Copacabana; dm R$40-90, d R$140-200; ❄@🛜) Top hostel honors go to this Greek-Brazilian run gem in a colonial-style '50s house tucked away in a Copacabana cranny. Four- to 10-bed dorms prevail throughout the home, chock-full of original architectural details and a hodgepodge of funky floorings. There's a lively bar and common areas.

WALK ON THE BEACH HOSTEL HOSTEL $

(Map p236; ☎2545-7500; www.walk-on-the-beach.com; Dias da Rocha 85, Copacabana; dm R$40-55; @🛜) Set in an unsigned two-story villa on one of Copacabana's rare quiet streets, this nicely designed hostel offers good-value fan-cooled dorm rooms (each with three to 12 beds). It has a lounge room and a small bar, and maintains a welcoming, low-key vibe.

BAMBOO RIO HOSTEL $

(Map p236; ☎2236-1117; www.bamboorio.com; Lacerda Coutinho 45, Copacabana; dm R$38-62, d R$120-180; ❄@🛜🏊) Yet another hostel set in a former villa, Bamboo Rio is a friendly, comfortable hostel with tidy air-conditioned dorm rooms (sleeping from five to 12), ample lounge space, a tiny pool and an inviting bar area. Overall, it's a nice choice for Copacabana, with a good traveler vibe.

CHE LAGARTO HOSTEL $

(Map p236; ☎3209-0348; www.chelagarto.com; Barata Ribeira 111, Copacabana; dm R$45-60; ❄@🛜🏊) This popular full-service hostel has a friendly, party atmosphere. The small rooftop pool with adjoining bar is a good place to meet other travelers, and the hostel arranges loads of activities – boat parties, nights out in Lapa, BBQs and more. There are two other Che Lagartos in Copacabana and one in Ipanema.

PURA VIDA HOSTEL $

(Map p236; ☎2210-8885; www.puravidahostel.com.br; Saint Roman 20, Copacabana; dm R$35-45, d without bathroom R$150-200; @) Pura Vida occupies a converted castle-like mansion (built in the 1920s) that was once the home of the Polish ambassador. Here you'll find huge dorm rooms with mostly single beds and polished wood floors, plus spacious common areas, including an outdoor veranda with bar.

EDIFICIO JUCATI HOSTEL, SERVICED APARTMENTS $$

(Map p236; ☎2547-5422; www.edificiojucati.com.br; Tenente Marones de Gusmão 85, Copacabana; s/d/tr/q R$190/220/250/280; ❄🛜) Near a small park, on a tranquil street, Jucati offers little in the way of atmosphere (there are no common areas), but does have large, simply furnished apartments with slate floors and small but serviceable kitchens. Have a look at the layout before committing. Most apartments have just one bedroom with a double bed and a living room with a bunk bed.

RESIDENCIAL APARTT SERVICED APARTMENTS $$

(Map p236; ☎2522-1722; www.apartt.com.br; Francisco Otaviano 42, Copacabana; s/d R$248/

APARTMENT AGENCIES

Blame It on Rio 4 Travel (Map p236; ☎3813-5510; www.blameitonrio4travel.com; Xavier da Silveira 15B, Copacabana) Created by a kind, helpful expat from New York, this professional agency rents many types of apartments and also has a travel agency, a few computers for internet use (R$10 per hour) and a laundry next door.

Rio Apartments (Map p236; ☎2247-6221; www.rioapartments.com; Av Rainha Elizabeth 85, Copacabana) A Swedish-run outfit with many apartment rentals in the Zona Sul.

Copacabana Holiday (Map p236; ☎2542-1525; www.copacabanaholiday.com.br; Barata Ribeiro 90A, Copacabana) Near the Cardeal Arcoverde metro station, this agency rents apartments in Copacabana and Ipanema.

402; ❄ 📶) This old-fashioned all-suites hotel doesn't have much charm, but the price and location are excellent. Basic one-bedroom suites have small kitchen units, a gloomy lounge room (with cable TV) and a sparsely furnished bedroom.

HOTEL IBIS HOTEL **$$**

(Map p236; ☎3218-1150; www.ibis.com; Ministro Viveiros de Castro 134, Copacabana; r not incl breakfast from R$269; ❄ 📶) The international chain opened its first Copacabana branch in 2012, and offers good value for its small, modern rooms with comfortable beds, sizable windows, wood floors and reliable wi-fi.

HOTEL SANTA CLARA HOTEL **$$**

(Map p236; ☎2256-2650; www.hotelsantaclara.com.br; Décio Vilares 316, Copacabana; s/d from R$240/260; 📶) Along one of Copacabana's most peaceful streets, this simple three-story hotel has some charming, old-fashioned features, and it's a nice alternative to the high-rises found elsewhere in the neighborhood. The rooms in back are a little gloomy; upstairs rooms are best (and well worth the extra reais), with wood floors, antique bed frames, writing desk and a balcony.

ATLANTIS COPACABANA HOTEL HOTEL **$$**

(Map p228; ☎2521-1142; www.atlantishotel.com.br; Bulhões de Carvalho 61, Copacabana; s/d/tr from R$310/330/380; ❄ 📶 🏊) Atlantis' rooms are clean and perfectly serviceable, but the whole place could use an update. The location, however – a short walk to either Ipanema or Copacabana beach – is excellent. The rooms above the 9th floor generally have fine views, and there is a modest pool and a sauna on the roof.

SOUTH AMERICAN COPACABANA HOTEL HOTEL **$$$**

(Map p228; ☎2227-9161; www.southamericanhotel.com.br; Francisco Sá 90, Copacabana; r from R$500; ❄ @ 📶 🏊) Solid value for its trim, modern rooms, this 13-story hotel is nicely located a short stroll from both Copacabana and Ipanema beaches. Rooms are set with pressed-wood floors, colorful bedspreads and a touch of artwork on the walls.

HOTEL VILAMAR HOTEL **$$**

(Map p236; ☎3461-5601; www.hotelvilamarcopacabana.com.br; Bolívar 75, Copacabana; s/d R$378/420; ❄ @ 🏊) This 15-story hotel, set on a quiet street in Copacabana, has narrow rooms with pressed-wood floors and cheery yellow bedspreads and curtains. Some bathrooms have Jacuzzi tubs.

AUGUSTO'S COPACABANA HOTEL **$$**

(Map p236; ☎2547-1800; www.augustoshotel.com.br; Bolívar 119, Copacabana; s/d R$380/440; ❄ @ 📶 🏊) Augusto's plays off the kitschy ancient Rome theme with murals of charioteers and lyre-playing toga-wearers. The rooms, however, are fairly straightforward with a light and airy feel, and modern bathrooms. Some rooms have balconies (but no views). The biggest rooms end in 1 or 8. There's also a small rooftop pool.

COPACABANA HOTEL RESIDÊNCIA SERVICED APARTMENTS **$$**

(Map p236; ☎3622-5200; www.atlanticahotels.com.br; Barata Ribeiro 222, Copacabana; s/d R$420/466; ❄ @ 📶 🏊) This is a fine choice for those seeking a bit more space. The clean, well-maintained suites all have small kitchen units and lounge rooms with good natural lighting. Keep in mind that busy Barata Ribeiro is awfully noisy; try to snag a top-floor apartment.

RIO GUESTHOUSE B&B **$$**

(Map p236; ☎2521-8568; www.rioguesthouse.com; Francisco Sá 5, Copacabana; d R$354-530; ❄ 📶) On a split-level penthouse overlooking Copacabana beach, the Australian-Brazilian hosts open up their home and rent out several comfortable rooms to guests. The highlight is undoubtedly the outdoor patio with gorgeous views over Copacabana.

DESIGN HOTEL PORTINARI HOTEL **$$**

(Map p236; ☎3222-8800; www.portinarihotelrio.com; Francisco Sá 17, Copacabana; r R$423-590; ❄ @ 📶) This stylish 13-story hotel demonstrates real design smarts. The rooms have tile floors, artful lighting and big windows, and each floor is decorated in a different style. The top-floor restaurant is set with tropical plants and boasts fine views through the floor-to-ceiling windows.

WINDSOR MARTINIQUE HOTEL HOTEL **$$**

(Map p236; ☎2195-5200; www.windsorhoteis.com.br; Sá Ferreira 30, Copacabana; s/d from R$376/400; ❄ 🏊) Near the Ipanema end of Copacabana, this is an all-glass high-rise with clean, but dated-looking rooms and a rooftop pool. It's just 30m to the beach, and the hotel provides a fine breakfast buffet.

RIO ROISS HOTEL HOTEL $$
(Map p236; ☎3222-9950; www.rioroiss.com.br; Aires Saldanha 48, Copacabana; s/d from R$276/354;) This friendly low-key place has fairly new carpets and flat-screen TVs, but otherwise rather dated rooms. For added space and bigger windows, opt for a corner room (any room ending in 2).

ACAPULCO HOTEL $$
(Map p240; ☎3077-2000; www.acapulcohotel.com.br; Gustavo Sampaio 854, Leme; s/d from R$385/410; @) The Acapulco hotel lies just a short stroll (one block) from the immortalized Copacabana beach. Recent renovations have made it an attractive option. Most rooms have a neat look about them with pressed-wood floors and colorful duvets and curtains.

REAL PALACE HOTEL HOTEL $$
(Map p236; ☎2101-9292; www.realpalacehotelrj.com.br; Duvivier 70, Copacabana; s/d R$426/460; @) Set on a quiet street a few blocks from Copacabana's famous beach, this simple 13-story hotel has small, sparsely furnished rooms. Tiles (of the faux-wood variety) cover the clean-swept floors, and the rooms all get decent light. There's a small rooftop pool, though it lies in shadow for most of the day.

MAR PALACE HOTEL $$
(Map p236; ☎2132-1501; www.hotelmarpalace.com.br; Av NS de Copacabana 552, Copacabana; r R$357; @) On Copacabana's busiest road, this sleek glass-and-steel high-rise building hides modest-sized rooms with faux-wood floors and large windows overlooking the street and the leafy plaza beyond. There's a tiny pool and a sauna on the top floor, as well as a workout room with views of Cristo Redentor.

ORLA COPACABANA HOTEL $$
(Map p236; ☎2525-2425; www.orlahotel.com.br; Av Atlântica 4122, Copacabana; d R$450-600;) The Spanish-owned Orla Copacabana has attractive, understated rooms, but the beach-facing location is the real draw. The standard rooms are too dark and cramped, so it's not worth staying here unless you book one of the deluxe rooms with those unobstructed ocean views.

PESTANA RIO ATLÂNTICA HOTEL $$$
(Map p236; ☎2548-6332; www.pestana.com; Av Atlântica 2230, Copacabana; s/d from R$638/691; @) Beautifully located along Copacabana beach, the Pestana has excellent amenities, decent service and a wide range of rooms. The best have wood floors, balconies and a bright, modern design scheme. Rooms at the lower end are carpeted, rather bland and too small to recommend.

PORTO BAY RIO INTERNACIONAL HOTEL $$$
(Map p236; ☎2546-8000; www.portobay.com.br; Av Atlântica 1500, Copacabana; s/d from R$600/660; @) One of Copacabana's top beachfront hotels, Porto Bay has stylish rooms with a light and airy feel that are painted in cool tones. Large white duvets, light hardwoods, elegant furnishings and simple artwork all complement each other nicely. Big windows let in lots of light, and most rooms have balconies.

SOFITEL RIO DE JANEIRO HOTEL $$$
(Map p236; ☎2525-1232; www.sofitel.com; Av Atlântica 4240, Copacabana; d from R$828; @) One of Rio's priciest hotels, the French-owned Sofitel does its best to impress. The excellent service, comfortable rooms, two lovely pools and beachfront location have earned many fans. All rooms have balconies and are tastefully furnished. Deluxe rooms and suites have ocean views.

COPACABANA PALACE HOTEL $$$
(Map p236; ☎2548-7070; www.copacabanapalace.com.br; Av Atlântica 1702, Copacabana; d from R$1150; @) Rio's most famous hotel has hosted heads of state, rock stars and other prominent personalities (Queen Elizabeth once stayed here, as did the Rolling Stones). The dazzling white facade dates from the 1920s, when it became a symbol of the city. Today accommodations range from deluxe rooms to spacious suites with balconies. Despite the price tag, some rooms could do with better upkeep. There's a lovely pool, excellent restaurants and fine service.

ASTORIA PALACE HOTEL $$$
(Map p236; ☎2545-9550; www.astoriapalacehotel.com; Av Atlântica 1886, Copacabana; s/d from R$502/532; @) Beautifully set overlooking the beach (and a stone's throw from the Copacabana Palace), the Astoria has rooms with a clean, modern design – though it's probably not worth the cost unless you get a room with a view.

MERCURE ARPOADOR
HOTEL **$$$**

(Map p236; ☑3222-9600; www.mercure.com; Francisco Otaviano 61, Copacabana; s/d R$503/665; ✳@☎🌊) This dapper all-suites hotel is well located in Arpoador, giving easy access to both Ipanema and Copacabana. Suites have sleek white-leather sofas that open into beds, kitchenettes, TVs with a stereo and DVD player, ambient lighting and comfortable bedrooms. All of the rooms have balconies, although there's no view.

ROYAL RIO PALACE
HOTEL **$$$**

(Map p236; ☑2122-9292; www.royalrio.com; Duvivier 82, Copacabana; r from R$520; ✳@☎🌊) Not far from the beach, this shiny glass-and-steel high-rise offers comfortable, modern lodging and decent amenities. The rooms are well maintained, and boast wood floors, a nice design aesthetic and sizable windows. There's a pleasant top-floor pool and two rarely used saunas.

🛏 Botafogo

EL MISTI
HOSTEL **$**

(Map p244; ☑2226-0991; www.elmistihostel.com; Praia de Botafogo 462, Casa 9; dm R$48-56, d without/with bathroom R$240/265; @☎) Located along Botafogo's hostel row, El Misti is a popular budget spot among Brazilian and foreign travelers for its cheap dorm rooms (with triple bunk beds) and lively atmosphere. It's a short walk from the Botafogo metro station. Free airport pick-up if you book for four nights or longer. There's a second El Misti in Copacabana.

VILA CARIOCA
HOSTEL **$**

(Map p244; ☑2535-3224; www.vilacarioca.com.br; Estácio Coimbra 84; dm/d from R$35/130; ✳@☎) On a peaceful tree-lined street, this low-key and welcoming hostel has six- to 15-bed dorms in an attractively decorated house. The common areas are a fine spot to mingle with other travelers.

ACE HOSTEL
HOSTEL **$**

(Map p244; ☑2527-7452; www.acehostels.com.br; São Clemente 23; dm R$25-46; ✳@) One block from the metro, this small well-run hostel has a range of rooms (the cheapest lack air-conditioning) and a roomy lounge/TV room.

OZTEL
HOSTEL **$$$**

(Map p244; ☑3042-1853; www.oztel.com.br; Pinheiro Guimarães 91, Botafogo; dm R$55-75, d R$240-290; ✳@☎) Evoking a Warholian aesthetic, Rio's coolest and most colorful hostel is like sleeping in an art gallery. The artsy front deck and bar is an inviting place to lounge but the real finds are the R$270 private rooms: with a garden patio under the nose of Christo, you'll be hard-pressed to find a groovier room in Rio.

🛏 Flamengo & Around

BROTHERS HOSTEL
HOSTEL **$**

(Map p242; ☑2551-0997; www.brothershostel.com; Farani 18; dm R$47-58, d R$140; ✳@☎) In a handsomely converted house, Brothers Hostel was started by four well-traveled Brazilian brothers. Some of the rooms are cramped, but the rock-loving bar is a good place to meet other guests.

BEIJA FLOR HOTEL
HOTEL **$**

(Map p241; ☑2285-2492; beijaflorhotel@yahoo.com; Ferreira Viana 20, Flamengo; s/d R$180/200; ✳☎) This remodeled hotel has clean rooms with tile floors, firm mattresses and modern bathrooms. On the downside, some rooms lack decent ventilation (opening onto an air shaft). It's on a quiet street within walking distance of the metro.

HOTEL FERREIRA VIANA
HOTEL **$**

(Map p241; ☑2205-7396; Ferreira Viana 58, Flamengo; s/d R$125/165; ✳) Not the nicest place in the area, but Ferreira Viana is relatively cheap. Your reais will buy you a small, dark room with tile floors and thin mattresses. Some rooms are better than others, so take a peek before committing.

HOTEL RIAZOR
HOTEL **$**

(Map p241; ☑2225-0121; www.hotelriazor.com.br; Rua do Catete 160, Catete; s/d R$135/170; ✳) The lovely colonial facade of the Riazor hides worn quarters short on comfort. The equation here is simple: bed, bathroom, TV, air-conditioning, and a door by which to exit the room and explore the city. You'll find a mix of travelers and lost souls here.

HOTEL REGINA
HOTEL **$$**

(Map p241; ☑3289-9999; www.hotelregina.com.br; Ferreira Viana 29, Flamengo; s/d from R$300/345; ✳@☎) On a quiet street off the main avenue through Flamengo, the handsomely renovated Regina boasts 117 rooms, each bright and modern, with wood or tile floors and sparkling bathrooms.

FAVELA CHIC

Favela sleeps are nothing new – intrepid travelers have been venturing Rio's urban mazes for nearly a decade – but as more and more of Rio's favelas are pacified, hostels and pousadas are popping up faster than the rudimentary constructions which make up the favelas themselves. Our favorites include the following:

Maze Inn (Map p241; ☑2558-5547; www.jazzrio.info; Casa 66, Tavares Bastos 414, Catete; dm R$60, s/d from R$120/150) Set in Tavares Bastos favela, the Maze Inn is a fantastic place to overnight for those looking for an alternative view of Rio. The rooms are uniquely decorated with original artworks by English owner and Renaissance man, Bob Nadkarni, while the veranda offers stunning views of the bay and Pão de Açúcar. Don't miss the bimonthly jazz parties (first and third Fridays of the month).

Vidigalbergue (☑7929-7999; www.vidigalbergue.com.br; Casa 2, Av Niemeyer 314, Vidigal; ✳@🛜) A safe 15-minute walk from Leblon brings you to this small hostel at the bottom of Vidigal favela, where these days there's even a tourist map to guide you around. The coup here is the stunning seaviews from all the dorms and the hospitality of the two English-speaking best-friend owners, Luis and Andre.

Pousada Favelinha (☑2556-5273; www.favelinha.com; Almirante Alexandrino 2023, Santa Teresa; dm R$45, d R$110; @) Located in the favela of Pereirão da Silva, Pousada Favelinha has four double rooms and a five-bed dorm, all with balconies that have stunning views over the city to Pão de Açúcar. There's also a terrace, a lounge and lots of insider info from the welcoming Brazilian-German owners. To get there, take the *bonde* to Colegio Asunção (Rua Almirante Alexandrino 2024) and enter the favela through the school grounds. While this is one of Rio's more peaceful favelas, it isn't for everyone – some love it, some don't.

Front-facing rooms *(luxos)* have sizable balconies for catching a breeze off the bay. It has a rooftop sauna and Jacuzzi.

IMPERIAL HOTEL HOTEL $$
(Map p241; ☑2112-6000; www.imperialhotel. com.br; Rua do Catete 186, Catete; r R$278-310; ✳@🛜🏊) The attractive colonial facade has only three stories but goes back endlessly to reveal clean and modern renovated rooms and suites. Some rooms are too dark to recommend, while others have better natural lighting and Jacuzzis.

AUGUSTO'S PAYSANDU HOTEL $$
(Map p242; ☑2558-7270; www.paysanduho tel.com.br; Paissandu 23, Flamengo; s/d R$208/231; ✳) On a quiet street lined with imperial palm trees, the Paysandu has a lovely art deco facade with rooms that don't quite measure up to the outside. Most have big old-fashioned windows, ceramic tile floors and high ceilings – and could use a scrub.

FLAMENGO PALACE HOTEL $$
(Map p241; ☑3235-2600; www.hotelflamengo palace.com.br; Praia do Flamengo 6, Flamengo; s/d from R$244/275; ✳🛜) The 14-story Flamengo Palace has basic but airy rooms

with simple furnishings, very firm mattresses and a clean overall design. Front-facing rooms cost just R$35 more but have excellent views of the bay; light sleepers however, may want to stay in the back where it is quieter.

🛏 Santa Teresa & Lapa

BOOKS HOSTEL HOSTEL $
(Map p250; ☑3437-3783; www.bookshostel. com; Francisco Muratori 10, Lapa; dm R$38-50, d without bathroom R$130-140; ✳@🛜) In the heart of Lapa and true to the nature of the neighborhood, this party hostel is the appetizer for your crazy night out. Dorms have graffiti art and there's a sociable *barraca*-style bar (rooms overlooking it don't allow for much sleep). All bathrooms are shared, and only some rooms have air-conditioning.

RIO HOSTEL HOSTEL $
(Map p250; ☑3852-0827; www.riohostel.com; Joaquim Murtinho 361, Santa Teresa; dm R$40-45, d R$150-160; ✳@🛜🏊) This Santa favorite provides travelers with a home away from home. The backyard patio with pool

is a great place to meet other travelers, and the hostel whips up different meals (R$18) nightly. There's also a kitchen for guests. The rooms are clean, and there are attractive double rooms, including private suites with fine views behind the pool.

TERRA BRASILIS HOSTEL $
(Map p250; ☎2224-0952; www.terrabrasilishostel.com; Murtinho Nobre 156, Santa Teresa; dm R$45-50, d R$200-230; @📶) Near Parque das Ruinas, this peaceful guesthouse has dorm rooms (sleeping six to 12) and private doubles, all with wood floors and French doors that open onto a veranda overlooking the city. The breezy patio with bar is a fine place to nurse a drink in the afternoon.

HOTEL MARAJÓ HOTEL $
(Map p250; ☎2224-4134; www.hotelmarajo.com.br; Joaquim Silva 99, Lapa; s/d R$100/120; ❄) A few paces from the Selarón steps, this basic hotel rents simple, fairly clean rooms, all with air-conditioning. It's perfectly located for taking advantage of Lapa's nightlife, if you don't mind the street noise.

★CASA BELEZA GUESTHOUSE $$
(Map p250; ☎8288-6764; www.casabeleza.net; Laurinda Santos Lobo 311; r R$220-300; ❄📶🏊) This lovely property dates back to the 1930s and was once a governor's mansion. Tropical gardens overlook the picturesque pool, and you can sometimes spot toucans and monkeys in the surrounding foliage. It's a small and peaceful operation, with just four guestrooms, and the kind family that runs the pousada also lives onsite.

CASA ÁUREA GUESTHOUSE $$
(Map p250; ☎2242-5830; www.casaaurea.com.br; Áurea 80, Santa Teresa; dm R$75, s/d without bathroom R$140/180, s/d R$200/250) Set in one of the neighborhood's oldest homes (from 1871), the two-story Casa Áurea has rustic charm with simple but cozy rooms and a large covered garden where you can lounge on hammocks, fire up the barbecue or whip up a meal in the open-air kitchen.

CASA MANGO MANGO GUESTHOUSE $$
(Map p250; ☎2508-6440; www.casa-mangomango.com; Joaquim Murtinho 587, Santa Teresa; r R$150-300 ; ❄@📶🏊) In an atmospheric 19th-century mansion, this friendly guesthouse has uniquely designed rooms, including several spacious but windowless rooms with separate sleeping lofts and two bright, beautifully designed rooms filled with artwork. The grounds have a small patio and pool, plus huge 200-year-old mango trees.

CAMA E CAFÉ HOMESTAY $$
(Map p250; ☎2225-4366; www.camaecafe.com; Paschoal Carlos Magno 90, Santa Teresa; r R$130-300; ⏲9am-5:30pm Mon-Fri, to 2pm Sat) A fine alternative to hotels and guesthouses, Cama e Café is a bed-and-breakfast network that allow travelers to book a room from local residents. The are several dozen options to choose from, with the majority of listings in Santa Teresa – although there are a few scattered options in the Zona Sul and western beaches.

Accommodations range from modest to lavish – indeed the best rooms are inside colonial homes with panoramic views and lush gardens.

CASA DA CARMEN E DO FERNANDO GUESTHOUSE $$
(Map p250; ☎2507-3084; www.bedandbreakfastrio.com.br; Hermenegildo de Barros 172; s/d from R$110/210; 📶🏊) This familial eight-room guesthouse attracts a laid-back crowd who feel right at home in the century-old building. The colorfully decorated lounge is adorned with artwork (including paintings by one of the owners) and has a comfy, lived-in feel, making it a fine place to watch a film, play music or enjoy the fine view through the oversized picture window.

Out back is a small pool and rustic terrace with equally impressive views. Rooms are simply furnished but enlivened with bright colors, and some have fine views.

CASALEGRE GUESTHOUSE $$
(Map p250; ☎8670-6158; www.casalegre.com.br; Monte Alegre 316; s/d from R$140/240; 📶) Casalegre has a rustic, art-loving bohemian vibe and its eight rooms are decorated with different works of art and vary in size (the cheapest two rooms share a bathroom). There's a strong communal vibe here, and the owners often host parties, yoga classes and other activities. It has an art gallery on the 1st floor and a small terrace in back.

CASA BIANCA GUESTHOUSE $$
(Map p250; ☎3233-1563; www.guesthousebianca.com; Murtinho Nobre 35; r from R$300; ❄📶) This beautiful 1930s-era mansion down the road from Parque das Ruinas has lovely details: stained-glass windows, tall ceilings, marble staircase and period furnishings.

Rooms are attractively set with wood floors and antique fixtures – two have excellent views (one of which has a private veranda). It's a quiet place, with just three rooms, and the friendly owner lives onsite.

CASTELINHO 38 HOTEL **$$**
(Map p250; ☎2252-2549; www.castelinho38.com; Triunfo 38, Santa Teresa; r R$207-426;) Another Santa charmer, Castelinho offers spacious rooms with high ceilings, wood floors and a light, airy design. It's set in a mid-19th-century mansion and has an outdoor terrace with a garden and lounge space.

VILLA LAURINDA GUESTHOUSE **$$**
(Map p250; ☎3648-2216; www.villalaurinda.com; Laurinda Santos Lobo 98, Santa Teresa; r R$180-300;) In a converted 1888 Victorian, the Villa Laurinda presents a serene portrait of life in Santa Teresa. At the house entrance is a lovely pool, ringed with tropical foliage and mango trees. The rooms are simply designed with wide plank floors and range from small to large; three of the rooms share a bathroom (others are en-suite).

You'll also find classically furnished common areas, including a small library with a grand piano.

CASA COOL BEANS GUESTHOUSE **$$**
(Map p250; ☎2262-0552; www.casacoolbeans.com; Laurinda Santos Lobo 136, Santa Teresa; d R$260-340;) Your expectations will easily be exceeded at this discreet 10-room B&B where the American owner's mantra focuses around personlized service. Each colorful room in the renovated 1930s Spanish-style villa was designed by a different Brazilian artist and it has a spacious sun deck and breakfast area. Book room 9 for the best views.

★**HOTEL SANTA TERESA** HOTEL **$$$**
(Map p250; ☎3380-0200; www.santa-teresa-hotel.com; Almirante Alexandrino 660, Santa Teresa; d from R$830;) Probably the finest boutique hotel in Rio, it's set in a lavishly restored building (part of a coffee plantation in the 19th century) with artfully designed rooms, an award-winning restaurant, ull-service spa, stylish bar and a pool with fine views over the city.

The design incorporates a certain tropical elegance with art and artifacts from across Brazil on display in common areas – and even in some rooms.

Barra da Tijuca & Western Rio

Few foreign travelers stay in the neighborhoods west of Leblon, as it's a hassle getting around without a car. However, you are close to some of Rio's best beaches – which get wilder the further west you go.

★**DON PASCUAL** GUESTHOUSE **$$**
(www.donpascual.com.br; Casa 12, Estrada do Sacarrão 867, Vargem Grande; r weekday/weekend R$240/330;) Surrounded by lush vegetation, this hidden gem has attractive rooms with a rustic-chic allure. Some of the rooms are split-level and incorporate reclaimed lumber into the cabin-like design. There's an enticing swimming pool and a restaurant that invites lingering. The downside? It's a long drive, and you'll need a car and excellent directions to get here. Call ahead for specifics.

RIO SURF 'N STAY HOSTEL **$$**
(Map p252; ☎3418-1133; www.riosurfnstay.com; Raimundo Veras 1140, Recreio dos Bandeirantes; surf package incl lessons & board rental 3-/7-nights from R$459/1020;) Just a short stroll to the fine surf off Macumba Beach, this converted house, which is owned by a New Zealander and a Brazilian, is the go-to spot for anyone who has come to Rio to learn to surf. The two dorm rooms (sleeping four or five people) and three private doubles are comfortably furnished, and the hosts do their best to make everyone feel at home.

There is a kitchen for guest use and a grassy lawn with palm trees that is fine for lazing about. Surf packages – that include lessons and accommodations – are available. Rio Surf 'N Stay is about a 40-minute bus ride from the Zona Sul; take bus 175 – Recreio from the coastal road along Copacabana, Ipanema or Leblon beaches.

LE RELAIS MARAMBAIA HOTEL **$$$**
(☎2394-2544; www.lerelaisdemarambaia.com.br; Estrada Roberto Burle Marx 9346, Barra da Guaratiba; r R$550-820;) Perched on the edge of the ocean in the peaceful community of Barra da Guaratiba, this boutique hotel (which opened in 2008) has five attractive rooms, each with wood floors, balconies and high-end fittings. Some rooms also have private Jacuzzis. It has a restaurant and a small outdoor terrace with pool that makes a great spot at sunset.

Understand Rio de Janeiro

Rio de Janeiro Today

Big things are happening in Rio. Center stage for the 2014 World Cup and host city of the 2016 Summer Olympics, the Cidade Maravilhosa (Marvelous City) has experienced enormous transformations in the past decade. Ambitious urban-renewal projects, new museums and concert halls, improved infrastructure and continued investments in the favelas are just a few other reasons why *cariocas* feel like their day in the sun has at long last arrived.

Best on Film

Cidade de Deus (director Fernando Meirelles, 2002) Oscar-nominated film showing the coexistence of brutality and hope in a Rio favela.

Orfeu Negro (Black Orpheus, director Marcel Camus, 1959) The Orpheus-Eurydice myth set during Rio's Carnaval with a ground-breaking bossa nova soundtrack.

Central do Brasil (Central Station, director Walter Salles 1998) Epic journey through unglamorized Brazil, set in Rio and the northeast.

Madame Satã (director Karim Aïnouz, 2002) Compelling portrait of Rio's gritty Lapa district during the 1930s.

Best in Print

Bossa Nova (Ruy Castro, 2000) A fascinating look at the poets, composers and musicians behind the music.

Samba (Alma Guillermoprieto, 1991) Portrait of life inside the favela Mangueira in the weeks leading up to Carnaval.

Brazil on the Rise (Larry Rohter, 2010) A journey through the culture, history and economic transformation of Brazil.

Rio de Janeiro (Ruy Castro, 2004) A short chronicle of intriguing episodes in Rio's history.

Boom Times

Rio's flourishing economy mirrors that of Brazil, with a burgeoning middle class fueling the city's growth. In 2012, Brazil officially surpassed the UK as the world's sixth largest economy. The economic policies of President Dilma Rousseff, the country's first female president in its near 200-year history, have maintained Brazil's good fortune – much to the surprise of many of her detractors. As a result, a consumption craze is on, and new restaurants, bars and boutiques open with startling frequency. The downside to all this is the high cost of living. A 2012 study by Mercer showed that Rio was the 13th most expensive city in the world – well ahead of London (25th) and New York (33rd). Rio also recently earned the distinction of having some of the world's highest hotel prices.

Game Face

In the run-up to the World Cup and Summer Olympics, Rio is investing billions of reais in improvements and infrastructure. Maracanã football stadium received an R$800 million upgrade, while Barra da Tijuca saw even larger investments (a staggering R$23 billion in total will be spent on the games) as the home of Olympic village and the majority of sporting venues. The city hasn't limited its focus to sports, however. Something more ambitious – and of greater impact for citizens and visitors alike – is happening in Rio's docklands, north of downtown. A once unsightly waterfront will see new gardens, bike paths, cultural spaces and museums (including the Santiago Calatrava–designed Museum of Tomorrow). Light rail will link the neighborhood with downtown. Meanwhile, work on the extension of the metro continues, with engineers hopeful they can complete the tunnels linking Barra and Ipanema before 2016.

Losers & Winners

Meanwhile, not everyone is set to benefit from the Olympic preparations, and those on the losing end are not surprisingly favela residents. According to the organization Rio on Watch, more than 8000 Brazilians have been evicted from their homes, and thousands of future evictions are anticipated in connection with the games. Amnesty International and other human-rights organizations have protested about the tactics employed: the forcible removal of families, while police use pepper spray to disperse the crowds, followed by bulldozers that quickly demolish the buildings.

Not all favela residents are on the losing side of development. Since the first favela improvement plan was unveiled in 1994, Rio has ramped up investments in its poorest communities, bringing better sanitation, transportation links and health centers – among other quality-of-life improvements. And with the arrival of permanent police posts inside favelas, many communities have become significantly safer. Dramatic developments include the arrival of a cable-car system through the Complexo do Alemão in the Zona Norte – the cable car slowly becoming a tourist attraction in its own right. And the system is set to be implemented in Morro da Providencia, Rio's oldest favela – and once among its most dangerous – as part of the port beautification scheme.

Civic Improvements

On other fronts, Rio has made strides towards improving security and tackling corruption. The *lei seca*, a zero tolerance drink-driving law passed in 2008, has reduced the number of traffic fatalities and injuries on the city's roads and highways. There have also been attempts to reduce corruption: more than 30 officers were arrested in 2011 for their suspected links to drug traffickers. Rio Public Safety Secretary José Mariano Beltrame – one of the principal architects behind the favela pacification program – has made tackling police corruption a priority.

Days of Celebration

Regardless of the great changes happening across the country, Brazil hasn't lost its unbridled joie de vivre, that infectious spirit of celebration that Prince Harry alluded to on a visit to the city in 2012 when he said, "Everything about Rio makes you want to dance." Indeed, with city coffers full and the Olympics on the horizon, the revelry has reached fever pitch, with record-breaking numbers (some five million expected in 2013) attending nearly 500 street parades of Rio's recent Carnaval.

if Rio were 100 people

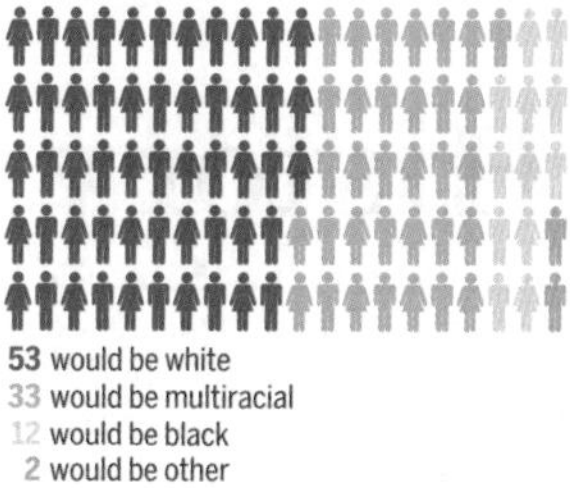

belief systems

(% of population)

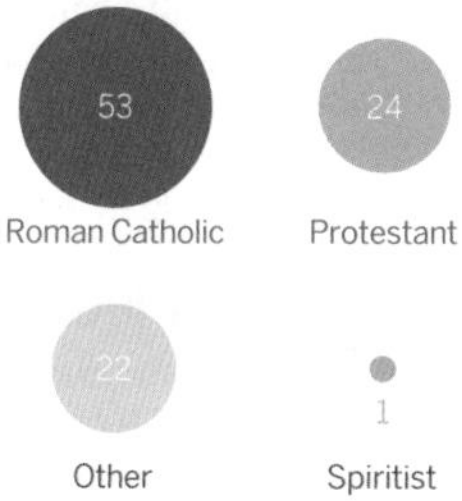

population per sq km

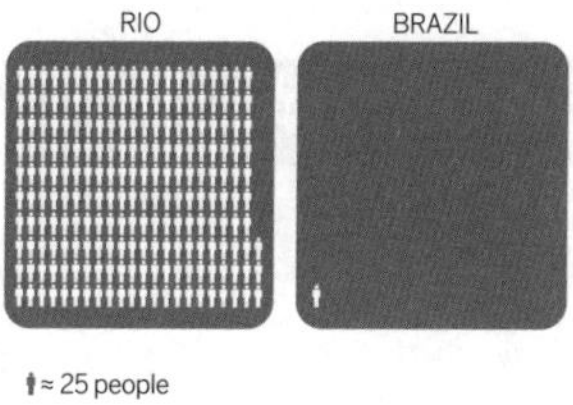

History

Discovered in the 1500s, Rio became a key settlement in Portugal's New World empire, particularly after the entire Portuguese court decamped here in the early 1800s. Magnificent churches and fine colonial streets still attest to the imperial wealth lavished on the city, though by the late 1800s Rio was already a divided city of haves and have-nots. The 20th century saw an influx of immigrants, explosive favela growth, the rise of a military dictatorship and a loss of prestige, when Brasília replaced Rio as the nation's capital. The last decade has seen boom days once again, with burgeoning financial growth.

Brazil is the only country in the New World that was both the seat of an empire (when the Portuguese king came over) and an independent monarchy (when Dom Pedro I declared independence).

The Portuguese Arrival

In the 15th century Portugal, ever infatuated with the sea, began its large-scale explorations that would eventually take Portuguese explorers to the coast of Brazil in 1500. A little over a year later, Gonçalo Coelho sailed from Portugal and entered a huge bay in January 1502. It was his chief pilot, Amerigo Vespucci, however, who would give the name to this bay. Mistaking it for a river (or possibly making no mistake at all since the old Portuguese 'rio' is another word for bay), he dubbed it Rio de Janeiro (River of January).

Of Noble Savages & Savage Nobles

Some believe that the indigenous Guanabara and Tupinambá (better known as the Tupi), inspired works such as Sir Thomas Moore's *Utopia* (1516) and Rousseau's Enlightenment-era idea of the 'noble savage'. This all started from the letters credited to Amerigo Vespucci on his first voyage to Rio in 1502. Common at the time was the idea that there existed on earth an Eden, and that it lay undiscovered. Vespucci claimed to have found that Eden, from his cursory observations of the Tupi. They were described as innocent savages, carefree and well groomed, with the unusual custom of taking daily baths in the sea. The fact that native women were freely offered to the strange foreigners probably added to the enthusiasm with which they spoke about the region upon their return to Portugal.

TIMELINE

8000 BC

Descendents of hunter-gatherers who crossed the Bering Strait from East Asia between 10,000 BC and 12,000 BC settle along Baía de Guanabara.

AD 1502

Portuguese explorer Gonçalo Coelho sails into Baía de Guanabara. His chief pilot, Amerigo Vespucci (after whom 'America' is named), dubbed the lovely setting Rio de Janeiro.

1565

After driving off the French and their indigenous allies, the Portuguese founded the first permanent settlement, São Sebastião do Rio de Janeiro.

In fact, the honeymoon didn't last long. The conquerors soon came to see the forest-dwelling *índios* as raw manpower for the Portuguese empire, and enslaved them, setting them to work on plantations. The *índios*, too, turned out to be different than the Europeans imagined. The Tupinambá were warlike and ate their enemies – through ritualistic cannibalism they believed they would receive the power and strength of the consumed opponent. They also didn't take to the work as the Portuguese had expected, and died in large numbers from introduced diseases. By the 17th century the Tupinambá had been completely eradicated. To fulfill their growing labor demands, the Portuguese eventually turned to Africa.

Africans in Brazil

The Portuguese began bringing blacks, stolen from Africa, into the new colony shortly after Brazil's founding. Most blacks were brought from Guinea, Angola and the Congo, and would constitute some three million souls brought to Brazil over its three-and-a-half centuries of human trafficking. The port of Rio had the largest number of slaves entering the colony – as many as two million in all. At open-air slave markets these new immigrants were sold as local help or shipped to the interior, initially to work on the thriving sugar plantations, and later – when gold was discovered in Minas Gerais in 1704 – to work back-breaking jobs in the mines.

Although slavery was rotten anywhere in the New World, most historians agree that the Africans in Rio had it better than their rural brethren. Those who came to Rio worked in domestic roles as maids and butlers and out on the streets as dock workers, furniture movers, delivery boys, boatmen, cobblers, fishermen and carpenters. The worst job was transporting the barrels of human excrement produced in town and emptying them into the sea.

As Rio's population grew, so too did the number of slaves imported to meet the labor needs of the expanding coffee plantations in the Paraíba Valley. By the early 19th century African slaves made up two-thirds of Rio's population.

Lots of illicit liaisons occurred between master and slave, and children born into mixed backgrounds were largely accepted into the social sphere and raised as free citizens. This contributed considerably to creating Brazil's melting pot. While escape attempts were fewer in Rio than in the more brutal climate of the northeast, there were attempts. Those seeking freedom often set their sights on *quilombos* (communities of runaway slaves). Some were quite developed – as was the case with Palmares, which had a population of 20,000 and survived through much of the 17th century before it was wiped out by Federal troops.

'Order and Progress', the slogan on Brazil's flag, comes from French philosopher Auguste de Comte (1797-1857), whose elevation of reason and scientific knowledge over traditional beliefs was influential on the young Brazilian republic.

1550–80

The Portuguese bring more than 2000 slaves to the new colony. Over the next 300 years, around three million people stolen from Africa will be relocated to Brazil.

1763

With gold flowing from Minas Gerais through Rio, the city grows wealthy and swells in population to 50,000; the Portuguese court transfers the capital of Brazil from Salvador to Rio.

1807

Napoleon invades Portugal and the Portuguese prince regent (later known as Dom João VI) and his entire court of 15,000 flee for Brazil. The royal family showers wealth upon Rio.

1822

Left in charge of Brazil after his father Dom João VI returns to Portugal, Dom Pedro I declares independence from Portugal and crowns himself 'emperor' of Brazil.

Abroad, the country was under pressure to outlaw slavery, and trafficking in human cargo was eventually banned in 1830. This move, however, did nothing to improve the lives of slaves already in Brazil, who would have to wait another two generations to gain their freedom. Despite the ban, the transportation of human cargo continued well into the 1850s, with 500,000 slaves smuggled into Brazil between 1830 and 1850. The British (out of economic self-interest) finally suppressed Brazil's trafficking with naval squadrons.

Pressure from home and abroad reached boiling point toward the end of the 19th century until finally, in 1888, from the steps of Royal Palace overlooking Praça Quinze de Novembro, slavery was declared abolished. Brazil was the last country in the New World to end slavery.

Rio's Early Days

In order to get the colony up and running the Portuguese built a fortified town on Morro do Castelo in 1567 to maximize protection from European invasion by sea and *índios* attack by land. They named their town São Sebastião do Rio de Janeiro, in honor of patron saint Sebastião – and namesake of King Sebastião of Portugal. Cobbled together by the 500 founding *cariocas* (residents of Rio), early Rio was a poorly planned town with irregular streets in the medieval Portuguese style. It remained a small settlement through the mid-17th century, surviving on the export of brazilwood and sugarcane. In Rio's first census (in 1600), the population comprised 3000 *índios*, 750 Portuguese and 100 blacks.

With its excellent harbor and good lands for sugarcane, Rio became Brazil's third most important settlement (after Salvador da Bahia and Recife-Olinda) in the 17th century.

The gold rush in Minas Gerais had a profound effect on Rio and created major demographic shifts on three continents. The rare metal was first discovered by *bandeirantes* (explorers and hired slave-hunters) in the 1690s and, as word spread, gold seekers arrived in droves. Over the next half-century an estimated 500,000 Portuguese arrived in Brazil and many thousands of African slaves were imported. Rio served as the natural port of entry for this flow of people and commerce to and from the Minas Gerais goldfields.

In the 18th century Rio morphed into a rough-and-tumble place attracting a swarthy brand of European immigrant. Most of the settlement was built near the water (where Praça XV de Novembro stands today), beside rows of warehouses, with noisy taverns sprinkled along the main streets. Rio was a rough city full of smugglers and thieves, tramps and assassins, and slaves on the run. Smuggling was rampant,

GOLD RUSH

During the 18th-century gold rush created by the discovery of gold in Minas Gerais, some 500,000 Portuguese immigrated to Brazil, while thousands of slaves were brought to into the country. Rio served as the entry port for people and commerce flowing to and from the goldfields.

1831

Brazil's first homegrown monarch, Dom Pedro I, proves incompetent and abdicates the throne. His son Pedro II takes power and ushers in a long period of growth and stability.

1888

Slavery is abolished in Brazil, the last country in the New World to do so. The law is signed by Princesa Isabel, admired by many blacks as their benefactress.

1889

A military coup, supported by Brazil's wealthy coffee farmers, overthrows Pedro II. The monarchy is abolished and the Brazilian Republic is born.

1900

Mayor Pereira Passos ushers in a period of urbanization, creating grand boulevards, opening up Copacabana (via tunnel), and improving public health and sanitation.

with ships robbed and the sailors murdered, and the police bribed. Gold flowing through the city created the constant menace of pirates. Adding a note of temperance to the place were the religious orders that came in small bands and built Rio's first churches.

Rio Under the King

In 1807 Napoleon's army marched on Lisbon. Two days before the French invasion, 40 ships carrying the Portuguese prince regent (later known as Dom João VI) and his entire court of 15,000 set sail for Brazil under the protection of British warships. After the initial landing in Bahia (where their unkempt state was met with bemusement), the royal family moved down to Rio, where they settled.

This had momentous consequences for the city as the king, missing the high culture of Europe, lavished his attention on Rio, envisioning a splendid European-style city for his new hometown. European artisans flooded the city. The British, rewarded for helping the king safely reach Brazil, gained access to Brazil's ports, and many Anglo traders and merchants set up shop in the town center. Anti-Napoleon French also arrived, as did other Europeans, creating an international air unknown until then. When the German prince and noted naturalist Alexander Philipp Maximilian arrived in Brazil in 1815 he commented on the many nationalities and mixtures of people he encountered.

Dom João VI fell in love with Rio. A great admirer of nature, he founded the botanical gardens and introduced sea bathing to the inhabitants of Rio. He had a special pier built at Caju, with a small tub at the end, in which he would immerse himself fully clothed as the waves rocked gently against it. (His wife Carlota Joaquina bathed in the nude.) This was long before Copacabana was opened to the rest of the city, remaining a virgin expanse of white sand framed by rainforest-covered mountains, reachable only by an arduous journey.

With the court came an influx of money and talent that helped build some of the city's lasting monuments, such as the palace at the Quinta da Boa Vista. Within a year of his arrival, Dom João VI also created the School of Medicine, the Bank of Brazil, the Law Courts, the Naval Academy and the Royal Printing Works.

Dom João VI was expected to return to Portugal after Napoleon was defeated at Waterloo in 1815, but instead stayed in Brazil. The following year his mother, mad Queen Dona Maria I, died, and Dom João VI became king. He refused demands to return to Portugal to rule, and declared Rio the capital of the United Kingdom of Portugal, Brazil and the Algarves. Brazil became the only New World colony to ever have a European monarch ruling on its soil.

History Reads

- *Brazil: Five Centuries of Change (Thomas E. Skidmore)*
- *The History of Brazil (Robert Levine)*
- *The New Brazil (Riordan Roett)*

1917

Samba is officially born, with the first recording of the song 'Pelo Telefone'. This song and others soon get wide airplay on the radio.

1923

The Copacabana Palace opens its doors. It becomes an icon of Rio's tropical glamor, with international jet-setters flying down during Rio's pre-Depression boom.

1928

Deixa Falar becomes the first *escola de samba* (samba school; called a 'school' because it's located next to a primary school), followed by Mangueira later that year.

1930

Getúlio Vargas comes into power. Inspired by European fascists, President Vargas presides over an authoritarian state, playing a major role in Brazilian politics for the next two decades.

Five years later Dom João VI finally relented to political pressure and returned to Portugal, leaving his 23-year-old son Pedro in Brazil as prince regent. In Portugal the king was confronted with the newly formed Côrtes, a legislative assembly attempting to reign in the powers of the monarchy. The Côrtes had many directives, one of which was restoring Brazil to its previous status as subservient colony. Word was sent to Dom Pedro that his authority was greatly diminished. According to legend, when Pedro received the directive in 1822, he pulled out his sword and yelled '*Independência ou morte!*' ('Independence or death!'), putting himself at the country's head as Emperor Dom Pedro I.

Portugal was too weak to fight its favorite son, not to mention the British, who had the most to gain from Brazilian independence and would have come to the aid of the Brazilians. Without spilling blood, Brazil had attained its independence and Dom Pedro I became the head of the Brazilian 'empire' (despite Pedro's claims to the contrary, Brazil was a regular monarchy, not an empire since it had no overseas colonies).

Dom Pedro I ruled for only nine years. From all accounts, he was a bumbling incompetent who scandalized even the permissive Brazilians by siring numerous illegitimate children. He also strongly resisted any attempts to weaken his power by constitutional means. Following street demonstrations in Rio in 1831, he surprised everyone by abdicating, leaving the power in the hands of his five-year-old, Brazilian-born son.

Rio's nearest *quilombo* in the 19th century was in Leblon – then quite distant from the city. Unlike other *quilombos*, it was headed by a white, progressive businessman, Jose de Seixas Magalhães, who hid and protected slaves in his Leblon mansion and his surrounding farmlands.

Until Dom Pedro II reached adolescence, Brazil suffered through a turbulent period of unrest, which finally ended in 1840 when Dom Pedro II, at the age of 14, took the throne. Despite his youth he proved to be a stabilizing presence for the country, and ushered in a long period of peace and relative prosperity. The period of industrialization began with the introduction of the steamship and the telegraph, and the king encouraged mass immigration from Europe.

Dom Pedro II's shortcomings during his half-century of rule were a bloody war with Paraguay (1864–70) and his slowness in abolishing slavery. He was well liked by his subjects, but they finally had enough of the monarchy and he was pushed from power in 1889.

The Belle Époque

Rio experienced boom days in the latter half of the 19th century. The spreading wealth of coffee plantations in Rio state (and in São Paulo) revitalized Brazil's economy, just as the city was going through substantial growth and modernization. Regular passenger ships began sailing to London (1845) and Paris (1851), and the local ferry service to Niterói began in 1862. A telegraph system and gas streetlights were installed

1932

Rio holds its first Carnaval parade. Mangueira wins, and quickly cements its status as the city's favorite samba school (a sentiment held by many today).

1937

President Getúlio Vargas announces a new constitution; he passes minimum wage laws in 1938, expands the military and centralizes power.

1942

Initially maintaining neutrality, Brazil enters WWII on the Allies' side, providing raw materials, plus 25,000 troops (the only Latin American nation to do so).

1950

Newly constructed Maracanã Stadium plays center stage in the FIFA World Cup. Brazil dominates until the final when, before 200,000 fans, it suffers a stunning loss to Uruguay.

HISTORY SITES

➡ Paço Imperial (p121) This former imperial palace was home to the royal family when they arrived from Portugal.

➡ Praça Quinze de Novembro (p124) Named after the date Brazil declared itself a republic (November 15, 1822), this plaza has witnessed a lot of historical action, including the crowning of two emperors and the abolition of slavery.

➡ Travessa do Comércio (p124) This narrow alley is a window into colonial Rio, with 18th-century buildings converted into bars and restaurants.

➡ Museu Histórico Nacional (p119) Set in the 18th-century royal arsenal, this museum houses Rio's best assortment of historical artifacts.

➡ Jardim Botânico (p79) Prince Regent Dom João VI ensured the city would have no shortage of green spaces, and ordered this verdant garden to be planted in 1808.

➡ Museu da República (p112) Formerly known as the Palácio do Catete, this mansion was Brazil's presidential home from 1896 to 1954. Getúlio Vargas was the last president to live here, and committed suicide in one of the upstairs rooms.

➡ Praça Floriano (p127) Centro's picturesque main square has long been the meeting ground for popular demonstrations, including student uprisings against the military dictatorship in the 1960s and victory celebrations following World Cup finals.

➡ Garota de Ipanema (p70) Famed spot where Tom Jobim and Vinícius de Moraes penned the 'Girl from Ipanema', whose international success was a major moment in the history of bossa nova.

in 1854. By 1860 Rio had more than 250,000 inhabitants, making it the largest city in South America.

For the wealthy, the goal of creating a modern European capital grew ever closer as the city embraced all things European – with particular influence from the customs, fashion and even cuisine of Paris. The poor, however, had a miserable lot. In the 1870s and 1880s, as the rich moved to new urban areas by the bay or in the hills, Rio's marginalized lived in tenement houses in the old center of town. There conditions were grim: streets were poorly lit and ventilated, with a terrible stench filling the narrow alleyways.

Rio's flood of immigrants added diversity to the city. On the streets, you could hear a cacophony of languages – African, Portuguese, English, French – mixing with the sounds of the *bonde* (tram), of carts drawn by mules, and the cadence of various dances – maxixes, lundus, polkas and waltzes.

1954

Following a political scandal, the military calls for the resignation of President Getúlio Vargas. He pens a melodramatic letter then shoots himself at his Rio palace.

1960

President Juscelino Kubitschek moves the capital of Brazil from Rio to the newly constructed Brasília; Rio's political and sociocultural prominence declines.

1963

Brazilian filmmakers create a new movement with Cinema Novo, which tackles Brazil's social problems. Director Glaubo Rocha leads the way with *Black God, White Devil.*

1964

President Goulart is overthrown by a military coup. Troops arrive in Rio and seize power. So begins the era of dictatorship, with generals running the show for the next 20 years.

The city went through dramatic changes in the first decade of 1900, owing in large part to the work of Mayor Pereira Passos. He continued the work of 'Europeanization' by widening Rio's streets and creating grand boulevards such as Av Central and Mem de Sá. The biggest of these boulevards required the destruction of 600 buildings to make way for Av Central (later renamed Rio Branco), which became the Champs Elysées of Rio, an elegant boulevard full of sidewalk cafes and promenading *cariocas*.

Passos also connected Botafogo to Copacabana by building a tunnel, paving the way for the development of the southern beaches. Despite his grand vision for Rio, his vision for the poor was one of wide-scale removal from the city center – a short-sighted policy that would dog the Rio (and Brazilian) government for the next 80 years. In truth, the *cortiços* (poor, collective lodgings) were breeding grounds for deadly outbreaks of smallpox, yellow fever and typhus. Citing the widespread health and sanitation problems, the city destroyed thousands of shacks. With no homes, the poor fled to the hills, later creating some of the earliest favelas (shanty towns). The city also exterminated rats and mosquitoes and created a modern sewage system.

By the time Passos' term ended in 1906, Rio was the Belle Époque capital par excellence of Latin America. Its only possible rival in beauty was Buenos Aires. One visitor who commented on Rio's transformation was former US President Teddy Roosevelt. In 1913, during a tour through town, he noted that since Brazil had become a republic in 1889, Rio de Janeiro had gone 'from a picturesque pest-hole into a singularly beautiful, healthy, clean and efficient modern great city.'

DOM PEDRO II

A true Renaissance man, Dom Pedro II had interests in many subjects – chemistry, philosophy, geology, poetry, anthropology – and he could speak over a dozen languages (including Arabic and Sanskrit). He corresponded with many great 19th-century figures including Richard Wagner, Alexander Graham Bell and Louis Pasteur.

Boom Days, Reform & Repression Under Vargas

At the end of the 19th century, the city's population exploded because of European immigration and internal migration (mostly ex-slaves from the declining coffee and sugar regions). By 1900 Rio boasted more than 800,000 inhabitants, a quarter of them foreign born (by contrast, São Paulo's population was only 300,000).

Following Passos' radical changes, the early 1920s to the late 1950s were one of Rio's golden ages. With the inauguration of some grand luxury resort hotels (the Glória in 1922 and the Copacabana Palace in 1923), Rio became a romantic, exotic destination for Hollywood celebrities and international high society, with Copacabana its headquarters. In some ways Rio's quasi-mythic status as a tropical arcadia spans its entire history, but in the 1940s and 50s its reputation as the urban Eden

1968

Caetano Veloso and Gilberto Gil and other musicians release 'Tropicália: ou Panis et Circencis'. Tropicália is born, a movement in music and art that takes aim at the military dictatorship.

1968

The government passes the repressive Institutional Act 5, which purges opposition legislators, judges and mayors from public office; most political parties are banned.

1968

The Brazilian economy booms, averaging an incredible 10% growth for the next six years. Rapid income growth continues into the 1970s.

1972

The era of megaprojects and skyrocketing deficits begins, with the 5300km Trans-Amazonian highway. It cost nearly US$1 billion, but was never completed.

THE ORIGINS OF THE FAVELA

In the Northeast of Brazil terrible droughts in the 1870s and '80s, coupled with the decline of the sugar industry, brought economic devastation. Offering a vision of hope, Messianic popular movements gained support among Brazil's poor. The most famous was led by Antônio Conselheiro (Antônio the Counselor), an itinerant preacher who had wandered for years through the backlands prophesying the end of the world, defending the poor and antagonizing the authorities. He railed against the new republican government and in 1893 eventually settled with his followers at Canudos, in the interior of northern Bahia. Within 1½ years Canudos had grown to a city of 35,000.

The republican government sensed plots in Canudos to return Brazil to the monarchy. After the first attempts to subdue Canudos failed, the government sent in a federal force of 8000 soldiers – many of whom hailed from Rio – in a war of extermination that nearly wiped out every man, woman and child from Canudos. The settlement was then burned to the ground to erase it from the nation's memory.

The soldiers and their wives – some of whom were survivors taken from the Canudos massacre – returned to Rio, where they were promised land in exchange for their victory. The government, however, reneged on the promise. The soldiers, who had camped out in front of the Ministry of War, then occupied the nearby hillside of Morro da Providência.

Oddly enough, as the first tenants put up makeshift shelters and settled in, they came across the same hardy shrub they found in the arid lands surrounding Canudos. Called 'favela', this plant caused skin irritations in all who came in contact with it – according to some accounts, the protective shrub even helped repel the army's initial invasions. Over time, hillside residents began calling their new home the Morro da Favela (perhaps in hopes that the plant would have protective benefits), and the name caught on. Within a generation, the word favela was used to describe the ever-increasing number of informal communities appearing around Rio – which quickly filled with a mix of former slaves and poverty-stricken inhabitants who came from the interior to seek a better life.

of Latin America was vouchsafed as the world was introduced to Carmen Miranda, a Rio icon.

This period was also when radical changes were happening in the world of music and Rio was beginning to celebrate its 'Brazilianness', namely its mixed heritage and race. Sociologist Gilberto Freyre's influential book *Masters and Slaves* (1933) turned things upside down as Brazilians, conditioned to think of their mixed-race past with shame, began to think differently about their heritage – as an asset that set them apart from other nations of the world.

1979–80

The decline of workers' wages leads to nationwide strikes. Unions call for justice and young workers join with intellectuals and activists to form Brazil's Workers' Party.

1985

After a cautious period of *abertura* (opening), Brazil holds an indirect presidential election. Tancredo Neves wins and millions of Brazilians celebrate the end of military rule.

1985

Neves dies of heart failure before taking office. His vice-presidential candidate, José Sarney, takes power but can't handle the rampant inflation and huge debt left by his predecessors.

1994

President Collor is impeached; Vice-President Itamar Franco takes power. He introduces a new currency, the real, which stabilizes the economy and ushers in an economic boom.

The 1930s was the era of President Vargas, who formed the Estado Novo (New State) in November 1937, making him the first Brazilian president to wield absolute power. Inspired by the fascist governments of Salazar in Portugal and Mussolini in Italy, Vargas banned political parties, imprisoned political opponents, and censored artists and the press.

Despite all this, many liked Vargas. The 'father' of Brazil's workers, he created Brazil's minimum wage in 1938. Each year he introduced new labor laws to coincide with Workers' Day on May 1, which were aimed at keeping Brazil's factory workers happy. His vision for Brazil was not to increase the country's output, but to improve the level of education among all Brazilians.

The Military Dictatorship

The world's fascination with Rio was severely curtailed during the rise of the military dictatorship of the 1960s. The era of repression began with press censorship, silencing of political opponents (sometimes by torture and violence) and an exodus of political defectors abroad (including musicians, writers and artists). There were numerous protests during that period (notably in 1968 when some 100,000 marched upon the Palácio Tiradentes). And even Rio's politicians opposed the military regime, which responded by withholding vital federal funding for certain social programs.

From 1987 to 1997, Brazilians suffered devastating hyperinflation, averaging 2000% annually. This meant rent doubled every 10 weeks, credit cards charged 25% a month interest and food and clothing prices went up 40% a month.

Despite the repression, the 1960s and '70s witnessed profound changes in the city, with the opening of tunnels and the building of viaducts, parks and landfills. In the realm of public transportation, modernization was on the way. In the 1970s builders connected Rio with Niterói with the construction of the bay-spanning bridge, while beneath the city, the first metro cars began to run.

Meanwhile, the Zona Sul saw skyscrapers rising over the beaches of Copacabana and Leblon, with a shift of the wealthy to places further away from neglected downtown Rio. The moving of Brazil's capital to Brasília in 1960 seemed to spell the end for Centro, which became a ghost town after hours and retained none of the energy of its past. By the 1970s, its plazas and parks were dangerous places, surrounded by aging office towers.

The center of old Rio remained a bleak place until around 1985, when Brazil held its first direct presidential election in 20 years. With the slow return to civilian rule, *cariocas* turned their attention to sadly abandoned parts of the city, like downtown. Over the next decade citizens, particularly local shop owners, launched a downtown revitalization campaign, sometimes collecting money by going door-to-door.

1994

The Favela-Bairro project means that, over the next decade, neglected communities have access to decent sanitation, health clinics and transportation.

2002

Lula is elected president. The former union leader serves a moderate first term, despite upper-class fears of radical agendas. Meanwhile, Brazil wins its fifth World Cup.

2003

President Lula launches the Bolsa Família program of cash payments to 11 million of Brazil's poorest families. The program helps reduce poverty by 27% during Lula's first term.

2006

Despite a corruption scandal in his party, Lula is reelected president. He presides over continued economic growth and receives record approval ratings.

By 1995 it was clear that the drive was a success. Whole blocks in downtown received much-needed facelifts. Handsomely restored buildings attracted new investment, with new shops and cultural centers opening their doors alongside book publishers and art galleries. And nightlife returned to Lapa.

A City Divided

Unfortunately, the latter half of the 20th century was also an era of explosive growth in the favelas, as immigrants poured in from poverty-stricken areas of the northeast and the interior, swelling the number of urban poor in the city. The Cidade Maravilhosa (Marvelous City) began to lose its gloss as crime and violence increased, and in the 1990s it became known as the Cidade Partida (divided city), a term that reflected the widening chasm between the affluent neighborhoods of the Zona Sul and the shanty towns spreading across the region's hillsides.

Set in Rio during the military dictatorship, Bruno Barreto's film *Four Days in September* (1997) is based on the 1969 kidnapping of the US ambassador to Brazil by leftist guerrillas.

As Rio entered the new millennium, crime remained one of the most pervasive problems afflicting the city. Violence continued to take thousands of lives, particularly in the favelas: in 2008, over 800 people were killed by police during gun battles between law enforcement and drug traffickers (12 police officers were also killed that year). Rio's middle and upper classes seemed mostly resigned to life inside gated and guarded condos, while poverty and violence surged in the slums nearby.

The government solution often failed to solve the problem. Crack troops would be sent in to take out a drug lord yet, whether or not their mission was successful, the heavy caliber raids often claimed innocent lives. This left many residents with a deep-rooted disdain for the police. Declaring war on the favelas was clearly not working; once the police left, drug lord in hand (or more likely dead), there was always someone else to take his place.

Although the first favela appeared on Rio's landscape in 1897, it wasn't until 1994 that the communities were included on maps.

A New Dawn

As a result of a worsening situation, Brazilian officials began to take a new approach. President Lula (full name Luiz Inácio Lula da Silva), who astutely saw the link between poverty and crime, announced in 2007 that Rio's favelas would receive US$1.7 billion to invest in running water, sanitation, roads and housing. He even paid a visit to the Cantagalo favela, a first for a Brazilian president. He later told a reporter that such investment – providing adequate services for the people – was the only way to combat drug lords.

On the local level, police began implementing a new approach to dealing with the drug traffickers in the favela. Led by a new wing called the Pacifier Police Division, they would drive the drug lords out as they

2007

Rio successfully hosts the Pan American Games, spending an estimated US$2 billion. Brazilian athletes rank third overall in total medal rankings (behind the US and Cuba).

2007

Rio bursts into celebration when Brazil wins the right to host the 2014 FIFA World Cup for the second time in the country's history.

2009

Jubilation erupts again as Rio is named host city of the 2016 Summer Olympics, making Brazil the first South American country in history to stage the event.

2010

Rio unveils Porto Maravilha, an R$8 billion project that will bring museums, parks, bike paths and infrastructure improvements to Rio's waterfront before the 2016 Olympics.

had done before, after which the police would stay behind in the community. In 2008 the favela Dona Marta became one of the first to be 'pacified', and millions of reais were invested in the community, repairing or sometimes replacing houses, improving sanitation and adding a new football (soccer) pitch – though the most dramatic improvement was adding a new funicular railroad that saved residents the 788-step slog to the top of the favela.

Favela visits by well-known figures are increasingly common. President Rousseff, US President Obama, Prince Harry and Lady Gaga have all visited Rio favelas in recent years.

The strategy proved remarkably successful, and it's been implemented in about 20 other favelas around Rio, benefiting an estimated 400,000 residents. President Dilma Rousseff, who succeeded Lula following the 2010 election, continues to implement the policies of her predecessor in hopes of bringing substantive changes to Brazil's poorest communities.

The success of the pacification program stems in large part from the cooperation (and funding) by all three levels of government – municipal, state and federal. Working with Rousseff is Eduardo Paes, Rio's popular mayor (elected to his second term in 2012) and Sergio Cabral, the state governor (whose second term will end in 2014). Both have been instrumental in carrying out Rio's favela improvements, as well as in developments affecting other facets of the city (notably in infrastructure and civic projects surrounding the 2016 Summer Olympics).

For insight into the often brutal tactics employed by police to combat drug traffickers, see the semi-fictional film *Tropa Elite* (Elite Squad, 2007), researched by former police officers and drug traffickers.

Local residents, for the most part, have been happy with the changes brought to their communities: improved social services, trash collection and the opening of over 150 new schools, plus a notable decline in violent crime. But with more than 900 favelas in the city (and over one million residents spread among them), Rio has a long way to go. The city for its part has set a goal of reaching all of Rio's favelas by the year 2020, at an estimated cost of R$8 billion.

2010

Rio launches Morar Caricoa, an ambitious R$8 billion favela improvement scheme to improve infrastructure and living conditions in all 1000 favelas by 2020.

2012

Rio's Carnaval continues to break records, with more than one million visitors drawn to the festival (29% more than expected), and revenues of nearly R$1.5 billion.

2013

To prepare for the 2014 FIFA World Cup (held in 12 Brazilian cities), Rio spends US$480 million to renovate Maracanã Stadium, where the final will take place.

2016

In the run-up to the Summer Olympics, Rio will spend an estimated R$35 billion on development, with much of the action happening in Barra da Tijuca.

The Sounds of Rio

Rio boasts a rich musical heritage, with live music as deeply connected to Rio culture as its beaches and mountains. Foremost of all is the city's signature sound – samba, which is heard all across town, particularly in the days and weeks leading up to Carnaval. Other styles contributing to Rio's lush soundtrack include rock, pop, jazz, Música Popular Brasileira (MPB), hip-hop and *forró* – all opportunities to showcase the city's outstanding pool of musical talent.

Samba

The birth of Brazilian music essentially began with the emergence of samba, first heard in the early 20th century in a Rio neighborhood near present-day Praça Onze. Here, immigrants from northeastern Brazil (mostly from Bahia) formed a tightly knit community in which traditional African customs thrived – music, dance and the Candomblé religion. Local homes provided the setting for impromptu performances and the exchange of ideas among Rio's first great instrumentalists. Such an atmosphere nurtured the likes of Pixinguinha, one of samba's founding fathers, as well as Donga, one of the composers of 'Pelo Telefone,' the first recorded samba song (in 1917) and an enormous success at the then-fledgling Carnaval.

Journalist, author and former dancer Alma Guillermoprieto vividly captures life in the favela, Mangueira, and preparations for the big Carnaval parade in her book *Samba*.

Samba continued to evolve in the homes and *botequims* (bars with table service) around Rio. The 1930s are known as the golden age of samba. By this point samba's popularity had spread beyond the working-class neighborhoods of central Rio, and the music evolved at the same time into diverse, less percussive styles of samba. Sophisticated lyricists like Dorival Caymmi, Ary Barroso and Noel Rosa popularized *samba canção* (melody-driven samba). (For insight into Noel Rosa's poetically charged and tragically brief life, check out the 2006 film *Noel: Poeta da Vila*.) Songs in this style featured sentimental lyrics and an emphasis on melody (rather than rhythm), foreshadowing the later advent of cool bossa nova. Carmen Miranda, one of the big radio stars of the 1930s, would become one of the first ambassadors of Brazilian music.

The 1930s were also the golden age of samba songwriting for the Carnaval. *Escolas de samba* (samba schools), which first emerged in 1928, soon became a vehicle for samba songwriting, and by the 1930s samba and Carnaval would be forever linked. Today's theme songs still borrow from that golden epoch.

Great *sambistas* (samba singers) continued to emerge in Brazil over the next few decades, although other emerging musical styles diluted their popularity. Artists such as Cartola, Nelson Cavaquinho and Clementina de Jesus made substantial contributions to both samba and styles of music that followed from it.

Traditional samba went through a rebirth over a decade ago with the opening of old-style *gafieiras* (dance halls) in Lapa. Today, Rio is once again awash with great *sambistas*. Classic *sambistas* like Alcione and Beth Carvalho still perform, while singers like Teresa Christina and Grupo Semente are intimately linked to Lapa's rebirth. Other talents on Rio's stages include Thais Villela, a rising star on the Lapa scene, and Diogo Nogueira, the deep-voiced samba son of legendary singer João Nogueira.

Another singer carrying on the tradition of her father is Mart'nália, daughter of samba legend Martinho da Vila. Meanwhile, the talented singer and songwriter Maria Rita, whose voice is remarkably similar to that of her late mother, Elis Regina – continues to create lush innovative samba-influenced albums.

Bossa Nova

In the 1950s came bossa nova (literally, new wave), sparking a new era of Brazilian music. Bossa nova's founders – songwriter and composer Antônio Carlos (Tom) Jobim and guitarist João Gilberto, in association with the lyricist-poet Vinícius de Moraes – slowed down and altered the basic samba rhythm to create a more intimate, harmonic style. This new wave initiated a new style of playing instruments and of singing.

Bossa nova's seductive melodies were very much linked to Rio's Zona Sul, where most bossa musicians lived. Songs such as Jobim's 'Corcovado' and Roberto Meneschal's 'Rio' evoked an almost nostalgic portrait of the city with their quiet lyricism.

By the 1960s, bossa nova had become a huge international success. The genre's initial development was greatly influenced by American jazz and blues, and over time, the bossa nova style came to influence those music styles as well. Bossa nova classics were adopted, adapted and recorded by such musical luminaries as Frank Sinatra, Ella Fitzgerald and Stan Getz, among others.

In addition to the founding members, other great Brazilian bossa nova musicians include Marcos Valle, Luiz Bonfá and Baden Powell. Bands from the 1960s like Sergio Mendes & Brasil '66 were also influenced by bossa nova, as were other artists who fled the repressive years of military dictatorship to live and play abroad. More recent interpreters of the seductive bossa sound include the Bahian-born Rosa Passos and the *carioca* Paula Morelenbaum.

BOSSA NOVA

Bossa Nova: The Story of the Brazilian Music that Seduced the World, by Ruy Castro, captures the vibrant music and its backdrop of 1950s Rio.

Tropicália

One of Brazil's great artistic movements, emerging in the late 1960s, was *tropicália*, a direct response to the repressive military dictatorship that seized power in 1964 (and remained in power until 1984). Bahian singers Caetano Veloso and Gilberto Gil led the movement, making waves with songs of protest against the national regime. In addition to penning defiant lyrics, *tropicalistas* introduced the public to electric instruments, fragmentary melodies and wildly divergent musical styles. In fact, the *tropicalistas'* hero was poet Oswald de Andrade, whose 1928 *Manifesto Antropofágico* (Cannibalistic Manifesto) supported the idea that anything under the sun could be devoured and recreated in one's music. Hence, the movement fused elements of US rock and roll, blues, jazz and British psychedelic styles into bossa nova and samba rhythms. Important figures linked to *tropicália* include Gal Costa, Jorge Benjor, Maria Bethânia, Os Mutantes and Tom Zé. Although *tropicália* wasn't initially embraced by the public, who objected to the electric and rock elements (in fact, Veloso was booed off the stage on several occasions), by the 1970s its radical ideas had been absorbed and accepted, and lyrics of protest were ubiquitous in songwriting of the time.

Tropical Truth: A Story of Music and Revolution in Brazil, by Caetano Veloso, describes the great artistic experiment of *tropicália* in 1960s Brazil. Although digressive at times, Veloso captures the era's music and politics.

Música Popular Brasileira (MPB)

Música Popular Brasileira (MPB) is a catchphrase to describe all popular Brazilian music after bossa nova. It includes *tropicália, pagode*

BRAZIL'S FAVORITE VOICE *TOM PHILLIPS*

One of Brazil's best-loved musicians still active on the scene today is Gilberto Gil, a Grammy-award winning singer and former minister of culture (from 2003 to 2008), who wasn't averse to singing a few songs following a meeting at, say, the World Economic Forum in Davos. The pop star made an unlikely government bureaucrat, considering his musical beginnings as an *engajado* (activist). During the 1960s he spent two years exiled in London after offending the dictatorship with his provocative lyrics.

A household name for decades, Gil hails from the northeastern state of Bahia. Born in 1942, he was raised in a middle-class family near Salvador. His career as a troubadour began in 1965, when he moved south to São Paulo with another Bahian musician, Caetano Veloso. Between them they were responsible for *tropicália,* an influential though short-lived cultural movement that blended traditional Brazilian music with the electric guitars and psychedelia of the Beatles. Years later Veloso even recorded a Tupiniquim (an indigenous group in the northeast) tribute to the Liverpudlian rockers – called 'Sugar Cane Fields Forever'.

Over the decades Gil has notched up hit after hit – morphing from quick-footed *sambista* to poetic balladeer to dreadlocked reggae icon.

Since the release of *Louvaçao* in 1967, Gil has recorded dozens of albums, including *Kaya N'Gan Daya,* a tribute to his idol Bob Marley. He's shared the stage with many performers over the years, even playing with the former UN General Secretary Kofi Annan (on bongos) in New York.

Though he's slowed down in recent years, the slender 70-something-year-old still performs – as he did at a 2012 concert on Copacabana beach, which he headlined alongside Stevie Wonder, attracting over 500,000 fans.

Here is some essential listening:

- ➡ *Gilberto Gil (Frevo Rasgado, 1968)* – Gilberto Gil
- ➡ *Tropicália, ou Panis et Circencis* (1968) – Gilberto Gil, Caetano Veloso, Gal Costa and Os Mutantes
- ➡ *Acoustic* (1994) – Gilberto Gil
- ➡ *Tropicália 2* (1994) – Gilberto Gil and Caetano Veloso
- ➡ *Refazenda* (1996) – Gilberto Gil
- ➡ *Quanta* (1997) – Gilberto Gil

(relaxed and rhythmic form of samba), and Brazilian pop and rock. All Brazilian music has roots in samba; even in Brazilian rock, heavy metal, disco or pop, the samba sound is often present.

MPB first emerged in the 1970s along with talented musicians such as Edu Lobo, Milton Nascimento, Elis Regina, Djavan and dozens of others, many of whom wrote protest songs not unlike the *tropicalistas.* Chico Buarque is one of the first big names from this epoch, and is easily one of Brazil's greatest songwriters. His music career began in 1968 and spanned a time during which many of his songs were banned by the military dictatorship – in fact his music became a symbol of protest during that era. Today the enormously successful *carioca* (resident of Rio) artist continues to write new albums, though lately he has turned his hand to novel writing.

Jorge Benjor is another singer whose career, which began in the 1960s, has survived up to the present day. Highly addictive rhythms are omnipresent in Benjor's songs, as he incorporates African beats and elements of funk, samba and blues in his eclectic repertoire. The celebratory album *África Brasil,* alongside his debut album *Samba Esquema Novo* (with recognizable hits like 'Mas, Que Nada!') are among his best.

RIO PLAYLIST

One of the world's great music cultures, Brazil has an astounding array of talented musicians. A list of our favorite songs could easily fill this section, but we've limited our highly subjective pick to 25 songs from 25 different artists.

- 'Canto de Ossanha' – Baden Powell
- 'Soy Loco Por Ti, America' – Caetano Veloso
- 'Alvorado' – Cartola
- 'Samba de Orly' – Chico Buarque and Toquinho
- 'Flor de Lis' – Djavan
- 'Aguas de Março' – Elis Regina (written by Tom Jobim)
- 'Hoje É Dia da Festa' – Elza Soares
- 'Sou Brasileiro' – Fernando Abreu and Mart'nália
- 'Namorinho de Portão' – Gal Costa
- 'Quilombo, O El Dorado Negro' – Gilberto Gil
- 'Desafinado' – João Gilberto
- 'Filho Maravilha' – Jorge Benjor
- 'A Procura da Batida Perfeita' – Marcelo D2
- 'Novo Amor' – Maria Rita
- 'Carinhoso' – Marisa Monte (written by Pixinguinha)
- 'Travessia' – Milton Nascimento
- 'Ultimo Desejo' – Noel Rosa
- 'Besta é Tu' – Novos Baianos
- 'Panis et Circenses' – Os Mutantes
- 'Acenda O Farol' – Tim Maia
- 'Garota de Ipanema' (Girl from Ipanema) – Tom Jobim
- 'Aquarela do Brasil' – Toquinho (written by Ary Barroso)
- 'Velha Infância' – Tribalistas
- 'Não me deixe só' – Vanessa da Mata
- 'Felicidade' – Vinicius de Moraes

Carlinhos Brown continues to make substantial contributions to Brazilian music, particularly in the realm of Afro-Brazilian rhythms. Born in Bahia, Brown has influences that range from *merengue* (fast-paced dancehall music originating in the Dominican Republic) to Candomblé music to straight-up James Brown–style funk (the US artist from whom Carlinhos took his stage name). In addition to creating the popular percussion ensemble Timbalada, he has a number of excellent albums of his own (notably *Alfagamabetizado*). Involved in many diverse projects, Brown was even nominated for an Oscar in 2012 for best original song ('Real in Rio' for the film *Rio*), which he and Sergio Mendes composed.

The Brazilian Sound, by Chris McGowan and Ricardo Pessanha is a well-illustrated, readable introduction to Brazilian music, with insight into regional styles and musicians (big-name and obscure). The useful discography lists essential albums to add to your collection.

Rock, Pop & Hip-Hop

MPB tends to bleed into other genres, particularly into rock and pop. One artist who moves comfortably between genres is Bebel Gilberto (the daughter of João Gilberto), who blends bossa nova with modern beats on jazz-inflected bilingual albums like *All in One* (2009). Another heiress of Brazilian traditions is the Rio-born Marisa Monte, popular at home and abroad for her fine singing and songwriting. Mixing samba, *forró* (traditional, fast-paced music from the northeast), pop and rock, Monte has been part of a number of successful collaborations in the music world. Her brief collaboration with Arnaldo Antunes and Carlinhos Brown resulted in the fine album *Tribalistas* (2003).

Other notable young singers who hail from a bossa line include Roberta Sá, whose most recent album, *Segunda Pele* (2012), features elements of bossa, jazz, and even reggae. From Fernanda Porto (whose music is often described as drum 'n' bossa, a blend of electronica and bossa grooves – check out her 2009 album *Auto-Retrato*). The expat singer-songwriter and performance artist Cibelle incorporates a mix of pop, folk and Brazilian sounds in her lush (mainly English-language) recordings like those on *The Shine of Dried Electric Leaves* (2006). She came to prominence as the main vocalist on Suba's noteworthy album *São Paulo Confessions* (1999). With a host of Grammy nominations to her name, Céu has many fans both at home and abroad. She has recorded three albums over the last seven years, creating dreamlike melodies with elements of *tropicália*, samba, reggae and jazz. Her latest, *Caravana Sereia Bloom* (2012), is a colorful work with songs inspired by a road trip across Brazil. Her first album, the self-titled *Céu* (2007) is still considered her best.

Brazilian hip-hop emerged from the favelas of Rio sometime in the 1980s, and has been steadily attracting followers ever since. Big names such as Racionais MCs first emerged out of São Paulo, but Rio has its share of more recent success stories. One of the best on the scene is Marcelo D2 (formerly of Planet Hemp) impressing audiences with albums like *A Procura da Batida Perfeita* (2003) and *A Arte do Barulho* (2008). Better known to international audiences is Seu Jorge, who starred in the film *Cidade de Deus* and performed brilliant Portuguese versions of Bowie songs on Wes Anderson's film *The Life Aquatic*. His best solo work is *Cru* (2005), an inventive hybrid of hip-hop and ballads, with politically charged beats.

Aside from Marcelo D2, most of today's hip-hop artists hail from São Paulo. A few names to look out for include Emicida, a youthful rapper admired for his cutting improvisational rhymes. Check out his funk-laden single 'Triunfo', one of his early breakthrough hits. Yet another *paulista*, Rael de Rima is a fast-rapping lyricist with a strong sense of musicality, often performing with guitar and a full back-up band. MC Criolo tackles themes like urban violence, police brutality and racism, which has made him a hit in the favelas. Following the release of his debut 2011 album, *Nó na Orelha*, he's earned a growing number of admirers. The *carioca* rapper MV Bill is a man with a message. His songs focus on youth facing the ever-present threats of drugs and violence. He's even written a book *(Falcão – Meninos do Tráfico)* and created a network of youth centers in Rio that offer kids – who might otherwise be on the street – classes in dancing, music and art.

Rock has its promoters, though it enjoys far less airtime than samba. Rio gets its share of mega-rockers on the world tour. It also has a few homegrown talents. The group Legião Urbana from Brasília remains one of the all-time greats among rock lovers. The band (which folded shortly after the death of lead singer Renato Russo in 1996) enjoyed enormous success in the 1980s and early 1990s, and has sold over 15 million records. Raul Seixas, Skank, O Rappa, Os Paralamas do Sucesso and the Rio-based Barão Vermelho are other essential names.

In other genres, indie-rock favorites Los Hermanos were a top band that created catchy albums before breaking up in 2007. Check out *Ventura* (2003) or *Bloco do Eu Souzinho* (2001), one of the seminal pop-rock albums of its time. Vanguart, fitting somewhere in the folk-rock genre, are also a group to watch. Their self-titled debut album (2007) channels samba, blues and classic rock.

RAUL SEIXAS

Raul Seixas (1945–1989) is often called 'the father of Brazilian rock'. Many of his wild rock anthems are well known, and it's not uncommon to hear shouts of *'toca Raul!'* (play Raul!) at concerts. Curiously, best-selling author Paulo Coelho co-wrote many of his songs.

Football

***Cariocas*, like most Brazilians, are football (soccer) mad. No one goes to work on big international game days, instead everyone packs into the neighborhood *botecos* or on the sidewalks out front to watch the game. After a big win the whole city celebrates with rowdy nights of partying. And should the team lose, the sadness in the air is palpable. Everyone cheers for the national team, but for most of the year, the club team is the one that matters most. Every *carioca* has a favorite team, and will never pass up the chance to see them play live amid the roaring crowds in Maracanã.**

Futebol, a book by Alex Bellos (2002), is a fascinating and humorous look at the culture behind Brazil's nationwide obsession, with stories of the legendary players and the way that football has shaped Brazilian society.

The Game, the Fans

It is widely acknowledged that Brazilians play the world's most creative and thrilling style of football. They are also generally known as lousy defenders, but no one seems to mind since they make attack so exciting. The fans, too, are no less fun to watch. Skillful moves and adroit dribbling past an opponent receive a Spanish bullfight-style 'olé!', while fans do their best to rev up the action by pounding huge drums (or the backs of the stadium seats), waving huge flags, launching fireworks and smoke bombs or sometimes sending suspicious fluids onto the seats below. Crowds are rambunctious, but no more prone to violence than in England, Spain or Italy, for instance.

The Clubs

Rio is home to four major club teams – Flamengo, Fluminense, Vasco da Gama and Botafogo – each with a diehard local following. Apart from a couple of short breaks for the Christmas–New Year holiday and Carnaval, professional club competitions go on all year. The major event in Rio's sporting calendar is the *classico*, when the four hometown teams play each other. Expect intense and bitter rivalry, matched in excitement only by encounters between Rio and São Paulo clubs.

Flamengo

The biggest of Rio's big four, Flamengo has an enormous fan base both in Rio and around the world – an estimated 36 million followers, which makes it the most popular football club in Brazil. Voted one of the most successful football clubs of the 20th century by FIFA, Flamengo certainly doesn't lack for cashflow, with annual revenue of over R$120 million. Famous players who have donned the iconic red-and-black jerseys include Zico, often hailed as the best player never to win a World Cup; Leonidas, leading scorer at the 1938 World Cup; Bebeto, Mario Zagallo and Romario. More recently, Ronaldinho Gaucho, two-time FIFA player of the year, played for Flamengo (2011–2012) before making a surprise move to Atlético Mineiro in 2012.

Flamengo plays its home games in Maracanã Football Stadium; a fan is called a Flamenguista.

Fluminense

Founded by sons of the elite in Laranjeiras back in 1902, Fluminense is a highly successful club that has contributed a number of top players to the national team. It has also been hailed as the 'champion of the century', for winning the largest number of Campeonato Carioca titles in the 20th century (28 in all), though its successes have diminished in the current century. Famous players include Didi (1949–1956), a superstar midfielder who helped Brazil win the World Cup in both 1958 and 1962, and Roberto Rivellino, who led Fluminense to the state championship in 1975 and 1976 (and was instrumental in Brazil's World Cup victory in 1970). Current stars include Fred (aka Frederico Chaves Guedes), who scored the fastest goal in Brazilian history (finding net 3.17 seconds after the game's start).

Fluminense plays its home games in Maracanã; a fan is known as a Tricolor (a reference to the maroon, green and white uniforms).

Vasco da Gama

Founded by Portuguese immigrants near the turn of the 20th century, Vasco remains the favorite club for *cariocas* of Portuguese descent. One of Vasco's all-time greats was Romario (who also played for Flamengo and Fluminense), a powerful striker who scored over 900 goals during his career. Another Vasco legend is Carlos Roberto de Oliveira, nicknamed Roberto Dinamite, who holds the record for the most appearances for the club and is its all-time highest scorer. His passion for Vasco runs deep, and he became president of the club in 2008.

Vasco plays its home games in the 25,000-seat Estadio São Januário in the Zona Norte; the uniforms are black with a white diagonal sash. A fan is called a Vascaíno.

Botafogo

Botafogo started out as a rowing club in the late 19th century, quickly embracing football after its popularization in the early 1900s. One of Brazil's oldest teams, Botafogo is the only club in Brazilian history to win titles in three different centuries. During the 1950s and '60s, some of Brazil's greatest footballers played for Botafogo, such as Garrincha, who overcame physical disabilities (including legs of uneven length) and became one of the best dribblers of all time. Other legends of the era include Nilton Santos, Amarildo and Quarentinha. Unfortunately, Botafogo's star power diminished significantly in the years after, and in 2002 it was even relegated to the second division after coming in last in the Brazilian League (though it quickly returned to the first division the following year).

Botafogo plays its home games at the Estádio Olímpico João Havelange (better known as Engenhão). The stadium was built for the 2007 Pan-Am games, and will also feature in the 2016 Summer Olympics. Botafogo players wear black-and-white striped jerseys; a fan is called a Botafoguense.

FLA-FLU

The intense interclub rivalry dubbed Fla-Flu (short for Flamengo-Fluminense) began back in 1911, when a group of disgruntled players from Fluminense left the club and went to Flamengo, creating a brand new team. Games attract huge crowds – over 175,000 in 1963, a world record for a club match.

Competitions

Apart from the World Cup, which takes place every four years, there are many other tournaments happening throughout the year. In addition to the following key competitions, other major championships include the Copa do Brasil, the Copa dos Campeões and the Copa América.

Campeonato Brasileiro

The premier competition inside Brazil is the Campeonato Brasileiro (Brazilian Championship). Between about late July and mid-November, 20-odd top clubs play each other once each, then the eight top teams advance to a knockout phase, which culminates in a two-leg final in mid-December to decide the national championship. Since the competition's inception in 1959, São Paulo's top four teams have dominated,

PELÉ

Pelé is one of the world's most famous players, and is still widely considered to be the greatest to have ever played the game. He's also not just a legendary footballer, Pelé was Brazil's first black government minister (for sport from 1995 to 1998) and has even been knighted by Queen Elizabeth II.

Pelé has come a long way since he was born Edson Arantes do Nascimento in a humble Minas Gerais town on October 23, 1940. Yet despite his stardom, his public image remains impeccable. He's never smoked or been photographed with a drink in hand, and has never been involved with drugs.

In a 22-year career, the teams on which Pelé played gained 53 titles, including three World Cups (the first, in Sweden in 1958, when he was just 17 years old) and back-to-back world club championships (with Santos in 1962 and 1963) among many others. Despite lucrative offers to play in Europe, Pele never did so – in fact, President Janio Quadros had Pelé declared a national treasure in 1971 so that he could not be transferred to a European club.

Pelé retired from the Brazilian team in 1971 and from Santos in 1974. In 1975 the New York Cosmos coaxed him north to the US, where he played until 1977, when the team won the American championship. He finally retired for good at the end of that year, after a game between the Cosmos and Santos in which he played the first half for the Cosmos and the second half with Santos.

In 1366 games (112 for the Brazilian team), he scored 1282 goals, making him Brazil's all-time highest goal scorer. When he scored his 1000th goal in 1969 in Maracanã stadium, he dedicated it 'to the children of Brazil'. Pele called getting the goal 'one of the greatest blessings a man could ever expect to receive from God.'

Pelé, who maintains an oceanfront home in Rio, continues to be a goodwill ambassador for sport, and still commands enormous respect – as evidenced by the roar of the crowd when he made a surprise appearance at the end of the Summer Olympics in London in 2012. In Brazil, Pelé is known simply as '*O Rei*' (the king).

followed by Flamengo (six titles), Vasco (four) and Fluminense (four). Underachieving Botafogo has won the championship only twice.

Copa Libertadores

The annual Copa Libertadores is South America's most important football tournament. It's contested by the best-performed clubs from South America and Mexico, and is watched by millions around the world – the event is broadcast in over 130 countries. It kicks off in February, with the final tournament staged between June and August. Since it was first held in 1960, Argentinean teams have won the most titles (22), followed by Brazil (16). Rio's Flamengo and Vasco da Gama have each won the tournament once.

The Estádio das Laranjeiras, built for Fluminense in 1905, was the first football stadium constructed in Brazil. It holds 8000 people and still stands today in Laranjeiras, next to the current governor's palace.

Campeonato Carioca

Each of Brazil's 26 states holds its own championship. Running from January through March, the Campeonato Carioca is the Rio state championship, and one of the oldest held in Brazil – contested since 1906. Although other teams around the state compete, the winner, not surprisingly, is usually one of the big four. Flamengo (32 titles) and Fluminense (31) have dominated, followed by Vasco (22 titles) and Botafogo (19).

Racial Barriers

In 1902, when Oscar Cox, an Anglo-Brazilian, and some of his friends created Rio's first club, Fluminense, it was initially an aristocratic and all-white affair. Black players would not break down the racial barriers until the 1920s when Vasco da Gama began championing black and multiracial players. By the 1930s, Brazil was already gaining fame for its talented players, some of whom were black or mulatto and came from poor families, thus inverting the elite-only sport into a sport for the poor and disenfranchised.

European Vacation

Until recently most of the best players left Brazil for more lucrative contracts with European clubs. Over the last decade, however, many Brazilian stars have returned home to play for more adoring fans and not insubstantial contracts. The strengthening of the real against the euro, along with Brazil's economic boom, has allowed top Brazilian clubs to offer salaries approaching the wages Brazilian players earn in Europe. TV rights and corporate sponsorship have also helped deepen the pockets of Brazilian clubs. The return of more players to Brazil, coupled with the ongoing growth of new talent into the big clubs, could help transform Brazil into one of the world's footballing giants – on the club level as well as the international level.

The Afro-Brazilian player and *carioca* Leonidas da Silva is one of Brazil's early football legends. He played for Vasco, Fluminense and Flamengo, leading each team to the state championship and helping to break down racial barriers. In 1938, he also scored the only bicycle kick goal in World Cup history.

The World Cup

Bringing the World Cup back to Brazil had long been a dream of the football-crazed nation. In 2007, when the nation learned that it had won the right to host the 2014 tournament, spontaneous celebrations erupted across town, and tens of thousands took to Copacabana beach to rejoice in the good news. The South American giant last staged the big sporting event in 1950, when Brazil lost in the dramatic final against Uruguay before some 200,000 fans in Rio's Maracanã stadium. This infamous day was later called '*maracanaço*' and is still in common parlance.

Brazil, the most successful football nation in the history of the game (with five World Cup victories), becomes the fifth country to host the event twice. Aside from Rio, where the opener and final take place, 11 other cities across the country will stage games; this too is historic, as it's the only time the World Cup has ever been held in more than 10 cities. Brazil has spent a staggering R$26 billion in preparation for the event, including stadium construction, upgrades to airports, roads and other infrastructure.

Architecture

The capital of Brazil for many years, Rio de Janeiro has been the architectural setting for the beautiful, the functional and the avant-garde. Today one can see a sweeping range of styles that span the 17th to the 20th centuries in buildings that often vie for attention alongside one another.

The Petrobras building (Av República do Chile 65, Centro) is often short-listed by media outlets as one of the world's ugliest buildings. Boxy, gray and uninspiring, the 1970s-era brutalist design looks like a cross between a half assembled Lego tower and a broken Rubiks cube.

Colonial & Imperial Rio

Vestiges of the colonial period live on in downtown Rio. Some of the most impressive works are the 17th-century churches built by the Jesuits. The best examples from this baroque period are the Convento de Santo Antônio and the Mosteiro de São Bento. The incredibly ornate interiors, which appear almost to drip with liquid gold, show little of the restraint that would later typify Brazilian architecture.

The artist mission (a group of artists and architects chosen to bring new life to the city) that arrived from France in the early 19th century introduced a whole new design aesthetic to the budding Brazilian empire. Neoclassicism became the official style and was formally taught in the newly founded Imperial Academy. The works built during this period were grandiose and monumental, dominated by classical features such as elongated columns and wide domes. Among the many fine examples of this period are the Museu Nacional de Belas Artes, the Theatro Municipal and the Casa França-Brasil (considered the most important from this period). The Casa has a few curious features: its alignment to the cardinal points, the large cross-shaped space inside and its monumental dome.

The end of the 19th century saw the continuation of this trend of returning to earlier forms and featured works such as the Real Gabinete Português de Leitura (Royal Reading Room). Completed in 1887, the Royal Reading Room shows inspiration from the much earlier manueline period (early 1500s), with a Gothic facade and the highlighting of its metallic structure.

The 20th Century

During the 20th century Rio became the setting for a wide array of architectural styles – including neoclassical, eclectic, art-deco and modernist works. During the same period Rio also restored some of its colonial gems (others fell to the wrecking ball), becoming one of Latin America's most beautiful cities.

This, of course, did not happen by chance. In the early 20th century, as capital of Brazil, Rio de Janeiro was viewed as a symbol of the glory of the modern republic and the president lavished beautiful neoclassical buildings upon the urban streetscape.

The early 1900s was also the period when one of Rio's most ambitious mayors, Pereira Passos, was in office. These twin factors had an enormous influence in shaping the face of Brazil's best-known city.

Mayor Passos (in office from 1902 to 1906) envisioned Rio as the Paris of South America, and ordered his engineers to lay down grand boulevards and create manicured parks, as some of Rio's most elegant buildings rose overhead. One of the most beautiful buildings constructed during this period was the Palaçio Monroe (Monroe Palace; 1906), a re-creation of a work built for the 1904 St Louis World's Fair. The elegant neoclassical Palaçio Monroe sat on the Praça Floriano and housed the Câmara dos Deputados (House of Representatives). Unfortunately, like many other of Rio's beautiful buildings, it was destroyed in 1976 in the gross 'reurbanization' craze that swept through the city.

The fruits of this early period were displayed at the International Exposition held in Rio in 1922. This was not only the showcase for neocolonial architecture and urban design; it also introduced Brazil's most modern city to the rest of the world. Another big event of the 1920s was the completion of the Copacabana Palace, the first luxury hotel in South America. Its construction would lead to the rapid development of the beach regions.

Rio's 1930s buildings show the influence of modern European architecture, which greatly impacted upon the city's design. Rio's modernism occurred in tandem with the rise of President Vargas, who wanted to leave his mark on Rio through the construction of public ministries, official chambers and the residences of government power. The Ministry of Health & Education, the apotheosis of the modernist movement in Brazil, is one of the city's most significant public buildings, as it's one of the few works designed by French architect Le Corbusier, who designed it in conjunction with several young Brazilian architects. (Another Le Corbusier-influenced design is the Aeroporto Santos Dumont, completed in 1937.)

The 1930s was also the era of the art-deco movement, which was characterized by highly worked artistic details and an abundance of ornamentation. Good specimens include the central train station and the statue of Cristo Redentor (Christ the Redeemer) on Corcovado.

Oscar Niemeyer

Oscar Niemeyer, one of the young Brazilians who assisted on Le Corbusier's project, would turn out to be a monumental name in architectural history. Working in the firm of Lúcio Costa at the time of his initial collaboration with Le Corbusier, Niemeyer – along with Costa – championed the European avant-garde style in Brazil, making a permanent impact on the next 50 years of Brazilian design. Costa and Niemeyer collaborated on many works, designing some of the most important buildings in Brazil.

In Rio, Niemeyer and Costa broke with the neoclassical style and developed the functional style, with its extensive use of steel and glass, and lack of ornamentation. The Museu de Arte Moderna (inaugurated in 1958) and the Catedral Metropolitana (begun in 1964) are good

ARCHITECTURAL ICONS

Copacabana Palace (p168) The neoclassical gem that came to represent a glitzy new era.

Arcos da Lapa (p136) The 18th-century aqueduct is a widely recognized landmark that also lies at the epicenter of Rio's resurgent music scene in Lapa.

Maracanã Football Stadium (p146) Brazil's temple to football and its largest stadium, fresh off a dramatic makeover in preparation for the 2014 World Cup.

Cristo Redentor (p110) Icon of Rio and much loved by *cariocas* (residents of Rio) regardless of religious affiliation.

Theatro Municipal (p120) The flower of the Belle Époque and the costliest opera house constructed outside of Europe.

examples of this style. One of the most fascinating modern buildings close to Rio is the Niemeyer-designed Museu do Arte Contemporânea (MAC) in Niterói. Its fluid form and delicate curves are reminiscent of a flower in bloom (though many simply call it spaceship like). It showcases its natural setting and offers stunning views of Rio.

Niemeyer, whose work is known for its elegant curves – the female form was one of his inspirations – became famous for his work designing the nation's capital. He was a longtime Rio resident, and remained passionate about architecture and quite active in the field, up until his death in 2012 at the age of 104.

A lifelong communist, Niemeyer spent much of the 1960s and 1970s in exile during the height of the military dictatorship. His political affiliations also prevented him from working in the US during the Cold War.

Recent Projects

The huge amount of investment pouring in from the Olympics and Brazil's ongoing economic boom has led to many new developments around the city.

In 2013, Rio officially inaugurated the Cidade das Artes (City of the Arts) in Barra da Tijuca. The controversial project, originally slated to open in 2008, ran significantly over budget (the projected R$86 million cost eventually ran to over R$500 million). The ultra-modern 90,000-sq-meter complex houses a high-tech 1800-seat concert hall, as well as theaters, a chamber music hall and terrace with picturesque views over Barra. The building is the new base of the Brazilian Symphony Orchestra, and designed by the Pritzker Prize-winning French architect Christian de Portzamparc.

The revitalization of Rio's derelict port area is also seeing a host of new developments. The Rio Museum of Art on Praça Mauá cleverly joins two existing buildings – one a neoclassical early 20th century mansion, the other a modernist building (and former rail station). The unusual juxtaposition serves as an apt metaphor for the mix of classical and contemporary works inside. It was slated for opening in 2013. Nearby, the dramatic Santiago Calatrava-designed Museum of Tomorrow juts out into the water, featuring the cantilevered roof and a sculptural facade for which Calatrava is so well-known. It's scheduled for completion in 2014.

In Copacabana, the cutting-edge Museu da Imagem e Som (Museum of Image and Sound), currently under construction, aims to enliven Copacabana's boxy skyscraper-lined waterfront. The design by New York architectural firm of Diller Scofidio + Renfro integrates the building into its dramatic setting – between seafront and hilly backdrop. Public access, outdoor ramps and open-air space ensures a building accessible to all. It's scheduled for completion in 2014.

Architecture in Print

The Curves of Time: the Memoirs of Oscar Niemeyer (Oscar Niemeyer)

When Brazil Was Modern: A Guide to Architecture, 1928-1960 (Lauro Cavalcanti)

Roberto Burle Marx: The Lyrical Landscape (Marta Iris Montero)

Survival Guide

Transportation

GETTING TO RIO DE JANEIRO

Flying is the easiest way to get to Rio, with many flights stopping first in São Paulo (one hour away). High-season prices for a return ticket from gateways in North America or Europe typically run from R$2000 to R$2600. Long-distance buses arrive in Rio from Chile and Argentina. Flights, cars and tours can be booked online at www.lonelyplanet.com.

Air

Direct flights from North America take about 10 hours from NYC (8½ hours from Miami); from the West Coast, count on 15 or more hours including a layover. From Europe, direct flights from London or Paris take about 12 hours.

Airports

GALEÃO (GIG)

Rio's Galeão international airport (Aeroporto Internacional Antônio Carlos Jobim) is 15km north of the city center on Ilha do Governador. It has left-luggage facilities, an internet cafe, ATMs and currency-exchange desks, pharmacies as well as a few shops and restaurants.

Bus

Premium Auto Ônibus (www.premiumautoonibus.com.br; R$12) operates safe air-con buses from the international airport to Rodoviária Novo Rio bus station, Av Rio Branco (Centro), Santos Dumont Airport, southward through the *bairros* of Glória, Flamengo and Botafogo, and along the beaches of Copacabana, Ipanema and Leblon to Barra da Tijuca (and vice versa) every 20 minutes from 5:40am to 10:30pm and will stop wherever you ask. It takes 75 minutes to two hours depending on traffic.

Heading to the airports, you can catch this bus from in front of the major hotels along the main beaches, but you have to look alive and flag them down.

Taxi

From Galeão, radio taxis charge a set fare of R$105 to Ipanema, which takes about an hour depending on traffic. Less-secure yellow-and-blue *comum* (standard) taxis should cost around R$50 to R$70, depending on traffic. *Comun* taxis from the international airport are generally safe, though the rare robbery does occur.

Keep in mind that traffic can lead to excruciatingly long delays on the return journey to the airport. On bad days it can take almost two hours from the Zona Sul, so leave yourself plenty of time.

SANTOS DUMONT (SDU)

Aeroporto Santos Dumont, used by some domestic flights, is by the bay, in the city center, 1km east of Cinelândia metro station. It has fewer facilities, with ATMs, a few shops and an internet cafe.

Bus

The Premium Auto Ônibus, which departs from Galeão, stops at Santos Dumont before continuing south to Copacabana and Ipanema.

Taxi

From the domestic airport, a radio taxi runs to Copacabana (R$51) and to Ipanema (R$63); and *comums* are around R$30.

Land

Long-Distance Bus

RODOVIÁRIA NOVO RIO

Buses arrive at the hugely improved **Rodoviária Novo Rio** (☎3213-1800; Av Francisco Bicalho 1), 2km northwest of Centro, which is fresh off a R$21 million facelift that ramped up security and turned the entire 2nd floor into a pleasant area with a respectable food court.

The people at the Riotur desk on the bus station's ground floor can provide information on transportation and lodging. If you arrive in Rio by bus, it's a good idea to take a taxi to your hotel, or at least to the general area where you want to stay. Traveling on local buses with all your belongings is a little risky.

A small booth near the exit at Novo Rio bus station organizes the yellow taxis out

CLIMATE CHANGE & TRAVEL

Every form of transport that relies on carbon-based fuel generates CO_2, the main cause of human-induced climate change. Modern travel is dependent on airplanes, which might use less fuel per kilometer per person than most cars but travel much greater distances. The altitude at which aircraft emit gases (including CO_2) and particles also contributes to their climate change impact. Many websites offer 'carbon calculators' that allow people to estimate the carbon emissions generated by their journey and, for those who wish to do so, to offset the impact of the greenhouse gases emitted with contributions to portfolios of climate-friendly initiatives throughout the world. Lonely Planet offsets the carbon footprint of all staff and author travel.

the front. Excellent buses leave every 15 minutes or so for São Paulo (six hours). Sample fares (with one bag) are about R$50 to the international airport, R$38 to Copacabana and Ipanema, and R$35 to Santa Teresa.

A handful of travel agents sell bus tickets, which will save you a time-consuming trek out to the bus station. **Guanatur** (☎2548-3275; www.guanaturismo.com.br; Rua Dias da Rocha 16A, Copacabana) and **Dantur** (☎2557-7144; www.dantur.com.br; Largo do Machado 29, Loja 47, Flamengo; ⏲9am-6:30pm Mon-Fri, to 1pm Sat) sell tickets for many lines.

GETTING AROUND RIO DE JANEIRO

Rio is a fairly easy city to navigate, with an efficient metro system, a public bike-sharing system and hurtling buses. The neighborhoods themselves are perfect for getting around on foot.

Bicycle

Rio has many kilometers of bike paths along the beach, around Lagoa and along Parque do Flamengo. In addition to a public bike-sharing scheme, you can rent bikes from stands along the east side of Lagoa Rodrigo de Freitas for around R$10 per hour and at various bike shops along the bike path between Copacabana and Ipanema.

Bike Rio (☎4063-3111; www.mobilicidade.com.br/bikerio.asp) Thanks to Itaú bank and Rio City Hall, you can now peddle yourself around the city on bright-orange bikes found at some 60 stations throughout Rio. After registering on the site, you can buy a monthly pass (R$10) or a day pass (R$5). Instructions are in English at the stations and the bikes are released via mobile phone or app. Foreigners can register online with a passport number.

Ciclovia (Map p236; ☎2247-0018; Francisco Otaviano 55, Copacabana; per hr/day R$15/50; ⏲9am-7pm Mon-Fri, 9am-4pm Sat, 10am-4pm Sun) One of several shops conveniently located on the cycle path between Ipanema and Copacabana.

Boat

Rio has several islands in the bay that you can visit by ferry. Another way to see the city is by taking the commuter ferry to **Niterói**. Niterói's main attraction is the **Museu do Arte Contemporânea**, but many visitors board the ferry just for the fine views of downtown and the surrounding landscape. The **ferry** (☎0800-721-1012; www.grupoccr.com.br/barcas) costs R$9 return and departs every 20 minutes from Praça Quinze de Novembro in Centro.

Ilha de Paquetá (☎0800-721-1012; www.grupoccr.com.br/barcas) Visitors can visit an island out in the bay by regular ferry – operated by the same company that runs ferries between Niteroi and Rio. The ferry takes 70 minutes and costs R$9 return, leaving every two to three hours between 5:15am and 11pm. The most useful departure times for travelers are 7:10am, 10:30am and 1:30pm.

Ilha Fiscal (☎2233-9165; Espaço Cultural da Marinha) Boats depart four times a day (1pm, 12:30pm, 2pm and 3:30pm) from Thursday to Sunday and include a guided tour of the Ilha Fiscal palace. It's a short ride (15 minutes) and costs R$15.

Bus

City Bus

Rio's new BRS (Bus Rapid System) bus scheme got an Olympic-size efficiency makeover in 2011, with a new streamlined system that now includes dedicated public transportation corridors in Copacabana, Ipanema, Leblon and Centro. Buses are frequent and cheap, and because Rio is long and narrow it's easy to get the right bus and usually no big deal if you're on the wrong one. Nine out of 10 buses going south from the center will go to Copacabana, and vice versa. Fares on most buses are around R$3.

METRO-BUS TICKETS

If you're not staying near a metro station or are traveling somewhere off the metro map, integrated metro-bus tickets can be a cheap and speedy way to get to a destination. The **Metrô Na Superfície** (metro buses; www.metrorio.com.br) consists of modern, silver buses that make limited stops as they shuttle passengers to and from metro stations. For most destinations, a one-way *metrô na superficie* (surface metro) ticket costs the same as a single metro ride (R$3.20) but includes both the bus and the metro ride (hold onto your ticket). If you're entering the metro and plan on connecting to a bus, be sure to request 'metro + *metrô na superficie*' tickets at the booth; otherwise, you'll just receive single-use metro tickets.

The most useful one for travelers staying in Leblon and western Ipanema is the metro bus marked 'Gávea'. This will take you to and from the metro station at Praça General Osório.

If you're going from the metro to Jardim Botânico, disembark at Botafogo station and catch the integrated metro bus from there. Stops are at Cobal do Humaitá, Rua Maria Angélica, the Hospital da Lagoa, the edge of Jardim Botânico, Praça Santos Dumont, Gávea Trade Center and PUC.

Other useful buses are the following Integração Expresso (R$4.15) lines:

- **Bus 513** connects Botafogo with Urca.
- **Bus 580** connects Largo do Machado with Cosme Velho (via Laranjeiras).
- **Bus 590** connects Cardeal Arcoverde station (Copacabana) with Leme.

You can also go to Barra by metro bus (the Expresso Barra). This operates much like the *metro na superficie*, with limited stops, but covers a much larger distance. The integrated metro-bus ticket costs R$4.35 and departs from Praça General Osório station, with stops at Posto 9 (Ipanema beach), Posto 12 (Leblon beach), São Conrado Fashion Mall, Praia do Pepino (São Conrado), Shopping Downtown, Barra Shopping and Casa Shopping, among others.

Every bus has its destination written on the front. If you see your bus, hail it by sticking your arm straight out (drivers won't stop unless flagged down).

Car

Driving & Parking

In the city itself, driving can be a frustrating experience even if you know your way around. Traffic snarls and parking problems do not make for an enjoyable holiday. Be aware that Rio has extremely strict drink-driving laws, with a fine of around R$2000 for those with a blood-alcohol content of over 0.06. Changing police checkpoints are set up nightly around the city.

Rental

Getting a car is fairly simple as long as you have a driver's license, a credit card and a passport. Most agencies require renters to be at least 25 years old, though some will rent (with an added fee) to younger drivers.

Prices start around R$100 per day for a car without air-conditioning, but they go down a bit in the low season. If you are quoted prices on the phone, make sure they include insurance, which is compulsory.

Car-rental agencies can be found at both airports or scattered along Av Princesa Isabel in Copacabana.

At the international airport, **Hertz** (☎0800-701-7300; www.hertz.com), **Localiza** (☎0800-979-2000; www.localiza.com) and **Unidas** (☎2295-3628; www.unidas.com.br) provide rentals. In Copacabana, among the many are **Hertz** (☎2275-7440; Av Princesa Isabel 500) and **Localiza** (☎2275-3340; Av Princesa Isabel 150).

Metro

Rio's **metro system** (www.metrorio.com.br; ⏲5am-midnight Mon-Sat, 7am-11pm Sun) is an excellent way to get around. During Carnaval the metro operates nonstop from 5am Saturday morning until at least 11pm on Tuesday. Both lines are air-conditioned, clean, fast and safe. The main line goes from Ipanema-General Osório to Saens Peña, connecting with the secondary line to Estácio (which provides service to São Cristóvão, Maracanã and beyond). The main stops in Centro are Cinelândia and Carioca. More stations are planned in the coming years, and the city plans to integrate the rest of Ipanema, Leblon and Barra into the transportation system.

A single ride ticket is called a *unitário* and costs R$3.20. To avoid waiting in lines, you can purchase a *cartão pré-pago* (prepaid card) with a minimum of R$10 or more; you can then recharge it (cash only, no change given) at kiosks inside some metro stations. If you're going somewhere outside of the metro's range (eg Cosme Velho or Barra), you can purchase metro-bus tickets. Free subway maps are available from most ticket booths.

Minivan

Minivans (called *vans* in Rio) are an alternative form of transportation in Rio and are usually much faster than buses. They run along Av Rio Branco to the Zona Sul as far as Barra da Tijuca. On the return trip, they run along the coast almost all the way into the city center. They run frequently, and cost between R$2 and R$4.50. They do get crowded, and are not a good idea if you have luggage. Call out your stop *('para!')* when you want to disembark.

Taxi

Rio's yellow taxis are prevalent throughout the city. They're generally a speedy way to zip around and are usually safe. The flat rate is around R$4.50, plus around R$1.60 per kilometer. Radio taxis are 30% more expensive than regular taxis.

Most people don't tip taxi drivers, but it's common to round up the fare.

In Rocinha and some other favelas, moto-taxis (basically a lift on the back of a motorcycle) are a handy way to get around, with short rides (usually from the bottom of the favela to the top or vice versa) costing R$2.

A few radio-taxi companies:

Coopertramo (☎2209-9292)

Cootramo (☎3976-9944)

Transcoopass (☎2209-1555)

Transcootour (☎2590-2220)

Train

The suburban train station, **Estação Dom Pedro II** (Central do Brasil; ☎2111-9494; Av Presidente Vargas, Praça Cristiano Ottoni, Centro) is one of Brazil's busiest commuter stations, but it's definitely not the safest area to walk around. To get there, take the metro to Central station and head upstairs. This is the train station that was featured in the Academy Award–nominated film *Central do Brasil* (Central Station).

Tram

Rio was once serviced by a multitude of *bondes* (trams), with routes throughout the city. The only remaining line, which connected Centro with Santa Teresa, suffered a tragic accident in 2011 that left five people dead and dozens injured. Since then the service has been suspended. At the time of press the *bonde* was expected to reopen in March 2014, in time for the World Cup.

If it does reopen, trams would travel from the **bonde station** (Lélio Gama 65) in Centro along two routes that date back to the 19th century. Both travel over the **Arcos da Lapa** and along Rua Joaquim Murtinho before reaching **Largo do Guimarães** on Rua Almirante Alexandrino, in the heart of boho Santa Teresa. From there, one line (Paula Matos) takes a northwestern route, terminating at **Largo das Neves**. The longer route (Dois Irmãos) continues from Largo do Guimarães uphill and southwest before terminating near the water reservoir at Dois Irmãos.

TOURS

There are many ways to experience Rio, whether by boat, helicopter, 4WD or good old-fashioned walking.

Bay Cruises

With its magnificent coastline, Rio makes a fine backdrop for a cruise. Tours depart from the **Marina de Glória** (Map p241), and you can purchase tickets in advance from 8am to 4pm Monday to Friday. You can see the bay on the following boat trips:

Marlin Yacht Tours (☎2225-7434; www.marlimyacht.com.br; Marina de Glória, Glória; cruise R$60-95) Offers several daily tours aboard its large 30-person schooners to Cagarras Island, stopping for a beach swim along the way. It also offers sunset cruises, sailing and diving trips, and is known for its fishing tours.

Biking Tours

Bike in Rio (☎8474-7740; www.bikeinriotours.com; tour R$65) Offers fun three-hour bicycle tours around Rio in small groups (eight people maximum). One itinerary takes in Parque do Flamengo and Copacabana, another goes around Ipanema and Lagoa, and a third explores Lapa and downtown Rio.

City Tours

A number of private guides lead customized tours around the city, taking in the major sights and nightlife, and organizing just about any experience Rio has to offer. Recommended guides include the following:

Brazil Expedition (☎9998-2907; www.brazilexpedition.com; city tours R$95) The friendly English-speaking guides from Brazil Expedition run a variety of traditional tours around Rio, including trips to Cristo Redentor, nightlife tours in Lapa, game-day outings at Maracanã football stadium and favela tours.

Marcelo Esteves (☎9984-7654; marcelo.esteves@hotmail.com) A highly experienced multilingual Rio expert offering private tours around the city.

Madson Araújo (☎9395-3537; www.tourguiderio.com) Professional English- and French-speaking guide offering custom-made day or night tours around Rio.

Favela Tours

Favela Tour (☎3322-2727; www.favelatour.com.br; R$65) Marcelo Armstrong's insightful tour pioneered favela tourism – his three-hour excursion takes in Rocinha and Vila Canoas.

Paulo Amendoim (☎9747-6860; pauloamendoim8@hotmail.com; tour R$65-75) Another recommended guide is Paulo Amendoim, the former president of Rocinha's residents association. He seems to know everyone in the favela, and leads a warm and personalized tour that helps visitors see beyond the gross stereotypes.

Be A Local (☎9643-0366; www.bealocal.com; per person R$65) Offers daily trips into Rocinha (you'll ride up by mototaxi, and walk back down), with stops along the way. It also organizes a night out at a *baile* (dance) funk party in Castelo das Pedras on Sunday.

Helicopter Tours

Helisight (☎2511-2141; www.helisight.com.br; per person 6-/15-/30-min flight R$210/520/720) Offering helicopter tours since 1991, Helisight has eight different itineraries, all giving gorgeous views over the city. There is a three-person minimum. Helipad locations are in Floresta da Tijuca facing Corcovado; on Morro da Urca, the first cable-car stop up Pão de Açúcar; and on the edge of Lagoa.

Hiking Tours

Jungle Me (☎4105-7533; www.jungleme.com.br; tour R$150) This top-notch outfit offers excellent hiking tours through Parque Nacional da Tijuca led by knowledgeable guides. The peaks-and-waterfalls tour offers challenging walks up several escarpments that offer stunning views of Rio followed by a refreshing dip in a waterfall. The wild-beaches-of-Rio tour takes you on a hike between scenic beaches in Rio's little-visited western suburbs.

4WD Tours

Jeep Tour (☎2108-5800; www.jeeptour.com.br) Travels to the Floresta da Tijuca in a large, open-topped 4WD. The tour includes a stop at the Vista Chinesa, then on to the forest for an easy hike and a stop for a swim beneath a waterfall, before making the return journey.

Rio by Jeep (☎3322-5750; www.riobyjeep.com) Another recommended outfit offering 4WD tours.

Walking Tours

Lisa Rio Tours (☎9894-6867; www.lisariotours.com; tours from R$110) Lisa Schnittger, a German expat who has lived in Rio for many years, leads a wide range of recommended tours. Some of her most popular excursions explore the colonial history of downtown, the bohemian side of Santa Teresa and Afro-Brazilian culture in Rio.

Rio Walks (☎2516-5248; www.riowalks.com.br; tours from R$50) This popular outfit leads walking tours around the historic center, strolls around Santa Teresa and a bar-hopping jaunt around Ipanema and Leblon.

Cultural Rio (☎9911-3829; www.culturalrio.com.br; tours from R$120) Run by the quirky Carlos Roquette, this tour offers visitors an in-depth look at social and historical aspects of Rio de Janeiro.

Directory A–Z

Business Hours

Standard opening hours in Rio are as follows:

Restaurants noon–3pm and 7–11pm.

Bars noon–2am Monday to Saturday; some open Sunday as well.

Nightclubs 11pm–5am Thursday to Saturday.

Shops 9am–6pm Monday to Friday, 9am–1pm Saturday.

Malls 10am–10pm Monday to Saturday, 3–10pm Sunday.

Banks 9am–3pm Monday to Friday.

Courses

Cooking

Cook in Rio (Map p236; ☎8761-3653; www.cookinrio.com) There aren't many cooking classes available in English in Rio, other than this notable exception, who offer one-day courses where you'll learn how to make a rich *moqueca* (seafood stew cooked in coconut milk) or a decadent pot of *feijoada* (black beans and pork stew).

Language

Most language institutes charge high prices for group Portuguese courses. You can often find a private tutor for less. Hostels are a good place to troll for instructors, with ads on bulletin boards posted by native-speaking language teachers available for hire.

Casa do Caminho Language Centre (Map p228; ☎2267-6552; www.casadocaminho-languagecentre.org; Ste 403, Farme de Amoedo 75, Ipanema) Offers competitively priced classes, with intensive group classes – three hours a day for five days for R$400, or 60 hours of class-time over a month for R$950. Profits go toward the Casa do Caminho (www.casadocaminhobrasil.org) orphanages in Brazil.

Instituto Brasil-Estados Unidos (IBEU; Map p236; ☎2548-8430; www.ibeu.org.br; 5th fl, NS de Copacabana 690, Copacabana; intensive 36hr course R$1560) One of the oldest, more respected language-institutions in the city.

Carioca Languages (Map p236; ☎2146-8414; www.carioca-languages.com; room 201, NS de Copacabana 807; 60hr course R$1000) Located in Copacabana, with a wide range of courses as well as private instruction.

Music

Maracatu Brasil (Map p242; ☎2557-4754; www.maracatubrasil.com.br; 2nd fl, Ipiranga 49; ⏰10am-6pm Mon-Sat) is one of the best places in Rio to study percussion. It's very active in music events throughout the city. Instructors here offer courses in a number of different drumming styles: *zabumba*, *pandeiro* and symphonic percussion, as well as guitar and other instruments. If you plan to stick around a while, you can sign up for group classes (from R$150 a

PRACTICALITIES

Newspapers & Magazines *Rio Times* (www.riotimesonline.com) is an English-language newspaper that publishes a free print version monthly, it also maintains a website that is updated regularly. *Veja* is the country's best-selling weekly magazine. In Rio it comes with a special *Veja Rio* insert, which details the city's weekly entertainment options; it is available on Sundays. *Jornal do Brasil* and *O Globo* are two of Brazil's leading daily newspapers.

Smoking Banned in restaurants and bars; some hotels have rooms for smokers.

Weights & Measures The metric system is used throughout Brazil.

month) or hire an instructor for private classes. On the 1st floor of the lime-green building, Maracatu sells instruments.

Electricity

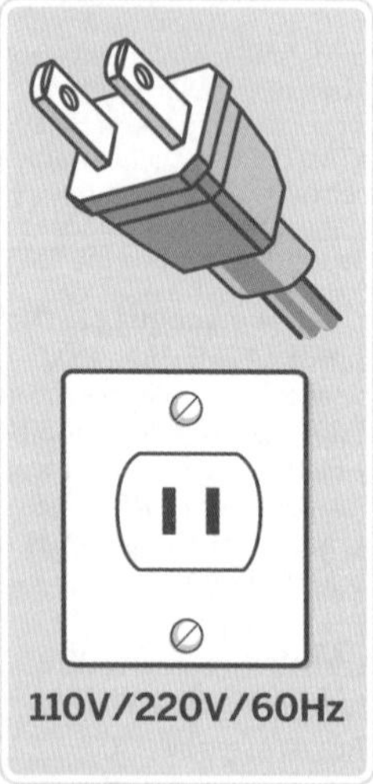

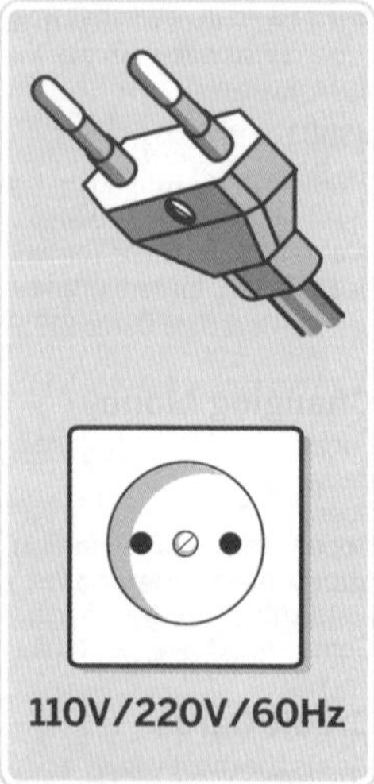

Embassies & Consulates

Many foreign countries have consulates or embassies in Rio. If they're not listed here, you'll find consulates listed in the back of Riotur's quarterly *Rio Guide*.

Argentinian Consulate (☎2553-1646; consar.rio@openlink.com.br; Praia de Botafogo 228, Sobreloja/1st fl 201, Botafogo)

Australian Consulate (☎3824-4624; www.dfat.gov.au/missions/countries/brri.html; 23rd fl, Av Presidente Wilson 231, Centro)

Canadian Consulate (☎2543-3004; www.brasil.gc.ca; 5th fl, Av Atlântica 1130, Copacabana)

French Consulate (☎3974-6699; http://riodejaneiro.ambafrance-br.org; 6th fl, Av Presidente Antônio Carlos 58, Centro)

UK Consulate (☎2555-9600; www.reinounido.org.br; 2nd fl, Praia do Flamengo 284 , Flamengo)

US Consulate (☎3823-2000; www.embaixada americana.org.br; Av Presidente Wilson 147, Centro)

Emergency

To call emergency telephone numbers in Rio you don't need a phone card. Useful numbers include the following:

Ambulance (☎192)

Fire Department (☎193)

Police (☎190)

Tourist Police (☎2332-4924; cnr Afrânio de Melo Franco & Humberto de Campos, Leblon; ⏲24hr) Report robberies to the tourist police; no major investigation is going to occur, but you will get a police form to give to your insurance company.

Gay & Lesbian Travelers

Rio is the gay capital of Latin America. There is no law against homosexuality in Brazil. During Carnaval, thousands of gay expatriate Brazilians and foreign tourists fly in for the festivities. Transvestites steal the show at all Carnaval balls, especially the gay ones. Outside Carnaval, the gay scene is fairly subdued. The most gay-friendly street in town is Farme de Amoedo in Ipanema, with cafes, restaurants and drinking spots.

You may hear or read the abbreviation GLS, particularly in the entertainment section of newspapers and magazines. It stands for Gays, Lesbians and Sympathizers, and when used in connection with venues or events basically indicates that anyone with an open mind is welcome. In general, the scene is much more integrated than elsewhere; and the majority of parties involve a pretty mixed crowd.

The **Rio gay guide** (www.riogayguide.com) is an excellent website full of information for gay and lesbian tourists in Rio, including sections on Carnarval, nightlife and bathhouses.

Internet Access

Most accommodations – including hostels and mid-range hotels – provide wi-fi access. The city has also implemented free wi-fi on the beach, running from Leblon up to Copacabana – though carrying your laptop out onto the sand isn't the brightest idea (that said, when the network is working, you can sometimes get service without crossing Av Atlântica).

Given the widespread availability of wi-fi and the popularity of smart phones, internet cafes are a vanishing breed, though there are still a few scattered around Copacabana and other areas of the Zona Sul. Most places charge between R$6 and R$12 an hour.

@Onze (Marquês de Abrantes 11, Flamengo; ⏲9am-11pm)

There's no Skype, but this peaceful spot serves up tasty sandwiches, salads, desserts and microbrews you can enjoy while browsing the web.

Cafe com Letras (Bartolomeu Mitre 207, Leblon; ⏲8:30am-8pm Mon-Fri, to 6pm Sat)

Blame It on Rio 4 Travel (Xavier da Silveira 15B, Copacabana)

Legal Matters

You are required by law to carry some form of identification. For travelers, this generally means a passport, but a certified copy of the relevant ID page will usually be acceptable.

In the last few years, Rio has gotten serious about drink-driving, and the penalties of driving under the influence are severe. Marijuana and cocaine are plentiful in Rio, and both are very illegal. An allegation of drug trafficking or possession provides the police with the perfect excuse to extract a not-insignificant amount of money from you – and Brazilian prisons are brutal places. If you are arrested, know that you have the right to remain silent, and that you are innocent until proven guilty. You also have a right to visitation by your lawyer or a family member.

Medical Services

Some private medical facilities in Rio de Janeiro are on a par with US hospitals. The UK and US consulates have lists of English-speaking physicians.

Hospitals

Clinica Galdino Campos (☎2548-9966; www.galdinocampos.com.br; Av NS de Copacabana 492, Copacabana; ⏲24hr) The best hospital for foreigners, with a high-quality care and multilingual doctors (who even make outpatient calls). The clinic works with most international health plans and travel insurance policies.

Pharmacies

Pharmacies stock all kinds of drugs and sell them much more cheaply than in the West. However, when buying drugs anywhere in South America, be sure to check the expiration dates and specific storage conditions. Some drugs that are available in Brazil may no longer be recommended, or may even be banned, in other countries. Common names of prescription medicines in South America are likely to be different from the ones you're used to, so ask a pharmacist before taking anything you're not sure about.

There are scores of pharmacies in town, a number of which stay open 24 hours.

Drogaria Pacheco (Av NS de Copacabana 115 & 534; ⏲24hr) In Copacabana.

Drogaria Pacheco (☎2239-5397; Av Visconde de Pirajá 592; ⏲24hr) Located in Ipanema.

Money

The monetary unit of Brazil is the real (R$, pronounced hay-*ow*); the plural is reais (pronounced hay-*ice*). The real is made up of 100 centavos. Most prices in this guide are quoted in reais, though some hoteliers prefer to list their rates in US dollars or euros.

ATMs

ATMs are the handiest way to access money in Rio. Unfortunately, there has been an alarming rise in card cloning, with travelers returning home to find unauthorized withdrawals on their cards. Use high-traffic ATMs inside bank buildings during banking-hours when possible. Always cover your hands when inputting your PIN, and check your account frequently to make sure you haven't been hacked.

ATMs for most card networks are widely available but often fussy. The best option is HSBC as it works with all cards and doesn't charge an exorbitant R$12 fee (except for some standalone HSBC ATMs on the Banco24Horas network in metro and bus stations). Citibank, Bradesco, Banco do Brasil and the Banco24Horas all charge fees.

You can find following bank's ATMs in the locations below:

Banco do Brasil With branches in Centro (Senador Dantas 105, Centro); Copacabana (Av NS de Copacabana 1292, Copacabana); and Galeão international airport (1st fl, Terminal 1, Galeão international airport).

Citibank Branches at Centro (Rua da Assembléia 100, Centro); Ipanema (Visconde de Pirajá 459A, Ipanema); and Leblon (Visconde de Pirajá 459A, Ipanema).

HSBC Located at Centro (Av Rio Branco 108, Centro); Copacabana (Av NS de Copacabana 583); Ipanema (Vinícius de Moraes 71, Ipanema); and Leblon (Cupertino Durão 219).

Changing Money

For exchanging cash, *casas de cambio* (exchange offices) cluster behind the Copacabana Palace Hotel in Copacabana and along Visconde de Pirajá near Praça General Osório in Ipanema.

Credit Cards

Visa is the most widely accepted credit card in Rio; MasterCard, American Express and Diners Club are also accepted by many hotels, restaurants and shops.

Credit-card fraud is rife in Rio, so be very careful. When making purchases keep your credit card in sight at all times. Have staff bring the machine to your table or follow them up to the cashier – don't give them your card.

To report lost or stolen credit cards, ring the following emergency numbers:

American Express (☎0800-891-2614)

Diners Club (☎0800-728-4444)

MasterCard (☎0800-891-3294)

Visa (☎0800-891-3680)

Tipping

In restaurants the service charge is usually included in the bill and is mandatory; when it is not included in the bill, it's customary to leave a 10% tip. If a waiter is friendly and helpful, you can give more.

There are many other places where tipping is not customary but is a welcome gesture. The workers at local juice stands, bars and coffee corners, and street- and beach-vendors, are all tipped on occasion. Parking assistants receive no wages and are dependent on tips, usually about R$4. Taxi drivers are not usually tipped, but it is common to round up the fare.

Post

Postal services are decent in Brazil, and most mail gets through. Airmail letters to the US and Europe usually arrive in a week or two. For Australia and Asia, allow three weeks.

There are yellow mailboxes on the street, but it's safer to go to a post office *(correios)*. Most post offices are open 8am to 6pm Monday to Friday, and until noon on Saturday.

Branches include **Botafogo** (Praia do Botafogo 324), **Copacabana** (Av NS de Copacabana 540) and **Ipanema** (Prudente de Morais 147).

Safe Travel

Rio gets a lot of bad international press about violence, though security has noticeably improved in the last few years. Regardless, to minimize your risk of becoming a victim, you should take some basic precautions. First off: dress down and leave expensive (or even expensive-*looking*) jewelry, watches and sunglasses at home.

Copacabana and Ipanema beaches have a police presence, but robberies still occur on the sands, even in broad daylight. Don't ever take anything of value with you to the beach. Late at night, don't walk on any of the beaches.

Buses are sometimes targets for thieves. Avoid taking them after dark, and keep an eye out while you're on them. Take taxis at night to avoid walking along empty streets and beaches. That holds especially true for Centro, which becomes deserted in the evening and on weekends, and is better explored during the week.

Get in the habit of carrying only the money you'll need for the day, so you don't have to flash a wad of reais when you pay for things. Cameras and backpacks attract a lot of attention. Plastic shopping bags nicely disguise whatever you're carrying. Maracanã football stadium is worth a visit, but take only your spending money for the day and avoid the crowded sections. Safety in the favelas has improved, but it's still best to go with a knowledgeable guide.

If you have the misfortune of being robbed, slowly hand over the goods. Thieves in the city are only too willing to use their weapons if given provocation.

Telephone

Public phones are nicknamed *orelhôes* (floppy ears). They take a *cartão telefônico* (phone card), which are available from newsstands and street vendors in denominations of R$5 to R$20.

To phone Rio from outside Brazil, dial your international access code, then 55 (Brazil's country code), 21 (Rio's area code) and the number.

To make a local collect call, dial 9090, then the number. For calls to other cities, dial 0, then the code of your selected long-distance carrier, then the two-digit area code, followed by the local number. You need to choose a long-distance carrier that covers both the place you are calling from and the place you're calling to. Carriers advertise their codes in areas where they're prominent, but you can usually use Embratel (code 21) or Telemar (code 31) nationwide.

To make an intercity collect call, dial 9 before the 0xx (the 'xx' representing the two-digit carrier as explained above, ie '21', '31' or a host of other Brazilian carriers). A recorded message in Portuguese will ask you to say your name and where you're calling from, after the tone.

Cell Phones

The cell phone is ubiquitous in Rio and goes by the name *celular*.

Brazil uses the GSM 850/900/1800/1900 network, which is compatible with North America, Europe and Australia, but the country's 4G LTE network runs on 2500/2690 (for now), which is not compatible with many North American and European smartphones, including initial releases of the iPhone 5. Cell phones have eight-digit numbers – though like São Paulo, Rio is expected to have nine digits in coming years.

Calls to cell phones are more expensive than calls to landlines. Cell phones have city codes like landlines, and if you're calling from another city, you have to use them. TIM (www.tim.com.br), Claro (www.claro.com.br), Oi (www.oi.com.br) and Vivo (www.vivo.com.br) are the major operators.

As of late 2012, foreigners can purchase a local SIM with a passport instead of needing a Brazilian CPF (tax ID number); a major bureaucratic roadblock dismantled.

If you have an unlocked GSM phone, you can simply buy a SIM card (called a *chip*) for around R$10 to R$16. Among the major carriers, TIM generally has the most hassle-free service. You can then add minutes by purchasing additional airtime from any newspaper stand. Incoming calls are free.

International Calls

International landline-to-landline calls from Brazil start from 66¢ a minute to the US and R$1.42 to Europe and Australia. Pay phones are of little use for international calls unless you have an international calling card or are calling collect. Most pay telephones are restricted to domestic calls, and even if they aren't, a 30-unit Brazilian phone card may last less than a minute internationally.

Without an international calling card, your best option is Skype. For international *a cobrar* (collect) calls, secure a Brazilian international operator by dialing 0800-703-2111 (Embratel).

Time

Brazil has four official time zones. Rio, in the southeastern region, is three hours behind Greenwich Mean Time (GMT) and four hours behind during the northern-hemisphere summer. Rio also observes daylight-saving time, pushing the clocks one hour forward from late November to late February.

Tourist Information

Riotur is the generally useful Rio city tourism agency. It operates a tourist information hotline, **Central 1746** (☎2271-7048, 1746; www.1746.rio.gov.br; ⏰24hr). Press 8 for tourist info then 1 for English.

Riotur's flashy new multilingual website, www.rioguiaoficial.com.br/en, is also a good source of information.

All of the Riotur offices distribute maps and the bimonthly *Rio Guide,* which is packed with information and major seasonal events. As well as branches at Galeão international airport's **Terminal 1** (☎3398-4077; Terminal 1, Domestic Arrival Hall, Galeão international airport; ⏰6am-11pm) and **Terminal 2** (☎3398-2245; Terminal 2, International Arrival Hall, Galeão international airport; ⏰6am-11pm), you'll find information kiosks at the following locations:

Riotur - Copacabana (☎2541-7522; Av Princesa Isabel 183; ⏰9am-6pm Mon-Fri) Good for information on events during Carnaval.

Copacabana Beach Kiosk (☎2547-4421; Av Atlântica, near Hilário de Gouveia; ⏰8am-8pm)

Riotur - Centro (☎2271-7000; www.rioguiaoficial.com.br; 9th fl, Praça Pio X; ⏰9am-6pm Mon-Fri)

Travelers with Disabilities

Rio is probably the most accessible city in Brazil for travelers with disabilities to get around, but that doesn't mean it's always easy. It's convenient to hire cars with driver-guides, but for only one person the expense is quite high compared to the cost of the average bus tour. If there are several people to share the cost, it's definitely worth it. For transport around the city, contact **Coop Taxi** (☎3295-9606).

The metro system has electronic wheelchair lifts, but it's difficult to know whether they're actually functional. Major sites are only partially accessible – there are about 10 steps to the gondola base of Pão de Açúcar, for instance; and although there is access to the base of Cristo Redentor, there are about two dozen steps to reach the statue itself. **Jeep Tour** (☎2108-5800; www.jeeptour.com.br) offers excursions for mobility-impaired travelers.

The streets and sidewalks along the main beaches have curb cuts and are wheelchair accessible, but most other areas do not have cuts. Most of the newer hotels have wheelchair-accessible rooms, but many restaurants have entrance steps.

Visas

Brazil has a reciprocal visa system, so if your home country requires Brazilian nationals to secure a visa, then you will need one to enter Brazil. US, Canadian and Australian citizens need visas, but UK, New Zealand, French and German citizens do not. You can check your status with the Brazilian embassy or consulate in your home country.

If you do need a visa, arrange it beforehand. Visas are not issued on arrival; and you won't be permitted into the country without it. Tourist visas are issued by Brazilian diplomatic offices. They are valid upon arrival in Brazil for a 90-day stay and are renewable in Brazil for an additional 90 days. In most Brazilian embassies and consulates, visas are processed in five to 10 days. You will need to present one passport photograph, a round-trip or onward ticket (or a photocopy of it) and a valid passport. If you decide to return to Brazil, your visa is valid for five years – though each year, you are allowed only a 90-day stay (or 180 days max if you renew it).

The fee for visas is also reciprocal. It's usually between US$20 and US$65, though for US citizens visas cost US$160.

Applicants under 18 years of age wanting to travel to Brazil must also submit a notarized letter of authorization from a parent or legal guardian.

Entry/Exit Card

On entering Brazil, all tourists must fill out an entry/exit card *(cartão de entrada/saida)*; immigration officials will keep half, you keep the other. They will also stamp your passport and, if for some reason they are not granting you the usual 90-day stay in Brazil, the number of days will be written beneath the word *Prazo* (Period) on the stamp in your passport.

When you leave Brazil, the second half of the entry/exit card will be taken by immigration officials. Don't lose your card while in Brazil, as it could cause hassles and needless delays when you leave.

Women Travelers

In Rio, foreign women traveling alone will scarcely be given a sideways glance. Although machismo is an undeniable element in the Brazilian social structure, it is less overt here than in many other parts of Latin America. Flirtation (often exaggerated) is a prominent element in Brazilian male-female relations. It goes both ways and is nearly always regarded as amusingly innocent banter. You should be able to stop unwelcome attention by merely expressing displeasure.

In the event of unwanted pregnancy or the risk thereof, most pharmacies in Brazil stock the morning-after pill (*a pílula do dia seguinte*), which costs about R$20.

Work

Brazil has high unemployment, and visitors who enter the country as tourists are not legally allowed to take jobs. It's not unusual for foreigners to find work teaching English in language schools, though. The pay isn't great, but if you negotiate you might be able make ends meet.

Volunteering

Río Voluntário (☎2262-1110; www.riovoluntario.org.br) Rio-based organisation supporting several hundred local volunteer organizations, from those involved in social work and the environment to health care. It's an excellent resource for finding volunteer work.

➡ **Iko Poran** (☎3852-2916; www.ikoporan.org) Also based in Rio, this volunteer organization links the diverse talents of volunteers with those required by needy organizations. Previous volunteers have worked as dance, music, art and language instructors, among other things. Iko Poran also provides housing options for volunteers.

➡ **Task Brasil** (www.taskbrasil.org.uk) UK-based Task Brasil is another laudable organization that places volunteers in Rio. Here, you'll have to make arrangements in advance and pay a fee that will go toward Task Brasil projects and your expenses as a volunteer.

➡ **Action Without Borders** (www.idealist.org) Visit its website for the best volunteer opportunities.

Language

Portuguese is spoken by around 190 million people worldwide, 90% of whom live in Brazil. Brazilian Portuguese today differs from European Portuguese in approximately the same way that British English differs from American English. European and Brazilian Portuguese have different spelling, pronunciation and, to some extent, vocabulary. For example, in Portugal, the word for 'train' is *comboio* and in Brazil you'd say *trem*.

Most sounds in Portuguese are also found in English. The exceptions are the nasal vowels (represented in our colored pronunciation guides by ng after the vowel), which are pronounced as if you're trying to make the sound through your nose, and the strongly rolled *r* (represented by rr in our pronunciation guides). Also note that the zh sounds like the 's' in 'pleasure'. The stressed syllables (generally the second-last syllable of a word) are indicated with italics. If you keep these few points in mind and read our pronunciation guides as if they were English, you'll have no problems being understood. The abbreviations (m) and (f) indicate masculine and feminine gender, whereas (sg) and (pl) stand for 'singular' and 'plural' respectively.

BASICS

Hello.	*Olá.*	o·*laa*
Goodbye.	*Tchau.*	tee·*show*
How are you?	*Como vai?*	*ko*·mo vai
Fine, and you?	*Bem, e você?*	beng e vo·*se*
Excuse me.	*Com licença.*	kong lee·*seng*·saa
Sorry.	*Desculpa.*	des·*kool*·paa
Yes./No.	*Sim./Não.*	seeng/nowng
Please.	*Por favor.*	por faa·*vorr*
Thank you.	*Obrigado.* *Obrigada.*	o·bree·*gaa*·do (m) o·bree·*gaa*·daa (f)
You're welcome.	*De nada.*	de *naa*·daa

What's your name?
Qual é o seu nome? — kwow e o *se*·oo *no*·me

My name is ...
Meu nome é ... — *me*·oo *no*·me e ...

Do you speak English?
Você fala inglês? — vo·*se* *faa*·laa eeng·*gles*

I don't understand.
Não entendo. — nowng eng·*teng*·do

WANT MORE?

For in-depth language information and handy phrases, check out Lonely Planet's *Brazilian Portuguese Phrasebook*. You'll find it at **shop.lonelyplanet.com**, or you can buy Lonely Planet's iPhone phrasebooks at the Apple App Store.

ACCOMMODATIONS

Do you have a single/double room?
Tem um quarto de solteiro/casal? — teng oom *kwaarr*·to de sol·*tay*·ro/kaa·*zow*

How much is it per night/person?
Quanto custa por noite/pessoa? — *kwang*·to *koos*·taa porr *noy*·te/pe·*so*·aa

Can I see it?
Posso ver? — *po*·so verr

campsite	*local para acampamento*	lo·*kow* *paa*·raa aa·kang·paa·*meng*·to
guesthouse	*hospedaria*	os·pe·daa·*ree*·a
hotel	*hotel*	o·*tel*
youth hostel	*albergue da juventude*	ow·*berr*·ge daa zhoo·veng·*too*·de
air-con	*ar condicionado*	aarr kong·dee·syo·*naa*·do
bathroom	*banheiro*	*ba*·nyay·ro
bed	*cama*	*ka*·maa
window	*janela*	zhaa·*ne*·laa

DIRECTIONS

Where is ...?
Onde fica ...? ong·de fee·kaa ...

What's the address?
Qual é o endereço? kwow e o eng·de·re·so

Could you please write it down?
Você poderia escrever num papel, por favor? vo·se po·de·ree·aa es·kre·verr noom paa·pel porr faa·vorr

Can you show me (on the map)?
Você poderia me mostrar (no mapa)? vo·se po·de·ree·aa me mos·traarr (no maa·paa)

at the corner	*na esquina*	na es·kee·naa
at the traffic lights	*no sinal de trânsito*	no see·now de trang·zee·to
behind ...	*atrás ...*	aa·traaz ...
in front of ...	*na frente de ...*	naa freng·te de ...
left	*esquerda*	es·kerr·daa
near ...	*perto ...*	perr·to ...
next to ...	*ao lado de ...*	ow laa·do de ...
opposite ...	*do lado oposto ...*	do laa·do o·pos·to ...
right	*direita*	dee·ray·taa
straight ahead	*em frente*	eng freng·te

EATING & DRINKING

What would you recommend?
O que você recomenda? oo ke vo·se he·ko·meng·daa

What's in that dish?
O que tem neste prato? o ke teng nes·te praa·to

I don't eat ...
Eu não como ... e·oo nowng ko·mo ...

Cheers!
Saúde! sa·oo·de

That was delicious.
Estava delicioso. es·taa·vaa de·lee·see·o·zo

Bring the bill/check, please.
Por favor traga a conta. porr faa·vorr traa·gaa aa kong·taa

I'd like to reserve a table for ...	*Eu gostaria de reservar uma mesa para ...*	e·oo gos·taa·ree·aa de he·zer·vaarr oo·maa me·zaa paa·raa ...
(eight) o'clock	*(às oito) horas*	(aas oy·to) aw·raas
(two) people	*(duas) pessoas*	(doo·aas) pe·so·aas

Key Words

bottle	*garrafa*	gaa·haa·faa
breakfast	*café da manha*	ka·fe daa ma·nyang
cold	*frio*	free·o
cup	*xícara*	shee·kaa·raa
dessert	*sobremesa*	so·bre·me·zaa
dinner	*jantar*	zhang·taarr
drink	*bebida*	be·bee·daa
entree	*entrada*	eng·traa·daa
fork	*garfo*	gaarr·fo
glass	*copo*	ko·po
hot (warm)	*quente*	keng·te
knife	*faca*	faa·kaa
lunch	*almoço*	ow·mo·so
market	*mercado*	merr·kaa·do
menu	*cardápio*	kaar·da·pyo
plate	*prato*	praa·to
restaurant	*restaurante*	hes·tow·rang·te
spicy	*apimentado*	aa·pee·meng·taa·do
spoon	*colher*	ko·lyerr

KEY PATTERNS

To get by in Portuguese, mix and match these simple patterns with words of your choice.

When's (the next flight)?
Quando é (o próximo vôo)? kwaang·do e (o pro·see·mo vo·o)

Where's the (tourist office)?
Onde fica (a secretaria de turismo)? ong·de fee·kaa (aa se·kre·taa·ree·aa de too·rees·mo)

I'm looking for (a hotel).
Estou procurando (um hotel). es·to pro·koorr·ang·do (oom o·tel)

Do you have (a map)?
Você tem (um mapa)? vo·se teng (oom maa·paa)

Is there (a bathroom)?
Tem (banheiro)? teng (ba·nyay·ro)

I'd like (a coffee).
Eu gostaria de (um café). e·oo gos·taa·ree·aa de (oom kaa·fe)

I'd like to (hire a car).
Eu gostaria de (alugar um carro). e·oo gos·taa·ree·aa de (aa·loo·gaarr oom kaa·ho)

Can I (enter)?
Posso (entrar)? po·so (eng·traarr)

Could you please (help me)?
Você poderia me (ajudar), por favor? vo·se po·de·ree·aa me (aa·zhoo·daarr) por faa·vorr

Do I have to (get a visa)?
Necessito (obter visto)? ne·se·see·to (o·bee·terr vees·to)

vegetarian food	*comida vegetariana*	ko·*mee*·daa ve·zhe·taa·ree·*a*·naa
with/without	*com/sem*	kong/seng

Meat & Fish

beef	*carne de vaca*	*kaar*·ne de *vaa*·kaa
chicken	*frango*	*frang*·go
crab	*siri*	*see*·ree
fish	*peixe*	*pay*·she
fruit	*frutas*	*froo*·tas
lamb	*carneiro*	karr·*nay*·ro
meat	*carne*	*kaar*·ne
oyster	*ostra*	*os*·traa
pork	*porco*	*porr*·ko
seafood	*frutos do mar*	*froo*·tos do maarr
shrimp	*camarão*	ka·ma·*rowng*
tuna	*atum*	aa·*toong*
veal	*bezerro*	be·*ze*·ho
vegetable	*legumes*	le·*goo*·mes

Fruit & Vegetables

apple	*maçã*	maa·*sang*
apricot	*damasco*	daa·*maas*·ko
asparagus	*aspargo*	aas·*paarr*·go
avocado	*abacate*	aa·baa·*kaa*·te
beetroot	*beterraba*	be·te·*haa*·baa
cabbage	*repolho*	he·*po*·lyo
capsicum	*pimentão*	pee·meng·*towng*
carrot	*cenoura*	se·*no*·raa
cherry	*cereja*	se·*re*·zhaa
corn	*milho*	*mee*·lyo
cucumber	*pepino*	pe·*pee*·no
garlic	*alho*	*aa*·lyo
grapes	*uvas*	*oo*·vaas
lemon	*limão*	lee·*mowng*
lettuce	*alface*	ow·*faa*·se
mushroom	*cogumelo*	ko·goo·*me*·lo
nut	*noz*	noz
onion	*cebola*	se·*bo*·laa
orange	*laranja*	laa·*rang*·zhaa
pea	*ervilha*	err·*vee*·lyaa
peach	*pêssego*	*pe*·se·go
pineapple	*abacaxí*	aa·baa·kaa·*shee*
plum	*ameixa*	aa·*may*·shaa
potato	*batata*	baa·*taa*·taa
pumpkin	*abóbora*	aa·*bo*·bo·raa
spinach	*espinafre*	es·pee·*naa*·fre
strawberry	*morango*	mo·*rang*·go
tomato	*tomate*	to·*maa*·te
vegetables	*legumes*	le·*goo*·mes
watermelon	*melancia*	me·lang·*see*·aa

Other

bread	*pão*	powng
cake	*bolo*	*bo*·lo
cheese	*queijo*	*kay*·zho
chilli	*pimenta*	pee·*meng*·taa
eggs	*ovos*	*o*·vos
honey	*mel*	mel
ice cream	*sorvete*	sorr·*ve*·te
jam	*geléia*	zhe·*le*·yaa
lentil	*lentilha*	leng·*tee*·lyaa
olive oil	*azeite*	a·*zay*·te
pepper	*pimenta*	pee·*meng*·taa

CARIOCA SLANG

Making an effort with the language is something Brazilians will greatly appreciate. *Díria* (slang) is a big part of the *carioca* dialect spoken by the residents of Rio. Here are a few words and phrases :

babaca ba·*ba*·ka – jerk

bunda *boon*·da – bottom/bum

Eu gosto de você. e·oo *gosh*·too zhi vo·*se* – I like you.

Falou! fa·*low* – Absolutely!/You said it!

Fique à vontade. feek a van·*tazh* – Make yourself at home.

fio dental *fee*·oo den·*tow* – dental floss, aka bikini

gata/gato *ga*·ta/*ga*·too – good-looking woman/man

Nossa! *no*·sa – Gosh!/You don't say! (lit: 'Our Lady')

sunga *soong*·ga – tiny swim shorts favored by *carioca* men

Ta ótimo!/Ta legal! ta *a*·che·moo/ta lee·*gow* – Great!/Cool!/OK!

Tudo bem? *too*·doo beng – Everything OK?

Tudo bem. *too*·doo beng – Everything's OK.

Valeu. va·*le*·o – Thanks.

Vamu nessa! va·moo·*ne*·sa – Let's go!

Signs

Banheiro	Bathroom
Entrada	Entrance
Não Tem Vaga	No Vacancy
Pronto Socorro	Emergency Department
Saída	Exit
Tem Vaga	Vacancy

rice	*arroz*	a·*hoz*
salt	*sal*	sow
sauce	*molho*	*mo*·lyo
sugar	*açúcar*	aa·*soo*·kaarr

Drinks

beer	*cerveja*	serr·*ve*·zhaa
coffee	*café*	kaa·*fe*
fruit juice	*suco de frutas*	*soo*·ko de *froo*·taas
milk	*leite*	*lay*·te
red wine	*vinho tinto*	*vee*·nyo *teeng*·to
soft drink	*refrigerante*	he·free·zhe·*rang*·te
tea	*chá*	shaa
(mineral) water	*água (mineral)*	*aa*·gwaa (mee·ne·*row*)
white wine	*vinho branco*	*vee*·nyo *brang*·ko

EMERGENCIES

Help!	*Socorro!*	so·*ko*·ho
Leave me alone!	*Me deixe em paz!*	me *day*·she eng paas
Call ...!	*Chame ...!*	*sha*·me ...
a doctor	*um médico*	oom *me*·dee·ko
the police	*a polícia*	aa po·*lee*·syaa

It's an emergency.
É uma emergência. — e *oo*·maa e·merr·*zheng*·see·aa

I'm lost.
Estou perdido. — es·*to* perr·*dee*·do (m)
Estou perdida. — es·*to* perr·*dee*·daa (f)

I'm ill.
Estou doente. — es·*to* do·*eng*·te

It hurts here.
Aqui dói. — a·*kee* doy

I'm allergic to (antibiotics).
Tenho alergia à (antibióticos). — *te*·nyo aa·lerr·*zhee*·aa aa (ang·tee·bee·o·tee·kos)

Where are the bathrooms?
Onde tem um banheiro? — *on*·de teng oom ba·*nyay*·ro

SHOPPING & SERVICES

I'd like to buy ...
Gostaria de comprar ... — gos·taa·*ree*·aa de kong·*praarr* ...

I'm just looking.
Estou só olhando. — es·*to* so o·*lyang*·do

Can I look at it?
Posso ver? — *po*·so verr

How much is it?
Quanto custa? — *kwang*·to *koos*·taa

It's too expensive.
Está muito caro. — es·*taa mweeng*·to *kaa*·ro

Can you lower the price?
Pode baixar o preço? — *po*·de bai·*shaarr* o *pre*·so

There's a mistake in the bill.
Houve um erro na conta. — *o*·ve oom *e*·ho naa *kong*·taa

ATM	*caixa automático*	*kai*·shaa ow·too·*maa*·tee·ko
credit card	*cartão de crédito*	kaarr·*towng* de *kre*·dee·to
post office	*correio*	ko·*hay*·o
tourist office	*escritório de turismo*	es·kree·*to*·ryo de too·*rees*·mo

TIME & DATES

What time is it?
Que horas são? — kee *aw*·raas sowng

It's (10) o'clock.
São (dez) horas. — sowng (des) *aw*·raas

Half past (10).
(Dez) e meia. — (des) e *may*·aa

morning	*manhã*	ma·*nyang*
afternoon	*tarde*	*taar*·de
evening	*noite*	*noy*·te
yesterday	*ontem*	*ong*·teng
today	*hoje*	*o*·zhe
tomorrow	*amanhã*	aa·ma·*nyang*

Question Words

How?	*Como é que?*	*ko*·mo e ke
What?	*Que?*	ke
When?	*Quando?*	*kwang*·do
Where?	*Onde?*	*ong*·de
Which?	*Qual?/Quais?* (sg/pl)	kwow/kais
Who?	*Quem?*	keng
Why?	*Por que?*	porr ke

Monday	*segunda-feira*	se·*goong*·daa·*fay*·ra
Tuesday	*terça-feira*	*terr*·saa·*fay*·raa
Wednesday	*quarta-feira*	*kwaarr*·taa·*fay*·raa
Thursday	*quinta-feira*	*keeng*·taa·*fay*·raa
Friday	*sexta-feira*	*ses*·taa·*fay*·raa
Saturday	*sábado*	*saa*·baa·do
Sunday	*domingo*	do·*meeng*·go

January	*janeiro*	zha·*nay*·ro
February	*fevereiro*	fe·ve·*ray*·ro
March	*março*	*marr*·so
April	*abril*	aa·*bree*·oo
May	*maio*	*maa*·yo
June	*junho*	*zhoo*·nyo
July	*julho*	*zhoo*·lyo
August	*agosto*	aa·*gos*·to
September	*setembro*	se·*teng*·bro
October	*outubro*	o·*too*·bro
November	*novembro*	no·*veng*·bro
December	*dezembro*	de·*zeng*·bro

TRANSPORTATION

boat	*barco*	*baarr*·ko
bus	*ônibus*	o·nee·boos
plane	*avião*	aa·vee·*owng*
train	*trem*	treng

a ... ticket	*uma passagem de ...*	*oo*·maa paa·*sa*·zheng de ...
1st-class	*primeira classe*	pree·*may*·raa *klaa*·se
2nd-class	*segunda classe*	se·*goom*·daa *klaa*·se
one-way	*ida*	*ee*·daa
return	*ida e volta*	*ee*·daa e *vol*·taa

What time does it leave/arrive?
A que horas sai/chega? aa ke *aw*·raas sai/*she*·gaa

Does it stop at ...?
Ele para em ...? e·le *paa*·raa eng ...

Please stop here.
Por favor pare aqui. poor faa·*vorr paa*·re aa·*kee*

bus stop	*ponto de ônibus*	*pong*·to de o·nee·boos
ticket office	*bilheteria*	bee·lye·te·*ree*·aa
timetable	*horário*	o·*raa*·ryo
train station	*estação de trem*	es·*taa*·sowng de treng

Numbers

1	*um*	oom
2	*dois*	doys
3	*três*	tres
4	*quatro*	*kwaa*·tro
5	*cinco*	*seeng*·ko
6	*seis*	says
7	*sete*	*se*·te
8	*oito*	*oy*·to
9	*nove*	*naw*·ve
10	*dez*	dez
20	*vinte*	*veeng*·te
30	*trinta*	*treeng*·taa
40	*quarenta*	kwaa·*reng*·taa
50	*cinquenta*	seen·*kweng*·taa
60	*sessenta*	se·*seng*·taa
70	*setenta*	se·*teng*·taa
80	*oitenta*	oy·*teng*·taa
90	*noventa*	no·*veng*·taa
100	*cem*	seng
1000	*mil*	*mee*·oo

I'd like to hire a ...	*Gostaria de alugar ...*	gos·taa·*ree*·aa de aa·loo·*gaarr* ...
bicycle	*uma bicicleta*	*oo*·maa bee·see·*kle*·taa
car	*um carro*	oom *kaa*·ho
motorcycle	*uma motocicleta*	*oo*·maa mo·to·see·*kle*·ta

bicycle pump	*bomba de bicicleta*	*bong*·baa de bee·see·*kle*·taa
helmet	*capacete*	kaa·paa·*se*·te
mechanic	*mecânico*	me·*ka*·nee·ko
petrol/gas	*gasolina*	gaa·zo·*lee*·naa
service station	*posto de gasolina*	*pos*·to de gaa·zo·*lee*·naa

Is this the road to ...?
Esta é a estrada para ...? es·taa e aa es·*traa*·daa *paa*·raa ...

(How long) Can I park here?
(Quanto tempo) Posso estacionar aqui? (*kwang*·to *teng*·po) *po*·so es·taa·syo·*naarr* aa·*kee*

I have a flat tyre.
Meu pneu furou. *me*·oo pee·*ne*·oo foo·*ro*

I've run out of petrol.
Estou sem gasolina. es·*to* seng ga·zoo·*lee*·naa

I've had an accident.
Sofri um acidente. so·*free* oom aa·see·*deng*·te

GLOSSARY

See p31 for more Carnaval terms.

açaí – juice made from an Amazonian berry

baía – bay

baile – dance party in the favelas

baile funk – dance, ball

bairro – neighborhood

baixo – popular area with lots of restaurants and bars

banda – street party

barraca – food stall

berimbau – stringed instrument used to accompany capoeira

bloco – see *banda*

bonde – tram

boteco – small neighborhood bar

botequim – bar with table service

cachaça – potent cane spirit

caipirinha – *cachaça* cocktail

Candomblé – religion of African origin

capoeira – Afro-Brazilian martial art

capela – chapel

carioca – resident of Rio

celular – cellular (mobile) phone

chope – draft beer

chorinho or **choro** – romantic, intimate samba

churrascaria – traditional barbecue restaurant

Cidade Maravilhosa – nickname for Rio de Janeiro (literally 'Marvelous City')

convento – convent

correios – post office

escola de samba – samba school

estrada – road

favela – shanty town

feijoada – black beans and pork stew

feira – open-air market

festa – party

forró – traditional fast-paced music from Northeast Brazil

frescobol – game played on the beach with two wooden racquets and a rubber ball

futebol – football (soccer)

futevôlei – volleyball played without the hands.

gafieira – dance club/dance hall

igreja – church

ilha – island

jardim – garden

lagoa – lake

largo – plaza

limão – lemon

livraria – bookshop

mar – sea

maracujá – passion fruit

maté – sweet iced tea

mirante – lookout

moqueca – seafood stew cooked in coconut milk

morro – mountain

mulatto – person of mixed black and white ancestry

museu – museum

onibus – bus

pagode – relaxed and rhythmic form of samba; first popularized in Rio in the 1970s

parque – park

posto – lifeguard station

pousada – guesthouse

praça – square

praia – beach

reais – plural of real

real – Brazil's unit of currency

rio – river

rodoviária – bus terminal

rua – street

salgados – bar snacks

sobreloja – above the store; first floor up

supermercado – supermarket

tacacá – a fragrant soup consisting of manioc paste, jambu leaves and fresh and dried shrimp

tambores – drums

Zona Norte – Northern Zone

Zona Sul – Southern Zone; specifically, the beach- and bay-side neighborhoods of Leblon, Ipanema, Copacabana, Botafogo, Flamengo and Glória.

Behind the Scenes

SEND US YOUR FEEDBACK

Things change – prices go up, schedules change, good places go bad and bad places go bankrupt. So if you find things better or worse, recently opened or long since closed, or you just want to tell us what you loved or loathed about this book, please get in touch and help make the next edition even more accurate and useful. We love to hear from travelers – your comments keep us on our toes and our well-traveled team reads every word. Although we can't reply individually to postal submissions, we always guarantee that your feedback goes straight to the appropriate authors, in time for the next edition. Each person who sends us information is thanked in the next edition – the most useful submissions are rewarded with a selection of digital PDF chapters.

Visit **lonelyplanet.com/contact** to submit your updates and suggestions or to ask for help. Our award-winning website also features inspirational travel stories, news and discussions.

Note: We may edit, reproduce and incorporate your comments in Lonely Planet products such as guidebooks, websites and digital products, so let us know if you don't want your comments reproduced or your name acknowledged. For a copy of our privacy policy visit lonelyplanet.com/privacy.

OUR READERS

Many thanks to travelers who used the last edition and wrote to us with helpful hints, useful advice and interesting anecdotes: Anthony De Lannoy, Tania Doyle, Stefano Garofoli, Freddy Guazzone di Passalacqua, Nigel Hartley, Fernanda Junqueira, Vedran Knezevic, Maira Lacerda, Wendy Liscia, Chris Milsom, Michaela Nilsson, Evgeny Podjachev, Luciano Rezende, Nicholas Russam, Grazyna Sanchez-Madejska, Lance Shoemaker, Panayiots Vorrias, Barbara Watson, Peggy Wilshire

AUTHOR THANKS

Regis St Louis

Many thanks to new and old friends who helped with tips and advice. In particular I'd like to thank Cristiano Nogueira, Jakki Saysell, Marcelo Esteves, Michael Waller, Thiago Mourão, Ian Papareskos, Eduardo Cruxen, Carina Jallad, Sophie Lewis, Kevin Raub and the folks at Riotur. At home I'd like to thank Cassandra, Magdalena and Genevieve for their continued love and support.

ACKNOWLEDGMENTS

Cover photograph: Two surfers waiting for a wave with Morro dois Irmãos in the background, Giordano Cipriani/4Corners ©.

THIS BOOK

This 8th edition of Lonely Planet's *Rio de Janeiro* guidebook was researched and written by Regis St Louis. The previous four editions were also written by Regis St Louis. This guidebook was commissioned in Lonely Planet's Oakland office, and produced by the following:

Commissioning Editor Kathleen Munnelly
Coordinating Editors Simon Williamson, Ross Taylor
Coordinating Layout Designer Wibowo Rusli
Managing Editor Bruce Evans
Senior Editors Karyn Noble, Andi Jones
Managing Cartographer Alison Lyall
Managing Layout Designer Jane Hart
Assisting Editors Trent Holden, Kate Morgan, Jeanette Wall
Assisting Cartographer Andy Rojas
Cover Research Naomi Parker
Internal Image Research Aude Vauconsant
Language Content Branislava Vladisavljevic, Annelies Mertens
Thanks to Ryan Evans, Larissa Frost, Genesys India, Jouve India, Catherine Naghten, Kerrianne Southway, Raphael Richards, Gerard Walker

Index

See also separate subindexes for:
EATING P222
DRINKING & NIGHTLIFE P223
ENTERTAINMENT P223
SHOPPING P224
SPORTS & ACTIVITIES P224
SLEEPING P225

Sights 000
Map Pages **000**
Photo Pages **000**

Sights 000
Map Pages **000**
Photo Pages **000**

Sights 000
Map Pages **000**
Photo Pages **000**

EATING

DRINKING & NIGHTLIFE

ENTERTAINMENT

SHOPPING

SPORTS & ACTIVITIES

Sights 000
Map Pages **000**
Photo Pages **000**

SLEEPING

Rio de Janeiro Maps

Map Legend

Sights
- Beach
- Buddhist
- Castle
- Christian
- Hindu
- Islamic
- Jewish
- Monument
- Museum/Gallery
- Ruin
- Winery/Vineyard
- Zoo
- Other Sight

Eating
- Eating

Drinking & Nightlife
- Drinking & Nightlife
- Cafe

Entertainment
- Entertainment

Shopping
- Shopping

Sleeping
- Sleeping
- Camping

Sports & Activities
- Diving/Snorkelling
- Canoeing/Kayaking
- Skiing
- Surfing
- Swimming/Pool
- Walking
- Windsurfing
- Other Sports & Activities

Information
- Post Office
- Tourist Information

Transport
- Airport
- Border Crossing
- Bus
- Cable Car/Funicular
- Cycling
- Ferry
- Monorail
- Parking
- S-Bahn
- Taxi
- Train/Railway
- Tram
- Tube Station
- U-Bahn
- Underground Train Station
- Other Transport

Routes
- Tollway
- Freeway
- Primary
- Secondary
- Tertiary
- Lane
- Unsealed Road
- Plaza/Mall
- Steps
- Tunnel
- Pedestrian Overpass
- Walking Tour
- Walking Tour Detour
- Path

Boundaries
- International
- State/Province
- Disputed
- Regional/Suburb
- Marine Park
- Cliff
- Wall

Geographic
- Hut/Shelter
- Lighthouse
- Lookout
- Mountain/Volcano
- Oasis
- Park
- Pass
- Picnic Area
- Waterfall

Hydrography
- River/Creek
- Intermittent River
- Swamp/Mangrove
- Reef
- Canal
- Water
- Dry/Salt/Intermittent Lake
- Glacier

Areas
- Beach/Desert
- Cemetery (Christian)
- Cemetery (Other)
- Park/Forest
- Sportsground
- Sight (Building)
- Top Sight (Building)

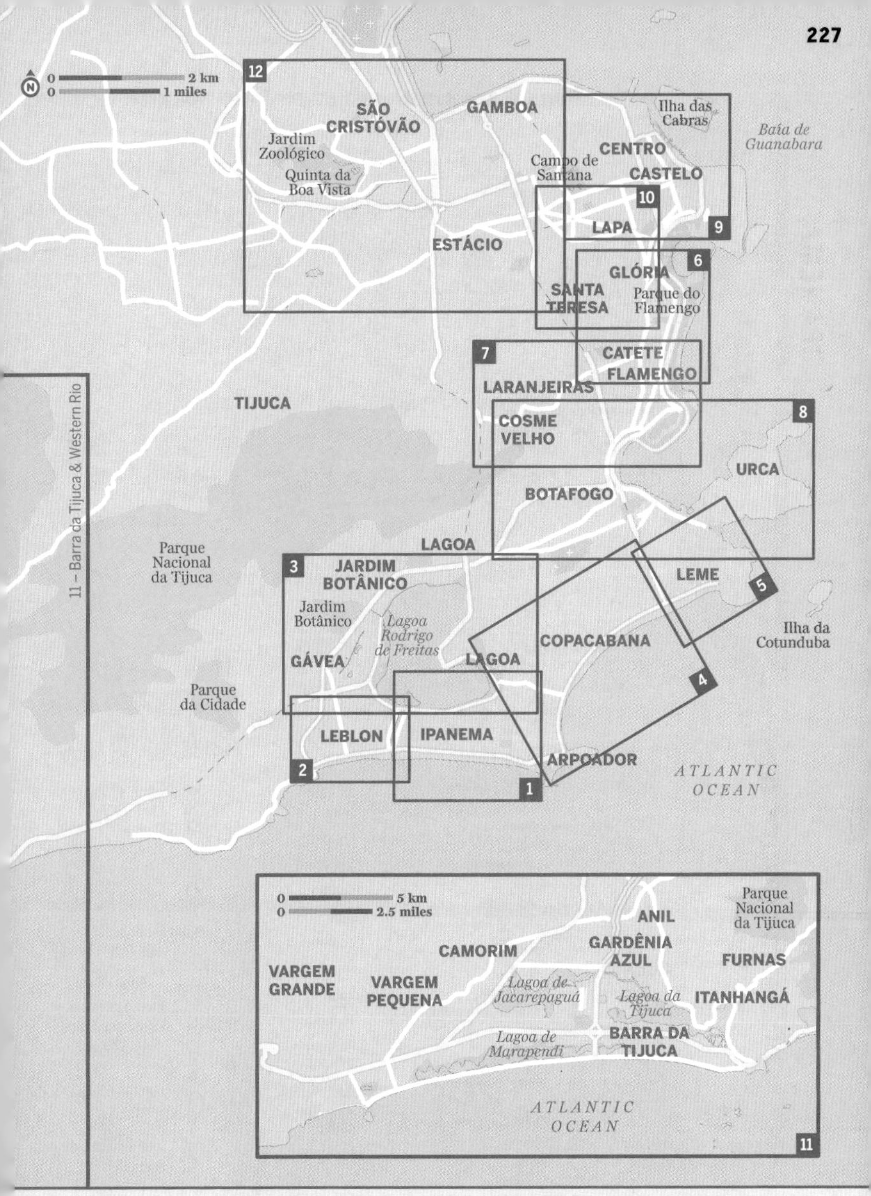
0 2 km
0 1 miles
12
SÃO CRISTÓVÃO
GAMBOA
Jardim Zoológico
Quinta da Boa Vista
Ilha das Cabras
Baía de Guanabara
CENTRO
Campo de Santana
CASTELO
10
LAPA
9
ESTÁCIO
6
GLÓRIA
SANTA TERESA
Parque do Flamengo
7
CATETE
FLAMENGO
LARANJEIRAS
TIJUCA
8
COSME VELHO
URCA
BOTAFOGO
11 – Barra da Tijuca & Western Rio
Parque Nacional da Tijuca
LAGOA
3
JARDIM BOTÂNICO
LEME
5
Jardim Botânico
Lagoa Rodrigo de Freitas
COPACABANA
Ilha da Cotunduba
GÁVEA
LAGOA
4
Parque da Cidade
LEBLON
IPANEMA
ARPOADOR
2
1
ATLANTIC OCEAN
0 5 km
0 2.5 miles
Parque Nacional da Tijuca
ANIL
GARDÊNIA AZUL
CAMORIM
FURNAS
VARGEM GRANDE
VARGEM PEQUENA
Lagoa de Jacarepaguá
Lagoa da Tijuca
ITANHANGÁ
Lagoa de Marapendi
BARRA DA TIJUCA
ATLANTIC OCEAN
11

AP INDEX

Key on p230

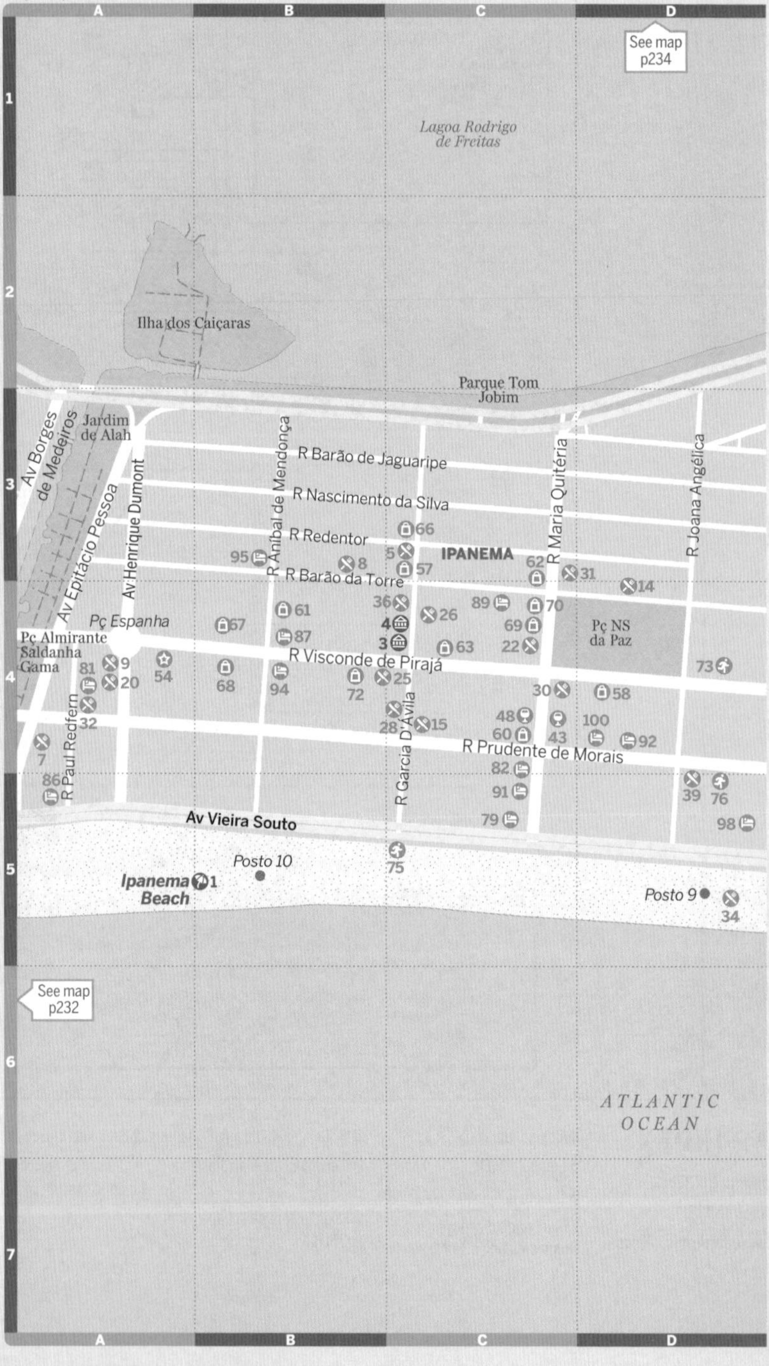
A
B
C
D
1
2
3
4
5
6
7
See map p234
Lagoa Rodrigo de Freitas
Ilha dos Caiçaras
Parque Tom Jobim
Jardim de Alah
Av Borges de Medeiros
Av Epitácio Pessoa
Av Henrique Dumont
R Aníbal de Mendonça
R Barão de Jaguaripe
R Nascimento da Silva
R Redentor
R Barão da Torre
IPANEMA
R Maria Quitéria
R Joana Angélica
Pç Espanha
Pç Almirante Saldanha Gama
Pç NS da Paz
R Visconde de Pirajá
R Paul Redfern
R Garcia D'Ávila
R Prudente de Morais
Av Vieira Souto
Posto 10
Ipanema Beach
1
Posto 9
See map p232
ATLANTIC OCEAN
3
4
5
7
8
9
14
15
20
22
25
26
28
30
31
32
34
36
39
43
48
54
57
58
60
61
62
63
66
67
68
69
70
72
73
75
76
79
81
82
86
87
89
91
92
94
95
98
100

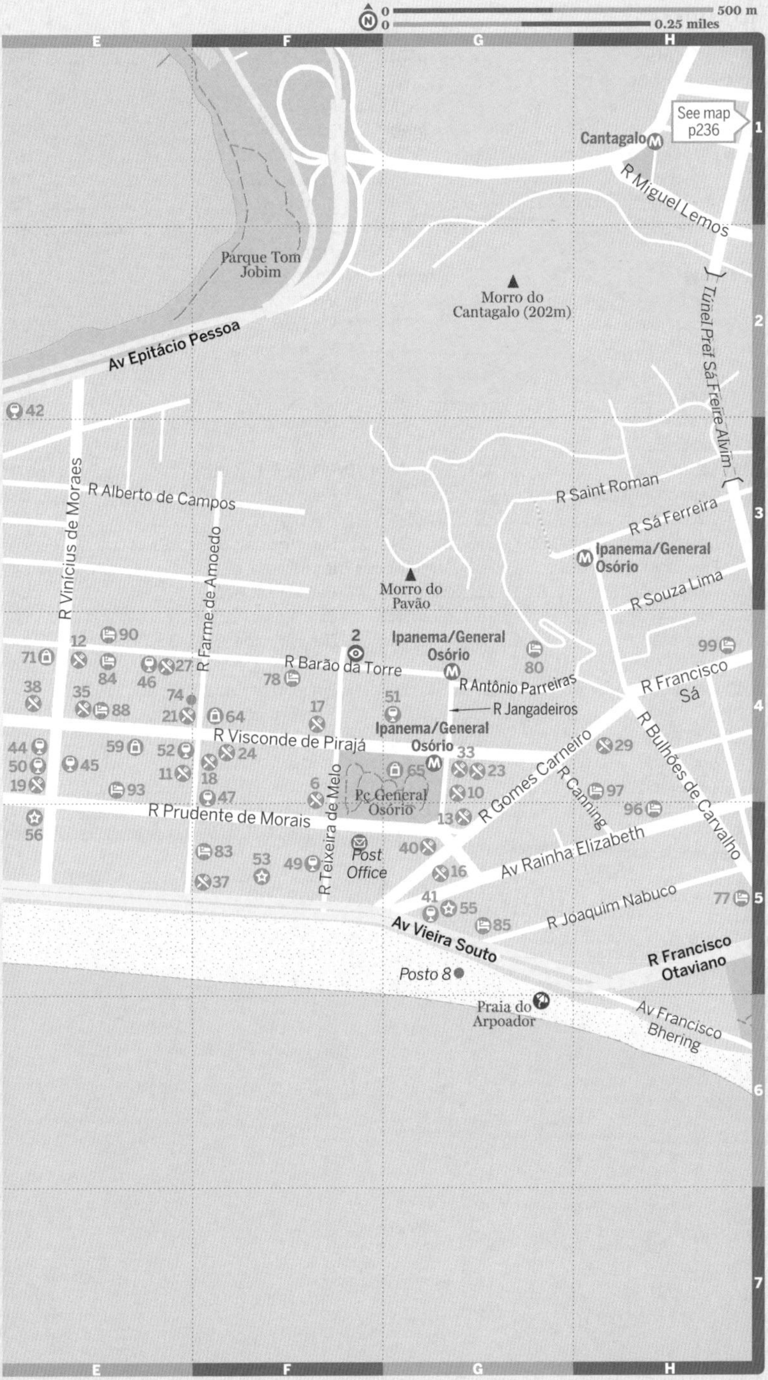
0 500 m
0 0.25 miles
E
F
G
H
1
2
3
4
5
6
7
See map p236
Cantagalo
R Miguel Lemos
Parque Tom Jobim
Morro do Cantagalo (202m)
Túnel Pref Sá Freire Alvim
Av Epitácio Pessoa
42
R Vinícius de Moraes
R Alberto de Campos
R Farme de Amoedo
R Saint Roman
R Sá Ferreira
Ipanema/General Osório
Morro do Pavão
R Souza Lima
90
12
2
Ipanema/General Osório
99
71
84
27
46
R Barão da Torre
78
80
38
35
88
74
21
64
17
51
R Antônio Parreiras
R Jangadeiros
R Francisco Sá
44
50
19
59
45
52
11
24
18
R Visconde de Pirajá
Ipanema/General Osório
33
65
23
29
R Bulhões de Carvalho
R Gomes Carneiro
R Canning
93
47
6
Pç General Osório
10
97
96
56
R Prudente de Morais
13
83
53
49
R Teixeira de Melo
Post Office
40
Av Rainha Elizabeth
37
16
41
55
85
77
R Joaquim Nabuco
Av Vieira Souto
R Francisco Otaviano
Posto 8
Praia do Arpoador
Av Francisco Bhering

IPANEMA *Map on p228*

Top Sights (p58)

1 Ipanema Beach ... B5

Sights (p59)

2 Elevador do Morro do Cantagalo ... F4
3 Museu Amsterdam Sauer ... C4
4 Museu H Stern ... C4

Eating (p59)

5 Alessandro E Federico ... C3
6 Amazônia Soul ... F4
7 Artigiano ... A4
8 Bazzar ... B3
9 Benkei ... A4
10 Brasileirinho ... G4
11 Cafeína ... E4
12 Capricciosa ... E4
13 Casa da Feijoada ... G5
14 Cavist ... D4
15 Delírio Tropical ... C4
Fasano Al Mare ... (see 85)
16 Felice Caffè ... G5
Fontes ... (see 54)
17 Frontera ... F4
18 Galitos Grill ... F4
19 Garota de Ipanema ... E4
20 Gula Gula ... A4
21 Koni Store ... E4
22 Koni Store ... C4
23 La Veronese ... G4
24 Laffa ... F4
25 Market ... B4
26 Mil Frutas ... C4
27 New Natural ... E4
28 Nik Sushi ... C4
29 Pintxo ... H4
30 Polis Sucos ... C4
31 Sorvete Brasil ... C3
32 Ten Kai ... A4
33 Terzetto Cafe ... G4
34 Uruguai ... D5
35 Vero ... E4
36 Via Sete ... C4
37 Vieira Souto ... F5
38 Yogoberry ... E4
39 Zazá Bistrô Tropical ... D5
40 Zona Sul Supermarket ... G5

Drinking & Nightlife (p67)

41 Bar Astor ... G5
42 Bar Lagoa ... E2
Baretto-Londra ... (see 85)
43 Barthodomeu ... C4
44 Barzin ... E4
45 Blue Agave ... E4
46 Delirium Cafe ... E4
47 Devassa ... F4
48 Empório ... C4
49 Galeria Café ... F5
50 Garota de Ipanema ... E4
Lord Jim ... (see 81)
51 Shenanigan's ... G4
52 Tô Nem Aí ... E4

Entertainment (p71)

53 Casa da Cultura Laura Alvim F5
54 Estação Ipanema A4
55 Studio RJ G5
56 Vinícius Show Bar E5

Shopping (p72)

Amsterdam Sauer .... (see 3)
Antonio Bernardo .... (see 36)
57 Aquim C3
Brasil & Cia .... (see 91)
58 Casa & Video D4
59 Catherine Labouré E4
Cavist .... (see 14)
60 Espaço Brazilian Soul C4
61 Espaço Fashion B4
62 Forum C3
Garota de Ipanema .... (see 50)
63 Gilson Martins C4
H Stern .... (see 4)
64 Havaianas F4
65 Hippie Fair G4
66 Isabela Capeto C3
67 Livraria da Travessa B4
68 Luko B4
69 Osklen C4
70 Redley C4
71 Toca do Vinícius E4
72 Wöllner Outdoor B4

Sports & Activities (p75)

73 Blyss Yôga D4
74 Casa do Caminho Language Centre E4
75 Escolinha de Vôlei C5
76 Spa Maria Bonita D5

Sleeping (p162)

77 Atlantis Copacabana Hotel H5
78 Bonita F4
79 Caesar Park C5
80 Casa Mosquito G4
81 Che Lagarto Ipanema A4
82 Everest Rio C4
83 Golden Tulip Ipanema Plaza F5
84 Hostel Harmonia E4
85 Hotel Fasano G5
86 Hotel Praia Ipanema A5
87 Hotel San Marco B4
88 Hotel Vermont E4
89 Ipanema Beach House C4
90 Ipanema Hotel Residência E4
91 Ipanema Inn C5
92 Ipanema Tower D4
Lighthouse Hostel .... (see 84)
93 Mango Tree E4
94 Mar Ipanema B4
95 Margarida's Pousada B3
96 Mercure Rio de Janeiro H5
97 Rio Hostel – Ipanema H4
98 Sol Ipanema D5
99 South American Copacabana Hotel H4
100 Visconti D4

LEBLON

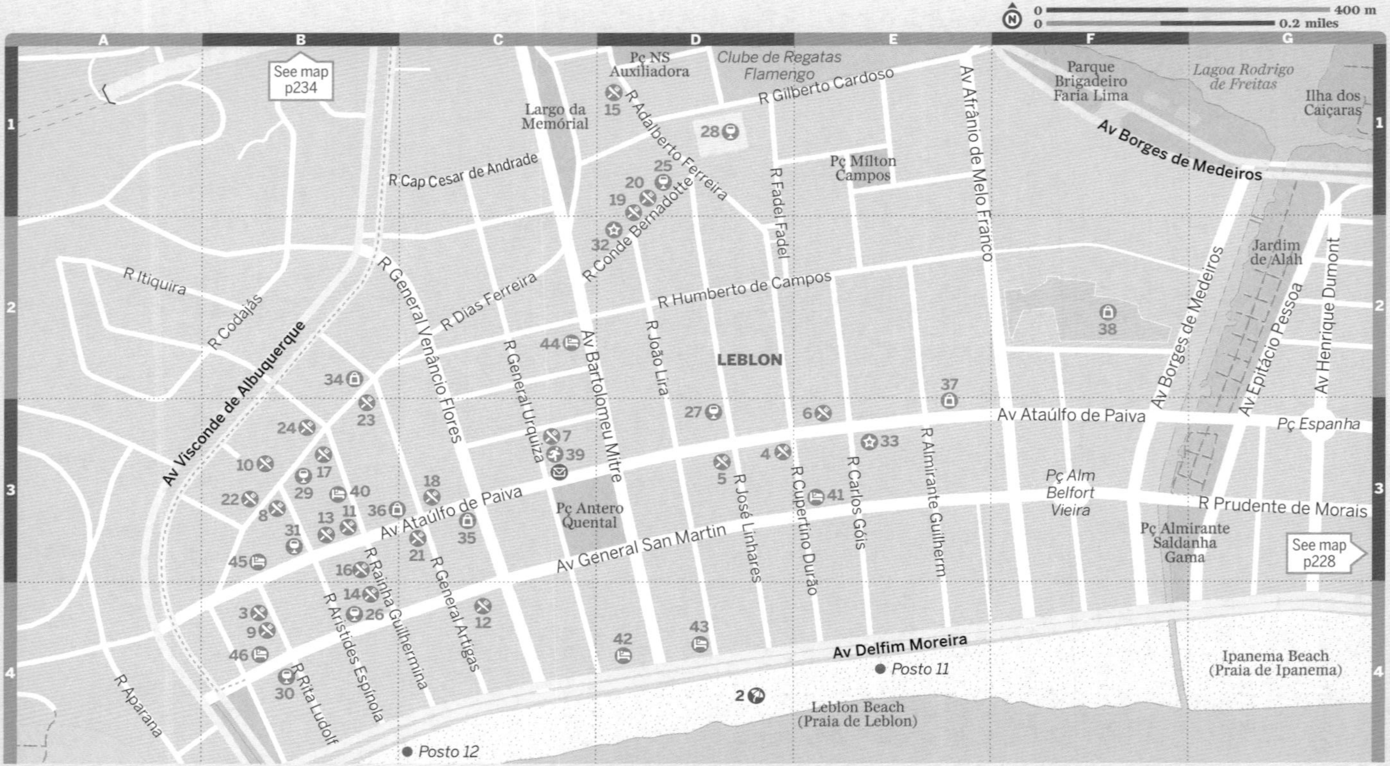

0 — 400 m
0 — 0.2 miles
A B C D E F G
1 2 3 4
See map p234
See map p228
Largo da Memórial
Pç NS Auxiliadora
Clube de Regatas Flamengo
R Gilberto Cardoso
Pç Mílton Campos
Av Afrânio de Melo Franco
Parque Brigadeiro Faria Lima
Lagoa Rodrigo de Freitas
Ilha dos Caiçaras
Av Borges de Medeiros
R Cap Cesar de Andrade
R Adalberto Ferreira
R Conde Bernadotte
R Fadel Fadel
Jardim de Alah
Av Henrique Dumont
Av Epitácio Pessoa
R Itiquira
R Codajás
R General Venâncio Flores
R Dias Ferreira
R Humberto de Campos
R General Urquiza
Av Bartolomeu Mitre
R João Lira
LEBLON
Av Visconde de Albuquerque
Av Ataúlfo de Paiva
Pç Espanha
R Almirante Guilherm
R Carlos Góis
R Cupertino Durão
R José Linhares
Pç Alm Belfort Vieira
R Prudente de Morais
Pç Antero Quental
Av General San Martin
Pç Almirante Saldanha Gama
R Rainha Guilhermina
R Aristides Espínola
R General Artigas
R Rita Ludolf
R Aparana
Av Delfim Moreira
Posto 11
Posto 12
Ipanema Beach (Praia de Ipanema)
Leblon Beach (Praia de Leblon)
2 3 4 5 6 7 8 9 10 11 12 13 14 15 16 17 18 19 20 21 22 23 24 25 26 27 28 29 30 31 32 33 34 35 36 37 38 39 40 41 42 43 44 45 46

Sights (p59)

1 Mirante do Leblon B5
2 Praia de Leblon D4

Eating (p65)

3 Armazém do Café B4
4 Bibi Crepes D3
5 Bibi Sucos D3
Café Severino .... (see 34)
6 Empório Arabe E3
7 Fellini C3
8 Galeto do Leblon B3
9 Gula Gula B4
10 Hortifruti B3
11 Jobi B3
12 Juice Co C4
13 Koni Store B3
14 Nam Thai B4
15 Plataforma D1
16 Prima Bruschetteria B3
Ráscal .... (see 38)
17 Sushi Leblon B3
18 Talho Capixaba C3
19 Universo Orgânico D1
20 Vegetariano Social Club D1
21 Vezpa C3
22 Yalla B3
23 Zona Sul Supermarket B3
24 Zuka B3

Drinking & Nightlife (p70)

25 Academia Da Cachaça D1
Bar d'hotel .... (see 42)
26 Bar Veloso B4
27 Bracarense D3
28 Cobal do Leblon D1
29 Esch Café B3
Jobi .... (see 11)
30 Melt B4
31 Pizzaria Guanabara B3

Entertainment (p71)

32 Teatro do Leblon D2
33 Teatro Leblon E3

Shopping (p74)

34 Argumento B2
Esch Café .... (see 29)
35 Kopenhagen C3
36 Lidador B3
Maria Oiticica .... (see 38)
37 Rio Design Center E3
38 Shopping Leblon F2

Sports & Activities (p75)

39 Body Tech C3
Dive Point .... (see 13)

Sleeping (p162)

40 Leblon Ocean Hotel Residência B3
41 Lemon Spirit Hostel E3
42 Marina All Suites D4
43 Marina Palace D4
44 Monsieur Le Blond C2
45 Ritz Plaza Hotel B3
46 Z.Bra Hostel B4

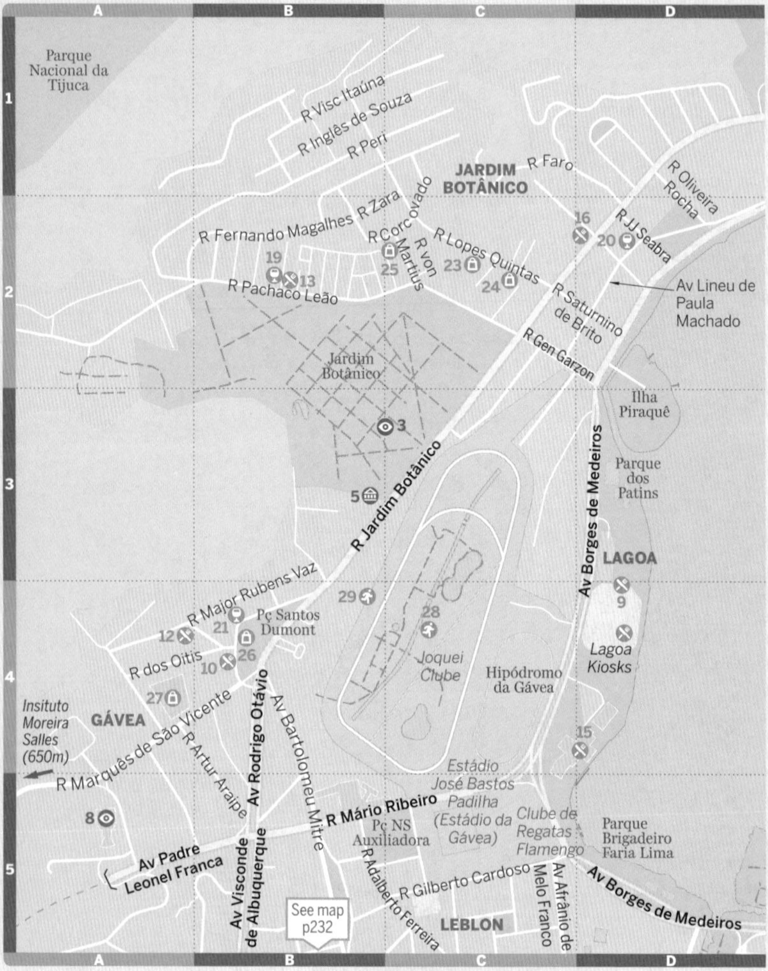

Top Sights **(p78)**

Sights **(p79)**

Eating **(p80)**

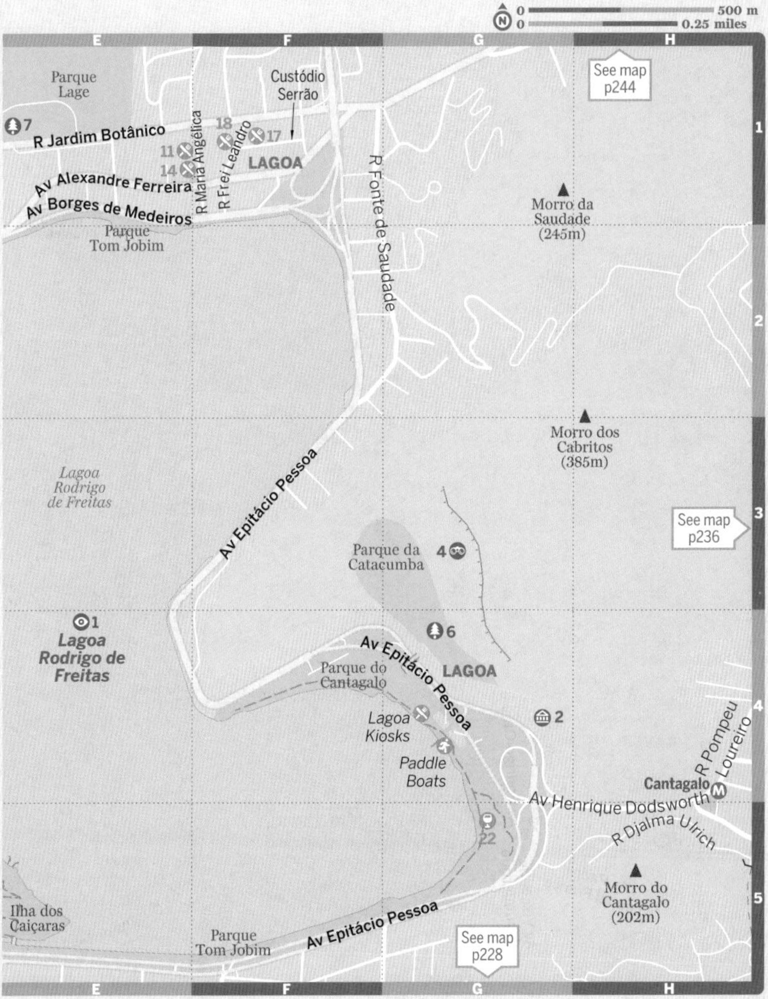

18 Oro F1

Drinking & Nightlife (p82)

- 00 .... (see 8)
- 19 Bar do Horto B2
- 20 Caroline Café D2
- 21 Hipódromo B4
- 22 Palaphita Kitch G5

Entertainment (p82)

- Miranda .... (see 15)

Shopping (p83)

- 23 Dona Coisa C2
- 24 Gabinete C2
- 25 O Sol C2
- 26 Praça Santos Dumont Antique Fair B4
- 27 Shopping da Gávea A4

Sports & Activities (p83)

- 28 Joquei Clube C4
- 29 Nirvana B4

Key on p238

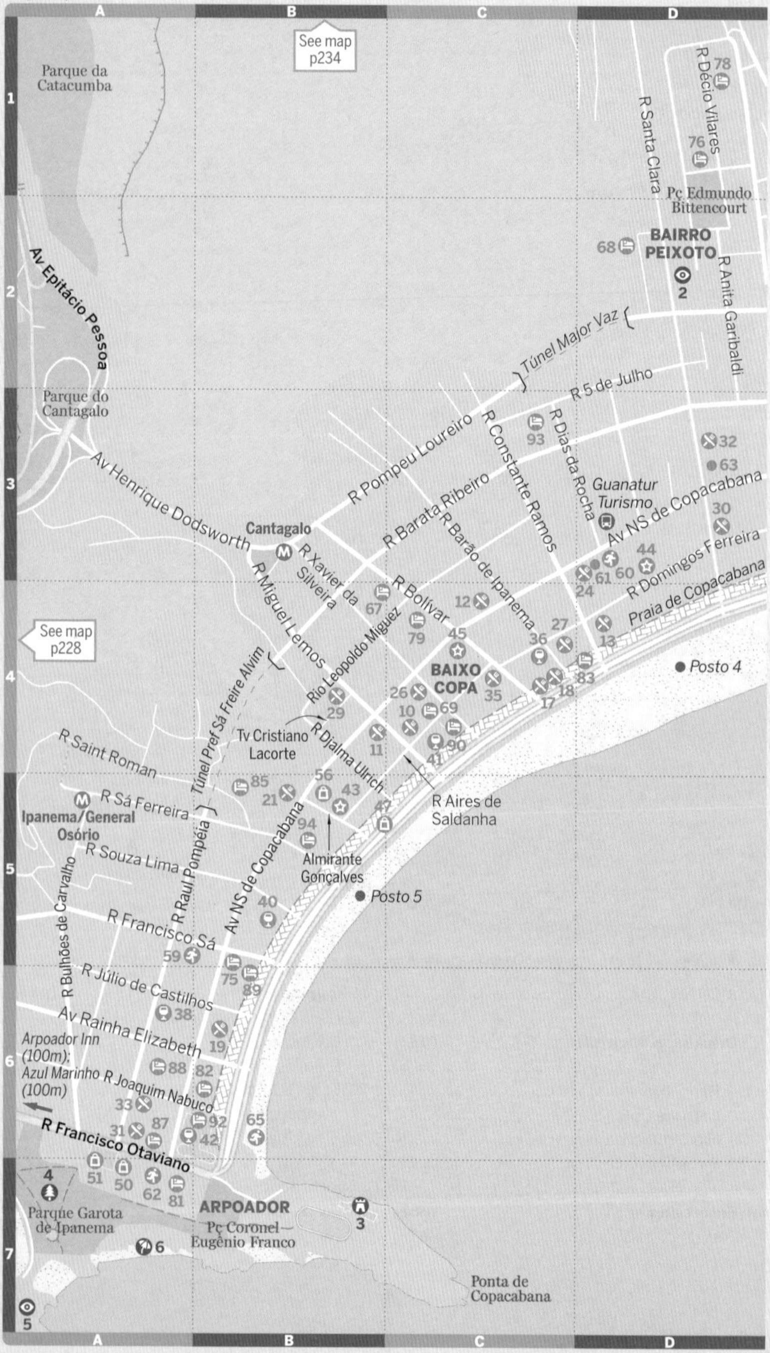
A
B
C
D
1
2
3
4
5
6
7
See map p234
See map p228
Parque da Catacumba
Av Epitácio Pessoa
Parque do Cantagalo
Av Henrique Dodsworth
Cantagalo
R Pompeu Loureiro
Túnel Major Vaz
R 5 de Julho
R Constante Ramos
R Dias da Rocha
R Santa Clara
R Décio Vilares
Pç Edmundo Bittencourt
BAIRRO PEIXOTO
R Anita Garibaldi
Guanatur Turismo
Av NS de Copacabana
R Domingos Ferreira
Praia de Copacabana
R Barata Ribeiro
R Barão de Ipanema
R Xavier da Silveira
R Bolívar
R Miguel Lemos
Rio Leopoldo Miguez
BAIXO COPA
Posto 4
Túnel Pref Sá Freire Alvim
Tv Cristiano Lacorte
R Djalma Ulrich
R Aires de Saldanha
Almirante Gonçalves
R Saint Roman
R Sá Ferreira
Ipanema/General Osório
R Souza Lima
R Raul Pompéia
Posto 5
R Bulhões de Carvalho
R Francisco Sá
R Júlio de Castilhos
Av Rainha Elizabeth
Arpoador Inn (100m); Azul Marinho (100m)
R Joaquim Nabuco
R Francisco Otaviano
ARPOADOR
Parque Garota de Ipanema
Pç Coronel Eugênio Franco
Ponta de Copacabana

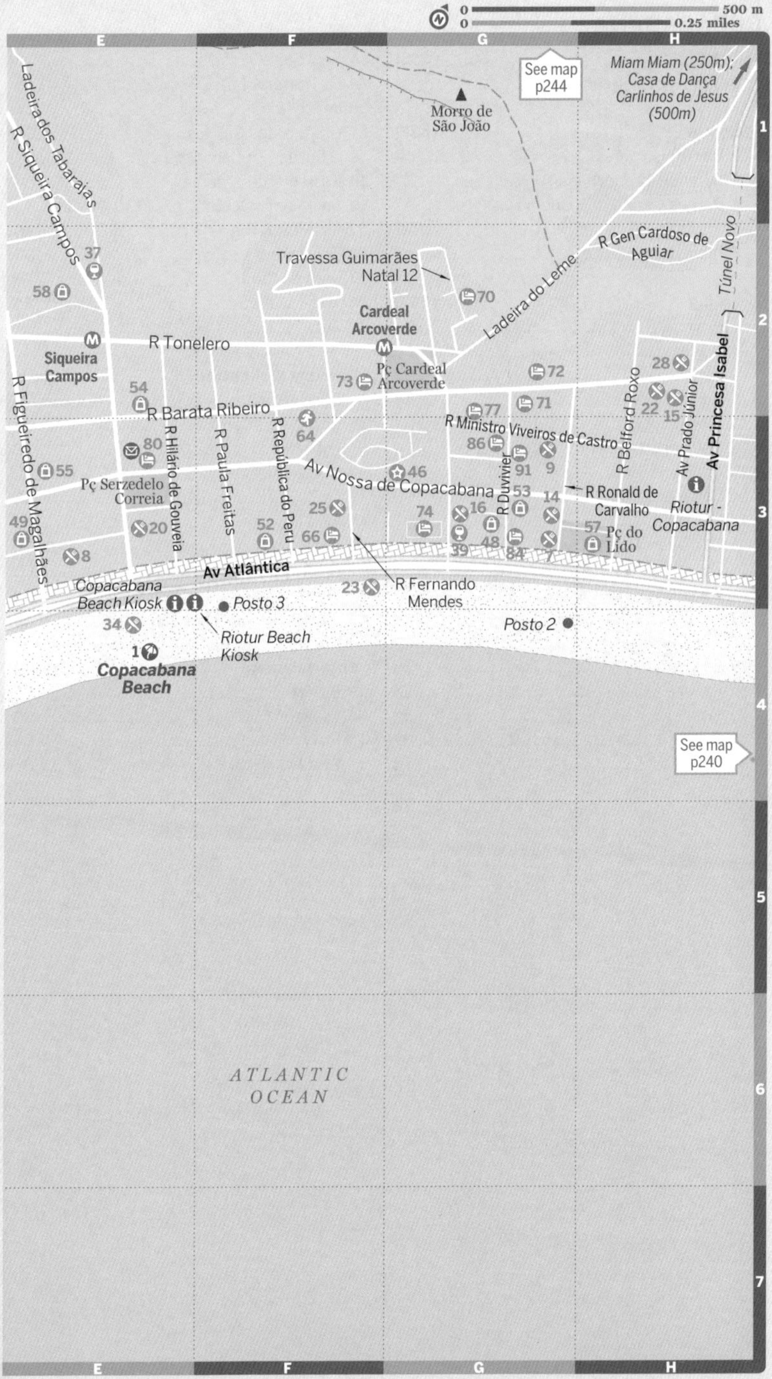

500 m
0.25 miles
E
F
G
H
1
2
3
4
5
6
7
See map p244
Miam Miam (250m); Casa de Dança Carlinhos de Jesus (500m)
Morro de São João
Ladeira dos Tabarajas
R Siqueira Campos
Travessa Guimarães Natal 12
R Gen Cardoso de Aguiar
Túnel Novo
Ladeira do Leme
Cardeal Arcoverde
Siqueira Campos
R Tonelero
Pç Cardeal Arcoverde
R Barata Ribeiro
R Figueiredo de Magalhães
R Hilário de Gouveia
R Paula Freitas
R República do Peru
R Ministro Viveiros de Castro
R Belford Roxo
Av Prado Júnior
Av Princesa Isabel
Av Nossa de Copacabana
R Duvivier
R Ronald de Carvalho
Riotur - Copacabana
Pç Serzedelo Correia
Pç do Lido
Av Atlântica
R Fernando Mendes
Copacabana Beach Kiosk
Posto 3
Riotur Beach Kiosk
Posto 2
Copacabana Beach
See map p240
ATLANTIC OCEAN

COPACABANA *Map on p236*

Shopping (p94)

47 Av Atlântica Fair B5
48 Bossa Nova & Companhia G3
49 Deu la Deu Vinhos E3
50 Draco Store A7
51 Galeria River A7
52 Gilson Martins F3
Havaianas .... (see 26)
53 Loja Fla G3
54 Lomography Gallery Store E2
55 Mundo Verde E3
56 Musicale B5
57 Praça do Lido Market H3
58 Shopping Siqueira Campos E2

Sports & Activities (p96)

59 Antaryamin A5
60 Body Tech (Copacabana) D3
61 Carioca Languages D3
62 Ciclovia A7
63 Instituto Brasil-Estados Unidos D3
64 Rio Samba Dancer F3
65 Surf Rio B6

Sleeping (p166)

66 Astoria Palace F3
67 Augusto's Copacabana B4
68 Bamboo Rio D2
69 Blame It on Rio 4 Travel C4
70 Cabana Copa G2
71 Che Lagarto G2
72 Copacabana Holiday G2
73 Copacabana Hotel Residência F2
74 Copacabana Palace G3
75 Design Hotel Portinari B5
76 Edificio Jucati D1
77 Hotel Ibis G2
78 Hotel Santa Clara D1
79 Hotel Vilamar C4
80 Mar Palace E3
81 Mercure Arpoador A7
82 Orla Copacabana B6
83 Pestana Rio Atlântica D4
84 Porto Bay Rio Internacional G3
85 Pura Vida B5
86 Real Palace Hotel G3
87 Residencial Apartt A6
88 Rio Apartments A6
89 Rio Guesthouse B6
90 Rio Roiss Hotel C4
91 Royal Rio Palace G3
92 Sofitel Rio de Janeiro B6
93 Walk on the Beach Hostel C3
94 Windsor Martinique Hotel B5

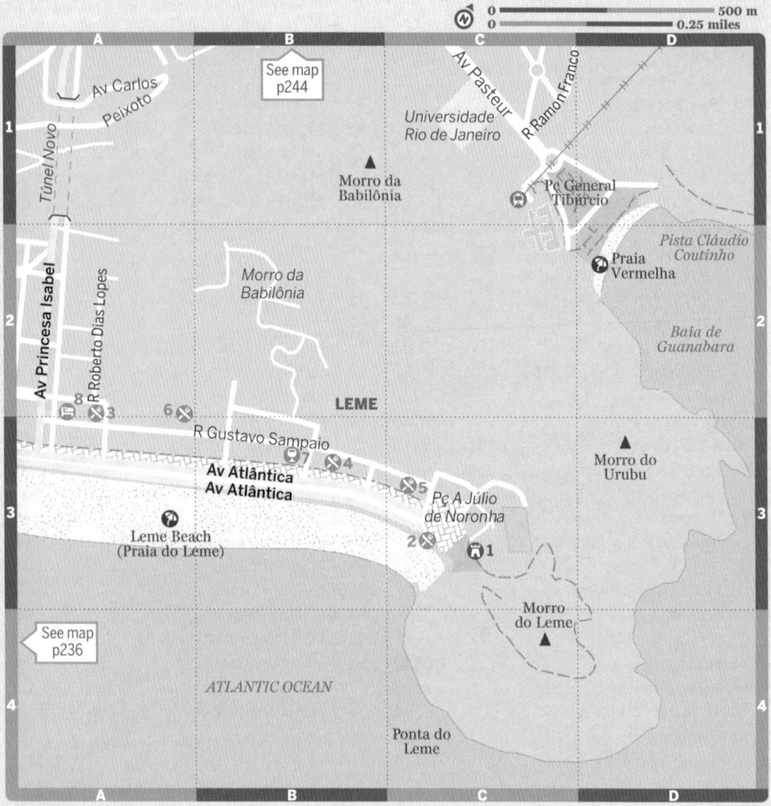

Sights (p87)
1 Forte Duque de Caxias C3

Eating (p87)
2 Carioca Com Você C3
3 Galeria 1618 .... A2
4 La Fiorentina B3
5 Marius C3
6 Shirley A2

Drinking & Nightlife (p91)
7 Sindicato do Chopp B3

Sleeping (p166)
8 Acapulco A2

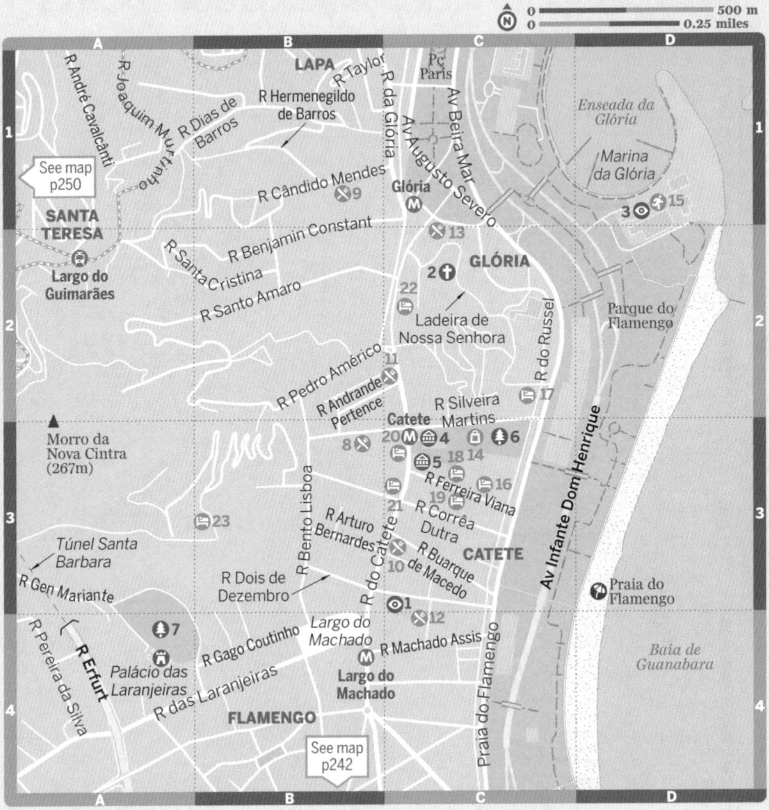

Sights (p112)
1 Centro Cultural Oi Futuro....................C3
2 Igreja de Nossa Senhora da Glória do Outeiro....................C2
3 Marina da Glória....................D1
4 Museu da República....................C3
5 Museu de Folclore Edison Carneiro....................C3
6 Parque do Catete....................C3
7 Parque Guinle....................A4

Eating (p114)
8 Cariocando....................B3
9 Casa da Suíça....................B1
10 Catete Grill....................C3
11 Estação República....................C2
12 Nanquim....................C4
13 Taberna da Glória....................C2

Entertainment (p115)
Centro Cultural Oi Futuro....................(see 1)
Espaço Museu Da República....................(see 4)
Maze Inn....................(see 23)

Shopping (p116)
14 Photography and Image Fair....................C3

Sports & Activities (p116)
Mar do Rio....................(see 15)
15 Marlin Yacht Tours....................D1

Sleeping (p169)
16 Beija Flor Hotel....................C3
17 Flamengo Palace....................C2
18 Hotel Ferreira Viana....................C3
19 Hotel Regina....................C3
20 Hotel Riazor....................C3
21 Imperial Hotel....................C3
22 Love Time....................C2
23 Maze Inn....................B3

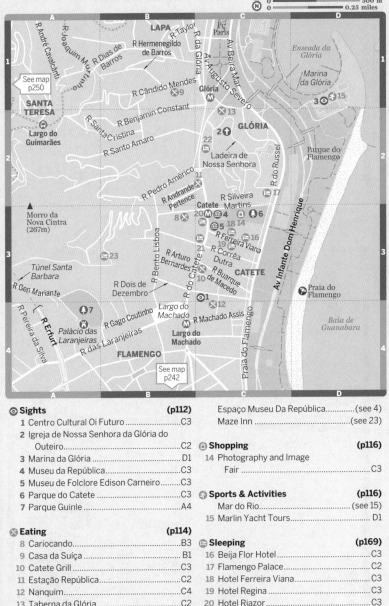

FLAMENGO, LARANJEIRAS & COSME VELHO

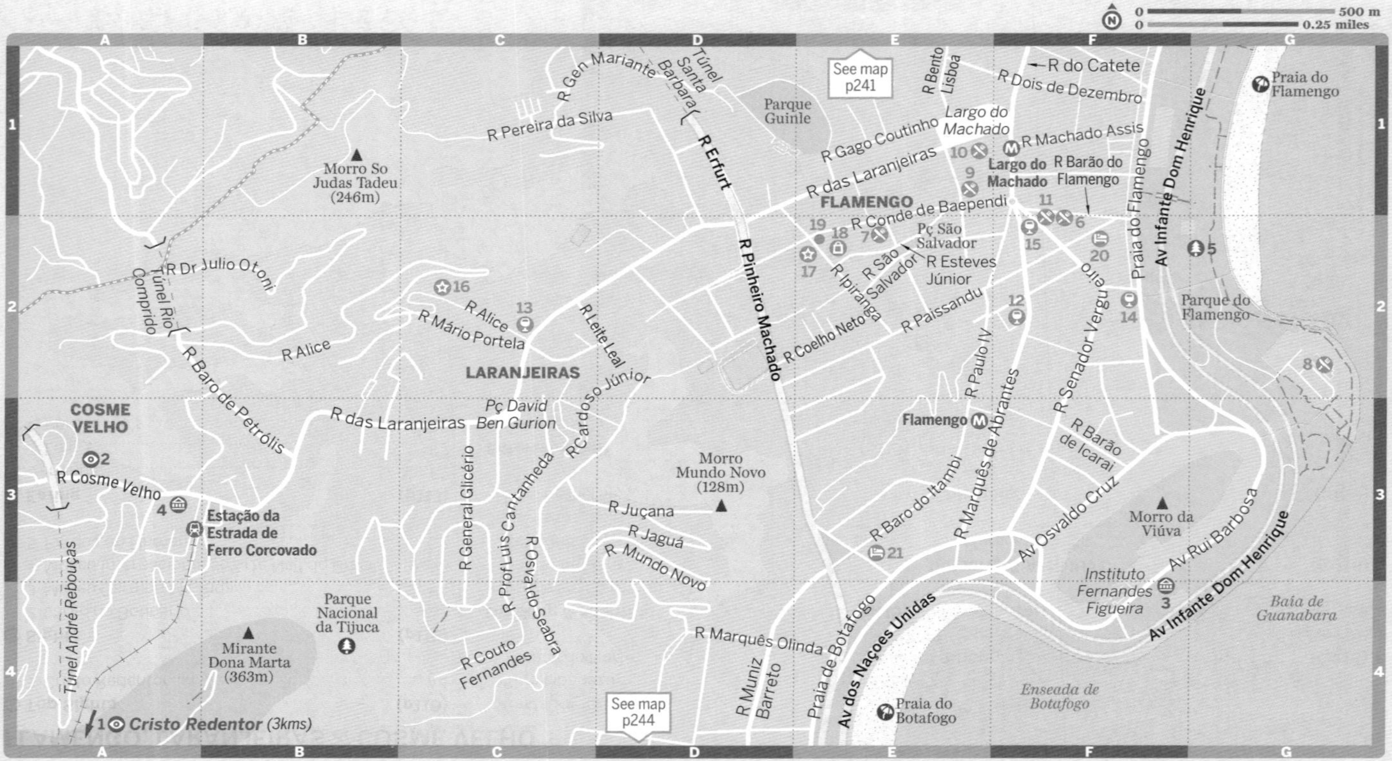
0 500 m
0 0.25 miles
See map p241
See map p244
R do Catete
R Dois de Dezembro
R Bento Lisboa
Largo do Machado
R Machado Assis
Largo do Machado
R Barão do Flamengo
Praia do Flamengo
Av Infante Dom Henrique
Praia do Flamengo
Parque do Flamengo
Parque Guinle
R Gago Coutinho
R das Laranjeiras
FLAMENGO
R Conde de Baependi
Pç São Salvador
R Esteves Júnior
R São Salvador
R Ipiranga
R Coelho Neto
R Paissandu
R Paulo IV
R Senador Vergueiro
R Marquês de Abrantes
Flamengo
R Barão de Icaraí
Av Osvaldo Cruz
Morro da Viúva
Av Rui Barbosa
Instituto Fernandes Figueira
Av Infante Dom Henrique
Baía de Guanabara
Enseada de Botafogo
Praia do Botafogo
Av dos Nações Unidas
Praia de Botafogo
R Muniz Barreto
R Marquês Olinda
R Baro do Itambi
Morro Mundo Novo (128m)
R Juçana
R Jaguá
R Mundo Novo
R Pinheiro Machado
R Erfurt
Túnel Santa Barbara
R Gen Mariante
R Pereira da Silva
Morro So Judas Tadeu (246m)
R Dr Julio Otoni
Túnel Rio Comprido
R Alice
R Mário Portela
R Alice
LARANJEIRAS
R Leite Leal
R Cardoso Júnior
Pç David Ben Gurion
R das Laranjeiras
R General Glicério
R Prof Luis Cantanheda
R Osvaldo Seabra
R Couto Fernandes
R Baro de Petrólis
COSME VELHO
R Cosme Velho
Estação da Estrada de Ferro Corcovado
Parque Nacional da Tijuca
Mirante Dona Marta (363m)
Túnel André Rebouças
1 Cristo Redentor (3kms)

FLAMENGO, LARANJEIRAS & COSME VELHO

Top Sights **(p110)**
1 Cristo Redentor ... A4

Sights **(p112)**
2 Largo do Boticário ... A3
3 Museu Carmen Miranda ... F4
4 Museu Internacional de Arte Naïf do Brasil ... A3
5 Parque do Flamengo ... G2

Eating **(p113)**
6 Intihuasi ... F2
7 Luigi's ... E2
8 Porcão Rio's ... G2
9 Restaurante Kioto ... E1
10 Sírio Libaneza ... E1
11 Tacacá do Norte ... F2

Drinking & Nightlife **(p115)**
12 Armazém do Chopp ... F2
13 Bar do Serafim ... C2
14 Belmonte ... F2
15 Devassa ... F2
Herr Brauer ... (see 6)

Entertainment **(p115)**
16 Casa Rosa ... C2
17 Severyna de Laranjeiras ... E2

Shopping **(p116)**
Maracatu Brasil ... (see 19)
18 Pé de Boi ... E2

Sports & Activities **(p116)**
19 Maracatu Brasil ... E2

Sleeping **(p169)**
20 Augusto's Paysandu ... F2
21 Brothers Hostel ... E3

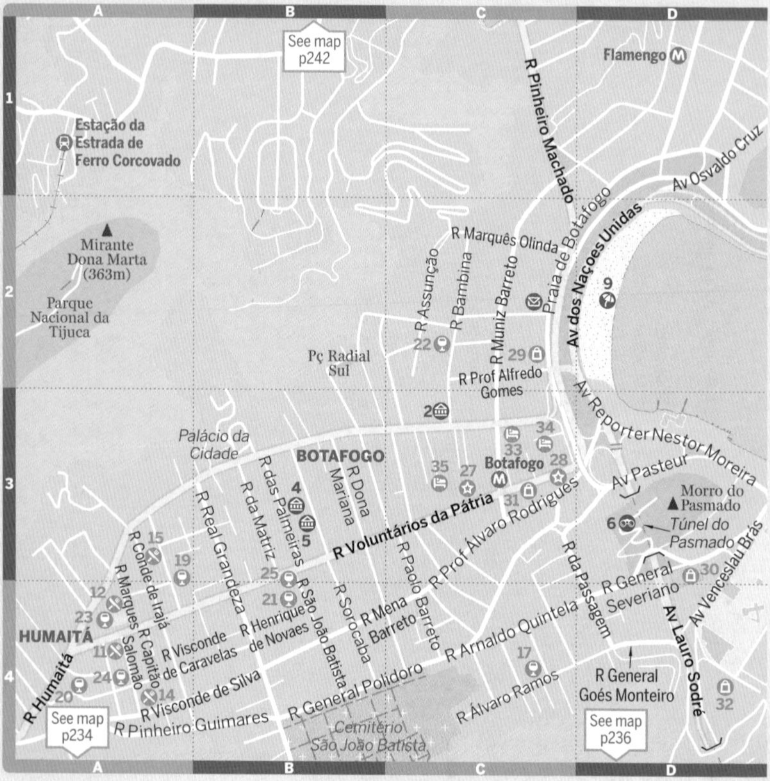

Top Sights (p99)

1 Pão de Açúcar G2

Sights (100)

2 Museu Casa de Rui Barbosa C3
3 Museu de Ciências da Terra E4
4 Museu do Índio B3
5 Museu Villa-Lobos B3
6 Pasmado Overlook D3
7 Pista Cláudio Coutinho G3
8 Praia da Urca F2
9 Praia de Botafogo D2
10 Praia Vermelha F4

Eating (p104)

11 Café Botânica A4
12 Cobal do Humaitá A4
Emporium Pax (see 29)
13 Garota da Urca G2
14 Meza Bar A4
15 Oui Oui A3
16 Zozô F4

Drinking & Nightlife (p104)

17 Bar Bukowski C4
18 Bar Urca G2
19 Beerjack Hideout A3
20 Botequim A4
21 Casa da Matriz B4

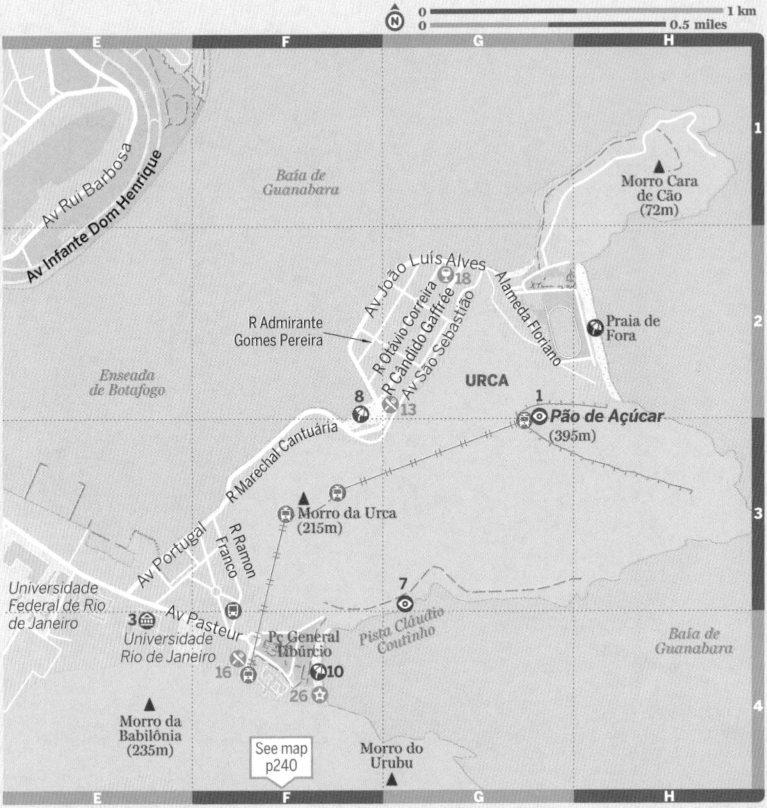

BOTAFOGO & URCA

22 Champanharia Ovelha Negra ... C2
Cobal do Humaitá ... (see 12)
23 Espírito do Chopp ... A4
Garota da Urca ... (see 13)
24 O Plebeu ... A4
25 Pista 3 ... B3

Entertainment (p106)

26 Circulo Militar da Praia Vermelha ... F4
27 Estação Botafogo ... C3
28 Estação Rio ... C3
Far Up ... (see 23)

Shopping (p106)

Artíndia ... (see 4)
29 Botafogo Praia Shopping ... C2
30 Casa & Gourmet ... D3
31 Livraria Prefácio ... C3
32 Rio Sul Shopping ... D4

Sleeping (p169)

33 Ace Hostel ... C3
34 El Misti ... C3
35 Vila Carioca ... C3

Key on p248

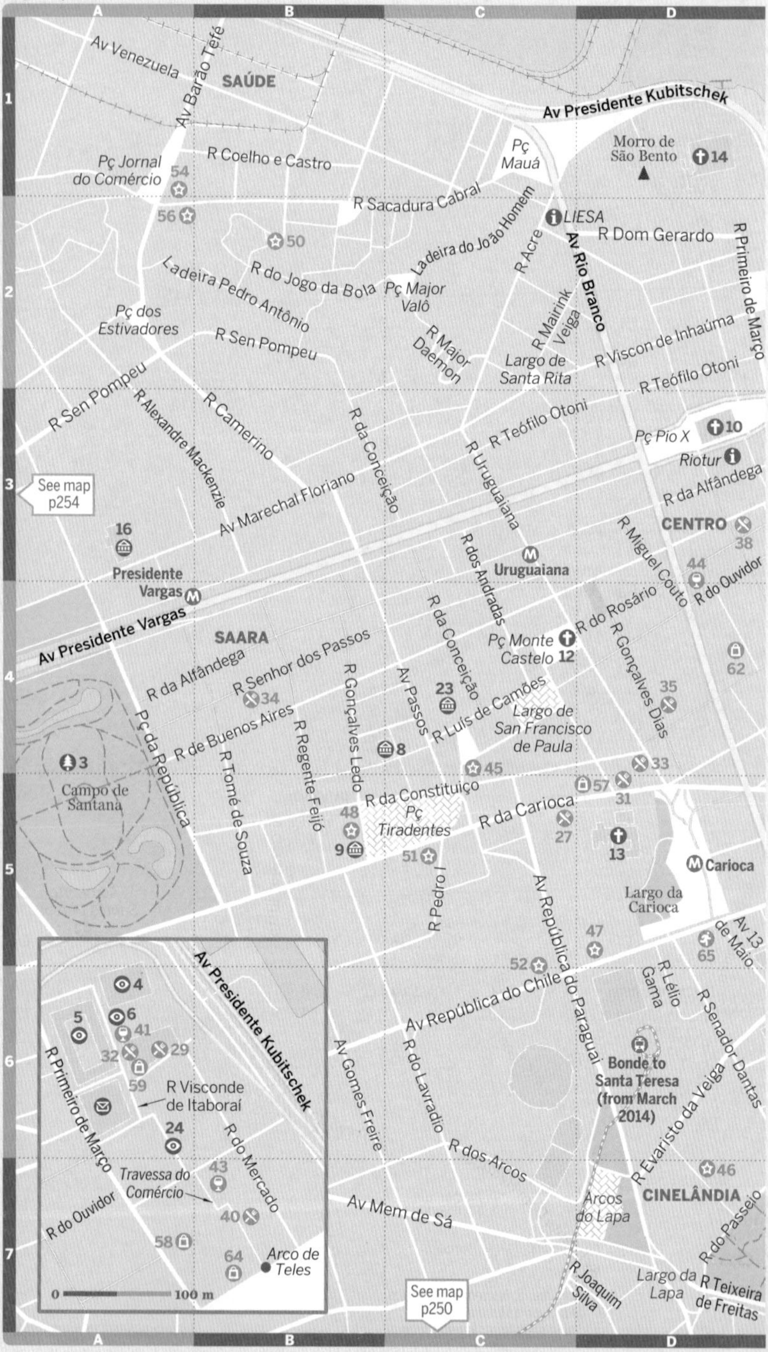
A
B
C
D
1
2
3
4
5
6
7
SAÚDE
Av Venezuela
Av Barão Tefé
Av Presidente Kubitschek
Pç Mauá
Morro de São Bento
14
Pç Jornal do Comércio
54
56
R Coelho e Castro
R Sacadura Cabral
LIESA
R Dom Gerardo
R Primeiro de Março
50
Ladeira do João Homem
R Acre
Av Rio Branco
R do Jogo da Bola
Ladeira Pedro Antônio
Pç Major Valô
Pç dos Estivadores
R Sen Pompeu
R Major Daemon
R Mairink Veiga
Largo de Santa Rita
R Viscon de Inhaúma
R Teófilo Otoni
R Alexandre Mackenzie
R Camerino
R da Conceição
R Uruguaiana
Pç Pio X
10
Riotur
R da Alfândega
See map p254
Av Marechal Floriano
16
Presidente Vargas
R dos Andradas
Uruguaiana
CENTRO
38
R Miguel Couto
44
R do Ouvidor
Av Presidente Vargas
SAARA
R da Conceição
R do Rosário
Pç Monte Castelo
12
R Gonçalves Dias
62
R da Alfândega
R Senhor dos Passos
R Gonçalves Ledo
Av Passos
23
R Luís de Camões
34
35
R de Buenos Aires
Largo de San Francisco de Paula
Pç da República
R Regente Feijó
R Tomé de Souza
8
3
Campo de Santana
45
33
57
31
R da Constituição
Pç Tiradentes
R da Carioca
48
27
9
51
13
Carioca
Largo da Carioca
R Pedro I
Av República do Paraguai
47
Av 13 de Maio
65
52
Av República do Chile
R Lélio Gama
R Senador Dantas
4
5
6
41
32
29
59
R Primeiro de Março
R Visconde de Itaboraí
24
R do Mercado
Travessa do Comércio
43
R do Ouvidor
40
58
64
Arco de Teles
0
100 m
Av Presidente Kubitschek
Av Gomes Freire
R do Lavradio
Bonde to Santa Teresa (from March 2014)
R Evaristo da Veiga
46
R dos Arcos
Av Mem de Sá
Arcos do Lapa
CINELÂNDIA
R do Passeio
R Joaquim Silva
Largo da Lapa
R Teixeira de Freitas
See map p250

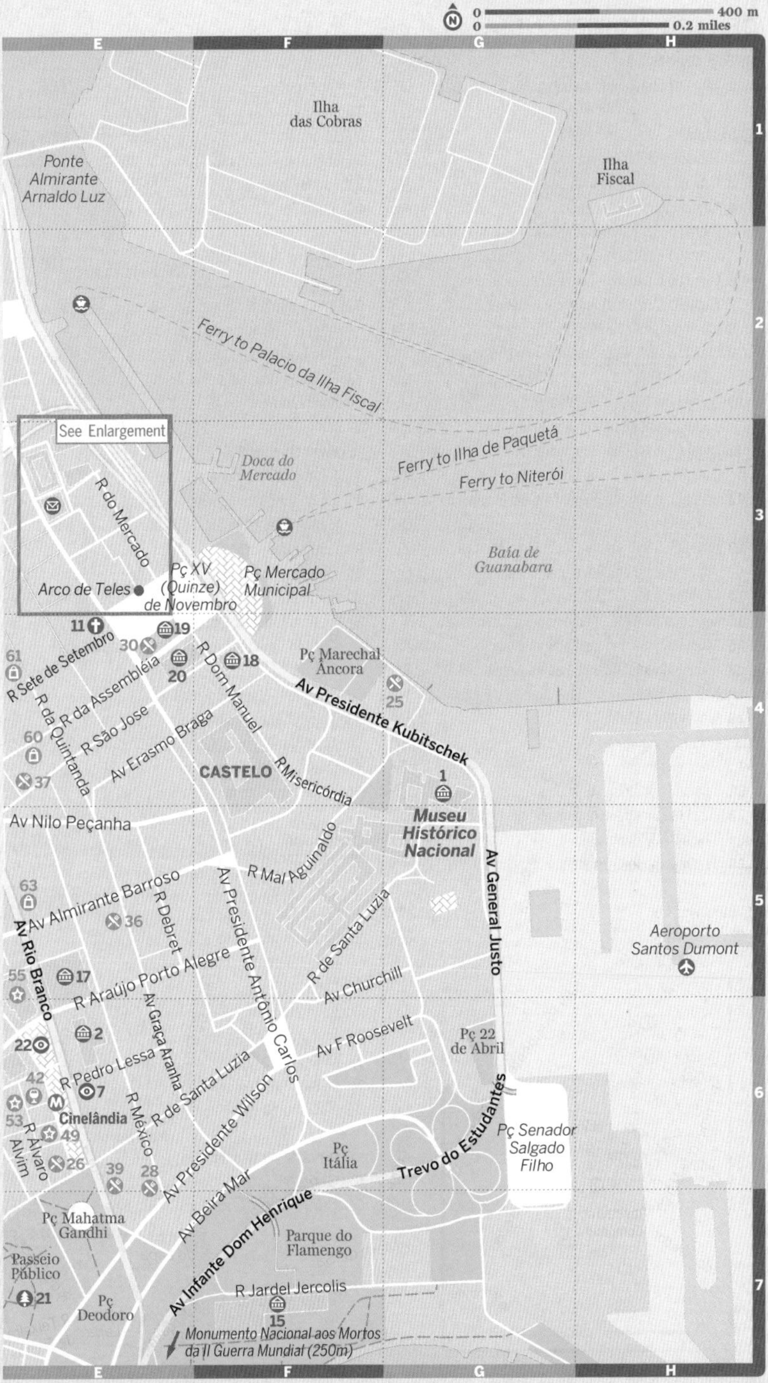

0 400 m
0 0.2 miles
Ilha das Cobras
Ponte Almirante Arnaldo Luz
Ilha Fiscal
Ferry to Palacio da Ilha Fiscal
See Enlargement
Doca do Mercado
Ferry to Ilha de Paquetá
Ferry to Niterói
R do Mercado
Baía de Guanabara
Arco de Teles
Pç XV (Quinze) de Novembro
Pç Mercado Municipal
Pç Marechal Âncora
R Sete de Setembro
R da Assembléia
R Dom Manuel
Av Presidente Kubitschek
R da Quintanda
R São Jose
Av Erasmo Braga
CASTELO
R Misericórdia
Museu Histórico Nacional
Av Nilo Peçanha
R Mal Aguinaldo
Av General Justo
Av Almirante Barroso
R Debret
Av Presidente Antônio Carlos
R de Santa Luzia
Av Rio Branco
Aeroporto Santos Dumont
R Araújo Porto Alegre
Av Churchill
Av Graça Aranha
Av F Roosevelt
Pç 22 de Abril
R Pedro Lessa
R México
R de Santa Luzia
Av Presidente Wilson
Trevo do Estudantes
Cinelândia
Pç Senador Salgado Filho
R Álvaro Alvim
Pç Itália
Av Beira Mar
Av Infante Dom Henrique
Pç Mahatma Gandhi
Parque do Flamengo
Passeio Público
R Jardel Jercolis
Pç Deodoro
Monumento Nacional aos Mortos da II Guerra Mundial (250m)

CENTRO & CINELÂNDIA *Map on p246*

SANTA TERESA & LAPA *Map on p250*

Top Sights (p135)
1 Escadaria Selarón ... F4

Sights (p136)
2 Arcos da Lapa ... F3
3 Casa de Benjamin Constant ... C5
4 Catedral Metropolitana ... E2
5 Centro Cultural Laurinda Santos Lobo ... B6
6 Fundição Progresso ... E3
7 Largo das Neves ... A4
8 Largo do Guimarães ... C6
9 Museu Chácara do Céu ... D5
Museu de Arte Sacra ... (see 4)
10 Parque das Ruínas ... D5

Eating (p137)
11 Aprazível ... C7
12 Bar Brasil ... E3
13 Bar do Mineiro ... C6
14 Cafecito ... C6
15 Cantinho do Senado ... D1
16 Ernesto ... F4
17 Espaço Lapa Cafe ... D2
18 Espírito Santa ... D5
19 Largo das Letras ... C6
Mangue Seco Cachaçaria ... (see 42)
20 Mike's Haus ... A8
21 Nega Teresa ... B6
22 Nova Capela ... E3
23 Sansushi ... D6
24 Santa Scenarium ... D1
25 Sobrenatural ... D6
Térèze ... (see 69)

Drinking & Nightlife (p139)
26 Adega Flor de Coimbra ... F4
27 Antônio's ... E3
28 Bar do Gomes ... B6
Bar dos Descasados ... (see 69)
29 Barzinho ... E3
30 Boteco do Gomes ... E3
31 Boteko do Juca ... E3
32 Choperia Brazooka ... E3
33 Goya-Beira ... B4
34 Leviano Bar ... E3

Entertainment (p140)
35 Beco do Rato ... G4
36 Carioca da Gema ... E3
37 Cine Santa Teresa ... C6
38 Circo Voador ... F3
39 Democráticus ... D3
40 Favellas ... E3
Fundição Progresso ... (see 6)
41 Lapa 40 Graus ... D3
42 Mangue Seco Cachaçaria ... D1
43 Mas Será O Benedito ... D2
44 Mistura Carioca ... E3
45 Parada da Lapa ... F3
46 Rio Scenarium ... D1
47 Sacrilégio ... E3
48 Sala Cecília Meireles ... F3
49 Semente ... F3
50 Teatro Odisséia ... F3
51 TribOz ... F4

Shopping (p142)
52 Feira do Rio Antigo ... D1
53 Flanar ... D2
54 La Vereda Handicrafts ... D6
55 Plano B ... E3
56 Scenarium Antique ... D1

Sports & Activities (p143)
Fundição Progresso ... (see 6)
57 Núcleo de Dança Renata Peçanha ... D2

Sleeping (p170)
58 Books Hostel ... E4
59 Cama e Café ... C6
60 Casa Áurea ... C7
61 Casa Beleza ... B7
62 Casa Bianca ... E5
63 Casa Cool Beans ... B7
64 Casa da Carmen e do Fernando ... F5
65 Casa Mango Mango ... E4
66 Casalegre ... B6
67 Castelinho 38 ... C6
68 Hotel Marajó ... F4
69 Hotel Santa Teresa ... C6
70 Rio Hostel ... E4
71 Terra Brasilis ... E5
72 Villa Laurinda ... B7

SANTA TERESA & LAPA

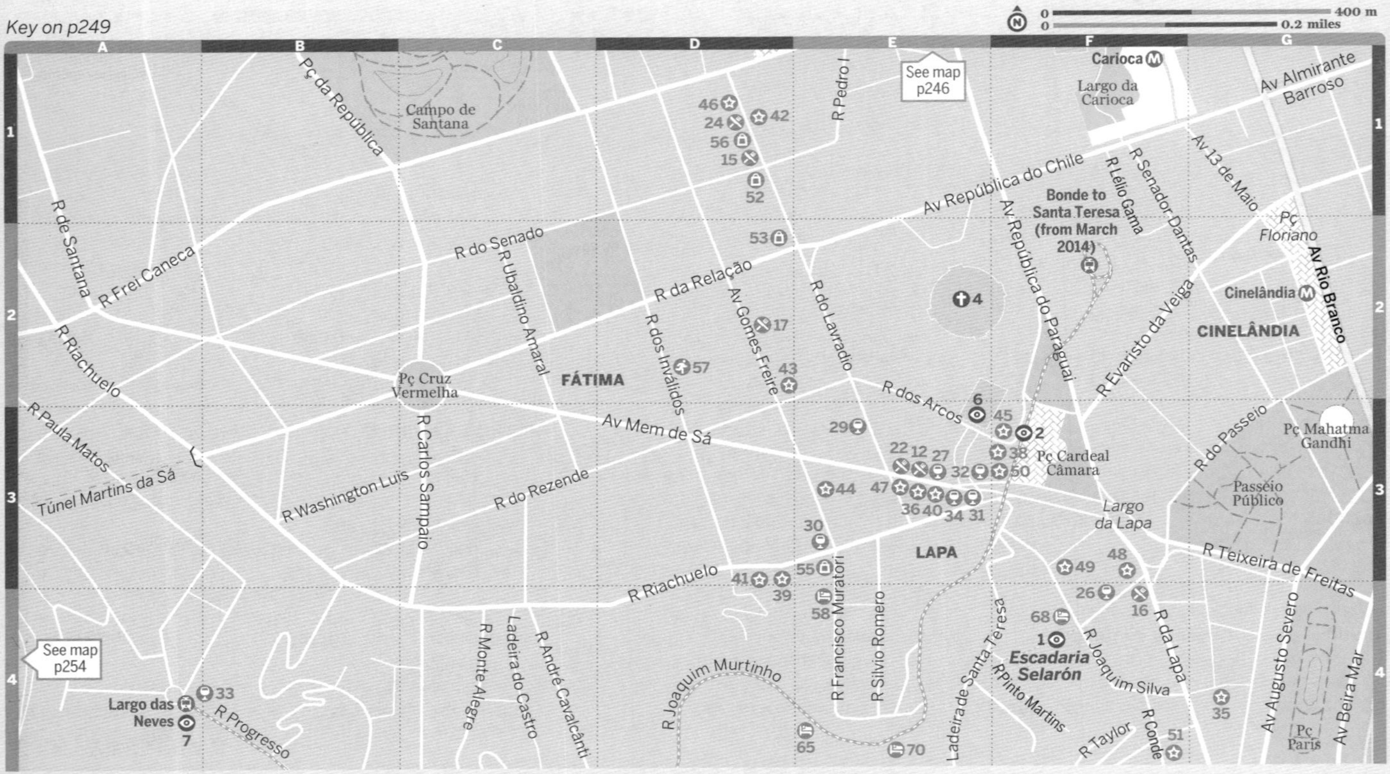

SANTA TERESA & LAPA

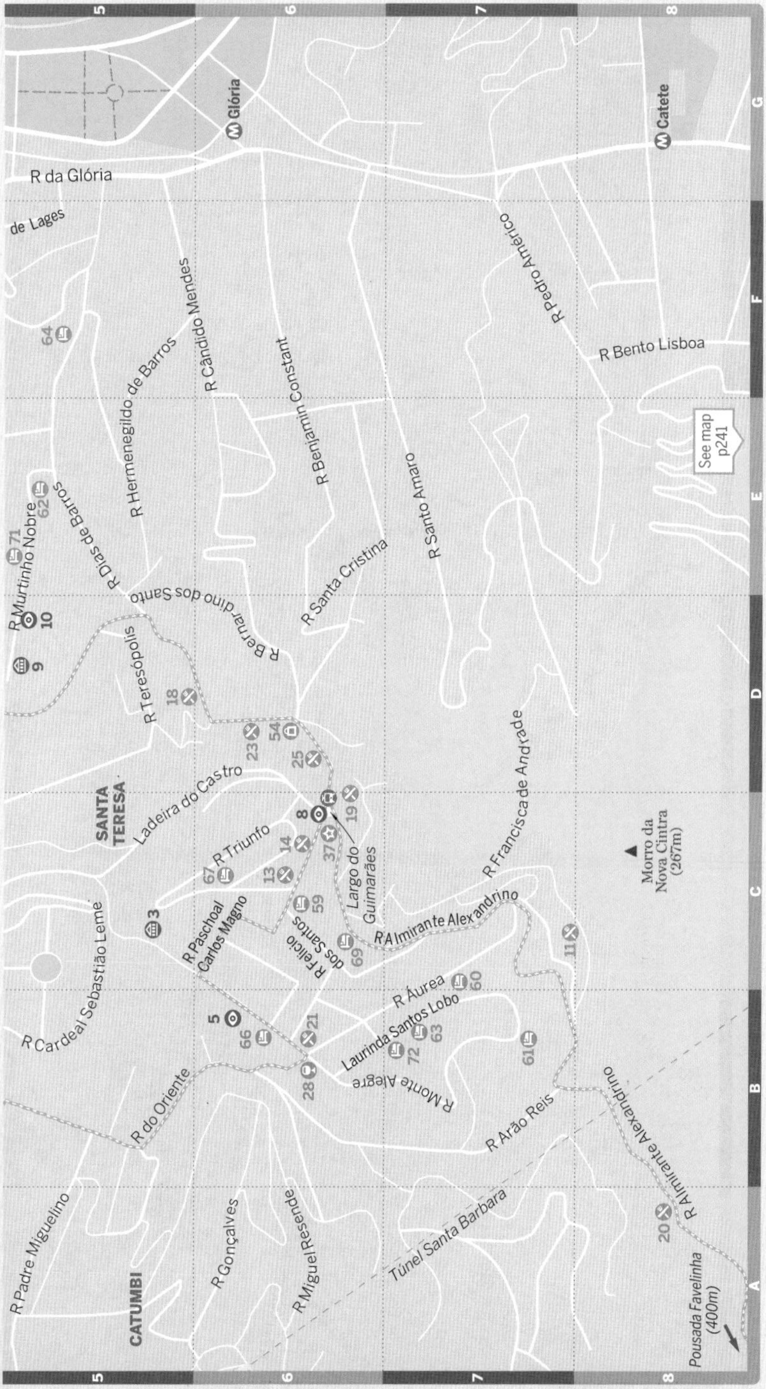

BARRA DA TIJUCA & WESTERN RIO

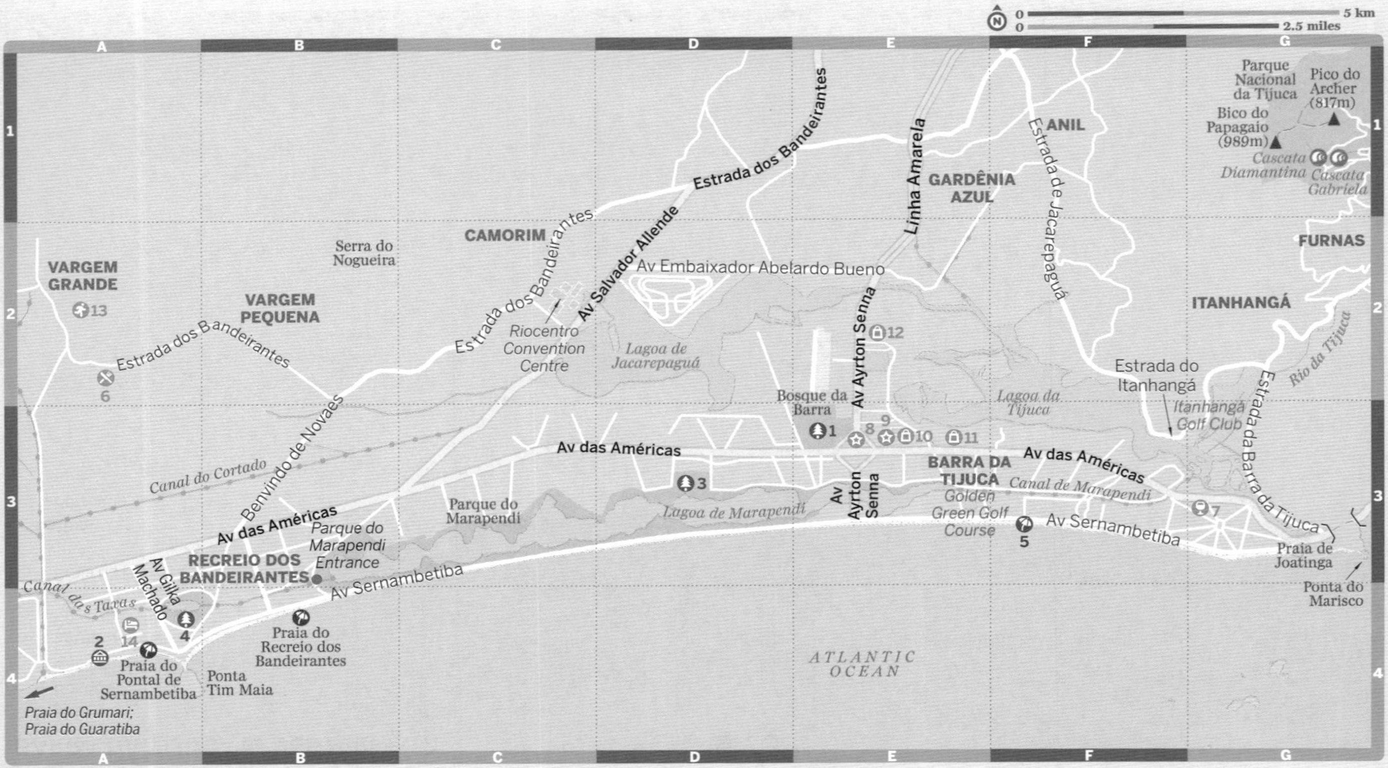

BARRA DA TIJUCA & WESTERN RIO

Sights (p153)
1 Bosque da Barra ... E3
2 Casa do Pontal ... A4
3 Parque do Marapendi ... D3
4 Parque Ecológico Chico Mendes ... A4
5 Praia da Barra da Tijuca ... F3

Eating (p156)
6 Barreado ... A2

Drinking & Nightlife (p157)
7 Nuth ... G3

Entertainment (p157)
8 Cidade das Artes ... E3
Citibank Hall ... (see 12)
9 UCI – New York City Center ... E3

Shopping (p157)
10 Barra Shopping ... E3
11 The Village ... E3
12 Via Parque Shopping ... E2

Sports & Activities (p25)
13 Rio Water Planet ... A2

Sleeping (p172)
14 Rio Surf 'N Stay ... A4

ZONA NORTE

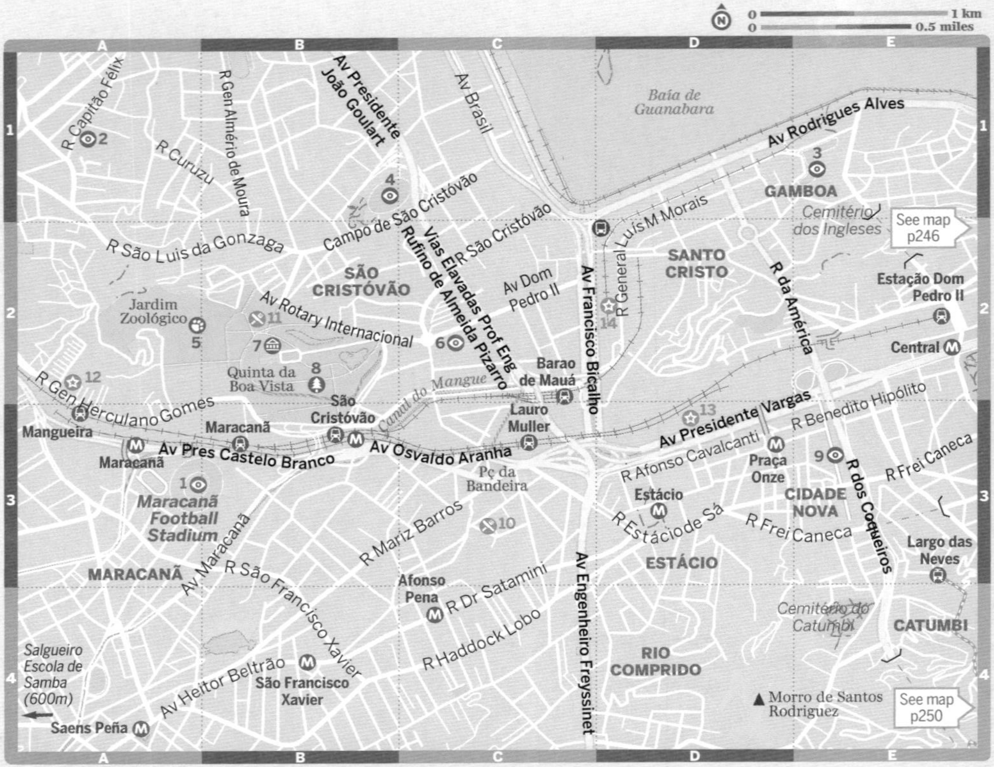

Top Sights (p146)
1 Maracanã Football Stadium A3

Sights (p148)
2 CADEG A1
3 Cidade do Samba E1
4 Feira Nordestina B1
5 Jardim Zoológico A2
6 Museu do Primeiro Reinado C2
7 Museu Nacional B2
8 Quinta da Boa Vista B2
9 Sambódromo E3
Sports Museum .... (see 1)

Eating (p149)
10 Aconchego Carioca C3
Barsa .... (see 2)
11 Restaurante Quinta da Boa Vista B2

Entertainment (p45)
12 Mangueira A2
13 São Clemente D3
14 Unidos da Tijuca D2